CONFLICT, HOLINESS, AND POLITICS IN THE TEACHINGS OF JESUS

CONFLICT, HOLINESS, AND POLITICS IN THE TEACHINGS OF JESUS

MARCUS J. BORG

TRINITY PRESS INTERNATIONAL
Harrisburg, Pennsylvania

Trinity Press International, P.O. Box 1321, Harrisburg, PA 17105
Trinity Press International is a division of the Morehouse Group

Cover art: Giraudon/Art Resource, New York. El Greco. Christ chasing the moneylenders from the temple, 1610–1614. Oil on canvas, 106 x 104 cm. St. Gines, Madrid, Spain.

Library of Congress Cataloging-in-Publication Data

Borg, Marcus J.
    Conflict, holiness, and politics in the teachings of Jesus /
Marcus J. Borg.
        p.   cm.
    Originally published: New York, N.Y.: E. Mellen, 1984, in series:
Studies in the Bible and early Christianity.
    Includes bibliographical references and index.
    ISBN 1-56338-227-X
    1. Jesus Christ – Political and social views. 2. Jesus Christ –
Views on Jewish ritual purity.   I. Title.
BS2417.P6B67   1998
232.9'54 – dc21   98-22816

Printed in the United States of America

98   99   00   01   02   10   9   8   7   6   5   4   3   2   1

Contents

Foreword to the New Edition

Marcus Borg and I might have met fifteen years earlier than we actually did, though we would not at that time have shared an interest in the historical Jesus. He was at Mansfield College, Oxford, writing his doctoral dissertation (the first version of the present book) from 1969 to 1972, under the guidance of Dr. George Caird, then principal of Mansfield College and subsequently Dean Ireland Professor of Exegesis at Queen's. At that time I was reading Greats (philosophy and ancient history) two streets away at Exeter College, and then beginning to study theology. We probably passed each other in the street, or in Blackwell's bookshop, a dozen times.

But I did not, then, know much about the historical study of Jesus. When I began my own doctoral work under George Caird in 1973, I was single-mindedly examining Paul; and George himself, who organized his time and his mind better than most, did not deviate from that topic in our conversations. The only time he mentioned Marcus to me was to hold him up as a shining example of someone who enters upon a doctoral program knowing what he wants to write about, and gets on and does it. Alas, the example fell on deaf ears. It took me three years to work out what I wanted to say about Paul, and another four to say it.

It was only after that, when I was teaching at McGill University in Montreal (where Caird had held the same chair thirty years earlier), that I began in earnest to study Jesus in his historical context. Between 1982 and 1984 I puzzled and probed and lectured and scribbled about Jesus, with Caird's little book *Jesus and the Jewish Nation*[1] as the spark that had set new ideas smoldering. At the Annual Meeting of the Society of Biblical Literature in November 1984 I attended a seminar exploring some ideas about Jesus' teaching in relation to the political conflicts within the Judaism of his day. Toward the end, someone mentioned, casually, that there was a new book on these topics by someone called Marcus Borg. I hunted for the book, bought it, took it home to Montreal, devoured it, and not long afterward made contact with its

---

1. London: Athlone Press, 1965.

author. This is the book I now have the privilege of introducing to a
new readership. I am grateful and honored.

Unlike many doctoral dissertations, this one transformed itself into
a book very successfully — perhaps because Borg let it lie, like a vin-
tage wine, for ten years before decanting it afresh. Its argument is
crisp and clear. It carves out fresh space which many readers of the
New Testament had never imagined existed, and then proceeds to fill
that space with historical reconstruction and exegetical detail that is
not only patient and well-documented but also creative and innova-
tive. It is not surprising that, unlike many volumes that fill the shelves
of second-hand stores five years after publication, this one is thought
worth republishing fourteen years on, twenty-six years after the original
thesis was completed. My task in what follows is briefly to introduce
the main themes of the book, and to raise questions that seem to me
to need exploring further.

It is a measure of Borg's achievement in this book that several original features of his treatment have since become almost commonplace
in the discipline. Of these, the most important, highlighted in the first
chapter, is without a doubt the reintegration of what we may loosely call
religion and politics. Generations of writers about Jesus had assumed
that the two were as incompatible in the first century in Palestine as
they have been supposed to be in the modern Western world, so that
to make Jesus a teacher of religion or theology was to make him apolitical, and to have him involved in politics was to remove him from
religious, spiritual, or theological concerns. The reconstructed Jesuses
both of Albert Schweitzer and the so-called "New Quest" gazed across
a great gulf at the revolutionary Jesuses invented by a line of writers
from H. S. Reimarus to S. G. F. Brandon. Neither had much to say to
the other. With a few clear paragraphs, Borg exposed the fallacy of this
assumption. To make Jesus a teacher of timeless religious truths is to
take him out of his context entirely; to say that he expected the world
to end and therefore did not bother to engage with current political
questions is to misunderstand eschatology; to make Jesus an existentialist philosopher is to commit a highly misleading anachronism. Equally,
to make Jesus a one-dimensional revolutionary is to forget that first-
century Jewish uprisings were motivated not least by zeal for Israel's
God and the law. Politics was based on religion; religion was necessarily
expressed in terms of national life.

Once we put Jesus in his context, therefore, his speech about God
and the Kingdom and his urging of a new social, cultural, and political
agenda on his contemporaries naturally belong together — are, indeed,
ultimately two ways of talking about the same thing. No well-taught

Jew of the first century would suppose that prayer and piety could be divorced from the vocation of Israel, both internally and vis-à-vis her pagan neighbors and adversaries; or that the crisis facing Israel internally and externally could be addressed without reference to Israel's God, and to God's will, as found in Scripture. Many of us who have written about Jesus in recent years now take this integration more or less for granted. We are thereby walking through a door which was unlocked not least by books like the present one.

Once we have said all this, we must explore the actual social and political situation that Jesus addressed, and the ways in which he addressed it. Here Borg makes three moves, each of which is vital to his case and, I believe, necessary in any historical reconstruction of Jesus, however much we may disagree with Borg in matters of actual analysis. First, Jesus was addressing a situation of *conflict*, both within Judaism and between Jews and pagans, and he was offering a particular agenda in relation to those conflicts. Second, Jesus was addressing more specifically a situation in which the quest for *holiness* on the part of some of his contemporaries was intimately bound up with certain social and political ambitions. Third, Jesus was not offering generalized "religious teaching," a new mode of spirituality, or a way by which people could be "saved" without reference to this-worldly realities; he was holding out an alternative *political* agenda for the people of God. Fourth, the *apocalyptic language* of Jesus was not about "the end of the world" as regularly conceived, but about the urgent challenge facing Israel in her present crisis. I shall introduce, and briefly discuss, each of these, before turning in conclusion to the highly significant twist in the tail of Borg's overall thesis.

First, then, the situation of conflict. In chapter 2, Borg offers a sketch of the complex situation of Jews under Roman rule in the century or so before the disastrous war of 60–70 C.E. Stressing the financial as well as the social and cultural burden of Roman rule, Borg argues that resistance to Rome was not, as often thought, confined to one party within Judaism, but characterized groups of all sorts and from all geographical areas. The Pharisees are explicitly included; they were not, after all, simply concerned with personal purity, but possessed, and acted upon, specific political aims. The chief priests were involved, too, in their own way. Concern for God's law and God's Temple were the motivating forces; resistance based on these could take a variety of forms, including armed violence. Although this account is necessarily brief, and needs filling in with a good deal more detail in the light of the last twenty years of research, in my judgment it is substantially on target.

The question of Pharisaic involvement, both in politics and in violence, is a particular point which should, I believe, be stressed.[2] The
arguments that Borg and others have advanced on this point have not
been rebutted, but neither have they yet made their way into the general awareness of New Testament scholars. The question of potential or
actual conflict between Jesus and the early Christians on the one hand
and non-Christian Judaism, including the Pharisees, on the other has
been highly contentious in recent decades, not least because everyone
is anxious, in this post-Holocaust world, to avoid the least suspicion
of anti-Judaism. This has resulted, in Borg's (and my) judgment, in a
downplaying of the role of the Pharisees within the broad spectrum of
resistance to Rome in the pre-66 period. It is, of course, true, as the
later rabbinic sources indicate repeatedly, that the pre-rabbinic Pharisaic movement was itself not homogeneous. The followers of Hillel and
Shammai, the two great sages of the Herodian period, disagreed not
merely on the finer points of Torah observance, but on what a loyal Jew
should do in the present political circumstances: should one actively
resist Rome, or be content to study and practice Torah? The debate
continued between 70 C.E., when the Temple was destroyed, and 132,
when the Bar-Kochba revolt began: should loyal, Torah-observant Jews
fight Rome, with a view to rebuilding the Temple, or should they be
content to let Rome rule the world as long as they themselves were
able to study and practice Torah privately? It was only after the final
disaster of 135 that the debate was effectively decided in favor of the
latter option. Strong evidence indicates that the former, the position
associated with the house of Shammai, was held by the majority prior
to 66. In other words (a significant conclusion for any discussion of
Jesus and the Gospels, and indeed Paul), the Pharisees in the period
we are concerned with, between the death of Herod the Great and
the outbreak of war in 66, were concerned with politics, not merely
with piety; with resistance and revolution, not merely with private
holiness.

But Borg's next main point is precisely that politics and piety were
not kept in separate compartments. In chapter 3 he shows that loyalty to Temple and Torah, the twin symbols around which resistance
to pagan rule organized itself, demanded holiness. The Temple was the
center of the great system of holiness, radiating out in concentric circles from the Holy of Holies at the heart of the Temple itself, through

---

2. The issue comes to a head in the closing pages of chapter 5. See, further, my
The New Testament and the People of God (London: SPCK, 1992), 185–203, on which the
following paragraph draws.

the outer courts, to Jerusalem, and then to the entire "holy land." Holiness, for those who claimed to take it seriously, meant separation, from pagans in the first instance, but then from those Jews who were failing to keep the Torah as precisely as the particular group thought necessary. This includes, though Borg does not develop this point, polemic not simply by strict Jews against lax ones, but by one kind of strict Jews against another (witness the hostility between the Pharisees and the writers of the Scrolls). But this situation generates, as he does show, increasing division within Jewish society, partly at least along rich/poor lines, as the poorer members of society found themselves unable to observe all the niceties of the Torah. As I have reread Borg's book one more time I am struck by the careful balance he maintains between resistance to Rome on the one hand and internal division within Jewish society on the other, both being dynamically related to the "holiness" agenda of various groups.

This is particularly significant in the light of subsequent discussions. I and others have argued at length that Jesus' prophetic critique of his Jewish contemporaries focused not least on their failure to be the light of the world, and their seeking instead to be the agents of God's judgment on the rest of humankind.[3] I remain convinced that this is vital and non-negotiable, and not to be wished away by those who, desiring to find a revolutionary Jesus, refuse to have him make any criticisms of his revolutionary contemporaries. Others, however (notably Dominic Crossan, in his rightly famous book *The Historical Jesus*[4]), have argued that the target of Jesus' criticisms was the internal social division within Jewish society, particularly that between the small rich elite and the impoverished majority. Crossan, indeed, has criticized my own work severely, if somewhat obliquely, for seeming in his eyes to ignore this element.[5] Since Marcus Borg himself, acting as a go-between to interpret Crossan's critique to me, has explained that Crossan perceives the Jesus of my reconstruction as being unconcerned about social justice within Jewish society, I am glad to have this chance to say that Borg's own balance, in chapter 3 of the present book, seems to me exactly right. Borg's more recent work sees Jesus' critique of holiness and purity as targeting primarily the ideology of native ruling elites rather

---

3. N. T. Wright, *Jesus and the Victory of God* (London: SPCK; Minneapolis: Fortress, 1992).

4. J. D. Crossan, *The Historical Jesus: The Life of a Mediterranean Jewish Peasant* (San Francisco: HarperCollins; Edinburgh: T. & T. Clark, 1991).

5. J. D. Crossan, "What Victory? What God?" in *Scottish Journal of Theology* 50, no. 3 (1997): 345–58, esp. 357f.

than national liberation movements. I confess I preferred his original position.[6]

What then was Jesus' counter-proposal, his agenda for Israel at this moment of crisis? In chapters 4–7, the heart of the book, Borg outlines his proposal. Jesus was a "holy man" who founded a "renewal movement," which was necessarily in competition with other renewal movements, offering a different vision of what Israel was supposed to be. Jesus' challenge to prevalent assumptions was focused in his table fellowship with sinners, which contrasted with the exclusive purity of the Pharisees' program: Jesus' own practice was a revolutionary (perhaps we should say a doubly revolutionary) weapon, both affirming God's work within Israel and denying the Pharisees' construal of that work. Genuine holiness, he was saying in action as well as word, was not a matter of separation from "sinners." The Pharisaic interpretations of the purity laws are to be understood as a reinforcement of their desire for strict national boundaries, and Jesus was protesting against that whole understanding of Israel's vocation and destiny. A good deal of synoptic gospel material comes up for review under this head: Borg has no difficulty, unlike several other contemporary scholars, in explaining Jesus' reported conflicts with the Pharisees in terms of this clash of agendas, while not for one minute suggesting that Jesus was "opposing Judaism." Jesus was a Jewish prophet of renewal and like all other such prophets was bound to come into conflict with others claiming the high ground of being loyal to Israel's God.

This exposition of Jesus' opposition to the Pharisees in particular would be further strengthened, I believe, by the sort of evidence collected by Mary Douglas, to whose work Borg refers once in his *Jesus: A New Vision*, once in his *Meeting Jesus Again for the First Time* (63 n. 14), and once in *Jesus in Contemporary Scholarship* (120f. n. 33), the latter two references both relating to the present point. While I do not believe that social science can supply historical detail simply by analogy, an understanding of how codes of purity operate within societies other than that of the modern West, and of how such codes interact with other cultural agendas, is enormously important in our understanding of what was going on in the interchanges between Jesus and his interlocutors. This point remains valid even if the controversies in question are deemed not to be authentic Jesus material: somebody in the early church thought they were important, and whoever wrote the stories had deep agendas which should be understood, not simply in terms of

---

6. See Borg, *Jesus in Contemporary Scholarship* (Valley Forge, Pa.: Trinity Press International, 1994), 115f., with 125 n. 72.

surface polemic, but of a complete cultural analysis. Equally, when we provide such an analysis it may well be that the objections to authenticity are seen to be based on a too shallow understanding of what was at stake. Borg's position points toward such an argument, and invites further work to fill it out.[7]

Instead of a holiness which separated Jew from Gentile, and observant Jew from non-observant, Borg's Jesus urged his hearers to a different paradigm. Instead of imitating God on the basis of the command "be holy, for I am holy," Jesus commanded them to be *merciful,* as their heavenly Father was merciful (Luke 6:36, which becomes thematic for Borg's thesis as a whole).[8] Israel's vocation depended on God's mercy; even so, mercy should be shown both toward outsiders and within their society. What results is the command to love one's enemies, and to pursue the way of peace. Jesus embodied his own teaching in his many acts which, by healing and transforming people, brought them within the circle of God's compassionate embrace.

The Hebrew root behind the word "mercy," *rahamim,* is the plural of the word for "womb." Borg therefore suggests, with an acknowledgement that this may be considered "daring," that one should speak of God's mercy as God's *womblikeness* (italics original), explaining this as meaning "nourishing, perhaps embracing" (see p. 146 below). This suggestion is repeated in Borg's subsequent writings about Jesus, and has become something of a trademark. While appreciating the overall point, I suspect the proposal is indeed "daring," but for philological rather than theological reasons. The Hebrew Bible is quite ready on occasion to use female imagery to describe God. But the root in question (*rhm*) is used roughly three times as often in the Hebrew Bible in the sense of "love, compassion" as it is in the sense "womb." I doubt very much whether a native speaker would consciously think of a womb when using some form of the root in its more general sense.

In one sense, in Borg's hypothesis, "mercy" is Jesus' substitute for "holiness"; in another, it is Jesus' radical modification of it. If "holiness" means separation, Jesus challenged it head on; if it means "the power of the holy, the other realm," as in Borg's use of the phrase "holy man" for Jesus, it can be seen as a power reaching out to heal, as opposed to creating exclusive boundaries. In some Jewish purity codes, uncleanness was regarded as infectious; Jesus' actions (touching a leper, for example) challenged this, indicating that it was genuine holiness, not unclean-

---

7. For a small start, see my *Jesus and the Victory of God,* chapter 9.
8. In this new edition, Borg uses "compassionate" and "compassion" instead of "merciful" and "mercy." See his explanation on pp. 16–17 below.

ness, that was infectious. The same debate underlies the controversies
to do with sabbath observance (chapter 6): Jesus chose to behave on
the sabbath in such a way as to symbolize his own agenda, his alternative paradigm for Israel, and he was opposed not because of petty
legalistic objections but because he was rightly perceived to be offering
a powerful alternative to existing programs. Jesus' response to the challenges of his interlocutors indicates that he saw the issue within the
historical context of Israel's present plight and concerns. He did not
oppose the sabbath law itself, merely the way in which the institution
had come to be used, as another badge of national set-apartness. It was
not, in other words, a question of whether the Torah was or was not
God-given, but a question of how it should be interpreted. Jesus was
offering a way of being Israel, of being the people of God, which, while
claiming to be based foursquare on Israel's traditions, offered a direct
challenge to the other contemporary interpreters of those traditions.

All the lines of Borg's argument so far draw the eye in one direction:
the Temple in Jerusalem (chapter 7). The Temple, as we have already
seen, was the focal point of Israel's holiness; it was also the spiritual
center of renewal movements and the ideological center of resistance
to Rome. Stressing the latter point, Borg offers a fresh reading of Jesus'
action in the Temple, in which his charge that the Temple was becoming a "den of robbers" (Mark 11:17 and parallels, quoting Jer. 7:11)
is directed at the way in which the Temple was regarded as "both a
guarantor of security and a focal point of liberation hopes" (186). The
Temple, like the sabbath institution, was meant to point beyond Israel
to God's purposes for the world; Jesus' contemporaries had turned this
ideal into a self-serving ideology.

Jesus' action in the Temple was not, then, a "cleansing" as commonly
understood. It was an acted parable of the Temple's destruction, echoed
in numerous prophetic sayings in which he is warning not of "the end
of the world" but of the end of *Israel's* world: of a disastrous and dev-
astating war in which those who did not turn away from the rush into
military revolt — those, in other words, who did not "repent" and heed
Jesus' warnings — would meet their doom. This would not be a matter
of arbitrary divine vengeance, but the straightforward consequence of
following the path of exclusive holiness rather than that of mercy.

Nor are these warnings to be seen as mere *vaticinia ex eventu*, written
up by the early church after 70 C.E. Drawing on Dodd's famous article,[9]

---

9. C. H. Dodd, "The Fall of Jerusalem and the 'Abomination of Desolation,'" *Journal of Roman Studies* 37 (1947): 47–54; reprinted in his *More New Testament Studies*
(Manchester: Manchester University Press, 1968), 69–83.

Borg argues powerfully that sayings like Luke 19:42–44 do not in fact
fit with the events of 70 C.E., are better explained as a network of allusions to biblical prophecy, and are highly likely to have come from Jesus
himself, and to refer, in classic prophetic/apocalyptic language, to the
destruction of Jerusalem at the hands of the Romans. This argument,
presented to the "Jesus Seminar," resulted in Luke 19:42–44 being
voted gray (="probably inauthentic") rather than black (="certainly
inauthentic"): Borg, in other words, convinced a sufficient number of
skeptics to vote red ("authentic") or pink ("probably authentic") for the
average result to be different from that which might have been expected
in that deeply anti-apocalyptic group.[10]

Borg is one of a number of writers who have placed the Temple firmly
in the center of their reconstructions of Jesus. E. P. Sanders, whose *Jesus
and Judaism* was in the press more or less at the same time as Borg's
book, does so even more, though he argues for the view that Jesus' purpose in announcing the Temple's imminent demise was to make way for
its rebuilding, a theme which Borg leaves to one side. Crossan, though
skeptical about the possibility of reconstructing much of the historical
detail, agrees with Borg and Sanders (and the present writer) to this extent, in seeing Jesus' action in the Temple as a deliberately provocative
theological/political symbol, and thus as the proximate historical reason for his arrest and subsequent execution. Despite the fact that some
scholars (such as G. Vermes) continue to deny that Jesus was interested
in the Temple or said anything very significant about it, I believe that
this theme must remain central to any Jesus research that intends to get
to the heart of the matter, and that Borg's insights, though no doubt
needing to be supplemented and balanced in various ways, remain vital
signposts to the true interpretation.

Jesus' warnings against the Temple, and his solemn announcement
of what would happen if Israel continued in her present course, were
regularly couched in language that we have come to refer to as "apocalyptic." Debate about the authenticity of such sayings tended, prior to
Borg, to assume that all such sayings referred to "the end of the world"
in some complete, cosmic sense: the end of the space-time universe
and the substitution of some different world altogether. The question
was then whether Jesus spoke of this end, or whether the sayings were
put into his mouth by his later followers. Borg brings a different perspective, one with far-reaching consequences. In chapter 8 he examines
the synoptic sayings in which threats are issued, looking both at the

---

10. Cf. R. W. Funk and R. W. Hoover, *The Five Gospels* (New York: Macmillan,
1993), 376.

content of the threats themselves and the warrants (i.e., the reasons
for the threats) which accompany them. He argues that the majority
of the relevant sayings speak of a contingent threat to Israel, within a
continuing historical order, whose warrant is that Israel has continued
to pursue the quest for holiness in a way contrary to the will of her
God. There remain a few sayings which seem to speak of a final "end,"
an imminent end to history itself, including the "coming of the son of
man"; these, Borg thinks, are not original to Jesus.

Borg is here building in part on the seminal insights of his teacher
and mine. In a number of works, culminating in his celebrated book *The
Language and Imagery of the Bible*,[11] George Caird argued that "apocalyptic" language regularly referred to this-worldly, space-time events
through the metaphorical lens of "cosmic" events. This is not to say,
as some critics have imagined, that such language ceased to have any
referent in the real world, denoting instead only the mental or spiritual
states of authors or readers. Rather, as Borg puts it: "The religious loyalties of first-century Jewish people thus suggest that only the imagery of
cosmic disorder and world judgment would have been adequate to speak
of the destruction of Jerusalem and the Temple" (227). I have elsewhere
affirmed the correctness of this reading of "apocalyptic" and developed
it in relation to the same material that Borg here studies, sometimes in
agreement, sometimes not.[12] Two comments seem appropriate here.

First, I believe Borg's argument has shown the way to a true reading
of these "apocalyptic" sayings. But I disagree with him (and with Caird,
as it happens) as to the *contingency* of the threats. I have argued at length
elsewhere that, though Jesus genuinely invited people of all sorts within
Israel to follow his alternative way of being Israel, he believed from the
start that the majority of his hearers would turn a deaf ear. This remains
a contentious minority opinion, but I believe it can be substantiated.

Second, I still find it strange that Borg, having swallowed the camel
of the "apocalyptic" genre of Jesus' sayings as a whole, should insist on
straining out the gnat of the "son of man" sayings within it. We have
good first-century evidence for how the book of Daniel was being read
(e.g., Josephus, 4 *Ezra*); there is plenty of evidence, against an earlier
scholarly near-consensus, that various different readers of Daniel 7 in
this period did understand the "son of man" figure messianically. (This
is not, of course, to say that there was anything approaching a unified
or "mainstream" view within the turbulent and many-sided Judaism of

---

11. London: Duckworth, 1980. Reissued, with a new introduction by N. T. Wright,
by Eerdmans (Grand Rapids), 1997. Cf. too G. B. Caird and L. D. Hurst, *New Testament
Theology* (Oxford: Oxford University Press, 1994), passim, esp. chapter 7.

12. *Jesus and the Victory of God*, esp. chapter 8.

the time.) The language of "coming on the clouds" and so forth, as
Caird already saw, belongs to the same category as the other language
mentioned above: a metaphorical lens through which appropriately to
describe this-worldly, concrete events, specifically God's judgment of
the wicked and vindication of the true Israel. I agree with Borg, and
with an increasing number of other writers, that "son of man" was not
a recognized title within Judaism at this period, denoting a supernatural
figure who would literally appear on the clouds of heaven. But Borg
never reckons with the fact that the book of Daniel as a whole, and
chapter 7 in particular, were read in the first century as revolutionary texts which promised God's deliverance to long-suffering Israel; and
that, within such a reading, the leader of a renewal movement might
well have alluded to the chapter, and its strange but central figure, as
a way of assuring his followers that the promise applied to them, and
even more so to him.[13]

After reading the first eight of Borg's nine chapters, I was left with
the questions: what did this Jesus think was going to happen next? Did
he think of himself as having a particular role to play (e.g., a messianic
role) within the present and immediately future events? Did he know,
or suspect, that he was shortly to die a violent death, and if so did he
give that death any interpretation? My own understanding of the broad
case that Borg had made by this point in the book allowed me, on
first reading, to go on without a break to think of answers to all these
questions. Jesus' prophetic critique of, and summons to, the Israel of his
day, leading up to his showdown in the Temple, provide to my mind a
setting within which it makes sense to see Jesus understanding himself
not only as a prophet, but as a would-be Messiah, albeit an unusual one
within the range of "royal" options in first-century Judaism. Further,
it makes sense of the evidence to suppose that he believed himself to
have a vocation to take Israel's sufferings upon himself and bring them
to their God-ordained climax in his own death.[14]

Borg does not examine these questions in the present book. Instead,
he moves in what seemed to me on first reading, and still seems to me
thirteen years later, an oblique direction. This is the more perplexing
in that, during these same years, it is this final, ninth chapter that has
provided the mainspring for Borg's developed writing about Jesus, first
in *Jesus: A New Vision*, then in *Jesus in Contemporary Scholarship*, and

---

13. Cf. *The New Testament and the People of God*, 291–97; *Jesus and the Victory of God*,
510–28.

14. I offered an initial version of these answers in "Jesus, Israel and the Cross," in
SBL 1985 Seminar Papers, ed. K. H. Richards (Chico, Calif.: Scholars Press), 75–95. For a
more worked-out statement see *Jesus and the Victory of God*, chaps. 11–12.

then in *Meeting Jesus Again for the First Time*. This is where Borg, building admittedly on hints earlier in the book about Jesus as a "holy man"
in touch with "the other world," begins to develop his understanding of
Jesus as a "sage."[15]

Borg creates space for this account with his description of mystical experience and the special mode of "knowing" it involves (240f.).
Other people in the Judaism of that day were "holy men" who "knew
God" in this special, intimate fashion; so did Jesus. Out of that knowing, though, he did what most others did not: he engaged in a prophetic
ministry, calling Israel to rediscover her own God and her true vocation
as the people of this God. Within this account, Jesus can be considered
a "sage," along with many others in various religious traditions. (Here
we see Borg's concern, throughout his writings, to locate what can be
said about Jesus on the wider history-of-religions map, not least, as he
has himself pointed out, in order to explain things clearly to students
from a secular background.) For Jesus the sage, what mattered was a
person's heart; Jesus pointed people along the way which would result
in the renewal of the heart, even though the way in question was the
way of death. "Thus Jesus internalized holiness" (255): the true holiness
was not as Jesus' contemporaries had imagined it, but rather "the path
of dying to the self and the world" (255). Those who grasped this, or
were grasped by it, would inevitably take a very different stance in the
community and politics of their day from those who did not.

All this brings us, finally, to the place where many books on Jesus
begin: the Kingdom of God. A brief but wide survey of the background
to this idea leads to the preliminary conclusion: "Kingdom of God" is
"Jesus' designation or 'name' for the primordial beneficent power of the
other realm"; it is "a symbol for the presence and power of God as
known in mystical experience" (261, 262). For Jesus, it was emphatically
a present reality, not something that was about to happen: the phrase
did not refer to the end of the space-time world, but "to the end of the
world of ordinary experience, as well as the end of the world as one's
center and security" (263). Jesus could and did invite people to enter
into this reality and to reorder their lives accordingly.

Am I, I wonder, the only reader to rub his eyes at this point and
wonder what happened to the solid rejection of existentialism with
which the book opened? The hands are the hands of Borg, but the voice
is the voice of Bultmann. Granted, Borg's Jesus is also a mystic and a

---

15. It is worth stressing that Borg's "sage" is very different from the would-be Cynic
sages of some other reconstructions of Jesus emanating from the Jesus Seminar and
elsewhere.

social prophet, while Bultmann's was neither. But both suppose that the "real" meaning of Jesus' apocalyptic Kingdom announcement was the invitation to his hearers to experience a new reordering of their interior personal worlds. This is hardly a criticism in itself, but it points to a major question that this chapter does not address. The phrase "Kingdom of God" and its cognates were, as is well known, not merely a general cipher for the presence of "the other," "the holy," "the numinous," or whatever, but summed up and expressed Israel's hope for liberation — the hope, in other words, that fueled the revolutionary movements that Borg made the starting point of his argument. What is missing in Borg's account of the meaning of "Kingdom of God" here is precisely that Israel-dimension which makes the rest of his book so striking: the sense that Jesus' mission was to *this* people at the great crisis and climax of their history. From my point of view, Borg had an opportunity here to close in on the heart of the matter, and did not take it. According to him, in this book at least, Jesus mounted a sustained critique of, and warning against, violent movements of nationalist liberation. *But it was precisely such movements that spoke of there being "no king but God."* Just as Jesus' agenda cut across theirs in the ways Borg has so fully argued up to this point, so his announcement of God's Kingdom flew directly in the face of theirs. Why does Borg not even consider this possibility?

To do so would not mean abandoning the "spiritual," "mystical," or "theological" dimension for which he has so carefully argued. It would mean integrating this dimension far more closely with the stress on Israel's national life which characterizes the rest of the book. Why should Jesus' challenge to Israel not have been thus: that she should, as a nation, as a community, recognize the presence and power of her own God in her midst, liberating her, albeit not in the way the revolutionaries had supposed? That, in a sense, is the conclusion toward which Borg seems to be heading, but he never works it out. Instead, he follows the line he has begun, interpreting as many "Kingdom" sayings as possible in terms of a present but hidden "spiritual" kingdom, and assigning those which cannot be treated in this fashion to the early church. When, in the closing pages, Borg ties together chapter 9 with the wider argument of the rest of the book, I am left full of admiration for an elegant conclusion, but full of puzzlement as to why it went this way. Borg insists that his exposition of Jesus' Kingdom preaching is integrated with "the concern for history unearthed throughout this study," but it seems to me that the integration is far looser than it need have been. What, after all, did Jesus think would happen? Was he disappointed? Did his violent death have anything to do with his vision and mission, and if so what?

Borg's Jesus, like Schweitzer's, died a failure. Israel as a whole did not

repent, did not embody the divine mercy and compassion in the way
that, according to him, she should have. The apocalyptic scenario thus
came to pass: Jerusalem and the Temple were indeed destroyed. Borg
is not concerned, in this historical treatment, to address the questions:
Does this matter? In what way, therefore, is his Jesus still worth listening
to? How do we move from Jesus the sage and Jesus the holy man, rooted
in first-century Palestine, to a Jesus who, as Borg in his other writings
stresses, might be followed and even worshiped today? How do we get
from his Jesus of history to his Christ of faith? And how does he avoid
the problems that, throughout the last century, have dogged the feet of
those who have postulated such a split? Why, ultimately, should we use
the word "Jesus" in connection with this "Christ"?

There is thus a sense in which Borg's Jesus is not totally unlike
some of those on offer within the nineteenth-century "Quest." He is
a teacher of spirituality, inviting people to discover the God-dimension
of reality and to reorder their personal and national lives accordingly. He criticizes those who, by implication, are not open to this
God-dimension, and so are engaging in activities, including violent
nationalist resistance and oppressive internal politics, which are a dis-
tortion of their true God-given vocation. They offer judgment, he offers
mercy; they exclude "sinners," he welcomes and heals them. Their holiness is outward, his is inward. This contrast is, after all, not so very
far from some traditional readings of Jesus and Judaism in which Jesus
offered his contemporaries something they did not previously have,
namely, mercy, grace, and a new sort of spirituality. Borg's analysis of
both sides of the contrast, especially his account of Jesus' program and
agenda, is of course quite different from traditional readings. But the
contrast itself, between an exclusive, external, and judgmental piety and
an inclusive, internal, and merciful one is strangely familiar. Not all will
welcome this, and not only for historical reasons.

Underneath these issues lies a critical question which is raised, and
sharpened, by the whole book. Did Jesus think that Israel's history was
reaching its climax, its single make-or-break moment? In many ways
this book seems to say "yes." Jesus, as a first-century Jew, saw Israel as
the focal point of the purposes of the creator God. The prophecies, including the threats of God's final judgment, were coming true in Jesus'
own generation. If they did not repent, this would be the end; not,
indeed, of the space-time world, but of Israel. But in other ways, particularly in the final chapter, things are not so clear. Was Jesus, after all,
simply one God-intoxicated holy man, one shrewd and spiritual sage,
among many? Was the significance of his address to his contemporaries
simply this, that he, like other holy men and sages in other traditions,

was pointing to a spiritual reality into which they could tap, which could radically transform their lives? And, if Borg replies that Jesus was also a social prophet, did he believe that his prophetic challenge was unique, climactic, and decisive, or was it, as far as he was concerned, simply one more in a long line of prophetic messages stretching back to Amos and forward into further generations?

Borg seems now inclined, a decade and more later, to go the latter route. His reinterpretation of the eschatological and apocalyptic sayings, reading them not as end-of-the-world warnings but as referring to a great this-worldly disaster, has enabled him to integrate them with the notion of a "present kingdom" which is, as it were, the first-century Jewish version of a more general truth and/or challenge addressed to all times, peoples, and places. Schweitzer gave his Jesus a continuing relevance, after the failure of his end-of-the-world eschatology, by claiming that his "personality" now confronts the whole world. The eschatological predictions of Borg's Jesus came true, but that, ironically, meant that he, too, died a failure: he had hoped they would not, had longed for Israel to repent and avoid the disaster. Borg gives him continuing relevance by fitting him into a wider category of spiritual teachers and social prophets, so that those who are not first-century Jews may have a chance to learn from him, and perhaps to change their lives and their societies accordingly. But, not to put too fine a point upon it: If it didn't work when Jesus himself tried it, why should we suppose it will now? Does the history of those who claim allegiance to Jesus give us grounds for optimism at this point?

My appeal to Borg the historian is this. Having located Jesus very credibly within the world of first-century revolutionaries, what stops us from locating him yet more precisely alongside other first-century would-be Messiahs? If Jesus could redefine the concept of holiness around his own program, learned in mystical experience from the one he called Abba, Father, why could he not similarly have redefined the concept of Messiahship? And, if so many other Jews in his world were expecting, not indeed the end of the space-time universe, but the climax of their own long and often tragic history, the great moment when their God, the creator of the world, would act once and for all to deliver them and so to bring divine justice and mercy to bear on Israel and the Gentiles alike, what stops us, with so many texts to urge us on, from saying that Jesus both shared that belief and expectation and, once more, redefined it in the light of his passionately held belief in the compassionate God? Why, in other words, can we not retain eschatology proper, that is, Israel's belief that world history, focused as it was upon Jewish history, was reaching its crown and culmination? Why should we be forced into the Procrustean either/or which poses, as the only alternatives, an old-fashioned "eschatological Jesus" who expected the end of the world and a wise or holy social prophet and mystic, who might in principle have uttered his challenging message at any time?

Further, if Jesus believed, as Borg insists, in the utter self-giving compassion of Israel's God, having discovered this in his own experience of prayer and mysticism, did it not strike him as strange that so few of his contemporaries seemed to share this intense knowledge? Did he never reflect, as the shrewd and discerning person Borg sees him to be, that this might constitute a special vocation for him personally? Did he never suppose that such a vocation might dovetail, not indeed with any and every "messianic" idea that this or that group might cherish, but with a calling that was nonetheless rooted in those well-known biblical prophecies of the shepherd who would come to rescue God's lost sheep? And, if such a shepherd was to accomplish the purpose of the self-giving, compassionate God, did Jesus never reflect on the biblical texts which spoke of the shepherd himself putting that self-giving love into practice as the ultimate outworking of his task? Finally, did he never reckon with the possibility that, if Israel's God was to come in person to liberate Israel and bring in the Kingdom, God might do so in and through the person of such an obedient shepherd? Since we have texts, and plenty of them, which suggest that Jesus of Nazareth did indeed think along these lines, and since they are significantly different both from what any other first-century Jew seems to have thought about himself and also from subsequent expressions of the church's faith, even the old criterion of dissimilarity, for which Borg rightly has little use, will suggest that we ought to take them seriously.

To do so would not undermine what I take to be the major thrust of this remarkable book. It would not even challenge the last chapter, for all I think it a somewhat strange conclusion to what has gone before. But it would suggest that there is further work, and further integration, to be done. Not all of it, of course, would cohere with the subsequent developments in Borg's own thinking. Indeed, in some ways he seems to me to have chosen to develop precisely the lines of thought in this book I regard as puzzling, and to neglect, or even to change his mind about, aspects which I still regard as valid and seminal. But this is the stuff both of friendship and scholarship. Indeed, since we both share an explicit personal allegiance to Jesus, it is the stuff of fellowship. What more could one ask?

N. T. WRIGHT

Lichfield Cathedral
February 1998

Abbreviations

Ant.	Josephus, *Jewish Antiquities*
Ap.	Josephus, *Against Apion*
Ap. and Ps.	R. H. Charles, ed., *Apocrypha and Pseudepigrapha of the Old Testament*, 2 vols. (Oxford, 1913)
ASTI	*Annual of the Swedish Theological Institute*
B.J.	Josephus, *Bellum Judaicum*
BJRL	*Bulletin of the John Rylands Library*
BZ	*Biblische Zeitschrift*
CBQ	*Catholic Biblical Quarterly*
CJT	*Canadian Journal of Theology*
ET	*Expository Times*
EvKomm	Evangelische Kommentare
HTR	*Harvard Theological Review*
HUCA	*Hebrew Union College Annual*
IDB	*Interpreter's Dictionary of the Bible*
Int	*Interpretation*
JBL	*Journal of Biblical Literature*
JBR	*Journal of Bible and Religion*
JE	*Jewish Encyclopedia*
JJS	*Journal of Jewish Studies*
JR	*Journal of Religion*
JRS	*Journal of Roman Studies*
JSS	*Journal of Semitic Studies*
JTS	*Journal of Theological Studies*
LXX	Septuagint
NEB	New English Bible
NovTest	*Novum Testamentum*
NTR	*New Theology Review*

NTS	*New Testament Studies*
RHPR	*Revue d'Histoire et de Philosophie religieuses*
RGG	*Religion in Geschichte und Gegenwart*
RQ	*Revue de Qumrân*
RSV	Revised Standard Version
RTPhil	*Revue de Théologie et de Philosophie*
S-B	Strack-Billerbeck, *Kommentar zum Neuen Testament aus Talmud und Midrash*
SJT	*Scottish Journal of Theology*
StEv	*Studia Evangelica*
StTh	*Studia Theologica*
TDNT	*Theological Dictionary of the New Testament*
ThZ	*Theologische Zeitschrift*
TLZ	*Theologische Literaturzeitung*
TU	*Texte und Untersuchungen*
TWNT	*Theologische Wörterbuch zum Neuen Testament*
USQR	*Union Seminary Quarterly Review*
Vita	Josephus, *Life*
ZAW	*Zeitschrift für die alttestamentliche Wissenschaft*
ZNW	*Zeitschrift für die neutestamentliche Wissenschaft*
ZTK	*Zeitschrift für Theologie und Kirche*

Introduction to
the New Edition

I am pleased to write a new introduction to the paperback edition of *Conflict, Holiness, and Politics in the Teachings of Jesus* (hereafter referred to as *CHP*). Completed in 1983, *CHP* was my first book-length treatment of the historical Jesus and was originally published by Edwin Mellen Press in 1984. Mellen is an excellent academic publisher and fills an important role in the publishing of scholarly books. But Mellen has historically been a low-volume publisher whose primary market has been scholars and research libraries. Thus, though *CHP* has often been cited by scholars in books and articles, it has not until now been available in a moderately priced edition.

The book's history goes back beyond 1984. Several of its central claims were part of my doctoral thesis, done at Oxford University from 1969 to 1972 under Prof. George B. Caird, a brilliant and well-known British New Testament scholar until his premature death in 1984. The foundational idea for my thesis came from a question Caird asked me at the beginning of my doctoral studies in 1969. As we were talking about possible topics, he said to me, "Let's assume that the Pharisees were not hypocrites — that they were not bad people, but good people, virtuous and devout. What then was the conflict between Jesus and the Pharisees about?" His question generated three years of research and writing on the traditions reporting conflict between Jesus and the Pharisees, set in the context of the social world of the Jewish homeland in the first century.

In the thesis which resulted, and on which this book is based, my central claims included the following. First, I made a sustained argument for rejecting apocalyptic eschatology as the foundational context for interpreting the teaching and activity of Jesus. Second (and instead), I argued that conflict between Jesus and some of his Jewish contemporaries (especially but not only the Pharisees) over "the shape" of Israel provides a more comprehensive context for interpreting Jesus' words and deeds. By "the shape" of Israel, I meant Israel's social-political structures, cultural dynamics, and historical direction: in short, "politics" in the broad sense of the word.

Third, much of my thesis made a case for the centrality of Jesus' in-

1

clusive meal practice. I argued that we see in it and the issues raised by it the central conflict of his ministry: between compassion and holiness as competing core values for Israel's life. I then integrated traditions about Jesus and the sabbath, Jerusalem, and the Temple into this frame-work of conflict. His opponents, I argued, were advocates of a politics of holiness (or purity), and Jesus was an advocate of a politics of compassion.

Together, these three claims point to the central meaning of the title of my thesis: "Conflict as a Context for Interpreting the Teachings of Jesus." To put my central argument very compactly: conflict about pol-itics (that is, about the shape and future of Israel), and not apocalyptic eschatology, provides a more comprehensive context for interpreting the traditions about Jesus. When I revised the thesis for publication as *Conflict, Holiness, and Politics in the Teachings of Jesus* in the early 1980s, these claims remained central, even as I rewrote much of the text and added fresh material.

For two reasons, the process of writing a new introduction to this book with which I have been involved much of my adult life has been interesting, even exciting. First, doing so has provided an opportunity to reflect on what has happened in the discipline regarding this book's central claims in the twenty-five years since I finished the thesis and the fifteen years since I completed CHP. Second, it has also led me to think about the extent to which I still see these issues the same way, and to what extent my perceptions have changed. It is interesting (and sometimes humbling) to read one's thoughts from fifteen and twenty-five years ago. I do see some things differently now.

These two reasons provide the structure for much of the rest of this introduction. I will begin by commenting on developments within Jesus research directly relevant to the book's argument. I will then describe a significant way in which my own thinking has changed and how this affects some points in the book.

Reflecting on *CHP*'s Central Claims

Much has happened in the historical study of Jesus in the lifetime of this book. Over the last fifteen years, the academic discipline of Jesus schol-arship has undergone a remarkable renaissance so that it is now routine to speak of a renewed quest or third quest for the historical Jesus.[1] In

---

1. For a description of what's happening in the discipline, see the first two chap-ters of my *Jesus in Contemporary Scholarship* (Valley Forge, Pa.: Trinity Press International,

this section, I will comment on *CHP*'s central claims in relationship to what is happening in the discipline.

The Undermining of Apocalyptic Eschatology

CHP's sustained challenge to apocalyptic eschatology as the primary context for interpreting the teaching and activity of the historical Jesus has fared well. When I began work on my thesis almost three decades ago, the mid-century scholarly consensus that apocalyptic eschatology was the historically correct context in which to interpret Jesus was still firmly in place. The consensus about an apocalyptic framework still seemed strong when I revised my thesis in the early 1980s. My challenge to the apocalyptic paradigm thus felt very much as if I were swimming against the tide, and I wondered whether my own position was simply eccentric.

Now that has changed. The consensus has been replaced by a strong division of opinion within the discipline. My hunch is that at least a slight majority of Jesus scholars in North America no longer think of Jesus within the framework of apocalyptic eschatology.[2] And even scholars who might disagree with that assessment would grant that the discipline is sharply divided on this issue. The consensus *as a consensus* is gone.

Apocalyptic eschatology is explicitly rejected by a large number of scholars, though for a variety of reasons. Burton Mack's understanding of Jesus as a Hellenistic-type Cynic sage who taught a witty and world-mocking wisdom separates Jesus from the apocalyptic traditions of Judaism.[3] On somewhat other grounds, Robert Funk's *Honest to Jesus* also rejects apocalyptic eschatology.[4] The Jesus Seminar, whose members include many who find both Mack's and Funk's understanding of Jesus to be too minimalist, has also consistently voted "black" on apocalyptic texts.[5] John Dominic Crossan, the best-known Jesus scholar in the world today, argues that Jesus abandoned the apocalyptic eschatol-

---

1994). For a solid journalistic account, see Russell Shorto, *Gospel Truth* (New York: Riverhead, 1997). For a conservative evangelical perspective, see Ben Witherington III, *The Jesus Quest* (Downers Grove, Ill.: InterVarsity Press, 1995).

2. For my account of why this has happened, see chapters 3 and 4 of *Jesus in Contemporary Scholarship.*

3. Burton Mack, *The Lost Gospel: The Book of Q and Christian Origins* (San Francisco: Harper, 1993).

4. Robert Funk, *Honest to Jesus* (San Francisco: Harper, 1996)

5. Robert Funk and Roy Hoover, *The Five Gospels* (New York: Macmillan, 1993).

ogy of John the Baptizer and replaced it with a sapiential eschatology.[6] In my own books published since *CHP,* I have consistently argued for a non-apocalyptic Jesus, seeing the apocalyptic texts as essentially "second coming of Jesus" texts created within the community after Easter.

Using a very different line of argument, N. Thomas Wright, arguably the most important British New Testament scholar of his generation, has also rejected what is commonly understood as apocalyptic eschatology. Unlike the previously mentioned scholars, Wright regards apocalyptic language (especially about "the coming son of man") as going back to Jesus, but sees such language as referring to historical events within the space-time world.[7] Thus apocalyptic eschatology is gone, though apocalyptic metaphors remain. Other scholars also accept apocalyptic language, but give it primarily a socio-political reading.[8]

Yet there are still influential voices affirming the apocalyptic paradigm. Among these is E. P. Sanders, who argues that Temple restoration eschatology was central to Jesus' mission and self-understanding. Specifically, Jesus believed that God would soon bring in the messianic age and replace the existing Temple with a new Temple, from which Jesus and the twelve would rule the messianic kingdom.[9] On quite different grounds, John Meier in his massive and impressive multivolume study of Jesus affirms a version of the mid-century consensus: Jesus spoke of the Kingdom of God as both present and imminent.[10] In his three books about Jesus, the Jewish scholar Geza Vermes maintains that imminent eschatology was central to Jesus.[11]

Moreover, there are a number of gospel and New Testament scholars who are not Jesus specialists who continue to see Jesus within

---

6. John Dominic Crossan, *The Historical Jesus: The Life of a Mediterranean Jewish Peasant* (San Francisco: Harper, 1991), and in several subsequent books.

7. N. Thomas Wright, *Jesus and the Victory of God* (Minneapolis: Fortress, 1996), 360–67, 512–19. See also chapter 10 of his *The New Testament and the People of God* (Minneapolis: Fortress, 1992).

8. See, for example, Elisabeth Schüssler Fiorenza, *In Memory of Her* (New York: Crossroad, 1983); and Richard Horsley, *Jesus and the Spiral of Violence* (San Francisco: Harper and Row, 1987).

9. E. P. Sanders, *Jesus and Judaism* (Philadelphia: Fortress, 1985), and *The Historical Figure of Jesus* (London: Penguin, 1993).

10. John P. Meier, *A Marginal Jew: Rethinking the Historical Jesus,* vol. 2 (New York: Doubleday, 1994). From a conservative point of view, Ben Witherington in *The Jesus Quest* also regards the apocalyptic sayings as authentic, but imminent eschatology disappears from his work. He argues that Jesus set no time limit for the coming of the son of man. As Crossan puts it, Witherington's Jesus proclaimed, "the end of the world was coming soon, maybe." Crossan, "Jesus and the Kingdom," in Marcus Borg, ed., *Jesus at 2000* (Boulder, Co.: Westview, 1997), 32.

11. Most recently, Geza Vermes, *The Religion of Jesus the Jew* (Minneapolis: Fortress, 1993).

the framework of apocalyptic eschatology. To what extent this is the residual effect of the earlier consensus or the product of sustained consideration is difficult to know. But in any case, what I thought of as very much a minority (and possibly eccentric) claim some fifteen years has now become a mainstream position.

Jesus' Inclusive Meal Practice

Prior to *CHP*, a few scholars (notably Joachim Jeremias and Norman Perrin) had argued that Jesus' table fellowship — his eating with "tax collectors and sinners" — was one of the most central features of his public activity. But there had been no extended study of *why* it was so central. They saw in it primarily a theological meaning: Jesus' inclusive table fellowship symbolized God's acceptance of sinners; it was an enacted parable of the forgiveness of sins.[12] But there was no consideration of whether it might have had other meanings in the social world of Jesus. The major section of *CHP* devoted to Jesus' meal practice sought to fill that need. I explored what was at stake in eating together in the Jewish homeland in the first century (especially among the Pharisees), and then located Jesus' meal practice and the controversy created by it within that framework.

Jesus' meal practice has become a central topic in the discipline. In the best-known scholarly study of Jesus in the last fifteen years, Crossan has made it central in his reconstruction of Jesus. He argues that "open commensality" was one of the two most central features of Jesus' activity (the other was "free healing"). Together, open commensality and free healing symbolized the shattering of social boundaries and affirmed unbrokered access to God (a sharing of material and spiritual resources), both revolutionary actions in a world constituted by boundaries and brokerage.

Though Crossan and I both emphasize Jesus' table practice, there are differences. Using cross-cultural anthropology, Crossan understands the significance of a shared meal primarily in the context of ancient peasant societies generally. He does not, so far as I can see, consider whether there might have been specifically Jewish meanings attached to table practice. That is, he does not emphasize what it would have meant in the Jewish homeland in the first century in particular. He does not connect Jesus' meal practice to issues of purity or to conflict

---

12. Joachim Jeremias, *New Testament Theology* (London: SCM, 1971), 114–16; Norman Perrin, *Rediscovering the Teaching of Jesus* (New York: Harper and Row, 1967), 107.

with the Pharisees. I mention this not as a defect, but as a difference between our arguments. In *CHP,* I make a case that table fellowship had specifically Jewish meanings, including the embodiment of a social vision for Israel.

Jesus and the Pharisees

Relatively few scholars have written much in the last twenty years about Jesus' conflict with the Pharisees. There are a variety of reasons. One is a post-Holocaust sensitivity to and awareness of the ways that Christian Scripture, theology, and scholarship have contributed to an anti-Jewish attitude throughout the history of Western culture. Hostile and uncritical portraits of the Pharisees as hypocrites and worse (already in the New Testament itself) have played their part.

The portions of the Gospels that report conflict between Jesus and the Pharisees have thus been analyzed primarily for the sake of exposing the scriptural roots of anti-Jewish attitudes. This is a vitally important task. We who are Christians need to be aware of how our sacred texts have become instruments of terror. But a perhaps unintended result is a strong tendency among scholars to see the conflict as reflecting late first-century tensions between Christian Jews and non-Christian Jews, and not as a conflict that goes back to Jesus himself.

A second reason is uncertainty about what the Pharisees were like in the first third of the first century. Scholars disagree about how much of the traditions associated with them can be traced back before the destruction of the Temple in 70 C.E.[13]

Thus recent scholarship has not had much to say about the historical Jesus and the Pharisees. Some explicitly deny that there was conflict. Burton Mack doubts that there were Pharisees (or even synagogues) in the Hellenistic environment of Galilee in the time of Jesus; in any case, his Cynic Jesus was sufficiently divorced from traditional Judaism so as to make conflict unlikely. On very different grounds, E. P. Sanders and Paula Fredriksen minimize any possible conflict with the Pharisees, to a large extent by seeing Jesus as quite similar to them. Dom Crossan is largely silent about them. The Jesus Seminar consistently voted the conflict traditions gray and black.

---

13. For an excellent compact summary of the history of research on the Pharisees, a review of the ancient sources, and a description of his own position, see Anthony J. Saldarini, "Pharisees," in *The Anchor Bible Dictionary,* ed. David Noel Freedman (New York: Doubleday, 1993), 5:289–303. See also his *Pharisees, Scribes and Sadducees in Palestinian Society* (Wilmington, Del.: Michael Glazier, 1988).

Yet conflict with the Pharisees is very well attested in the Jesus tradition. True, some of it is stylized and stereotyped, obviously reflecting
redaction by the authors of the Gospels and the intensity of conflict late
in the first century. This is most obvious in Matthew 23, with its rep-
etitious "Woe to you scribes and Pharisees, hypocrites," and its vitriolic
vilification of them as "serpents" and "brood of vipers."

But conflict between Jesus and the Pharisees is strongly attested
in the earlier layers of the tradition. It is widespread in both Q and
Mark. Even Thomas reports it. The conflict is also found in multiple
forms of the tradition: short indictment sayings, pronouncement stories, and parables. Moreover, in the early layers of the tradition, the
critique of the Pharisees is not indiscriminate but centers on issues of
meal practice, purity issues, and the sabbath. Furthermore, the conflict
is restricted to the public ministry of Jesus: the Pharisees are not part of
the arrest and trial narratives. This suggests that the gospel tradition did
not indiscriminately stereotype them as the enemies of Jesus. And thus
the question asked by my thesis supervisor remains: "Let's assume that
the Pharisees were not hypocrites — that they were not bad people, but
good people, virtuous and devout. What then was the conflict between
Jesus and the Pharisees about?"

My own understanding of what the Pharisees were like in the time
of Jesus depends on the work of others. I am not a scholar of the rabbinic tradition, and I have not done my own independent study of the
Pharisees in the rabbinic tradition. But I have read most of the scholarly
literature produced about the Pharisees in the last hundred years. For
my *gestalt* of the Pharisees, I am primarily indebted to the work of the
Jewish scholar Jacob Neusner. In a series of works published in the 1960s
and 1970s, Neusner argued that the Pharisees were a table fellowship
group committed to the intensification of purity. They were a renewal
movement committed to extending priestly standards of purity to nonpriests (that is, to Jews in general), and table fellowship was central to
their practice. Table companionship and the state of purity in which the
meals were eaten embodied their vision of what Israel was to be.

The significance of Neusner's work for my own is crystallized in two
of his statements about the centrality of table fellowship among the
Pharisees. First, no fewer than 229 of the 341 rabbinic traditions attributed to the Pharisaic "schools" of Hillel and Shammai pertain to
table fellowship. Second, legal matters of cleanness (purity) and proper
tithing of agricultural produce were the two matters of primary concern
to the Pharisees.[14] The congruence between Neusner's description of

---

14. For elaboration and documentation, see chapter 4 of this book.

the Pharisees and the way they are portrayed in the early layers of the gospel tradition is remarkable.

If Neusner is significantly wrong about the Pharisees, then I would need to revise my own understanding of the conflict between Jesus and the Pharisees.[15] But if he is in general correct, then the conflict between Jesus and the Pharisees is to a considerable extent about the social vision that flows from taking the traditions of Israel seriously. For the Pharisees, the core value of their social vision was holiness/purity; the core value of Jesus' social vision, I argue, was compassion.

Jesus and Purity

As is apparent, my understanding of Jesus and the Pharisees is directly connected to my emphasis on the centrality of purity issues in the Jewish homeland in the time of Jesus. To make explicit the connection to the title of CHP, I argue that holiness in first-century Judaism was understood primarily as purity, so that "holiness" and "purity" are virtually interchangeable terms. I argue that holiness/purity was central not only to the Pharisees, but also to the Essenes, some of the resistance fighters, and the Temple elites and their retainers (including many of the scribes). I conclude that a "quest for holiness" or a "quest for purity" (phrases which I use as synonyms) was the dominant cultural dynamic in the Jewish homeland in the first century. It created a social world ordered as a purity system, one with sharp social boundaries.

Though a number of scholars have cited my analysis of purity in the social world of Jesus with approval, some significant voices in the discipline have strongly rejected it as seriously and misleadingly off-target. E. P. Sanders thinks that purity issues had little significance in the relationship between Jesus and the Pharisees. Paula Fredriksen has argued that I have consistently and systematically misunderstood purity.[16]

---

15. In his essay in *The Anchor Bible Dictionary* (see n. 13 above), Saldarini finds Neusner's account of the Pharisees persuasive and integrates it into his own synthesis. N. T. Wright's understanding of the Pharisees and Jesus' conflict with them is also compatible with mine, even though he disagrees with some of Neusner's later comments on Jesus and the Pharisees. See his *The New Testament and the People of God*, 181–203, and *Jesus and the Victory of God*, 371–98.

16. In her essay "Did Jesus Oppose the Purity Laws?" *Bible Review* 11 (June 1995): 18–25, 42–47, Fredriksen speaks of my "thorough misunderstanding of the purity laws" and asserts that I have frequently "reiterated and elaborated on this error." See also her "What You See Is What You Get: Context and Content in Current Research on the Historical Jesus," *Theology Today* 52 (1995): 75–97. Presumably her denial that conflict about holiness/purity was important will be a theme in her forthcoming book-length treatment of the historical Jesus.

To some extent, the disagreement depends upon different ways of reading the Jesus tradition. But to a large extent, it hinges on the definition of purity. There are minimalist and maximalist definitions; purity can be defined very narrowly or very broadly. A minimalist definition would confine purity issues to conflict about specific purity laws in Leviticus.[17] On the other hand, a maximalist definition such as that offered by cultural anthropologist Mary Douglas virtually identifies purity systems with culture: a purity system is an orderly system of classifications, lines, and boundaries. Purity is concerned with a place for everything and everything in its place; impurity is things "out of place."[18]

My own understanding of purity is somewhere in the middle between a minimalist and maximalist definition. I think there is only limited usefulness in defining a purity system so broadly as to be virtually synonymous with culture. Its limited usefulness is that it makes the point that all cultural classifications (and thus all language) divide up the world so that some things are valued more than others, and some things are "out of place." But if all cultures are purity systems, then the notion loses most of its precision.

Thus I define "purity system" and "purity society" more narrowly than Douglas does, and more broadly than Sanders and Fredriksen do. To Douglas's definition of purity as a cultural system of classification, I add that a purity system is one that explicitly uses the language of purity (pure and impure, clean and unclean). If one accepts a middle-range definition of purity rather than a narrow definition, it seems clear that holiness/purity was a dominant cultural dynamic in the Jewish homeland of the first century.[19]

This does not mean that I see Judaism as intrinsically a purity system. I think the emphasis upon purity was the product of particular historical

17. See books cited in n. 9 above. At the "Jesus in Context" symposium sponsored by Duke Divinity School in February 1998, Sanders said only two Gospel texts deal with purity issues: Mark 1:40–44 (cleansing a leper), and Mark 7:18–19. He understands the latter as abolishing food laws, and argues that Jesus did no such thing. I agree that Jesus did not abolish food laws but I do not think this was the meaning of Mark 7:15 (a few verses earlier) in its historical setting. Needless to say, I see many more texts as dealing with purity, explicitly as well as implicitly.

18. Mary Douglas, *Purity and Danger: An Analysis of Concepts of Pollution and Taboo* (London: Routledge and Kegan Paul, 1966).

19. In addition to the exposition in chapters 3–4 of this book, see my *Jesus in Contemporary Scholarship*, 107–12. In subsequent scholarship, Jerome Neyrey's work is very helpful; see his *The Social World of Luke-Acts* (Peabody, Mass.: Hendrickson, 1991), 271–304, and "The Idea of Purity in Mark's Gospel," in *Semeia* 35, ed. John H. Elliott (Decatur, Ga.: Scholars Press, 1986), 91–128. See also Bruce Malina, *The New Testament World: Insights from Cultural Anthropology*, rev. ed. (Louisville: Westminster/John Knox, 1993), 149–83.

circumstances. Moreover, voices of opposition to the purity system were also Jewish voices. That is, the critique of purity is not a critique of Judaism, but a critique of a particular way of construing Judaism.

For my understanding of the role of purity in first-century Judaism, I am once again primarily dependent upon Jacob Neusner. As I said in the previous section about the Pharisees, if Neusner is significantly mistaken about the Pharisees and the idea of purity in first-century Judaism, then I would have to rethink much of CHP. But, as in the case of the Pharisees, the congruence between his analysis of purity and what we find in the early layers of the gospel tradition is impressive.

Where I Have Changed My Mind

The major change concerns how I see the role of the Temple and Jerusalem in the social world of Jesus, and thus the meaning of Jesus' prophetic threats against the Temple and Jerusalem. In CHP, I argued that the Temple as the center of the purity system was also a focal point of Jewish resistance to Rome. I saw the Temple with its ideology of holiness as central to what I sometimes called Jewish nationalism. Jesus' critique of the Temple was thus a critique of its role in Jewish nationalism, which I saw as responsible for the catastrophic war of revolt against Rome from 66 to 70.

I now see the Temple's role in the social world of Jesus very differently. I continue to see it as the center of the purity system. But rather than seeing the Temple as the center of Jewish national aspirations, I see it as the center of a native domination system. This change is accompanied by a modification in my understanding of the role of purity in the social world of Jesus. Rather than seeing purity as operating in a fairly undifferentiated way through the society as a whole, I now see purity as primarily the ideology of the ruling class, centered in the Temple.

This change is the result of the single most important development in how I see the social world of the Jewish homeland in the first century, and Jesus in relationship to that world. Namely, in the years since I finished the first edition of this book in 1983, I have become aware of the importance of economic class analysis for understanding the sociopolitical dynamics of Jesus' world.

In particular, I have been struck by the illuminating power of cross-cultural studies of the political and economic structures of premodern societies. The use of such studies is one of the most important examples of a major development in biblical scholarship in the last twenty years, namely, an increasingly interdisciplinary approach.

Of particular importance for biblical scholars has been a model of the political-economic structure of "preindustrial agrarian societies." Among Hebrew Bible scholars, two of the most familiar names who have made use of this model are Norman Gottwald and Walter Brueggemann. Among Jesus scholars, the pioneers are Richard Horsley and Dom Crossan.[20] Their use of the model has been followed by many, though not by all. Indeed, one of the major divisions in the discipline today is between scholars who use this model and those who do not.

Because this model and its illuminating power may not be familiar to all readers, I begin with a summary.[21] Preindustrial agrarian societies (sometimes shortened to "peasant societies") emerged when agriculture became sufficiently productive to support cities. Over time, these societies (which lasted in different forms until the Industrial Revolution) were increasingly marked by a sharp class division, of both power and wealth, between city-dwellers and rural people. In very broad strokes, urban and rural corresponded to the two primary social classes.

In the city lived "the urban ruling elites" and their "retainers." The former were about 1 to 2 percent of the total population and consisted of the political and economic elites: the ruler, traditional aristocracy, high government and religious officials, and their extended families. The "retainers" (about 5 to 8 percent of the population) were a "service class" attached to the elites. They included middle- and lower-level government officials, the army, some of the priesthood, most scribes, some urban merchants, and the servants of the elites.

The second major social class was rural. Though made up mostly of peasants, and most often called "the peasant class," it also included people who were not agricultural producers, such as fishers, laborers, and artisans, as well as radically marginalized people such as beggars, outcasts, and other "expendables." The rural class was typically around 90 percent of the population.

The relationship between urban elites and rural peasants was one of economic exploitation. Generalizing across cultures, urban elites and their retainers (together, 6 to 10 percent of the population) typically acquired two-thirds of the annual production of wealth. Rural peasants — 90 percent of the population — made do with the remaining one-third.

---

20. See books by Crossan and Horsley cited in nn. 6 and 8 above. See also Horsley's *The Liberation of Christmas: The Infancy Narratives in Social Context* (New York: Crossroad, 1989); *Sociology and the Jesus Movement* (New York: Crossroad, 1989); and, with Neil Asher Silberman, *The Message and the Kingdom: How Jesus and Paul Ignited a Revolution and Transformed the Ancient World* (New York: Grosset/Putnam, 1997).

21. I have also described the model elsewhere. See in particular chapter 5 of *Jesus in Contemporary Scholarship* and chapter 6 of *The God We Never Knew* (San Francisco: Harper, 1997).

This is the glaring economic fact about such societies: gross economic inequality between urban elites and rural peasants.

Yet the wealth was generated by the peasants, for in these societies agricultural production was the primary source of wealth. So how did the elites manage to extract two-thirds of the production of peasants for their own use? Through two primary means. The first was taxation of peasant agricultural production. The second was direct ownership of agricultural land, on which peasants paid rent, or worked as sharecroppers or day-laborers. The effect on peasant life was dramatic. Marked by subsistence existence in good times, peasant life was vulnerable to a bad crop or even the death of an animal. Infant mortality and disease rates were high, and life expectancy was remarkably low.

To complete the model: in addition to this relationship of economic exploitation between urban elites and rural peasants, such societies were also politically oppressive and typically legitimated by religious ideology. In these societies ruled over by a few men (and thus they were patriarchal societies as well), ordinary people had no power over the shape or direction of society. Moreover, these societies were typically legitimated by religion. The religion of the elites declared that God or the gods had ordained the social order. Kings ruled by divine right.

Together, these three elements constituted the "domination system" of the ancient world, to use Walter Wink's useful shorthand phrase.[22] Such societies were marked by "systemic injustice" — injustice built into the very structures of society. The issue was not the personal virtue or wickedness of the elites. Elites as individuals could be decent and good people. The issue, rather, was the injustice built into the system itself.

The kind of society portrayed by this model was common throughout the ancient Near East (and, indeed, in most parts of the world for a very long time). To illustrate its illuminating power by applying the model briefly to the biblical tradition, ancient Egypt was a classic domination system. Strikingly, the history of ancient Israel began with the story of liberation from the domination system of Egypt. A few hundred years later, the conflict between Moses and Pharaoh was resumed within Israel itself. With the emergence of kingship, the domination system was reestablished, and soon legitimated by a royal theology. As Walter Brueggemann puts it, Solomon became a new Pharaoh and Egypt was reborn in Israel.[23]

---

22. Wink, *Engaging the Powers*. See also his crystallization of his trilogy on the powers, *The Powers That Be*.

23. Walter Brueggemann, *The Prophetic Imagination* (Philadelphia: Fortress, 1978), chapter 2.

Seeing the history of ancient Israel within this framework greatly illuminates the message of the classical prophets. Like Moses before them,
the great social prophets of ancient Israel were to a large extent God-
intoxicated voices of religious social protest against the ruling elites of
palace and temple. In the name of God and Israel's covenant traditions, they indicted the domination system and its legitimation by royal
theology.

The model illuminates the social world of Jesus as well. The domination system continued into his time. I see no reason to think that the
Jewish homeland in the first century was exempt from the most common form of political economy in the ancient world. To put that only
slightly differently, I see no reason to think that her economic and political structures differed significantly from her neighbors. Even though
certain laws of the Hebrew Bible (especially those concerning the ju-
bilee year) mandated a more egalitarian society, there is little reason
to think that they had much impact in Herodian and Roman Palestine. Indeed, there is reason to think that conditions for peasants were
worsening. Despite the fact that the Torah promised that land would remain in the hands of peasant families in perpetuity, there is persuasive
evidence that land was increasingly being acquired by wealthy elites.[24]

At the top of the domination system was Roman imperial control,
with its system of tribute and taxation. Below the Romans were the
native ruling elites, made up primarily of the Herodian families and
the native aristocracy, much of which consisted of the high priestly
families. To a considerable extent, the native domination system was
thus centered in the Herodians and in the Temple in Jerusalem. The
Temple was thus a profoundly ambiguous institution. On the one hand,
it was the center of traditional Jewish devotion and pilgrimage. It was
the dwelling place of God on earth and the place where sacrifices were
offered for certain kinds of sins and impurities. On the other hand, it
was the center of an economically exploitative domination system. The

---

24. Referring to this development as "the commercialization of land," Crossan argues
that in the time of Jesus, a "traditional agrarian empire" (in which peasants still owned
their land, even though taxed heavily) was being replaced by a "commercialized agrarian
empire" (in which land was treated as a commodity to be bought and sold, with elites
acquiring more of it). See Crossan, "Jesus and the Kingdom," 23–24, with footnotes and
bibliography. Other important studies include David Fiensy, *The Social History of Palestine
in the Herodian Period* (Queenston: Edwin Mellen, 1991), and the forthcoming book by
K. C. Hanson and Douglas Oakman, *Palestine in the Time of Jesus: Social Structures and Social Conflicts* (Minneapolis: Fortress, 1998). For an excellent relatively compact exposition
of tensions brought about by economic and social changes in Galilee, see Sean Freyne,
"The Geography, Politics, and Economics of Galilee and the Quest for the Historical
Jesus," in Bruce Chilton and Craig A. Evans, ed., *Studying the Historical Jesus: Evaluations
of the State of Current Research* (Leiden: Brill, 1994), 75–121.

high priest and the traditional high priestly families were not only the religious elite, but the political and economic elites. During the time of Roman governors, the high priesthood was primarily responsible for domestic political rule. Tithes (which were really taxes on agricultural production) were paid to the Temple and priesthood.[25] High priestly families were major landowners, despite the Torah's prohibition of land ownership by priests.[26]

This perception of the role of the Temple in the domination system has affected my understanding of the role of holiness/purity in the social world of Jesus. I no longer see the emphasis upon holiness/purity as the dominant cultural dynamic of postexilic Judaism as a whole, but more particularly as the religious ideology of a domination system centered in the Temple. That the Temple was seen as the center of purity seems well established: it was geographically the center of a world of purity maps. Moreover, the oral elaboration of the laws of purity in Leviticus was done primarily by scribal retainers attached to the Temple. As Neusner wrote more than two decades ago, "You shall be holy as I your God am holy" (Lev. 19:2) was the central subject of scribal exposition.[27] And it is worth noting that the emphasis upon proper tithing of agricultural produce as a purity issue served the economic interest of the elites.

Thus I see holiness/purity primarily as the ideology of the Temple elites and their scribal retainers. I see the Pharisees, with their emphasis upon purity and tithing, as sharing that ideology, whatever their actual relationship to the Temple and its scribal retainers.

This change in my understanding of the social world of Jesus has affected how I see Jesus' attitude toward Jerusalem and the Temple. In CHP, I saw Jesus' act of overturning tables in the Temple as well as his prophetic warnings to Jerusalem to be indictments of Jerusalem and the Temple as the center of Jewish nationalist aspirations and resistance. Then, and specifically, I interpreted the words accompanying the Temple act in Mark 11:17, "You have made it a den of robbers," as an indictment of the Temple as a center of nationalist violence. My justification was that the words echo Jer. 7:11, where "robbers" has connotations of "violent ones."

Now I see Jesus' Temple act quite differently. Namely, the act of overturning the tables of the money-changers is more plausibly an in-

---

25. These were in addition to Herodian and Roman taxation.

26. The Torah's prohibition of land ownership by priests was interpreted to mean that, though they could own land, they could not work it. See E. P. Sanders, *Judaism: Practice and Belief*, 63 B.C.E.–66 C.E. (Philadelphia: Trinity Press International, 1992), 77, 147.

27. See pp. 73–77, 95–96 in this book.

dictment of the Temple as the center of an economically exploitative system legitimated in the name of God. The allusion to Jer. 7:11 in Mark 11:17 (if it goes back to Jesus) thus fits perfectly. In their context in Jeremiah, the words indict the Temple elites of Jeremiah's day, who had made the Temple "a den of robbers." Rather than it being a center of justice for widows and orphans, it had become the den of the elites who pillaged the populace, all the while saying, "This is the temple of the Lord, the temple of the Lord, the temple of the Lord," and "We are safe" (Jer. 7:1–15). Similarly, I now see Jesus' verbal warnings to Jerusalem and the Temple not as an indictment of Jewish nationalism or separatism, but as an indictment of city and temple as the center of the domination system.

This change in my perception of the Temple and its role in the purity system has not affected the most central claims of CHP. I continue to see the issue between Jesus and his opponents as social-political (and, of course, within a religious framework). But I no longer see the central political issue as a misguided nationalism generated by the dynamic of holiness, but as a domination system legitimated by the ideology of holiness/purity. The "villains" (if one may speak of such) thus change. They were not those yearning for liberation from Rome, but those who profited from and legitimated (consciously or unconsciously) the domination system. Again, the issue was not personal virtue, but involvement in systemic injustice legitimated by an emphasis upon "holiness." Against the politics of holiness, Jesus not only protested, but advocated an alternative core value for shaping Israel's life — a politics of compassion.

Thus I no longer see the conflict between purity and compassion as having much to do with how to deal with the collision course with the Roman enemy. Rather, the conflict was about politics and justice: about whether compassion or purity was to be the core value shaping Israel's collective life. To use different language, the conflict was about whether compassion or purity was to be the core value of the Kingdom of God.

Finally, to echo and emphasize a point I made earlier, my understanding of Jesus as a sharp critic of the politics of holiness/purity does not set Jesus over against Judaism. The emphasis upon holiness/purity was Jewish, but it was not Judaism. Instead, it was a form of Judaism advocated by the elites and their retainers. Rather than representing Judaism or the Jews of their day, they might fairly be seen as the oppressors of the vast majority of the Jewish people in that time. How far purity was affirmed by those in the peasant class is difficult (and perhaps impossible) to know. One can imagine that it was internalized in peasant psyches, for the underclass in a society often internalizes the

ideology of the dominant class. But often the underclass rejects the ideology of the elites, and it is easy to imagine forms of peasant Judaism
quite different in emphasis and practice. In any case, my argument is
that holiness/purity was the core value of the Temple elites and their
scribal retainers.

This Edition of *CHP*

I have done only a "light editing" of the body of CHP. I have made
minor stylistic changes here and there, but I have neither revised
the argument nor updated the footnotes. It thus, with very minor
modifications, describes how I saw things in the early 1980s.

There is one major change in word-choice about which I want
to comment. I have consistently changed "mercy" and "merciful" to
"compassion" and "compassionate." The justification for the change is
very simple. Namely, the most common connotations of "mercy" and
"merciful" in modern English often do not express the meanings of
the relevant gospel and biblical texts. In English, "mercy" and "merciful" commonly have two closely related dimensions of meaning.[28]
First, showing mercy typically presumes a situation of wrongdoing. One
is merciful to somebody who has done wrong and toward whom one
would therefore be entitled to act otherwise. Showing mercy is thus
often associated with contexts of guilt, whether legal ("pardon") or
theological ("forgiveness"). Second, the language of mercy commonly
presumes a power relationship of superior to inferior; one is merciful to
somebody over whom one has power. But in most synoptic contexts,
these meanings are not only not called for, but are often inappropriate.

The word "compassion" avoids these connotations. As its Latin roots
suggest, compassion means "to feel with." To be compassionate means
to feel the feelings of another, and then to act accordingly. Strikingly,
in Hebrew and Aramaic, it is semantically associated with the word for
"womb."[29] To be compassionate is to feel for somebody as a mother feels
for the children of her womb. It also has connotations of life-giving and
nourishment. In the Hebrew Bible, God is often spoken of as compassionate. God feels for and cares for the children of God's womb, and
God is angered when the children of God's womb are the victims of
injustice and suffering. One of the most powerful expositions of this

---

28. See, for example, the first three definitions of mercy in the *Oxford English
Dictionary*.

29. See, for example, Phyllis Trible, *God and the Rhetoric of Sexuality* (Philadelphia:
Fortress, 1978), chaps. 2 and 3.

notion is found in Abraham Heschel's treatment of the prophets of ancient Israel.[30]

The change from mercy to compassion affects one of the central contrasts of the book. Whereas in the first edition I spoke of a contrast between holiness and mercy, I now speak of a contrast between holiness/purity, on the one hand, and compassion, on the other hand. Whereas I then spoke of a politics of holiness versus a politics of mercy, I now speak of a politics of holiness (or purity) versus a politics of compassion.

To conclude this introduction, I want to thank N. Thomas (Tom) Wright for writing a foreword to this edition. This book originally brought us together some fifteen years ago. We have become good friends, even as we are scholars with somewhat different positions.[31] I appreciate the attention Tom has paid to this book in his own work, and appreciate his willingness to introduce the paperback edition, even though the way in which I have changed my mind makes my argument somewhat less supportive of his own position.

To comment briefly about the differences Tom cites in his foreword, they are primarily about three matters. First, we disagree about whether sayings about "the coming of the son of man" go back to Jesus. I do not think so, and Tom does. I understand them as "second coming" sayings created in the post-Easter community: the early Christian movement after Jesus' death began to speak of his return as "the son of man" of Daniel 7. However, this disagreement is not major. As noted earlier, Tom does not think they should be interpreted within the framework of apocalyptic eschatology.

Second, unlike me, Tom attributes a messianic consciousness to Jesus, on the grounds that doing so enables us to accommodate more of the synoptic material. (Tom, it should be noted, does not seek to integrate the Gospel of John into his portrait.)

Third, Tom argues that Jesus saw his own death as playing a central role in his vocation of bringing about the real return of Israel from exile. I remain unpersuaded about both claims, though I am open, I trust, to further light. But for now, the understanding of Jesus as the Messiah and of his death as salvific both still seem to me to be post-Easter products of the early Christian community. In short, I see both "Messiah" and "salvific death" as post-Easter metaphors for speaking about the

---

30. Abraham Heschel, *The Prophets* (New York: Harper and Row, 1962).

31. We are currently co-authoring a book on Jesus in which our differing positions will be set out side by side. To be called *The Meaning of Jesus: Two Visions*, it will be published by HarperSanFrancisco in late 1998.

significance of Jesus. Metaphors can be true of course (and as a Christian, I think these metaphors are true). But their truth is neither literal nor dependent on historical factuality. Their metaphorical truth as post-Easter affirmations does not depend upon them ever having been ideas in the mind of Jesus, or intentions of Jesus himself.

But these differences should not obscure our major agreements or our mutual affection. We agree that the political dynamics of first-century Jewish Palestine are central to glimpsing the historical Jesus. We agree that there was conflict between Jesus and some of his Jewish contemporaries (including the Pharisees) about the historical shape and direction of Israel. We agree that Jesus' relationship to Jerusalem and the Temple is central to a historical reconstruction of Jesus. We agree that Jesus offered an alternative to the quest for holiness in its different forms, as advocated by Pharisees, Temple elites, Essenes, and at least some within the resistance movements. We see Jesus as thoroughly Jewish and passionately concerned with one of the most central of Jewish questions: what was Israel to be? His was a Jewish voice offering a Jewish alternative within the Judaisms of the turbulent first century.

CHAPTER ONE
Introduction

In the history of comprehensive reconstructions of the mission and teaching of Jesus, the stone which one generation of critics rejects often becomes for a new generation the cornerstone of a new edifice.[1] The outstanding example of a neglected stone recovered and made central by a daring act of salvage occurred at the turn of this century. Before Johannes Weiss and Albert Schweitzer wrote their epochal works,[2] Jesus' sayings of eschatological crisis and his world-denying imperatives had largely been neglected by nineteenth-century scholarship. The context within which it interpreted the teaching of Jesus did not leave room for them, a situation to which Schweitzer vividly drew attention.[3] The neglected stone, the sayings of eschatological crisis, now became the cornerstone. The understanding of Jesus' ministry was articulated within the framework of his expectation of the imminent irruption of the transcendent Kingdom of God: the end of the world as we know it, resurrection, judgment, and the coming of the messianic Kingdom. The new cornerstone inevitably determined both the shape and size of the new edifice: it set the overall context within which Jesus' mission was viewed, and largely controlled the number of stones which could be fitted into the new building. The context set by this cornerstone has dominated twentieth-century New Testament scholarship.

But, as was the case with the constructions which preceded it, this construction also left its debris. In the ensuing edifice no place could be found for the traditions about Jesus which reflect a concern with the institutions of Judaism, which manifest conflict with his contemporaries about the shape and destiny of Israel, and which indicate an awareness of the religio-political threat to Israel by Rome.

---

1. See H. J. Cadbury, *The Peril of Modernizing Jesus* (New York, 1937), 46.

2. J. Weiss, *Die Predigt Jesu vom Reiche Gottes* (Göttingen, 1st ed. 1892, 2d ed. 1900); the first edition is available in English, trans. and ed. R. H. Hiers and D. L. Holland, *Jesus' Proclamation of the Kingdom of God* (Philadelphia, 1971). A. Schweitzer, *Das Messianitäts- und Leidensgeheimnis* (Tübingen, 1901), available in English as *The Mystery of the Kingdom of God* (London, 1914), and *Von Reimarus zu Wrede* (Tübingen, 1906), available in English as *The Quest of the Historical Jesus* (London, 1910).

3. Cf. *Quest*, 398, where Schweitzer writes of the results produced by his predecessors: "Many of the greatest sayings are found lying in a corner like explosive shells, from which the charges had been removed."

The present study is based upon the assumption that stones of such weight should not be left lying about, neglected or dismissed as unusable. What the new cornerstone will be is still unclear, though there are indications that it may emerge from the renewal of interest in the social matrix of the Palestinian base of the Jewish movement, about which we shall say more in the latter part of this introduction. This study reflects that interest and is another contribution to the quest for a more comprehensive historical reconstruction of the ministry of Jesus than that provided by the eschatological context.

The context within which this study places the teaching of Jesus is conflict: the conflict between Rome and Israel as the setting within which conflict occurred between Jesus and his contemporaries concerning the structures and purpose of Israel. Selecting a context, of course, cannot be arbitrary but must grow out of and be justified by the material which the context seeks to interpret. Thus the final justification of conflict as a context for interpreting the teaching of Jesus will be the study as a whole, but preliminary observations establish a prima facie case for utilizing this context.

Conflict was endemic in first-century Palestine. The society of which Jesus was a part had been promised universal sovereignty and yet found itself in a colonial situation under a mighty and often ruthless world power with its own claims to universal sovereignty. Not surprisingly, Jewish conflict with the colonial power was widespread and utilized a variety of means, ranging from the dispatch of official delegations, to nonviolent protests, to guerilla warfare, culminating in the tragic war of liberation of 66–70 C.E.

In this situation Jesus spoke repeatedly of the Kingdom of God, the term which expressed the hope of Israel for universal sovereignty. That he was crucified as a leader of the national liberation movement on the orders of a second-rank and second-rate Roman colonial administrator points to conflict with either Rome or Jewish authorities or both. That he may have been innocent of sedition does not counter the significance of his mode of death, for whether guilty of the specific charge or not, violent death as a political criminal does not occur in the absence of conflict.

Besides these terse observations, there is also the distinctive character of the tradition in which Jesus stood. The Hebrew Bible (Christian Old Testament) has aptly been characterized as the description of "the struggle to structure a historic community so that its life is an expression of loyalty to one God."[4] Religion (loyalty to Yahweh) and politics (struc-

---

4. C. F. Sleeper, "Political Responsibility according to I Peter," *NovTest* 10 (1968):

turing a historic community) are here combined, two phenomena which the modern world tends to separate. In the same way, the Torah was not only divine revelation, but also the constitution of the community of Israel. It embraced all of life, functioning as religious law as well as civil, criminal, and international law. Moreover, it concerned not only the present structuring of the community, but also its destiny and purpose. Hence what might be political matters in other traditions are in fact intertwined with religion in this tradition. "Moses," Josephus writes, "did not make religion a part of virtue, but he saw and ordained other virtues [viz.: justice, fortitude, temperance, universal agreement of the members of the community with one another] to be parts of religion."[5]

Thus to be a religious figure in this tradition was quite different from being a religious figure in a tradition which defines religion as, for example, what persons do with their solitude. It meant to face questions about the purpose, structure, and destiny of the historic community of Israel. What did it mean to be the people of God? In particular, in a setting in which Israel's sovereignty was denied and its very existence threatened by the imperial combination of Hellenistic culture and Roman military power, what did it mean to be Israel, the people of promise destined to rule Yahweh's created order? Groups within Judaism had their conflicting answers to this question.

Jesus too, I will argue, had his answer, an answer which, because of the distinctive nature of the tradition which he shared with his contemporaries, would have affected the social structures and institutions of his own people, and which did involve him in conflict with his contemporaries. This conflict between Jesus and his contemporaries, in the setting of Israel's conflict with Rome, is the subject of this study.[6]

To speak of conflict in this sense is to speak of Jesus' concern about groups, history, and politics. It is also to engage in the quest of the historical Jesus. The validity of both enterprises is called into question by two obstacles: the prevalent exclusion of politics from the concern of Jesus; and the assignment of priority to a method which minimizes what may be attributed to Jesus. The burden of this introductory chapter is to examine and undermine these two obstacles.

---

284. See also T. M. Parker, *Christianity and the State in the Light of History* (London, 1955), 5–15; G. E. Wright, *The Old Testament and Theology* (New York, 1969), 97–120.

5. *Ap.* 2.16.

6. Conflict as *historical* conflict thus distinguishes this study from (though it is not necessarily antithetical to) studies which understand conflict in cosmic terms as between the divine and demonic. See, for example, R. Leivestad, *Christ the Conqueror* (London, 1954), subtitled, "Ideas of Conflict and Victory in the New Testament"; J. Kallas, *Jesus and the Power of Satan* (New York, 1968); J. Becker, *Das Heil Gottes* (Göttingen, 1964); and J. M. Robinson, *The Problem of History in Mark* (London, 1957).

The Exclusion of Politics

That Jesus was not concerned about politics was virtually a consensus earlier in this century. As C. J. Cadoux observed near mid-century, one could fill a good-sized notebook with quotations claiming that Jesus excluded political questions from his concern.[7] Reasons for this exclusion vary. By far the most common and formidable reason throughout the middle third of this century was based on Jesus' claimed eschatological orientation and a hermeneutic derived from it. However, before turning to that, various other reasons that are offered or implied need to be scrutinized.

Noneschatological Exclusion of Politics

According to one common assumption, the only two options for a Jew in first-century Palestine were violent revolutionary nationalism or a nonpolitical stance. Since most writers do not see Jesus as a violent revolutionary, they conclude that he was apolitical. Such is implied by L. H. Marshall's statement that the difficulty which the Jewish leaders experienced in convincing Pilate that Jesus was dangerous proved that he "had not dabbled in politics."[8] The assumption is that to dabble in politics meant to be culpable of treason against Rome. W. Lillie similarly writes that Jesus remained aloof from the whole political set-up of the time, "in spite of the attractions of Zealot policy."[9] Again, two options are posed: aloofness or zealotism.

To define "to be political" as equivalent to "to be a Zealot" is a strange way of using words. Supporting the status quo in a revolutionary situation is not apolitical, but is also a political stance. Moreover, there is a range of political stances between violent revolution and unqualified allegiance to the present order. More importantly, this exclusion of politics concentrates solely on Rome and ignores the fact that questions about the structure and purpose of Israel were also political questions. That Jesus was indifferent to politics cannot be demonstrated on the grounds that he did not lead the local unit of the national liberation front.

A second position affirms that the focus of Jesus' ministry was on eternal religious and moral principles quite divorced from the vagaries of the historically conditioned conflicts of his time. Scholarly voices

---

7. C. J. Cadoux, *The Historic Mission of Jesus* (London, 1941), 163.
8. L. H. Marshall, *The Challenge of New Testament Ethics* (London, 1946), 149.
9. W. Lillie, *Studies in New Testament Ethics* (London, 1961), 90.

from earlier in this century frequently made the claim. A. H. M'Neile argued that the aims of Jesus were "utterly remote from anything political," for his Kingdom was not of this world; instead, he consistently penetrated beneath earthly hopes and ideas to spiritual principles.[10] J. Mackinnon claimed that Jesus was so totally absorbed in the moral and spiritual life that he had no time for the "crass politics" of the day.[11] More startling yet was the judgment of E. F. Scott: Jesus deliberately aimed to keep clear of the "stormy politics of his age"[12] and had to labor under the burden of carrying on "a purely religious work in a heated political atmosphere."[13]

In fairness to the above writers, we should note that they may have given a very narrow scope to the term "politics," whereas this study uses it in a broad sense: the concern about the structure and purpose of a historical community. Perhaps they simply mean that Jesus did not seek a seat on the Sanhedrin or serve in the civil service or become involved in palace intrigues or guerilla warfare, all of which is correct.

But for several reasons, to use that as a basis for claiming that politics was of no interest to Jesus is misleading. First, to claim that Jesus was concerned about religion but not politics bifurcates religion and politics in a manner alien to the ancient world, though such separation is very common in modern Western societies.[14] Of course, Jesus may have transcended the interrelationship of politics and religion, though he would virtually cease to be a first-century Jewish religious figure if he did; moreover, this is a claim that needs to be demonstrated rather than asserted on the basis of a theological affirmation of his uniqueness.

Second, not only does this position separate religion from politics, but it also separates Jesus from his historical milieu. It assumes that the conflict situation of his people had no significant influence on his teaching, evidenced especially in Scott's statement that the chief en-

---

10. A. H. M'Neile, *The Gospel according to St. Matthew* (London, 1957), xxii.

11. J. Mackinnon, *The Historic Jesus* (London, 1936), 49. Cf. J. W. Flight, *IDB*, 3:514: "He avoided political complications in his teaching, for he was concerned with man's relation to God and to his fellow men, and not to the Roman political order."

12. E. F. Scott, *The Ethical Teaching of Jesus* (London, 1924), 78.

13. E. F. Scott, *The Crisis in the Life of Jesus* (New York, 1952), 29. Cf. Parker, *Christianity and the State*, 17, n. 6: "We may suppose, too, that, especially with His knowledge of the disaster in which the political ferment of the time would end, He knew that, not merely to take sides, but even to give political issues prominence in His teaching, would divert attention from His redemptive mission."

14. Cadoux, *Historic Mission*, 164–65; and chapter 2 of the present writer's *Conflict and Social Change* (Minneapolis, 1971), where multiple reasons are explicated for the modern Christian's tendency to separate religious and political questions.

cumbrance to Jesus' "purely religious work" was the heated political atmosphere. Substituting the name of an earlier figure of Jewish history in a parallel statement demonstrates the extraordinary character of this claim: "It was the chief difficulty of Jeremiah (Amos, Isaiah, Ezekiel, etc.) that he had to carry on a purely religious work in a heated political atmosphere."

On the contrary, Israel's historical crises led those figures to address the nation; the crises were not unfortunate hindrances that obscured a purely religious mission that they would have undertaken in any case. To separate Jesus in this way from his historical situation is reminiscent, according to Amos Wilder, "of those orchids that are said to live on air. They bloom up off the ground and nourish themselves on ozone" and have nothing to do with the dust of life.[15] If there is no continuity between Jesus and these earlier figures, this must be demonstrated, not assumed; and popular opinion in his day connected him to these earlier figures.[16]

Third, the emphasis on Jesus' religious concern is frequently motivated by the conviction that his teaching has an eternal significance which is not conditioned by the historical particularity of first-century conflicts.[17] Jesus as the incarnate Son of God must have been concerned primarily about eternal issues, not about the contingencies of a historical situation subject to rapid change, or else his teaching would risk irrelevancy to a later generation. However, to take seriously the Christian understanding of "incarnation" means precisely that God in Christ did become enmeshed in the circumstances of human life in a particular time and place, which need not (and perhaps cannot?) exclude the turbulent political questions of that time and place.

Interestingly, with some exceptions that will be noted later, the relatively few studies which do take conflict seriously also tend to restrict the alternatives to aloofness or Zealotism and to see the political question primarily in relation to Rome, largely ignoring the struggle within Judaism over the shape and purpose of Israel. This was true of H. S. Reimarus in the late 1700s, whose book is usually seen as the first in the quest for the historical Jesus: Jesus intended to liberate the Jewish people from Rome.[18] The same tendencies characterize the representa-

---

15. A. Wilder, *Otherworldliness and the New Testament* (London, 1955), 67.
16. Mark 6:15 par., 8:28 par. There are also numerous indications that Jesus (or the tradition) saw himself in the category of prophet: Mark 6:4; Luke 4:24, 13:33–34; and the frequent allusions to passages from the prophets.
17. See R. H. Hiers, *Jesus and Ethics* (Philadelphia, 1968), 132–47, for a survey of those who take this position.
18. H. S. Reimarus, *Von dem Zwecke Jesu und seiner Jünger* (1778), available in two

tives of this tradition in this century: R. Eisler,[19] J. Carmichael,[20] and the late S. G. F. Brandon,[21] whose scholarly work provoked a spate of critical articles and short studies.[22] Perhaps the durable disinclination of mainstream scholarship to treat seriously the political dimension is partially due to the "unwelcome" results of affirming the political pole of this unrealistically limited pair of alternatives.[23] Yet the fascination and merit of these studies stem from their proper even if inadequate recognition of the intense conflict situation of first-century Palestine, a recognition which they have been permitted nearly to monopolize.

Thus the arguments for the noneschatological exclusion of politics are countered relatively easily, however much they persist on the popular level. But in fact the major causes of the neglect of the political dimension are the peculiar characteristics of the two contexts for interpreting the teaching of Jesus which have dominated New Testament studies throughout much of this century. The first is the *time dimension* of the context proposed by Weiss and Schweitzer; the second is the *individualistic/ahistorical dimension* of the existential context.

English editions: *The Goal of Jesus and His Disciples,* trans. G. W. Buchanan (Leiden, 1970); *Reimarus: Fragments,* ed. C. H. Talbert and trans. R. S. Fraser (Philadelphia, 1970).

19. R. Eisler, *The Messiah Jesus and John the Baptist* (London, 1931).

20. J. Carmichael, *The Death of Jesus* (London, 1963).

21. S. G. F. Brandon, principally in *Jesus and the Zealots* (Manchester, 1967), though his earlier *The Fall of Jerusalem and the Christian Church* (London, 1951), and later *The Trial of Jesus* (London, 1968), are also relevant. His thesis is conveniently adumbrated in "Jesus and the Zealots," *StEv* 4=*TU* 102 (1968): 8–20. Brandon, it should be noted, affirms only a bond of common sympathy between Jesus and the Zealots, not identity.

22. Some (though not all) of the following literature also subscribes to the dichotomy Zealot/nonpolitical: O. Cullmann, *Jesus and the Revolutionaries* (New York, 1970); M. Hengel, *Was Jesus a Revolutionist?* (Philadelphia, 1971), with very valuable bibliography, and "War Jesus Revolutionär? Sechs Thesen eines Neutestamentlers," *EvKomm* 2 (1969): 694–96, plus *Victory over Violence: Jesus and the Revolutionists* (Philadelphia, 1973); J. W. Bowman, *Which Jesus?* 97–118; W. Klassen, "Jesus and the Zealot Option," *CJT* 16 (1970): 12–21; W. R. Farmer, "The Revolutionary Character of Jesus and the Christian Revolutionary Role in American Society," *Perkins School of Theology Journal* 22 (1969): 37–59; W. A. Beardslee, "New Testament Perspectives on Revolution as a Theological Problem," *JR* 51 (1971): 15–33; J. Gnilka, "War Jesus Revolutionär?" *Bibel und Leben* 12 (1971): 67–78; H. Merkel, "War Jesus ein Revolutionär?" *Bibel und Kirche* 26 (1971): 44–47; R. Pesch, "Der Anspruch Jesus," *Orientierung* 35 (1971): 53–56, 67–70, 77–81; G. Grespy, "Recherche sur la signification politique de la mort du Christ," *Lumière et Vie* 20 (1971): 89–109; G. Baumbach, "Die Zeloten — ihre geschichtliche und religionspolitische Bedeutung," *Bibel und Liturgie* 41 (1968): esp. 19–25; A. Richardson, *The Political Christ* (Philadelphia, 1973).

23. H. G. Wood, "Interpreting This Time," *NTS* 2 (1955–56): 262, notes that Eisler's "bizarre attempt to turn Jesus into a half-hearted Zealot leader . . . confirmed rather than challenged the current neglect of the study of the political relations of the ministry."

Imminent Eschatology and the Exclusion of Politics

The demonstration that history and politics were of no concern to Jesus is commonly credited to Weiss and Schweitzer.[24] For them, the conviction that the coming of the Kingdom and the end of the world as we know it were identical, and that this was imminent, excluded politics and history. In the face of imminent supernatural intervention by God to bring about the messianic age, concern with the structures and historical fate of Israel would have been absurd. There was (literally) not time for that. This eschatological relativization of political questions is the substructure of Schweitzer's treatment of the question of tribute to Caesar. "How," he asks, "could one be concerned at all about such things?" As an earthly institution the state's duration extended only to the dawn of the Kingdom; since this was near, due within months, "what need had one to decide if one would be tributary to the world-power or no? One might as well submit to it, its end was in fact near."[25] So also with the question of the validity and meaning of the Torah, the constitution of the historic community's life: that question, Schweitzer affirms, had no significance for Jesus and was first posed by history, by the delay of the parousia.[26] Time — that is, the near end of it — excluded all such questions.

However valid their understanding of Jesus' mission was,[27] subsequent developments, precisely on the time question, mean that their imprimatur can no longer be invoked for the exclusion of politics. Very few scholars have been willing to follow them in the immediacy which they attach to the expectation of the end. Most compelling to most scholars are, on the one hand, the firm presence in the tradition of present sayings about the Kingdom, as well as future sayings, and, on the other hand, hesitancy about the immediacy of the end. Some argue that Jesus put no limit on the time of the end,[28] others that, though he expected the end in the lifetime of some of his contemporaries, he nevertheless envisioned a community that would live for a few decades between his death and the end,[29] and still others

---

24. N. Perrin, *The Kingdom of God in the Teaching of Jesus* (London, 1963), 20–21 and 21n, 51–52.

25. Schweitzer, *Mystery*, 119.

26. Ibid.

27. As argued in chapter 8 of this study, the exegetical base for understanding the crisis which Jesus announced as "the end of the world" is very narrow.

28. A. L. Moore, *The Parousia in the New Testament* (Leiden, 1966); on very different grounds, so also N. Perrin in his study of the Jesus tradition: *Rediscovering the Teaching of Jesus* (New York, 1967), 202–6.

29. E.g., E. G. Kümmel, *Promise and Fulfilment* (London, 1961).

that the identification of the Kingdom with the end of history is unwarranted.[30]

When once an extension of historical time is granted, whether indefinite or limited to a few decades, then the structures and historical fate of Israel again become important questions. How was Israel to live? What was to be its relationship to Rome? Or, if it was the purpose of Jesus to create a new community, what was to be its relationship to Israel? Was it to seek to transform Israel? Such questions impinge when an extension of time is granted.

Yet the undermining of the time dimension has been obscured by the continued use of the vocabulary made prominent by Weiss and Schweitzer, even though the meaning of the terms has shifted drastically. For them, the use of terms like "eschatological," "final," "end," "Kingdom of God," etc., was precise and consistent: such language referred to the supernatural act of God whereby the world would be radically changed (including resurrection of the dead, last judgment, and the coming of the messianic age).

But to any student of the synoptics, it is obvious that "eschatology" is now used in a variety of senses. Without cataloguing them, three can be noted. First, it continues to be used in the imminent literal sense given to it by Weiss and Schweitzer. Second, in studies influenced by neo-orthodoxy, in both Barthian and Bultmannian forms, it refers to the eternal which stands over every moment of time and thus is not concerned at all with a literal future, whether near or distant.[31] Third and finally, sometimes it characterizes a decisive act of God in history, even though it may have some continuity with the past and does not obviate a historical future.[32]

---

30. In addition to proponents of "realized eschatology," see esp. the following articles: S. Aalen, " 'Reign' and 'House' in the Kingdom of God in the Gospels," *NTS* 8 (1962): 215–40; M. Rist, "Jesus and Eschatology," in J. C. Rylaarsdam, ed., *Transitions in Biblical Scholarship* (Chicago, 1968), 193–215; G. B. Caird, "Les eschatologies du Nouveau Testament," *RHPR* 49 (1969): 217–27; J. Carmignac, "Les dangers de l'eschatologie," *NTS* 17 (1970–71): 365–90.

31. Discussed by J. Moltmann, *The Theology of Hope* (New York, 1967), 39–58. On 39–40, he notes that dialectical theology "makes the *eschaton* into a transcendental eternity, the transcendental meaning of all ages, equally near to all the ages of history and equally far from all of them." This is the same "whether eternity was understood in transcendental terms, as in Barth, who spoke of the unhistorical, supra-historical or 'proto-historical,' or whether the *eschaton* was understood in existentialist terms, as in Bultmann, who spoke of the 'eschatological moment.' " See also H. C. Kee, *Jesus in History* (New York, 1970), 265, n. 4, who notes the shift in meaning "from a pronouncement about the future to an understanding of existence in the present."

32. E. Jenni, *IDB*, 2:126, describes this as a broad definition of eschatology, which is concerned with "a future in which the circumstances of history are changed to such an extent that one can speak of a new, entirely different state of things, without, in so doing,

This multiplicity of senses is not in itself reprehensible, since few people would claim that a word can have one and only one meaning. What is culpable is when the sense in which the term is used is not specified. When a writer describes the teaching of Jesus as set in an eschatological framework, what is meant? That Jesus lived with an imminent expectation of "the end"? Or that this hour (and every hour) is the hour of existential decision? Or that Jesus was convinced that something of utter decisiveness and newness was happening in his generation? And when it is said, for example, that Israel faced its last hour, are we to understand that it was Israel's last hour because of the coming messianic age and final judgment, or because of a historical happening that was decisive for Israel? This ambiguity lies at the root of statements that eschatology is among the words which "have lost nearly all precise exegetical meaning"[33] and that "eschatology" ought to be banned from the vocabulary of theology.[34]

This ambiguity makes possible the transfer of a family of implications which logically have their home under one sense of the term to another sense of the term, where they turn out to be illegitimate children. Thus implications legitimately derived from eschatology in the sense advocated by Weiss and Schweitzer often continue to be recited even when eschatology is used in a substantially different sense.

Both of these aspects of the diffusion of eschatology are well illustrated in Norman Perrin's early work on the Kingdom of God, a useful survey of Jesus research from Schweitzer through the 1950s. Perrin considers that the decades of research since Weiss have confirmed that Jesus' understanding of the Kingdom of God has its background in apocalyptic thought.[35] In his survey, he regularly uses this conviction as a systematic tool to criticize presentations of Jesus' teaching which speak of politics, or of a concern to reform Judaism, or of human response as

necessarily leaving the framework of history." Cf. S. B. Frost, *Old Testament Apocalyptic* (London, 1952), 32.

33. J. C. Beker, "Biblical Theology Today," in M. Marty and D. G. Peerman, eds., *New Theology Number Six* (London, 1969), 27. So also O. Cullmann, *Salvation in History* (London, 1967), 79.

34. Carmignac, "Les dangers de l'eschatologie," passim, but esp. 388–90.

35. Perrin, *Kingdom of God*, 20, 51–52, 84, 118, 149–50, 153, 170, and esp. 158–59. Perrin's subsequent book on the Kingdom of God, *Jesus and the Language of the Kingdom* (Philadelphia, 1976), revises his earlier understanding considerably. Most notably, he now sees Kingdom of God as a *symbol* rather than a *concept*, though he still sees the decisive background as apocalyptic. For a work which develops further Perrin's understanding of symbol, see B. B. Scott, *Jesus, Symbol-Maker for the Kingdom* (Philadelphia, 1981), esp. 1–11.

playing an important role, or which interpret Jesus' teaching in terms of a continuing world order.[36]

All of this is consistent until Perrin presents his own understanding of the eschatology of Jesus. Reaffirming *that Kingdom of God is an apocalyptic concept* in the teaching of Jesus, he then qualifies it substantially, arguing that Jesus departed from the apocalyptic understanding of history in favor of a prophetic understanding.[37] Furthermore, Jesus' teaching may not be interpreted in terms of a linear understanding of time.[38] Finally, Jesus' eschatological teaching did not necessarily involve either the end of time or cosmic catastrophe,[39] nor did it yield any guidance as to the manner or time of consummation.[40] But what then is left of the original assertion that Kingdom of God is an apocalyptic concept in the teaching of Jesus?[41] Nothing of that which is normally connoted by the term "apocalyptic," nor of that which Weiss and Schweitzer meant. Once the apocalyptic conception of the Kingdom of God has been so thoroughly qualified, continuing to insist that Jesus' teaching must be understood within that framework is misleading. Cosmic events and end of time are gone — is "apocalyptic," especially when Weiss is credited with the demonstration of its centrality, still a felicitous term to describe an expectation devoid of this?

Perrin's work cogently illustrates the often unacknowledged shift in meaning of terms like "eschatological," "apocalyptic," "final," "end." Moreover, this shift enables Perrin (illegitimately) to use implications deriving from eschatology in the sense argued by Weiss to discredit those understandings of the teaching of Jesus which speak of politics, even though Perrin himself uses these terms in a sense radically different from their use in the seminal works of Weiss and Schweitzer.

In fact, it appears that Perrin's own understanding of eschatology is very close to the third definition cited above: to refer to a decisive

---

36. Perrin, *Kingdom of God*, 21 and 21, n. 4; 51–52, 84, 157.

37. Ibid., 176–78, 185. The prophetic understanding which Jesus accepted is that God acts in history, challenging Israel to repent; the apocalyptic understanding which he rejected is that history is a predetermined plan leading to a predetermined climax, in which the focus is on the end, not on moments within history.

38. Ibid., 185.

39. Ibid., 185, 190.

40. Ibid., 198.

41. Apparently two things: there will be a future consummation of that which has begun in the ministry of Jesus, though "how, when, and where" are unspecified (190); and that Jesus and the apocalyptic writers share in common the use of "Kingdom of God" in connection with the future hope (41n; and the list of differences between Jesus and the apocalypticists which he there adduces adds more force to the question whether "apocalyptic" is an appropriate term to describe the expectation of Jesus).

act of God in history, whereby something new enters and decisively changes history, even though it may have continuity with the past and does not obviate a historical future. But, crucially, this does not exclude politics in the sense of a concern for the structure and purpose of the historical community of Israel. This broad characterization of eschatology has been adopted by many Hebrew Bible scholars, who find that the prophetic passion about the historical present and future of Israel, involving immediately recognizable political questions, is eschatological in this sense.

This shift in the meaning of eschatology so that the time dimension is understood in other than the literally imminent sense given to it by Weiss and Schweitzer means that one can no longer claim that eschatology excludes the questions which we have labeled political. However, another strong current of New Testament scholarship also excludes history and politics from Jesus' concern: the ahistorical and individualistic character of a dominant hermeneutic, deriving from a demythologized eschatology and allied to existential philosophy.

Existentialism and the Exclusion of Politics

That the existentialist understanding of human existence is both individualistic and ahistorical has often been observed.[42] Indeed, this may be a major reason for its attractiveness in a century in which for several decades New Testament scholars (along with other theologians) were agreed "that the Christian kerygma has nothing in common with history and that church and world, faith and knowledge, lie on two completely different planes."[43] Whether or not existentialism is a viable hermeneutic whereby one moves from the question of *explicatio* (what the teaching of Jesus *did* mean) to *applicatio* (what it *does* mean for twentieth-century life) is beyond the scope of this study. What must be observed, however, is that the existential hermeneutic often operates not only as a vehicle of interpretation whereby the teaching of Jesus is clothed in contemporary dress, but also as a context for the historical understanding of the teaching itself.

For example, Rudolf Bultmann, arguably the most famous New

---

42. See, e.g., J. Moltmann, "Toward a Political Hermeneutics of the Gospel," *USQR* 23 (1968): 308–11; C. Braaten, *History and Hermeneutics* (Philadelphia, 1966), passim; Cullmann, *Salvation in History*, 24–28 and passim.

43. K. Koch, *The Rediscovery of Apocalyptic* (London, 1972), 63. His lament seems directed to the continental situation in particular; on 63–70 he mentions in passing some of the cultural factors at work.

Testament scholar of the twentieth century, affirmed that Jesus' language about the end can be demythologized by means of existential
philosophy. But then he also attributed this understanding to Jesus
himself. According to Bultmann, Jesus pressed "the whole contemporary mythology...into the service of this conception of human
existence," namely, that "every hour is the last hour."[44] Existential
thought has moved from the role of interpretation to inclusion in
historical assertions about Jesus.

Similarly, Hans Conzelmann argued that though Jesus spoke of the
nearness of the Kingdom in temporal terms, he really meant the nearness existentially: its "meaning lies in qualifying the human situation
in view of the coming of the kingdom."[45] Jesus himself is presented
as an existentialist. Moreover, the purpose of the "new quest for the
historical Jesus" of the 1950s and 1960s was to uncover "the understanding of existence implicit in Jesus' history" in order to compare it to
the existential encounter that is mediated by the kerygma.[46] The new
quest was thus a quest for Jesus' understanding of existence in existential terms. That Jesus therefore sounds like a twentieth-century German
existentialist in works stemming from this school is not surprising —
though, upon reflection, one may agree that it is "somewhat staggering"
that "Jesus is practically indistinguishable from a German kerygmatic
theologian of the twentieth century."[47]

Searching for Jesus' understanding of existence is not illegitimate,
even though data for this purpose may be more difficult to obtain than
the data sought by the "old questers."[48] What is illegitimate is the
attribution of the ahistorical and individualistic characteristics of existentialism to Jesus, which inevitably occurs when existentialism is the
context for explicating the historical meaning of his teaching. This not
only demythologizes but dehistoricizes the New Testament in general

---

44. R. Bultmann, *Jesus and the Word*, 52. See also the criticism by Bowman,
Which Jesus? 52–53: Bultmann finds the substitution of existentialist eschatology for
mythological eschatology "present *in the mind and teaching of Jesus*" (italics added).

45. H. Conzelmann, quoted in J. M. Robinson, *A New Quest for the Historical Jesus*
(London, 1959), 18.

46. Robinson, *New Quest*, 94.

47. Koch, *The Rediscovery of Apocalyptic*, 69. Cf. the remark of D. Nineham, "Jesus
in the Gospels," in N. Pittenger, ed., *Christ for Us Today* (London, 1965), 57: the Jesus
of the new quest seems "culturally rootless, or even to have his roots in the culture of
twentieth-century Germany."

48. See the excellent analysis by V. A. Harvey, *The Historian and the Believer* (London,
1967), 179–94. On 193 he concludes that insofar as the new quest concentrates on Jesus'
existential selfhood, it solicits "the heaviest possible assent to a historical judgment which,
in this particular case, is most tenuous."

and Jesus in particular.[49] Like any self-respecting context, it will not tolerate anything that does not cohere with it.

But skepticism with regard to this exclusion is justified on several grounds. There is the tradition in which Jesus stood, notable for its concern with both community and history. There are the sayings attributed to him which refer to impending historical events and which pertain to the structures and institutions of Judaism. Even the "eschatological" imagery (notably the Kingdom of God!) is corporate; the eschatological language itself does not lead to individualism, but existential reinterpretation of the eschatology does.[50] Historical research as such does not pronounce these items to be unauthentic or declare them to be mythological nuts which need to be shelled by an individualizing hermeneutic; rather, the existentialist perspective cannot fit them into its frame of reference.

Thus the case for the exclusion of politics by the time dimension of imminent eschatology and by the ahistorical/individualistic dimension of the existential perspective evaporates. Regarding the former, precisely the immediacy of the end has been modified or rejected by much of subsequent scholarship. Regarding the latter, the exclusion is due to the illegitimate intrusion of a perhaps viable hermeneutic into assertions about the historical Jesus. The collapse of the case for exclusion does not mean, of course, that one can thereby conclude that Jesus was concerned about the structures and historical destiny of Israel. That requires demonstration which can be done only through detailed exegetical study.

To the credit of the imminent eschatological context and the existential context, both do account for the element of crisis and the urgency of decision in a way in which their predecessors most often did not. The ministry of Jesus did not consist of articulating timeless moral principles or religious doctrines intended for generations yet unborn, but brought a decisive crisis to those who heard him, i.e., Israel. Any understanding of Jesus' mission and teaching must do justice to this crisis and urgency. But because of what they exclude, the imminent eschatological and existential contexts are less than adequate.

---

49. A complaint articulated by N. A. Dahl, "The Problem of the Historical Jesus," in C. Braaten and R. Harrisville, eds., *Kerygma and History* (New York, 1962), 163–65. He concludes, "It is pertinent to ask now whether, in view of the historical sources, it is not an impermissible extreme, conditioned by existence philosophy, to describe the historical Jesus merely as the Bearer of the Word which calls for decision."

50. See A. Wilder, *Eschatology and Ethics in the Teaching of Jesus* (New York, 1950), 53–70, who questions the individualistic character of Bultmann's existential reinterpretation on the grounds that the mythology of both the Old and New Testaments has a corporate and social referent.

For in identifying the crisis with the last (literally) crisis of world history, and by then demythologizing this by means of an individualistic
and ahistorical hermeneutic, so much of the Gospel tradition is left
unaccounted for.

The eschatological and existential context, by mid-century the
dominant context, either excluded or ignored much of the material attributed to Jesus. The wisdom sayings of Jesus were often dismissed as
unauthentic — not because they failed any of the usual tests for authenticity (most of them are Q), but because they did not cohere with
the picture of Jesus as an eschatological prophet.[51] The sayings warning
of the fall of the Temple and Jerusalem as an event within history with
historical causes were dismissed — not because they are poorly attested
(they are found in Q, Mark, L and John), but because the expectation of the fall of the Temple as a strictly eschatological event excludes
historical causation.[52]

Disputes about the meaning of the Torah were seen not as going
back to Jesus, but as the product of the early Christian movement, necessitated only by the delay of the parousia.[53] Or, if the disputes were
held to be genuine, it was because, it was claimed, Jesus saw the Torah
as one of the structures which held people in bondage to inauthentic existence, not because the disputes may have had any positive significance
vis-à-vis the structures and purpose of Israel. The critique of the Pharisaic program for Israel which is implied (and sometimes made explicit)
in the table fellowship of Jesus was either ignored or else understood in
individualistic terms as a conflict of dispositions (humility versus pride,
hypocrisy versus sincerity, etc.). The expulsion of the merchants from
the Temple, when treated at all, was said to have been done in preparation for the *eschaton.* It could then be demythologized into an acted
expression of the call to authentic existence — and not assigned any
significance vis-à-vis politics or history. The numerous intimations that
Jesus warned the leaders of Israel that the promises of God would go
to others if they did not respond were dismissed because they presuppose a historical future, presumably beyond Jesus' vision. The Kingdom
of God — an expression which would seem to have an indisputable
prima facie connection to Israel's collective future (even though with
universal overtones), and thereby have political implications — was

---

51. R. Bultmann, *The History of the Synoptic Tradition* (New York, 1963), 101–8. On
102–4, he lists twenty-six such sayings, all of which are regarded as nondominical. For
a critique, see W. D. Davies, *The Setting of the Sermon on the Mount* (Cambridge, 1964),
381–83, 457–60.

52. Kümmel, *Promise and Fulfilment,* 100–102.

53. Schweitzer, *Mystery,* 119.

understood either in superterrestrial terms, or as the *eschaton* which stands over every moment, demanding decision.

One can well agree with the lament that scholars "have internalized, de-temporalized, de-historicized, cosmologized, spiritualized, allegorized, mysticized, psychologized, philosophized and sociologized the concept of the Kingdom of God,"[54] not necessarily for the sake of avoiding the political implications, but avoiding them nevertheless. This study contends that what is needed is a context, growing out of and supported by the synoptic material, which can incorporate both the unmistakable elements of crisis and urgency and the implicit and often explicit concern with the structures and historical destiny of the people of God.[55]

A Way Forward

In the 1970s, a new emphasis in New Testament studies began to emerge. Rather than tending to exclude politics, this development highlights the social and political factors shaping the emergence of the Christian movement and the ministry of the historical Jesus. Though this trend does not have a generally agreed upon "label," it seeks to integrate the social sciences with the study of Christian origins. It makes deliberate use of insights and models derived from anthropology, sociology, and psychology. Scholarly works illustrating this emphasis include those by Gager, Theissen, Scroggs, Rubenstein, Malherbe, and Kee.[56]

Several other important works provide a more meticulously detailed picture of the historical and cultural setting of Judaism and its neighbors than previously available, especially those by Hengel and Neusner.[57]

---

54. G. W. Buchanan, *The Consequences of the Covenant* (Leiden, 1970), 55.

55. Three New Testament studies have sought to take the political dimension of Jesus' ministry seriously. All focus on Luke. See L. Gaston's provocative and useful *No Stone on Another* (Leiden, 1970); John Yoder, *The Politics of Jesus* (Grand Rapids, 1972); Richard Cassidy, *Jesus, Politics and Society* (Maryknoll, N.Y., 1978). Yoder concentrates on showing that the teaching of Jesus provides a viable social ethic even for Christians in the twentieth century; Cassidy attends to Jesus' stance on certain perennial social issues: riches and poverty, the status of women, nonviolence, etc.

56. John Gager, *Kingdom and Community: The Social World of Early Christianity* (Englewood Cliffs, 1975); see extensive review articles by David Bartlett, Jonathan Smith, and David Tracy in *Zygon* 13 (1978): 109–35. Gerd Theissen, *Sociology of Early Palestinian Christianity* (Philadelphia, 1978). Robin Scroggs, *Paul for a New Day* (Philadelphia, 1977); "The Sociological Interpretation of the New Testament: The Present State of Research," *NTS* 27 (1980): 164–79; "The Earliest Christian Communities as Sectarian Movement," in J. Neusner, ed., *Christianity, Judaism and Other Greco-Roman Cults* (Leiden, 1975), 2:1–12. Richard Rubenstein, *My Brother Paul* (New York, 1972). Abraham Malherbe, *Social Aspects of Early Christianity* (Baton Rouge, 1977). Howard Kee, *Christian Origins in Sociological Perspective* (Philadelphia, 1980). See also Patrick Henry, *New Directions in New Testament Study* (Philadelphia, 1979), esp. 180–202.

57. M. Hengel, *Die Zeloten* (Leiden, 1961; 2d ed., 1976); *Judaism and Hellenism,*

Contributing significantly to this picture are two major reference works, the thoroughly revised edition of Schürer's *The History of the Jewish People in the Age of Jesus Christ* and *The Jewish People in the First Century: Compendia Rerum Iudaicarum ad Novum Testamentum.*[58]

Of course, there is nothing new about studies of the background of Christianity, or even of the new Testament against its background. However, most often the background has been treated as a "backdrop," as a setting which at best might illuminate some references made by the actors who appear on the stage of the New Testament. What is new in this emphasis, which has a precedent though not direct progenitor in the "Chicago School" of New Testament interpretation much earlier in this century, is the treatment of the background not as setting but as a set of *factors* which shaped the early Christian movement and to which the movement tried to respond.

The background has become foreground, though the change has not produced a simple reduction to social causation. Instead, most of the studies stress the reciprocal relation between social factors (e.g., political instability, economic conditions and taxation, rural and urban dynamics, social disruption, social and religious norms) and the practices and ideology of the early Christian movement.

A number of realizations important for this book have emerged. First, though scholars recognized long ago that early Palestinian Christianity was a sect, the significance of this fact has not been more thoroughly explored. Many of the characteristics of sectarian movements also characterize it. In particular, like most sects, it originated in protest and sought to create a new world, both a new social world and a new way of perceiving reality. Second, there is a new awareness of the social function of religious norms and practices and of the effect of social factors (especially socio-religious norms) on the psyches of people. Third, there is a sharper perception of the social realities behind the texts, which in turn leads to the realization that many of these texts, whatever transcultural dimensions of meaning they may also have, initially had a pointed connection to the social matrix of the day.

For this investigation, the most pertinent of these works is the German scholar Gerd Theissen's study of the "Jesus movement," a renewal

---

2 vols. (Philadelphia, 1974); *Jews, Greeks and Barbarians* (Philadelphia, 1980). Neusner's numerous works on Judaism will be referred to throughout.

58. Emil Schürer, *The History of the Jewish People in the Age of Jesus Christ*, ed. Geza Vermes et al. (Edinburgh: vol. 1, 1973; vol. 2, 1979); S. Safrai and M. Stern, eds., *The Jewish People in the First Century: Compendia Rerum Iudaicarum ad Novum Testamentum*, 2 vols. (Assen, 1974). See also the multivolume *Christianity, Judaism and Other Greco-Roman Cults*, ed. J. Neusner (Leiden, 1975).

movement within Judaism brought into being by Jesus and operating in Palestine and Syria from roughly 30 C.E. to 70 C.E.[59] Theissen concentrates on traditions preserved in the synoptic Gospels and on the social dynamics of first-century Palestinian society. Along with the Pharisees, Essenes, and freedom fighters, the Jesus movement was one of four renewal movements competing for the religious loyalty of the Jewish people.

The major portion of Theissen's book is devoted to a careful analysis of the social factors (socio-economic, socio-ecological, socio-political, socio-cultural) affecting all of the movements, and the responses of the movements to these factors. Both the factors and the responses were shaped by the advent of Roman political power and the encroachment of Hellenistic culture. Each renewal movement, including the Jesus movement, offered a program defining what it meant to be the people of God in that setting. All emphasized intensification of the Torah, but in different ways and with different effects.

For the Essenes, Pharisees, and freedom fighters, the intensification was intended to produce greater differentiation from and solidarity over against the Gentiles, but the effect was to produce sharper divisions within Jewish society. The Jesus movement with its even more radical intensification of Torah became the "peace party" and an inclusive movement, initially including the outcasts within Jewish society and within a few decades Gentiles as well. Early Palestinian Christianity thus emerged as one of several socio-religious groups engaged in a struggle intimately connected to political, economic, and social factors. By moving politics and conflict to the foreground, this new emphasis is congruent with the present study, which sees the conflict between Rome and Judaism as the setting within which conflict occurred between Jesus and his contemporaries about the shape and purpose of the people of God.

Method and This Study

The second major obstacle to the viability of this study is whether sufficient historical knowledge of Jesus is available. New Testament scholarship in this century has developed a number of criteria for evaluating the historical authenticity of traditions attributed to Jesus in the Gospels: the criterion of multiple attestation of sources and forms, the

---

59. Theissen, *Sociology of Early Palestinian Christianity.*

environmental criterion, the criterion of coherence, and the criterion of dissimilarity.

Central to the question of how much can be known about the historical Jesus is the debate in contemporary scholarship about whether *priority* is to be assigned to the criterion of dissimilarity as the method for distinguishing the teaching of Jesus from what must be attributed to the church.[60]

The criterion appears in a negative form, in which it is used to *exclude* from the teaching of Jesus anything which can be attributed to either Judaism or early Christianity. In its negative form, it must, logically, produce a minimal picture of Jesus' teaching. This criterion also appears in a positive form, in which it is used to *include* as primitive tradition anything which does not reflect known interests of early Christianity, without supposing that sayings which reflect Christian interests must be excluded.

Only the negative form of the criterion claims sovereignty over the other criteria, for it excludes from the teaching of Jesus anything (no matter how well attested by, e.g., multiple sources) which reflects either Judaism or the church. *Only* that which is dissimilar can be accepted.[61] Because the early Christian movement not only may have "Christianized" the teaching, but also may have "Judaized" it, one can grant authenticity only when the tradition "can be shown to be dissimilar to characteristic emphases *both* of ancient Judaism and of the early

---

60. The opposing positions are most comprehensively presented by Perrin, *Rediscovering*, 15–53, and F. G. Downing, *The Church and Jesus* (London, 1968), esp. 93–131, though the whole book is germane. Two subsequent articles of special value are M. D. Hooker, "Christology and Methodology," *NTS* 17 (1970–71): 480–87; and H. K. McArthur, "The Burden of Proof in Historical Jesus Research," *ET* 82 (1970–71): 116–19. Other selected literature: E. Käsemann, *Essays on New Testament Themes* (London, 1964), 15–47; N. Perrin, *What Is Redaction Criticism?* (London, 1970), 68–74; Dahl, "The Problem of the Historical Jesus," 138–71; H. Conzelmann, *RGG* 3, 3:623–51; H. K. McArthur, *In Search of the Historical Jesus* (New York, 1969), 139–44; Cullmann, *Salvation in History*, 187–93; R. H. Fuller, *A Critical Introduction to the New Testament* (London, 1966), 94–98, and *The New Testament in Current Study* (London, 1963), 40–42; J. Jeremias, "The Present Position in the Controversy Concerning the Problem of the Historical Jesus," *ET* 69 (1957–58): 333–39; H. E. W. Turner, *Historicity and the Gospels* (London, 1963), chapter 3; A. W. Cramer, "In All the Prophets I Awaited Thee," *NovTest* 8 (1966): 102–5; L. E. Keck, "Bornkamm's *Jesus of Nazareth* Revisited,: *JR* 49 (1969): 1–17; W. G. Kümmel, "Norman Perrin's 'Rediscovering the Teaching of Jesus,'" *JR* 49 (1969): 49–66; R. T. France, *Jesus and the Old Testament* (London, 1971), 15–24; D. G. A. Calvert, "An Examination of the Criteria for Distinguishing the Authentic Words of Jesus," *NTS* 18 (1971–72): 209–19.

61. This position is held by Perrin, *Rediscovering*, 32–48; Käsemann, *Essays*, 37; Conzelmann, *RGG* 3, 3:623; cautiously by Fuller, *Current Study*, 41, and *Introduction*, 94–98; H. Zahrnt, *The Historical Jesus* (London, 1963), 107–8, who adds: "There is today general agreement on this basic principle of method," a statement which may be appropriate in the continental situation out of which he writes.

Church,"[62] only when Jesus is separated from both "friend and foe."[63] Advocates grant that this method can produce only a minimal picture of the teaching of Jesus, but the "brutal fact" is that the nature of the tradition forces this method upon us.[64] Nor is this brutal necessity all loss, for this rigorous method permits the recovery of that which is most distinctive about Jesus.[65]

But whether primacy of authority should be assigned to this criterion is questionable on several grounds.[66] There is no assurance that that which is most distinctive (which is what the criterion unearths) is also most characteristic (which is what historical inquiry seeks). It may simply be that which is most eccentric.[67] Moreover, given our limited knowledge of both ancient Judaism and the ancient church, the claim that a saying is unparalleled (and hence authentic) is based on an argument from silence.[68] When dissimilarity does appear, one cannot be certain that the Jesus level of the tradition has been reached, but only that a stage of tradition has been reached that is so opaque that the interests of the community are no longer known.

Finally, the picture of Jesus which this criterion must logically produce is discontinuous both from the community out of which he came and from the community which saw its origin in him. Nor can the criteria of coherence and multiple attestation enable one to move beyond discontinuity when they are subordinated, as they are here, to the criterion of dissimilarity. Jesus is "reduced to what is neither Jewish or Christian,"[69] imprisoned between "the Scylla of Judaism and the Charybdis of primitive Christianity."[70] A method which cannot by its very nature affirm any continuity between Judaism and Jesus, Jesus and the church, is unacceptable. What is needed is a method which can uncover both continuity and discontinuity.

Yet Perrin and Käsemann, two of the most prominent proponents of the primacy of this criterion, do make a considerable number of affir-

---

62. Perrin, *Rediscovering,* 39; italics added.

63. Käsemann, *Essays,* 37.

64. Perrin, *Rediscovering,* 43. Perrin's rigor led J. L. Martyn, USQR 23 (1968): 133, puckishly to subtitle Perrin's book, "How the Earliest Church Is Our Enemy, and How We Shall Defeat It in Order to Recover the Actual Teaching of Jesus."

65. Perrin, *Rediscovering,* 39.

66. See esp. Downing, *The Church and Jesus,* 111–17; and Hooker, "Christology and Methodology," 480–85.

67. Downing, *The Church and Jesus,* 116; Hooker, "Christology and Methodology," 481; Cramer, "In All the Prophets I Awaited Thee," 104.

68. Downing, *The Church and Jesus,* 114–15; Hooker, "Christology and Methodology," 482.

69. Keck, "Bornkamm's *Jesus of Nazareth* Revisited," 4–5, n. 11.

70. McArthur, *In Search of the Historical Jesus,* 142–43.

mations about the historical Jesus.[71] In particular, Perrin's portrait of the teaching of Jesus is reasonably full, generally persuasive, and compelling. But this is because Perrin *in practice* does not subordinate the other criteria to the criterion of dissimilarity. Some examples may be cited, all of which are identified by Perrin as important and authentic. Jesus' table fellowship with tax collectors and sinners is so thoroughly authenticated by multiple attestation that it needs no further authentication;[72] such is also the case with the exorcisms.[73] Though Mark 7:15 and Matt. 8:11 have obvious relevance to questions faced by the early Christian movement (whether purity laws continued to have significance, and the question of the Gentiles), they are yet regarded as authentic because of their dissimilarity to Judaism.[74] *Abba* is accepted as authentic, despite its use within early Christianity.[75]

At other times Perrin grants authenticity because a unit of tradition reflects the "clear vision of one mind, the depth of comprehension of one individual's vision and understanding," or because of the "vividness and power of the story itself," even though the story concerns "a question of great concern to both first-century Judaism and the early Christian Church."[76]

Perrin is almost certainly correct to accept these elements as authentic. What is important to note is that he can do so only by refusing in practice what he affirms in principle: the priority of the criterion of dissimilarity. Instead, he uses, wisely and skillfully, a variety of criteria.[77] We may conclude that the preeminent role assigned to the criterion of dissimilarity in its negative form is both unjustified and misleading.

However, in its positive form, the criterion of dissimilarity is not subject to the above limitations. In its positive form, it includes as au-

---

71. Perrin, *Rediscovering*, 54–206. Though Käsemann's article, *Essays*, 15–47, is programmatic rather than comprehensive, he concludes it with a survey of selected distinctive elements which is by no means minimal; see also the section on Jesus in his *Jesus Means Freedom* (London, 1969), 21–32.

72. Perrin, *Rediscovering*, 46, 104–8; on 104–5, he specifically grants that this table fellowship was an important feature of the life of the early church which, on the criterion of dissimilarity, should exclude it from the Jesus tradition.

73. Ibid., 65, 136–37.

74. Ibid., 149–50, 161–64.

75. Rom. 8:15, Gal. 4:6. Here Perrin tries to maintain the application of the criterion of dissimilarity by arguing that the Pauline occurrences are not representative of early church tradition since they "are the only examples of it" (41). How many examples of an Aramaic term would one expect in Greek documents written to Greek-speaking churches?

76. Perrin, *Rediscovering*, 78, 133; see also 96, 120, 128.

77. This illustrates the impression of the present writer that abstract discussions of method are not nearly as illuminating as witnessing the actual method which an author uses.

thentic those traditions which do not reflect known emphases of early
Christianity. As such, it can be used as one of several criteria, for it
does not exclude traditions which reflect Judaism or early Christianity. These can be judged by the criteria of multiple attestation and
coherence, and the environmental criterion. But it *includes* as primitive tradition elements which do not reflect known interests of early
Christianity,[78] "which it is improbable that the Church in light of its
theological development should ever have invented."[79]

In this form, the criterion has great utility for this study. For we are
interested in issues which were not of notable interest to the church
once it had left the Jewish homeland. The conflicts within Judaism
about the structures and purpose of Israel were not of immediate concern to Christian communities in the Mediterranean world. Nor was
the question of Judaism's relationship to Rome. By the time the Gospels
were written, early Christianity was firmly in the Gentile world; the outcome of Israel's crisis was known and probably not of great interest to
Gentile Christians.[80] The political question for early Christian communities was primarily the fact that Christianity was an illegal religion in
the empire, not a political question involving Israel.

Thus, where an interest in the structures and historical fate of Israel
is perceived, it must be primitive tradition, dating at least to the Christian movement within geographical Palestine — and there is warrant,
as we shall see, for attributing their concerns primarily to Jesus. This
study contends that there is a large amount of material that still links
the mission of Jesus to the structures and destiny of Israel, and that this
material, because it cannot easily be attributed to the creative activity
of the church, has great claim to authenticity. The tendency of the developing tradition, of course, was to universalize and individualize these
elements so that they could be of continuing relevance to the life of
the church.[81] Thus, in some cases, the relationship to Israel's historical
crisis is not on the surface, but perceptible nevertheless.

---

78. C. F. D. Moule, *The Phenomenon of the New Testament* (London, 1967), 61–62,
designates such an element as "a feature in the tradition asserting itself despite a tendency
in its transmitters militating against it." Turner, *Historicity and the Gospels*, 73, terms it the
"method of residues."

79. W. D. Davies, *Christian Origins and Judaism* (London, 1962), 13; he terms such
elements "self-authenticating."

80. See esp. G. B. Caird, *Jesus and the Jewish Nation* (London, 1965), 5–6; C. H.
Dodd, *Historical Tradition in the Fourth Gospel* (Cambridge, 1963), 215–17.

81. See C. W. F. Smith, *The Jesus of the Parables* (Philadelphia, 1948), 43: "Jesus spoke
originally to a particular nation in a definite historical situation. There seems every likelihood that sayings that had their first application to the Jewish people, with their sense
of corporate responsibility, were, when the nation was no longer the important factor,
applied universally to the individual or in particular to the Christian disciple."

To conclude this discussion of method, this study, in common with most studies, will use a variety of criteria: the positive form of the criterion of dissimilarity; multiple attestation, both of sources and forms, which has application not only to sayings and incidents, but also to themes and motifs; the "environmental" criterion (traditions which reflect a Palestinian background may be regarded as early); and coherence. Because the use of the criteria is complex, their adequacy cannot be demonstrated by an abstract discussion, but only in actual use.

What this study will attempt, then, is to argue that there is much in the Gospels that suggests conflict as a context for interpreting the teaching of Jesus and that, when once this context is established, there is much else that coheres with it. As such, it moves toward a reconstruction of the teaching of Jesus, even though its limits prevent it from being fully comprehensive.

"Reconstruction" is out of vogue, probably because it smacks of speculation; yet historical investigation involves reconstruction.[82] The perennial problem in synoptic studies, identified in this chapter, is the existence of a relatively extensive body of traditions which, by the commonly accepted criteria of authenticity, have more or less equal claims to being regarded as primitive, but which are not amenable to explanation in terms of any single coherent reconstruction of the mission of Jesus. Granted this situation, the comprehensiveness — the explanatory power — of a reconstruction is the final test of both context and method.[83] Thus the contention of this study is that conflict is a context which permits a coherent interpretation of these apparently primitive traditions.

The first task, therefore, is to describe the conflict setting within which the ministry occurred. This entails the explication of the cultural (i.e., politico-religious) dynamic of first-century Judaism which shaped its institutions and dominated its life as the people of God (chapters 2 and 3). Both early Palestinian Christianity — the Jesus movement —

---

82. See Koch, *The Rediscovery of Apocalyptic,* 125: "The commentators of today shun the imputation of producing a historical reconstruction like the plague. But to investigate history does in fact mean reconstruction." Such reconstruction, he adds, involves connecting the conditions of Hellenistic and Roman society to the late biblical period and presenting "the connection between the Old and New Testaments . . . as a stirring and forward-striving history of hope and action, of believing and speaking, of suffering and conquering."

83. Cf. Downing, *The Church and Jesus,* 189, who suggests that the way forward in Jesus research (including especially progress on the question of method) is the articulation of "a large range of over-all reconstructions" which can then be "sketched, elaborated, compared, defended."

and Jesus (chapters 4 through the conclusion) addressed Israel as a nation facing a crisis, offering it an alternative course with identifiable
political historical consequences, different from those portended by its
present cultural dynamic. This cultural dynamic can best be discerned
by examining the phenomenon of Jewish resistance to Rome.

CHAPTER TWO

The Multiform Character of Jewish Resistance to Rome

Religious renewal movements are spawned and sustained by a perceived difference between how things are and how they ought to be. They are thus shaped by two factors: loyalty to an inherited tradition (or otherwise we could call them new movements rather than renewal movements) and contemporary circumstances which call for change. Sometimes a third factor enters as well, the religious experience of the leader and/or adherents. When this is the case, the perceived difference may be between what is disclosed by that religious experience and the present state of affairs. In any event, contemporary circumstances are the medium within which renewal movements grow and the conditions to which they must respond, directly or indirectly.[1]

The social matrix within which the Jesus movement emerged in Palestine was one of conflict created by the presence of Gentile political and cultural power and the diverse responses given within Jewish society to the question, "What does it mean to be a faithful Jew under these circumstances?" In this chapter we shall describe the varied pressures brought by the Roman occupation as well as the resistance which emerged among the Jewish people. Contrary to the picture commonly drawn by scholarship and generally accepted until recently, resistance to Rome in first-century Palestine was not concentrated within a revolutionary party, whether known as the "Zealots" or by some other name, but embraced people from all segments of the population, cutting across geography, sectarian allegiances, and social classes.

---

1. See Gerd Theissen, *Sociology of Early Palestinian Christianity* (Philadelphia, 1978), 114: "Our analysis of the Jesus movement in Palestine was based on a sociological theory of conflict: religious renewal movements develop out of social tensions and attempt to give new impulses for their resolution."

The Social Matrix

> It was now that the war opened, in the twelfth year of the principate of Nero, and the seventeenth of the reign of Agrippa, in the month of Artemisius.[2]

With that solemn dating, Josephus announces the outbreak of the Jewish War of Independence in 66 C.E., which culminated in the destruction of Jerusalem and the Temple in 70 and the heroic mass suicide of the last of the Jewish resisters some four years later in besieged Masada.[3] The war was the most dramatic event in the two hundred years of turbulent Roman-Jewish relationships stretching from the inclusion of Palestine in the Roman empire in 63 B.C.E. to the Second Jewish War of 132–35 C.E.

During this entire period, Palestine was a society under pressure. It was characterized by three dimensions of conflict: vertically between the Jewish people and the Roman occupiers; horizontally between Jews and Gentiles sharing the same land; and internally among the Jewish people themselves.

The ineptitude of Roman colonial administration was partially responsible. Rome experimented with various forms of rule. Rome ruled indirectly, through client kings such as Herod the Great and his sons, and directly, through Roman prefects in Judea beginning in 6 C.E. There was centralized rule, as in the days of Herod and then again under the later prefects when Palestine was a single administrative district, and decentralized rule, with Palestine divided into three administrative districts from 4 B.C.E. to 41 C.E.

As a result, no form of government developed the stability that stems from long duration.[4] Moreover, the rulers designated by Rome were often incompetent or insensitive or both. The man whom history calls Herod *the Great* was not deemed such by his Jewish subjects. Taxing them heavily and spending vast sums on Hellenistic building projects,

---

2. *B.J.* 2.284.
3. For a history of the resistance, see especially David Rhoads, *Israel in Revolution: 6–74 C.E.* (Philadelphia, 1976). See also S. G. F. Brandon, *Jesus and the Zealots* (Manchester, 1967), 65–145; W. R. Wilson, *The Execution of Jesus* (New York, 1970), 85–90; S. Perowne, *The Later Herods* (London, 1958), 1–108; B. Reicke, *The New Testament Era* (London, 1969). For Masada, see Y. Yadin, *Masada: Herod's Fortress and the Zealots' Last Stand* (New York, 1966).
4. Cf. Theissen, *Sociology of Early Palestinian Christianity*, 66: "It was impossible for any form of government to develop which was legitimated by a long period of power and tradition.... No institution was given a chance of becoming powerful enough to be able to control the difficult territory. Palestine lived in a constant state of constitutional crisis."

including temples to pagan deities, he was also brutal.[5] The prefects who began direct rule of Judea in 6 C.E. were second-rank and often second-rate Roman colonial administrators, sometimes simply incompetent, sometimes corrupt, sometimes deliberately provocative of Jewish sensitivities.

But even if Roman administrators had been competent and enlightened, the conflict probably could not have been avoided. For the Roman occupation impacted Jewish religious, social, political, and economic life. The Torah was the divinely revealed constitution of Israel, comprising not only ritual law, but also civil, criminal, and international law. Roman hegemony introduced a second system of law, and though the Romans largely permitted local administration to be governed by Jewish law, there were conflicts, some of them intrinsic, others due to bad judgment. According to the Torah, Israel was to be a theocracy ruled by God through God's anointed one: earlier in Israel's history the King, and since the exile the high priest. No foreigner was to rule over Israel.[6] Roman rule clearly violated the latter, even during the reign of Herod.

Moreover, both Rome and Herod fundamentally undermined the high priesthood by changing it from a lifetime office to an appointment which could be, and was, changed at whim. Because the land itself was viewed as holy, stipulations of the oral Torah prohibited Gentile religious practices and even Gentile ownership of land.[7] Of course, under Roman occupation the Jewish people were powerless to enforce these laws. Jewish religious loyalties were also offended by specific Roman practices, as in Pilate's violation of the law against graven images and the emperor Caligula's odious plan to erect a statue of himself in the holy of holies of the Temple.[8]

---

5. Cf. M. Stern, "The Jewish People in the First Century," in S. Safrai and M. Stern, eds., *The Jewish People in the First Century: Compendia Rerum Iudaicarum ad Novum Testamentum* (Philadelphia, 1974), 1:175: "His rule was regarded as a tyranny." The comment with which Stern ends his section on Herod (1:216–77) aptly characterizes Herod's reputation among his subjects: "He figures in the New Testament as a slayer of infants."

6. Deut. 17:14–15. Cf. T. Sanh. 4:10: "A King cannot be appointed outside the land of Israel, nor can one be appointed unless he be eligible for marriage into the priestly families" (i.e., a full Israelite).

7. For the land of Israel as the outermost of the ten concentric circles of holiness, see M. Kel. 1:6–9. See also 4 Ezra 9:8, 13:48. For the application of the Noachian laws, including the prohibition of idolatry, to "resident aliens," i.e., Gentiles, see G. F. Moore, *Judaism in the First Centuries of the Christian Era: The Age of the Tannaim* (Cambridge, 1937), 1:339. For the prohibitions of Gentile ownership see M. Av. Zar. 1:8. The oral Torah also required the payment of tithes from every field in Israel, which few if any Gentiles would do. See J. Neusner, *A Life of Yohanan ben Zakkai*, 2d ed. (Leiden, 1970), 15, citing L. Ginzberg, *On Jewish Law and Lore* (Philadelphia, 1945), 86ff.

8. For the incident under Pilate, see Josephus, *B.J.* 2.167–77, and *Ant.* 18.55–62.

Social tensions arose as well. Jewish identity, primarily religious and ethnocentric, was threatened by the presence of Gentiles and Hellenistic practices. On the one hand, there was the danger of assimilation, always present when a small culture is engulfed by a more powerful cosmopolitan culture. The tendency toward discarding distinctive Jewish practices was exacerbated by economic conditions, as we shall see later. On the other hand, there was open antagonism between Jew and Gentile. Anti-Semitism was rife in the empire as a whole.[9] The intensity of the antagonism is indicated by the fact that at the outbreak of the War of Independence in 66 c.e., Gentile majorities massacred Jews in Caesarea, Scythopolis, Ashkolos, Ptolemais, Tyre, Hippos, Gadara, and Damascus. In Tiberias, the Gentile minority was massacred by Jews.[10]

Active resistance to Rome and its client kings was widespread in the century from the accession of Herod the Great in 37 b.c.e. to the outbreak of the rebellion in 66 c.e. There were conspiracies and demonstrations against Herod, usually resulting in martyrdom. At Herod's death in 4 b.c.e., revolts erupted throughout the country; Roman troops ended the rebellion by crucifying two thousand Jews near Jerusalem. The imposition of direct Roman taxation in 6 c.e. was greeted by a revolt led by Judas the Galilean and a Pharisee named Saddok. Massive nonviolent protests were directed against actions of Pilate in the 20s and 30s, and against the emperor Caligula's insane scheme to have a statue of himself erected in the Temple in Jerusalem in the early 40s. On several occasions, delegations of Jews appealed to the emperor to protest colonial administration.

A guerilla movement operated intermittently throughout the century, attacking both Romans and collaborationist Jews.[11] In addition to political opposition directed against Rome, domestic political instability was created by the Herodian and Roman policies of elevating relatively unknown families to positions of leadership. Aristocratic families, as is still the case in more traditional parts of the Middle East, were important elements in the political structure. Under Roman rule, the leading families were no longer sanctioned by long tradition, but simply by Roman power.

See also C. H. Kraeling, "The Episode of the Roman Standards at Jerusalem," *HTR* 35 (1942): 163–89. For Caligula's attempt, see Josephus, *B.J.* 2.184–203, and *Ant.* 18.216–309; Philo, *Legatio*, 184–348; and Tacitus, *Hist.* 5.9. See also the more complete analysis later in this chapter.

9. See A. N. Sherwin-White, *Racial Prejudice in Imperial Rome* (Cambridge, 1967), 86–101; and L. Poliakov, *History of Anti-Semitism* (New York, 1965).

10. Theissen, *Sociology of Early Palestinian Christianity*, 69.

11. See note 3 above.

Even so, one might think that all of this could be of little concern to the average person living in first-century Palestine. Still a largely rural agricultural society, composed of small villages and towns inhabited largely by farmers who went each day to their fields, Palestine had only a few cities. Though the citizenry would have been aware of Gentiles, we can imagine that most might have continued their traditional religious practices quite oblivious to the Roman occupation. During Jesus' lifetime and ministry, there were relatively few occupation troops in the country. The Roman governor was normally resident in the recently constructed city of Caesarea on the Mediterranean coast, traveling to Jerusalem only for the major Jewish festivals; and in Galilee, Rome still ruled indirectly through the client-king Herod Antipas, son of Herod the Great.

So it might have been, except for the economic impact of Roman rule, which brought a double system of taxation, adding Roman taxes to those mandated by divine revelation in the Torah. Both had their greatest impact upon farmers, who still constituted the vast majority of the population of Palestine.

To understand this, we need to examine the religious taxes required by the Torah and the economic situation of the Jewish farmer. The Torah was designed primarily for an agricultural society, and its system of taxation therefore applied primarily to agricultural produce, "whatever is used for food and is kept watch over and grows from the soil," i.e., whatever is tilled.[12]

Many Jewish farmers were still small landholders, producing primarily grain, vegetables, fruits, wine, oil and dates, as well as sheep, cattle, and goats. As did most farmers in the ancient world, they produced everything (and little more) for their own use; a small portion would be sold or bartered for absolute necessities, and there was little opportunity for savings. One or two years of bad crops could easily result in the loss of the farm, with the farmer then becoming a "hireling" or worse.[13]

Jewish agriculture was tied to the sabbatical cycle; in every seventh year, the land was to be left fallow. During the other six years, the tithes referred to in various portions of the written Torah combined as follows:

1. Every year, the "wave offering" or "first fruits" offering; the exact amount was not specified, but ranged from 1 percent to 3 percent of the produce.

---

12. M. Maas. 1:1.
13. For the plight of the small landowner, see J. Klausner, *Jesus of Nazareth* (Boston, 1964), 179–80; on agriculture generally, 174–80. See also F. C. Grant, *The Economic Background of the Gospels* (London, 1926), 55–64, and S. Applebaum in *Compendia*, 2:646–64.

2. Every year, the first tithe of 10 percent, to be given to the priests or Levites for the support of the theocracy.

3. In the first, second, fourth, and fifth years of the cycle, a "second tithe," also of 10 percent.

4. In the third and sixth years, the "poor man's tithe" of 10 percent.

There were other taxes as well, such as the annual Temple tax of a half shekel (about one day's wages), but these were relatively minor.[14] The amount of taxation on agricultural produce, required by the Torah, was slightly over 20 percent.

To this system of taxation, the Romans added their own: crop and land taxes, a poll tax (the famous "tribute" tax), customs, and tolls.[15] Many of these could be exorbitant, especially customs and tolls; though certainty about the exact percentage is impossible, the figure of 25 percent has been cited; moreover, since they were added each time a product crossed an administrative boundary, they accumulated.[16] The famous poll tax was comparatively modest. Levied on everybody except children and old people, it amounted to about one day's wages. Though all of these taxes affected the farmer directly or indirectly, the land and crop taxes had the greatest impact. The former was 1 percent of the value of the land; the latter was 12.5 percent of the produce.[17]

Thus Jews in Palestine were subject to two systems of taxation, both of which they were powerless to affect. The one was dictated by Roman policy, over which they had no control, and the second was required by divine revelation. For the small landowner who farmed his own land, the burden was extraordinary: in addition to his need to save for the sabbatical year, the double system demanded from 35 to 40 percent of his produce, perhaps even more.[18]

---

14. For the Jewish taxation system, see Grant, *The Economic Background of the Gospels*, 92–106, and his list of twelve taxes on 94–96; S. Safrai in *Compendia*, 2:818–25; and the useful notes on the tractates *Maaseroth* and *Maaser Sheni* in H. Danby's edition of *The Mishnah* (London, 1933), 67, 73.

15. For Roman taxation, see F. M. Heichelbaum in T. Frank, ed., *An Economic Survey of Ancient Rome* (Baltimore, 1938), 231–45; Schürer-Vermes, *The History of the Jewish People in the Age of Jesus Christ*, 1:372–76, 401–7; Stern in *Compendia*, 1:330–33; Grant, *The Economic Background of the Gospels*, 89–91; Klausner, *Jesus of Nazareth*, 187–88.

16. Stern, *Compendia*, 1:333. Klausner, *Jesus of Nazareth*, 188, cites the much lower figure of 2.5 percent, but adds that because of the cumulative effect, the price of an article in the Roman market could be as much as a hundred times the price in its place of origin.

17. Heichelbaum, in Frank, *An Economic Survey of Ancient Rome*, 231–32, 235; Stern in *Compendia*, 1:331.

18. Cf. the summary statement by Grant, *The Economic Background of the Gospels*, 105: "If we may hazard an approximation, where no exact figures are available, the total taxation of the Jewish people in the time of Jesus, civil and religious combined, must have

The impact of the economic crunch was severe, producing signs of social disintegration, such as widespread emigration,[19] a growing number of landless "hirelings," and a social class of robbers and beggars.[20] Moreover, the double obligation faced the population with an economic dilemma which was at the same time a test of religious loyalty. In addition to paying the Roman taxes, enforced by Roman police power, should one, could one, also pay the taxes required by the Torah? Many could survive only by being nonobservant. The price they paid for nonobservance was social and religious ostracism by those who sought to be faithful. Under Roman rule, such ostracism was the only form of Jewish sanction left, and a large social class was born, known as "the people of the land," the *amme ha aretz.* Hence the double system of taxation, in addition to causing economic hardship and political resentment, also accelerated the tendency toward assimilation and loss of Jewish identity, not because of the attractiveness of Hellenistic culture, but because of economic exigency.

The introduction of Roman rule thus brought a crisis into all aspects of Jewish life, religious, social, political, and, because of the economic impact, into the smallest hamlet of the Palestinian countryside. No wonder there was conflict with Rome. The conflict seemed incapable of resolution. The needs of Roman *Realpolitik* demanded its presence and power in Palestine, both as a buffer against the Parthian empire to the east and to insure the security of Egypt, the breadbasket of the empire.[21] Rome was probably puzzled by the recalcitrance of its Jewish subjects and unable sympathetically to understand their sensitivities.

After all, Rome had had treaties of alliance with Judea in the time of the Maccabees, and its present presence in Palestine could plausibly be attributed to Jewish invitation. Three times it had been asked to enter directly into Jewish affairs — in 63 and 4 B.C.E., and 6 C.E. Moreover, the decrees of Julius Caesar in 45 B.C.E. guaranteed to Judaism certain rights not normally given to peoples of the empire: the status of *religio licita,* exemption from emperor worship and conscription, and

---

approached the intolerable proportion of between 30 and 40 percent; it may have been higher still."

19. The laws of tithes did *not* apply to Jews living in the Diaspora; Grant, *The Economic Background of the Gospels,* 94, n .1; Safrai in *Compendia,* 2:816. Apparently this is connected to the holiness *of the land.* The land of Israel and its produce were thought to belong to God in a special way. On the significance of the land, see especially W. D. Davies, *The Gospel and the Land* (Berkeley, 1974); on agricultural laws and the land, see 54–58.

20. Theissen, 34–35.

21. F. C. Grant, *Roman Hellenism and the New Testament* (London, 1962), 86–88; C. Colpe, "East and West," in H. J. Schultz, ed., *Jesus in His Time* (Philadelphia, 1971), 19–27; Neusner, *Yohanan ben Zakkai,* 28–29.

concessions to Jewish sensitivities about images and the sabbath. Had the empire not behaved benevolently toward its Jewish subjects? But to Jewish eyes (equally understandably), Rome looked quite different.[22] Though Rome may once have been an ally, it was now an unwanted imperial ruler. Rome could pacify Palestine only by letting go of it, which Rome was not prepared to do.

As already noted, resistance to Roman rule in Jewish Palestine was widespread throughout the entire period. What was the source of resistance from the Jewish side? The most common historical reconstruction attributes the resistance primarily to one group, the Zealots, founded in 6 C.E. by Judas the Galilean, who are described as strongest in Galilee and operating as an ideologically distinct party within Judaism.[23] The strength of this view, which until recently was nearly a consensus, can be seen in the virtually standard formula in introductions to the New Testament: first-century Judaism contained four parties, namely, Pharisees, Sadducees, Essenes, and Zealots.

Two full-length studies of Jewish nationalism by W. R. Farmer and M. Hengel participate in the consensus[24] as do studies of the political dimension of the New Testament.[25] This view leads to two frequent though not logically necessary inferences. First, it suggests that resistance was confined to one group and thus not a vital issue for most people. Those who advocated it became Zealots; those who did not remained aloof and fundamentally accepted Roman imperial order. Closely related is a natural corollary: the Pharisees in contrast to the militant Zealots are viewed as essentially pacifist and apolitical.[26] Secondly, it suggests that the conflict with Rome throughout

---

22. For unbecoming Jewish literary portraits of Rome, see Ass. Moses 8:1–5; Ps. Sol. 17:13–15; 1QpHab 3:4–6:12.

23. For a survey of the secondary literature affirming this view, see M. Smith (who does not accept it), "Zealots and Sicarii, Their Origins and Relation," HTR 64 (1971): 1 and notes 1–8. Participating in the consensus as well as explicitly affirming their concentration in Galilee are G. F. Moore, *Judaism in the First Centuries of the Christian Era* (Cambridge, Mass., 1927–30), 1:287; D. S. Russell, *Between the Testaments* (London, 1960), 37; W. Knox, *St. Paul and the Church of Jerusalem* (Cambridge, 1925), 21–22, n. 45; J. Jeremias, *The Parables of Jesus* (New York, 1963), 74; E. Lohmeyer, *Lord of the Temple* (Edinburgh and London, 1961), 21; S. Johnson, *Jesus in His Own Times* (London, 1958), 18–19; J. Parkes, *The Foundations of Judaism and Christianity* (London, 1960), 126, 165; L. Finkelstein, *The Pharisees* 3 (Philadelphia, 1962), 5; C. H. Dodd, *The Founder of Christianity* (London, 1971), 7.

24. W. R. Farmer, *Maccabees, Zealots, and Josephus* (New York, 1956); M. Hengel, *Die Zeloten* (Leiden, 1961). Farmer argues that "zeal" was a watchword of resistance to pagan power before 6 C.E., but still finds the origin of "Zealot" as a party term in 6 C.E.

25. O. Cullmann, *The State in the New Testament* (New York, 1956), and *Jesus and the Revolutionaries*; Brandon, *Jesus and the Zealots*; D. R. Griffiths, *The New Testament and the Roman State* (Swansea, 1970).

26. Affirming the pacifist and/or apolitical character of the Pharisees as a whole, are,

the first century had little to do with loyalties shared by the majority of the population or with the attempt of the mainstream to struc- ture their corporate life so that it would manifest loyalty to Yahweh. Moreover, locating the resistance in Galilee operates in yet another way to sequester the resistance from the mainstream, since some schol- ars have made a distinction between the "boorishness" of Galilee, on the one hand, and Jerusalem as the center of intellectual life, on the other hand. The unenlightened boors of Galilee are then identified with the nationalists, and the Torah intellectuals with the pacifist, ur- bane, anti-revolutionaries, thereby severing the link between Torah and resistance.[27]

Thus, the implication follows, faithful Jews could easily avoid the question of the Roman conflict so long as they avoided the tightly knit liberation front which operated out of Galilee. The teaching of Jesus and indeed the whole New Testament seem to support this view: they are silent about a movement specifically known as the Zealots (except for an alleged reference to "Simon the Zealot").[28] Therefore, finally, the conflict between Rome and Judaism was of little explicit concern to Jesus or the early Christian movement.

However, this consensus and the inferences derived from it are very weakly grounded in the ancient sources. There is no evidence that "Zealot" was a party designation until 66 C.E. when Josephus's narrative uses it for the first time. He uses the term not as a blanket designation for the resistance movement, but to designate one (or two?) group(s) of Jewish revolutionaries in Jerusalem who were often engaged in civil war with other revolutionary groups.[29]

In his narrative of events prior to the war, Josephus most commonly uses the pejorative term *lestai* ("bandits," "brigands") to describe the guerilla wing of the resistance movement. The pejorative connotation of

---

above all, Finkelstein, *The Pharisees,* passim, and H. Loewe, *Render unto Caesar* (Cam- bridge, 1940), 20–33. See also R. Travers Herford, *The Pharisees* (London, 1924), 186–87, and *Judaism in the New Testament Period* (London, 1928), 69, 77; C. Roth, "The Pharisees in the Jewish Revolution of 66–73," *JSS* 7 (1962): 63, whose judgment is remarkable since the rest of his article shows that Pharisaic involvement was considerable; Moore, *Judaism,* 1:77; J. T. Pawlikowski, "On Renewing the Revolution of the Pharisees: A New Approach to Theology and Politics," *Cross Currents* 20 (1970): 433, n. 13.

27. This is especially true of Finkelstein, *The Pharisees,* where the typology of rural patriotic boor versus urban pacifist intellectual governs his work.

28. Or, in one notable case, the silence is used in an argument from silence: since Jesus castigated Pharisees and Sadducees by name, the silence about the Zealots must point to a basic sympathy toward them. See Brandon, *Jesus and the Zealots,* 200–201.

29. At the earliest, it is used to refer to the followers of a certain Menahem in *B.J.* 2.444 and recurs in 2.564, 651; however, Smith, "Zealots and Sicarii," 16, may be correct that it is not used as a party designation until *B.J.* 4.138–61. It does not appear at all in the *Antiquities,* whose narrative concludes in 66 C.E.

lestai is unfair to the resistance fighters, for they were often motivated by genuine piety, as has long been recognized.[30] Josephus's apologetic purpose does explain his use of the opprobrious term *lestai* to describe the resistance movement,[31] but it cannot explain why he uniformly avoids the term "Zealot" before the war, especially since for him it is an equally opprobrious term.[32] The conclusion consistent with the evidence from Josephus and the other ancient sources is that "Zealot" was not a party term at all before the war.[33]

The disappearance of the term is of some importance. Without a label, we are perhaps less likely to think of one distinctive organization as the bearer of resistance. Moreover, a patient analysis of the ancient sources demonstrates that resistance to pagan cultural influence and military power was not confined to one group, no matter how designated, but involved elements from all the major groups. This claim, which corrodes decisively the consensus understanding of the conflict between Rome and Judaism, and which is one of the keys to understanding the politics of Jesus, now requires demonstration.

Analysis of the Jewish Resistance

To demonstrate mainstream involvement in the conflict with Roman power, we shall examine six specific periods of resistance beginning with the time of Herod, treating them as case studies rather than repeating

---

30. At least since H. Graetz's first edition in 1856 of his *Geschichte der Juden von den ältesten Zeiten bis auf die Gegenwart*, according to Baumbach, "Die Zeloten — ihre geschichtliche und religionspolitische Bedeutung," 2–3. The claim has been amplified especially by Farmer, *Maccabees, Zealots, and Josephus*, and Hengel, *Die Zeloten*.

31. His *Bellum Judaicum* undoubtedly caters to the Roman viewpoint (*Ap.* 1.50; *Vita*, 363–64) so that the primary cause of the war had to be assigned to elements within the Jewish homeland, not to Rome itself. At the same time, considering the perils to which the Diaspora would have been subject had the Mediterranean world concluded that rebellious Judaism was essential Judaism, he was concerned to show that the rebels were not true Jews.

32. The Zealots active during the war are described as malcontents, miscreants, brutal, arrogant, zealous for vice, etc.; see *B.J.* 2.442–45, 651; 4.160–65; 7.269–70.

33. For an extended elaboration of this claim, including evidence from the rabbinic tradition, Justin Martyr, Hegesippus, Hippolytus, and the New Testament, see the present writer's "The Currency of the Term 'Zealot,'" *JTS* 22 (1971): 504–12. Compare F. J. Foakes Jackson and K. Lake, *The Beginnings of Christianity* (London, 1920), 1:421–25, and Smith, "Zealots and Sicarii," 1–19, who reach the same conclusions. In passing, it should be noted that the designation of Simon as *ho zelotes* in Luke's two lists of the disciples (Luke 6:15, Acts 1:13) is not counter-evidence, since it can be translated either as "the zealous one." or "the Zealot." In the absence of any evidence that *zelotes* was a party name, it should be translated with a lower-case *z* as "the zealous one."

a chronicle of the whole era, which has been done many times before.[34] A consideration of the high priests and politics will then be added.

Herod's Reign (37–4 B.C.E.)

The several decades prior to Herod the Great had been chaotic. They included the first Roman occupation of Jerusalem and the Temple by Pompey in 63 B.C.E. and frequent civil strife between various Jewish disputants for national leadership. Yet there had at least been the possibility that Judea would continue to be governed by a Maccabean high priest and the Sanhedrin. But the advent of Herod made it clear to the Jewish people that they had fallen under Gentile power. To faithful Jews, Herod's two greatest faults were his reduction of Jewish autonomy on the one hand, and, on the other, his Gentile associations and Romanizing policy.

With Herod Jewish self-rule vanished. The traditional life-long tenure of the high priest was replaced by a high priesthood subject to Herod's whim and recall.[35] The power of the Sanhedrin, seat of Jewish authority for structuring their national life, was effectively destroyed when Herod began his reign by murdering all but a few members of the Jewish senate.[36] Sovereignty thus passed from a Jewish high priest and Torah assembly to the Herodian court and civil service, modelled along Hellenistic lines.[37] The preceding era of the Hasmonean queen Alexandra Salome (76–67 B.C.E.), who made the Pharisees her closest advisers,[38] came to be regarded in Pharisaic tradition as a "golden age, in which even the earth brought forth crops of miraculous size — grains of wheat as large as kidneys, barley as large as olives, and lentils like golden denarii."[39] The Pharisees had been free to structure Israel's corporate life on their understanding of the Torah. Now that freedom was gone.

---

34. See, e.g., Brandon, *Jesus and the Zealots*, 65–145; W. R. Wilson, *The Execution of Jesus* (New York, 1970), 85–90; S. Perowne, *The Later Herods* (London, 1958), 1–108; B. Reicke, *The New Testament Era* (London, 1969), 1–95; E. Mary Smallwood, *The Jews under Roman Rule* (Leiden, 1976), 60–119, 144–80, 256–92; Rhoads, *Israel in Revolution,* 47–93.

35. For lists of Herodian high priests, see E. M. Smallwood, "High Priests and Politics in Roman Palestine," *JTS* 13 (1962): 3; J. Jeremias, *Jerusalem at the Time of Jesus* (London, 1969), 377.

36. *Ant.* 14.175, 15.6; Ass. Moses 6:3.

37. For Herod's emasculation of the high priesthood and Sanhedrin, see A. H. M. Jones, *The Herods of Judaea* (Oxford, 1938), 79–85; A. Schalit, *König Herodes* (Berlin, 1969), 98–109.

38. *Ant.* 13.408–11.

39. D. S. Russell, *The Jews from Alexander to Herod* (London, 1967), 74.

Herod's Gentile associations and Romanizing policy only worsened the situation. He himself was an Idumean and thus, of non-Jewish descent, was not entitled to be king.[40] Moreover, his kingship was conferred on him de jure by the Romans[41] and obtained de facto only with the help of the Roman general Sosius, who with Herod successfully laid siege to Jerusalem in 37 b.c.e.[42]

That Herod was but an intermediary for Roman power was repeatedly made clear by his policies as king. His elaborate building projects, following Hellenistic architecture, included temples dedicated to Caesar.[43] He introduced foreign practices, especially in the form of athletic games and public entertainment which, Josephus writes, "corrupted the ancient way of life" and led to the neglect of those customs "which had formerly induced piety in the masses."[44] His loyalty to Rome led faithful Jews to suspect him of introducing graven images into the country,[45] and their suspicions were justified when Herod had a golden Roman eagle erected over the Temple gate.[46]

Jewish reaction to Herod was widespread. On two different occasions the Pharisees, apparently en masse, refused to take oaths of allegiance to Herod and Caesar, as did the Essenes on the first occasion.[47] These were not simply isolated acts of public disobedience, but, according to Josephus, manifested their enduring intent to undermine Herod.[48] Persons faithful to the law protested to Herod when they suspected that he had introduced human images into his theater, and ten of them formed a conspiracy to assassinate him.[49] That the conspiracy had popular support is seen from the fact that the informer who betrayed the conspiracy was spontaneously lynched in front of a large crowd, none of whom would cooperate in the identification of the perpetrators of extralegal justice.[50]

Herod's desecration of the Temple with the eagle of imperial Rome

---

40. See note 6 above.

41. *Ant.* 14.381–89; *B.J.* 1.282–85; cf. Strabo 16.765; Appian, *Bell. Civ.* 5.75; Tacitus, *Hist.* 5.9.

42. *Ant.* 14.468–86; *B.J.* 1.345–53.

43. *B.J.* 1.403–7, 414; *Ant.* 15.326–30.

44. *Ant.* 15.267.

45. *Ant.* 15.277–79.

46. *B.J.* 2.650; *Ant.* 17.151. That the eagle symbolized Rome is affirmed by V. G. Simkhovitch, *Toward the Understanding of Jesus* (New York, 1925), 17; Buchanan, *The Consequences of the Covenant*, 24; Johnson, *Jesus in His Own Times*, 149; and suggested by Smallwood, *The Jews under Roman Rule*, 99.

47. *Ant.* 15.369–71, 17.41–45; *Baba Batra* 3b.

48. *Ant.* 17.41.

49. *Ant.* 15.277–89.

50. *Ant.* 15.289–90.

led two Pharisaic scholars and their forty students in 4 B.C.E. to destroy the eagle, for which act they were executed.[51] The strong public
support enjoyed by these martyrs is shown by the widespread disturbances following their deaths.[52] In addition to the above more or less
public acts of protest, Herod's reign was marked by the continuing activity of guerilla groups.[53] Thus Herod, no matter how great his skill
as a practitioner of *Realpolitik,* in spite of his extension of the Kingdom to near Davidic proportions and his magnificent rebuilding of the
Jerusalem Temple, was viewed by many faithful Jews as a disaster.[54]

Several insights emerge from this case history. First, the groups
protesting varied, both in their tactics and composition. They included
not only guerillas operating clandestinely, but also Pharisees engaging
in acts of civil disobedience and direct action.[55] That which united the
protestors was sorrow and anger at the loss of autonomy, loyalty to the
practices enjoined by Torah, and concern for the holiness of the land
and Temple. All were threatened by the penetration of Gentile power
under Herod, the friend of Rome.

Events Following Herod's Death

With the death of Herod in 4 B.C.E., multiple attempts were made to
regain a modicum of Jewish autonomy by diverse groups using diverse
means. Out of loyalty to the Pharisaic scholars so recently executed by
Herod, a large group of people petitioned Herod's son and successor,
Archelaus, to appoint a new high priest. It led to armed conflict in
which the revolutionaries (Josephus's term) killed part of a cohort, and
Archelaus responded by slaying three thousand of them in the Temple.[56]

Shortly thereafter, provoked by an attempt on the part of a Roman
official to seize unlawfully the royal riches in Jerusalem, Jewish pilgrims
arriving for Pentecost (with the Judeans greater both in numbers and
enthusiasm than the Galileans and Idumeans)[57] laid siege to the troops

---

51. *B.J.* 1.548–655; *Ant.* 17.149–67.

52. *B.J.* 2.4–13; *Ant.* 17.204–18.

53. See A. Schalit, "Herod and His Successors," in H. J. Schultz, ed., *Jesus in His Time*
(Philadelphia, 1971), 40–41.

54. Cf. *Ass. Moses* 6:6, where he is compared to the Egyptians of the exodus era.

55. See G. Allon, "The Attitudes of the Pharisees to the Roman Government and
the House of Herod," *Scripta Hierosolymitana* vii (1961). Though sufficient evidence is
perhaps lacking to speak of the "absolute" opposition of the Pharisees to Herod, as Allon
does, he is correct to reject the apolitical view of the Pharisees and to conclude that "the
main line of the Pharisaic majority ... was resistance to Roman rule and the striving for
political liberty and popular rule" (70, 78).

56. *B.J.* 2.4–13; *Ant.* 17.204–18.

57. *B.J.* 2.43; *Ant.* 17.254.

of the offending official. In the ensuing battle Roman troops set fire to the porticoes of the Temple and then plundered the Temple treasury.[58] Horrified by this desecration of their sacred place, the people rallied in even greater numbers and affirmed themselves to be waging a war for national independence.[59] The quest for autonomy spread beyond Jerusalem. In Galilee, Judas, son of the "brigand chief Ezekias,"[60] seized and occupied the leading city of Sepphoris. In Perea, a slave named Simon crowned himself king and amassed a large military force.[61] In central Judea, Athronges gathered forces which attacked Romans and royalists.[62] Indeed, "the whole of Judea [was] one scene of guerilla warfare."[63] Only the arrival of the legions of the Roman general Varus quelled the revolution. Varus conquered and burned Sepphoris, and shortly after the rebels in fear deserted Jerusalem, he completed his task by crucifying two thousand Jews near the holy city.[64]

In Rome a quite different attempt to achieve autonomy was under way. Fifty Jewish "deputies," clearly men of prominent status, petitioned Augustus to place Palestine under a governor sent from Rome rather than continue under control of the Herods.[65] Often interpreted by scholars as a request for direct Roman rule and thus indicative of a quietist political stance,[66] the delegation in fact sought to return control of the nation's domestic affairs to the high priest and Sanhedrin under the jurisdiction of a Roman governor, much as in the time of Persian hegemony. Josephus himself uses the word "autonomy" to describe their goal.[67] Indeed, it was reasonable to suppose that greater authority over the internal corporate life of Judea would be given to the Jewish senate under a Roman governor than it possessed under the Herodian court.[68] But this attempt, like the insurrections of the same year, failed.

Attention must be drawn to several points. First, the groups involved

---

58. B.J. 2.39–50; Ant. 17.250–64; Ass. Moses 6:9.

59. B.J. 2.53; Ant. 17.267.

60. B.J. 2.56; Ant. 17.271.

61. For the likelihood that the prominence of names such as Simon and Judas in this period reflects deliberate emulation of the Maccabean freedom fighters, see W. R. Farmer, "Judas, Simon and Athronges," NTS 4 (1958): 147–55.

62. Ant. 17.269–84; B.J. 2.55–65.

63. B.J. 2.65.

64. B.J. 2.66–75; Ant. 17.286–95; Ass. Moses 6:8–9.

65. B.J. 2.80–93; Ant. 17.299–14.

66. E. Schürer, for example, in his classic A History of the Jewish People in the Time of Jesus Christ (Edinburgh, 1893ff.) I.ii.43. In this judgment he is followed by many modern scholars.

67. B.J. 2.80; Ant. 17.300.

68. Simkhovitch, Toward the Understanding of Jesus, 12–25, rightly emphasizes the nationalistic purpose of the delegation. He concludes, 25: "They wanted independence; but

in the actions embraced a broad cross-section of the population. In terms of geography, all sections of the country were involved, though Judeans (not Galileans) were most prominent. In terms of sectarian affiliation, one may safely affirm that segments of most or all groups were involved: first, people acting out of loyalty to the Pharisaic scholars; second, people identified simply as pilgrims to the pentecost festival; third, prominent men, probably including Sadducees, presenting the appeal for greater autonomy in Rome; fourth, countryfolk in the provinces.

Moreover, ten years before the founding of a group allegedly known as Zealots, we find massive resistance to Rome. The fundamental point is clear: the movement against Rome cannot be assigned to one group or geographical area. The loyalties exhibited by the insurrectionaries include loyalty to the scholars who defended Torah and Temple, and loyalty to the Temple after its firing by Roman troops. The purpose of the protests was quite constant: to secure the requisite freedom to enable the community to structure its own historical life in accord with the Torah.

Finally, the impress of 4 B.C.E. upon the Jewish mind must be noted. These events, including the burning and robbing of the Temple, armed conflict throughout the nation, and mass crucifixion, constituted the first Jewish experience of direct Roman authority in several decades. This gives some validity to the comment that "in Jewish eyes 'the war of Varus' was to rank with the tyranny of Antiochus Epiphanes."[69] Such is suggested by the Assumption of Moses, a Jewish document probably composed sometime between 6 C.E. and 29 C.E. It recites the activity of Varus and then sees the immediate future in language derived from the experience under Antiochus, indicating that Rome was understood to be the present manifestation of the persecuting beast.[70] Indeed, Rome's

---

if no independence was to be had, the next best thing was cultural home rule under a Sanhedrin of their own choosing, autonomy that would grant them their own religious traditions. Such autonomy was unthinkable under a Herodian prince. It was quite conceivable under a Roman governor." So also Allon, "The Attitude of the Pharisees," 72; W. Förster, *Palestinian Judaism in New Testament Times* (Edinburgh and London, 1964), 101; P. Winter, *On The Trial of Jesus* (Berlin, 1961), 13–14, 154, n. 18; J. Neusner, *A Life of Yohanan ben Zakkai*, 2d ed. (Leiden, 1970), 14; Bruce, *New Testament History*, 73.

69. Perowne, *The Later Herods*, 15.

70. Ass. Moses 6:8–9; 8–9. This rejects the suggestion of Charles that 8–9 really do describe Antiochus and actually belong before chapter 6 (*Ap. and Ps.*, 2:420). There is no evidence in the (admittedly few) manuscripts for such a dislocation. T. W. Manson, *The Servant Messiah* (Cambridge, 1953), 30–31, and P. Richardson, *Israel in the Apostolic Church* (Cambridge, 1969), 220 and n. 2, also reject Charles's rearrangement of the text. Smallwood, *The Jews under Roman Rule*, 113, also notes that a second-century Hebrew chronicle, *Sedar Olam*, places the "War of Varus" on the same level as the great war of 66–70 C.E.

activity in ensuing decades was experienced repeatedly as insensitive, oppressive, and provocative.

6 C.E. and the Census

The involvement in these events is also cross-sectional and cross-geographical. The dethronement of Archelaus and his replacement by a Roman governor was achieved by a second delegation to Rome of prominent men, presumably as in 4 B.C.E. in the quest of greater autonomy.[71] The Sanhedrin did generally enjoy more autonomy under Roman governors (prefects) than under Herod, and in this respect the delegations were perceptive. Yet the advent of the Roman governor Coponius[72] in 6 C.E. brought the imposition of the *kensos* or *tributum capitis*, a tax based upon a census which at least since the time of the Maccabees had been understood as the mark of national subjugation.[73]

In Jerusalem an otherwise unidentified "popular faction" deposed the high priest Joazar, viewed as a quisling because he had urged cooperation with the census.[74] The call to revolt issued by Judas the Galilean included as co-articulator the Pharisee Saddok.[75] Though the Galilean origin of Judas is usually used as an indicator that resistance was strongest in Galilee, the opposition instigated by Saddok and him must have occurred in Judea (where the "populace responded gladly"),[76] since it was there, not in the Galilee of Herod Antipas, that the census took place. Furthermore, their protest against taxation represented Pharisaic thought, for some Pharisaic sages understood taxation by a foreign power as robbery and Gentile rulers as robbers, not entitled to taxes nor possession of any part of the land.[77] Thus the broad base of Jewish opposition to Roman power is again demonstrated.

---

71. *Ant.* 17.342–44; *B.J.* 2.111.

72. *Ant.* 18.2; *B.J.* 2.117. For the title of the Roman governors as "prefect" rather than "procurator," see J. Vardaman, "A New Inscription Which Mentions Pilate as 'Prefect,'" *JBL* 81 (1962): 70–71.

73. 1 Macc. 13:41–42 dates independence to the lifting of the Seleucid tax on Judea (1 Macc. 13:39): "In the year 170 [i.e., 142 B.C.E.], Israel was released from the Gentile yoke." See also E. Stauffer, *Christ and the Caesars* (London, 1955), 115, who cites Herodotus to the effect that tribute is a sign of the loss of sovereignty.

74. *Ant.* 18.3, 16.

75. *B.J.* 2.118; *Ant.* 18.4–10.

76. *Ant.* 18.6.

77. Neusner, *Yohanan ben Zakkai*, 15.

Pilate

The administration of Pilate (26–36 c.e.) illustrated the insensitivity and arrogance to which Roman colonial administration could descend and the loyalties which engendered massive Jewish response using a variety of means. Appointed by the Roman anti-Semite Sejanus,[78] whose political star ascended with the virtual de facto abdication of the emperor Tiberius, Pilate either through naivete or malice offended against the central institutions of Judaism.[79]

Shortly after Pilate's appointment as governor, a cohort of his troops entered Jerusalem with images of the emperor attached to its standards and placed them in the fortress Antonia adjacent to the Temple.[80] Not only did this contravene customary Roman policy, but it violated the Torah's prohibition of graven images and desecrated the Temple by the presence of pagan cult objects on the Temple hill.[81] The magnitude of the offense is suggested by the fact that Jerome and Theophylact preserve, apparently independently of Josephus, the memory that Pilate deposited images in the Temple.[82] A vast throng of both Jerusalemites and country folk protested vigorously and nonviolently to Pilate in Caesarea. Pilate relented only when he learned that they were prepared to

---

78. Philo, In Flaccum, 1; Legatio, 159–61. Cf. P. Maier, "Sejanus, Pilate, and the Date of the Crucifixion," Church History 37 (1968): 3–13. The natural inference from Philo is that Sejanus's anti-Semitism was directed at the Jews in Italy. On the other hand, Eusebius, apparently dependent on Philo, states that Sejanus intended to destroy "the whole race" (Eccl. His. II.5.7). Whether Eusebius's statement is based on a lost writing of Philo, a misreading of Philo, or his own editorial purposes is difficult to ascertain. In any case, it is clear that Sejanus's anti-Jewish reputation was both well known and feared (see Legatio, 161).

79. For summary statement of the harshness of Pilate's term see Philo, Legatio, 302; Wilson, The Execution of Jesus, 18–22; H. Cohn, The Trial and Death of Jesus (New York, 1971), 7–17.

80. B.J. 2.167–77; Ant. 18.55–62.

81. For an analysis, see C. H. Kraeling, "The Episode of the Roman Standards at Jerusalem," HTR 35 (1942): 263–89, who emphasizes the gravity of the incident by comparing it to the later threat posed by Caligula: "Yet what was threatening in these later years [the time of Caligula] was only what had actually occurred probably in 26 A.D., when the Roman standards with their images of the emperor were set up on the Temple hill as the numina of the garrison's worship" (286). Affirming the standards to be cult objects are E. M. Smallwood, "Jews and Romans in the Early Empire," History Today 15 (1965): 316; Smallwood, The Jews under Roman Rule, 161; P. Maier, "The Episode of the Golden Roman Shields at Jerusalem," HTR 62 (1969): 112; A. D. Nock, "The Roman Army and the Roman Religious Year," HTR 45 (1952): 239. In the Dead Sea Scrolls, 1QpHab 6 refers to the practice of the kittim (Romans) sacrificing to their standards and worshiping their weapons of war.

82. Jerome, Commentary on Matthew, and Theophylact, Commentary on Mark, cited by G. R. Beasley-Murray, A Commentary on Mark Thirteen (London, 1957), 71. In Jewish tradition, Megillath Taanith 18 may refer to the day when the standards were removed; if so, the day was observed annually as one on which fasting was not permitted.

die. Notable here is the large number of faithful Jews, almost certainly including Pharisees, apparently pursuing routine lives in Jerusalem and Judea, suddenly erupting into action out of loyalty to Torah and Temple, using tactics for which guerilla movements are not known.

Pagan religious objects provided a further source of offense in Pilate's coinage, though no specific Jewish reaction is reported. In a departure from the practice of previous governors, his coins depicted implements used in pagan worship, notably the priest's staff and the ladle with which sacrificial wine was poured.[83]

Apparent cross-sections of the population are again involved shortly after the incident of the standards when Pilate appropriated Temple funds to build an aqueduct.[84] According to Josephus, "tens of thousands" (probably an overstatement) of Jews gathered in Jerusalem to protest. Pilate transformed the nonviolent protest into a violent action by turning his disguised troops loose with clubs. In an incident the details of which are otherwise unknown, Pilate's troops slew Galilean pilgrims *while they were sacrificing*. To do so, his troops would have had to enter that part of the Temple to which Jews alone were permitted ingress.[85] Another protest, this time involving the people acting through the four sons of Herod and others in authority, erupted when Pilate set up imageless votive shields dedicated to Tiberius in Herod's palace in Jerusalem.[86] Besides these nonviolent (from the Jewish side) protests during Pilate's tenure, at least one violent insurrection occurred.[87]

Emerging clearly is the impression that these incidents did not stem from a well-organized resistance movement (though that may have been operative). Rather, masses of mainstream Jews reacted spontaneously out of loyalty to Torah and Temple. They were concerned that the holiness of Jerusalem and the nation should not be despoiled by ac-

---

83. Smallwood, "Jews and Romans in the Early Empire," 316, and Stauffer, *Christ and the Caesars*, 119.

84. *B.J.* 2.175–77; *Ant.* 18.60–62.

85. Luke 13:1. For the incident, see J. Blinzler, "Die Niedermetzelung von Galiläern durch Pilatus," *NovTest* 2 (1958): 24–49. He argues convincingly that it occurred at a Passover; the language requires that it occurred in the Temple; it cannot be identified with any incident reported by Josephus or Philo; the silence of Josephus is of no significance (30–38).

86. Philo, *Legatio*, 299–305. The translator of the Loeb edition treats this as an alternate version of the incident of the standards recorded by Josephus. However, Maier, "The Episode of the Golden Roman Shields," 111–13, has demonstrated convincingly that two incidents are involved; so also H. W. Hoehner, *Herod Antipas* (Cambridge, 1972), 176–80; Förster, *Palestinian Judaism*, 101; and Bruce, *New Testament History*, 33. No specific law, so far as we know, was violated by *imageless* shields; Maier, 116–18, speculates that it was perhaps hypersensitive ultraorthodox reaction against an unpopular governor, primed by the earlier incident of the standards.

87. Mark 15:7. Cf. Smallwood, *The Jews under Roman Rule*, 164.

tions blatantly in contradiction to the conditions which should prevail in Yahweh's land, and they used means ranging from peaceful protest to violence. Nor can a special role be assigned to Galilee; instead, Jerusalem was most often the center.

Caligula

The details of the emperor Caligula's odious attempt to erect a statue of himself in the holy of holies of the Temple in 40 c.e. and the fortunate circumstances whereby it was averted do not need rehearsal.[88] What needs attention is the Jewish reaction to this most ominous menace which threatened to repeat the days of Antiochus Epiphanes. A broad cross-section of the population, including the aristocracy, thronged to the cities of Ptolemais and Tiberias to petition Petronius, the Roman official charged with Caligula's mission. Though the protest was nonviolent, and though the crowd expressed its willingness to be slaughtered, all three ancient authorities agree that the crowd would in fact have gone to war rather than permit such a desecration of the Temple.[89] What is striking is that any rigid distinction between a great mass of Jews committed to at the most nonviolent resistance, on the one hand, and a smaller group committed to violent insurrection, on the other hand, disappears. Instead the Jewish nation as a whole was prepared to fight, if necessary, to defend its holy place.

Cumanus

Two incidents, both involving individual Roman soldiers, mobilized large numbers of Jews during the administration of the governor Cumanus (48–52 c.e.). The aberrant actions of two soldiers cannot serve as indicators of official Roman policy, of course, but the incidents do illustrate the loyalties for which Jews were willing to risk their lives. During Passover a Roman soldier among those posted on the roof of the Temple as a precaution against uprisings made a rude gesture (of either a sexual or excretory nature) to the pilgrims gathered in the Temple courts. The crowd (presumably a general cross-section

---

88. B.J. 2.184–203; Ant. 18.261–309; Philo, Legatio, 184–348; Tacitus, Hist. 5.9.

89. Philo, Legatio, 108, 215; even the Diaspora is envisioned as joining in armed defense of the holy place. Josephus, who most vividly emphasizes the nonviolent nature of the protest, hints that more than nonviolent resistance was possible in Ant. 18.270: "The Jews, though they regarded the risk involved in war with the Romans as great, yet adjudged the risk of transgressing the Law to be far greater." Tacitus, Hist. 5.9, also notes the intention of the Jews to resort to arms.

as it was composed of Passover pilgrims) assailed Cumanus about this "blasphemy against God." He then sent more troops into the Temple area, the crowd panicked, and a large number were killed.[90] This insult against and violence in the Temple were soon followed by an affront of equal magnitude against the Torah. While hunting for revolutionaries on a search and destroy mission in Judea, a member of a Roman patrol publicly destroyed a copy of the Torah. An undifferentiated multitude of Jews, "roused as though it were their whole country which had been consumed in the flames,"[91] protested to Cumanus that they would rather perish than permit the Torah to be defiled thus. So forceful was the demonstration that Cumanus, fearing a revolution, executed the offending soldier in front of the protestors.[92]

In these episodes under Cumanus, characteristics common to the previous ones are repeated. Out of loyalty to Temple and Torah, Jews in greater numbers than those who could credibly be attributed to a guerilla movement, using public tactics for which clandestine liberation fronts are not known, protested vociferously to the governing authorities. Though the protests were nonviolent from the Jewish side, the protestors were not only willing to die, but the authorities rightly or wrongly feared that they might resort to armed insurrection. Once again, no particular prominence is assigned to Galilee or Galileans. In all the incidents surveyed thus far (and indeed in all of the ones reported by Josephus and other ancient sources), Galilee plays an explicit role in only a minuscule number. The center instead is Jerusalem and Judea. Clearly the Pharisees were often involved, since loyalty to Torah was one of the identifying marks of the Pharisees (though not of them alone) and of those who looked to them as models of fidelity. But also the protests must have involved some of the *amme ha aretz* who, though unable or unwilling fully to comply with the Torah, still valued the central institutions of Judaism.

Priests and Resistance

One socio-religious class has not been mentioned much in these case studies: the priesthood, and in particular high priests. Though their social and political position produced immense pressures to support the established order, there is evidence that some of them from time to time also participated in anti-Roman activities.

---

90. *B.J.* 2.223–27; *Ant.* 20.105–12. According to Josephus, "thousands" were killed; his use of numbers is often suspect.

91. *B.J.* 2.230.

92. *B.J.* 2.228–31; *Ant.* 20.113–17.

There is considerable evidence that the Roman authorities suspected even the high priestly circles of potential disloyalty. First, the Romans followed the custom of Herod, who retained custody of the high priest's garments as insurance against insurrection.[93] About 37 c.e., Vitellius, governor of Syria, returned the garments to the Temple. When the Roman governor Fadus sought to regain custody less than a decade later, the Roman authorities feared that such action might result in revolt.[94] Yet they deemed it worth the risk, eventually sending a delegation to Caesar to settle the question. Second, the rapid replacement of high priests under several governors may well point to political suspicions. In the fifty-two years following 15 c.e., seventeen high priests were appointed. Since two of these served thirty years, the remaining twenty-two years saw an extraordinarily high figure of fifteen high priests. It is a reasonable conjecture that those with a long tenure had achieved a *modus vivendi* with the governor.[95] Conversely, some of those who served very short terms may have been considered politically unreliable. Third, the Roman refusal to appoint a new high priest after the war of 66–70 reflected a fear that he would become a nationalistic rallying center.[96]

That these suspicions were at least partially justified is shown by the behavior of the high priestly circles shortly before and during the war of 66–70.[97] The cessation of sacrifices on behalf of Caesar, the act which initiated the war, was ordered by Eleazar, captain of the Temple (ranking second only to the high priest) and son of the high priest Ananias.[98] During the war the former high priest Ananus was one of the two generals charged with the defense of Jerusalem. Of the two commanders of Idumea, one was a chief priest and the other a son of the high priest Ananus.[99]

Not too much must be claimed, of course. The high priests by virtue of their public position and vulnerability to Roman removal were required to be diplomatic, and many no doubt deserved the epithet "collaborator." But the suspicions of Rome and the behavior of some

---

93. *Ant.* 18.92.

94. *Ant.* 20.6–14, esp. 7.

95. W. Knox, *St. Paul and the Church of Jerusalem,* 62–63; so also Scott, *The Crisis in the Life of Jesus,* 30: to ensure high priestly fidelity, "the high office changed hands every few years at the discretion of the imperial power."

96. A. Guttmann, "The End of the Jewish Sacrificial Cult," *HUCA* 38 (1967): 147–48.

97. See, above all, Smallwood, "High Priests and Politics," 22–31.

98. *B.J.* 2.049.

99. Smallwood, 29, and Jeremias, *Jerusalem,* 198.

do justify the claim that they were not immune to Jewish loyalties or to the Jewish quest for greater autonomy.[100]

Finally, the Essenes have appeared hardly at all in these case histories. The reason, of course, is obvious. As people who had deliberately withdrawn from the cities and villages of Palestine to the community at Qumran, they did not figure in public events prior to the outbreak of the war in 66 C.E. Yet their literary deposit, in particular the Rule of War, shows that they too harbored anti-Roman attitudes and envisioned a future terrestrial combat in which they would fight against Rome.[101] Consistent with this, their sexual tabus suggest a conscious emulation of the ancient Israelite warrior,[102] indicating that readiness for holy war was a feature of the sect. Indeed, there is persuasive circumstantial evidence that they fought in the war of 66–70 C.E. One of the six military provinces was commanded by John the Essene.[103] Josephus notes that the Essenes were tortured by the Romans during the war,[104] and archaeological evidence demonstrates that Qumran was destroyed between 66 and 70 C.E.[105] Though these last two items could simply mean that the people of Qumran were the innocent victims of Roman atrocities, they do fit well the hypothesis that they were combatants.[106] In either instance, Qumran completes the case that opposition to Rome transcended traditional party divisions in Judaism.

Summary

The common view of the Sadducees as collaborators, Pharisees as quietists, and Zealots as Galilean militants needs substantial revision. The predilection of modern historians to see these designations as corresponding to real differences vis-à-vis attitudes toward Rome (however meaningful the distinctions are concerning other questions) can only be misleading, just as it would mislead a future historian to make the

---

100. Cf. the judgment of P. Winter, "Sadducees and Pharisees" in Schultz, ed., *Jesus in His Time*, 49–50. Granting that the usual view of the Sadducees as collaborators is largely true, he argues, "it would be wrong on this account to say that they had no national sympathies," for they "had a concern for the preservation of old traditions and national institutions."

101. See esp. O. Betz, "Jesu Heiliger Krieg," *NovTest* 2 (1958): 116–37, esp. 116–24.

102. M. Black. *The Scrolls and Christian Origins* (London, 1961), 16–17.

103. *B.J.* 2.567.

104. *B.J.* 2.152–53.

105. See, e.g., M. Burrows, *The Dead Sea Scrolls* (New York, 1955), 82.

106. H. H. Rowley, "The Qumran Sect and Christian Origins," *BJRL* 44 (1961): 116–37, esp. 116–24.

natural assumption that party designations in the United States corresponded to real differences vis-à-vis the question of the Vietnam war,
during which there were "hawks" and "doves" in both major parties.
For these vignettes demonstrate that Jewish resistance to Rome had its
sources not in a single sect operating underground as a guerilla movement, occasionally confronting the Romans directly in open warfare,
but in loyalties embraced by diverse groups.

Several times Pharisees are named. At other times, though the opposition is not identified by party, broad segments are involved. Of course,
there were differences in the means employed by the mainstream and
the underground, but even these were not differences in principle. That
is, one cannot make a distinction between these groups on the basis
of an in-principled commitment to nonviolent protest and avoidance
of armed revolution on the one hand, and those committed to revolution, on the other.[107] For as Josephus, Philo, and Tacitus make clear, the
massive groups who demonstrated nonviolently at the time of Caligula
were in fact willing to take up arms in opposition to Rome, a willingness which Josephus in his last work states was also operative generally
in Jewish defense of their traditions.[108] Moreover, resistance was not
a specialty of the "unenlightened boors" of Galilee,[109] but centered in
Jerusalem, the summit of Jewish religious and intellectual life.

Finally, beginning as we did with the reign of Herod, we have seen
that opposition to non-Jewish power was not an innovation beginning
with the advent of direct Roman rule in 6 c.e., but was continuous
with loyalties extant before then. Running throughout the episodes of
resistance are the twin themes of Torah and Temple, the two most important institutions of Judaism. Moreover, what it meant to be loyal
to Torah and Temple had been decisively shaped by the Jewish experience since the exile. Understanding the dynamics of Jewish resistance
to Rome requires that we see it in this larger framework. Only by doing so can we complete the picture of the social matrix within which
the Jesus movement competed with other renewal movements for the
loyalty of the Jewish people.

---

107. Wink, "Jesus and Revolution," 41, agrees with our judgment that all parties
shared an anti-Roman attitude and then argues that what differentiated them was their
strategy where "their ways parted sharply."

108. *Ap.* 2.272, 292.

109. See also Hoehner, *Herod Antipas*, 56–58, who refutes the stereotype of the
Galileans as more prone to unrest.

CHAPTER THREE

The Dynamics of Jewish Resistance to Rome: The Quest for Holiness

The concern of the Jewish tradition to structure the life of a community within history so that it reflects loyalty to Yahweh is frequently expressed as an *imitatio dei:* "Israel should reflect in her community life the character and activity which she ascribes to God."[1] During the postexilic period, the content of the *imitatio dei*, the paradigm in conformity with which the national community developed, was *holiness*, understood as separation from everything impure. Intensifying through the Maccabean period and into New Testament times, resting on the two foundational institutions of Torah and Temple, animating the major renewal groups of the period, and drawing part of its vitality from its utility as a program of survival in an increasingly threatening world, the quest for holiness became the dominant cultural dynamic of Israel's corporate life. It is here that we find an adequate understanding of the source of Israel's resistance to Rome and a context for understanding the politics of Jesus.

The Postexilic Development

The small Jewish community living in the hills surrounding Jerusalem after the return from exile in Babylon in the sixth century B.C.E. founded its life on Torah and Temple. They became respectively the constitution and religio-political center of its corporate life.

The dominant role of these two institutions is illustrated by the rabbinic tradition's telescoping of the restoration of the Temple and the promulgation of the Torah by Ezra into the same generation.[2] The last of the men of the Great Synagogue, Simeon the Just, similarly links

---

1. L. E. Toombs, *IDB*, 1:647.
2. G. F. Moore, *Judaism in the First Centuries of the Christian Era: The Age of the Tannaim* (Cambridge, 1937), 1:6–7, 33.

Torah and Temple: "By three things is the world sustained: by the Law, by the Temple service, and by deeds of loving kindness."[3]

Sociologically, loyalty to these central institutions functioned to insure the survival of Israel. Without fidelity to them, the cohesion and solidarity of the society would have disintegrated through the corrosive effects of native Canaanean and cosmopolitan Hellenistic culture. No Jew could deny their fundamental significance and yet remain within the community's limits of tolerance, even though disagreement about their meaning was both permitted and common.

However, Torah and Temple in themselves did not determine the historical characteristics which the postexilic community developed. Rather, that was determined by the dominant motif in the light of which the community interpreted the Torah and the function of the Temple: holiness. The quest to embody holiness in national life saw its goal articulated in the recurrent theme of the priestly code, which probably received its final form during the exile: "Speak to all the community of Israel: *You shall be holy*, because I, Yahweh your God, am holy."[4] Upon the achievement of holiness depended the future security of the nation.[5]

Moreover, holiness was understood primarily as entailing separation. Just as the holiness of God was understood to be God's separation from all that defiles,[6] so the holiness of Israel, living by an *imitatio dei*, meant separation.[7] Indeed, holiness was identified with separation in the Tannaitic midrashim, an identification which L. Baeck traces to the pre-Maccabean period.[8] *Parush* (separation) and *qadosh* (holiness) were used as synonyms. "You shall be holy" was rendered as "You shall be *perushim*."[9] So also with Yahweh's holiness — "Just as I am *parush*, so ye shall be *perushim*."[10]

The quest for holiness accounts for the movement of internal reform within Judaism, with its greater emphasis on sabbath observance, proper tithing, prohibition of marriage with non-Jews, etc.[11] It also ac-

---

3. M. Aboth 1:2. Simeon lived ca. 280 or 200 B.C.E.

4. Lev. 19:1–2; 11:44–45; 20:7, 26.

5. Lev. 15:31, 18:28, 20:22, 25:18, 26:14–41; Mal. 3:8–12.

6. S. Schechter, *Some Aspects of Rabbinic Theology* (London, 1909), 205; 199–218 explicate holiness as a controlling idea in Judaism.

7. Cf. J. S. Chesnut, *The Old Testament Understanding of God* (Philadelphia, 1968), 133: "Israel is to be holy as the special, separated people of the holy God."

8. L. Baeck, *The Pharisees and Other Essays* (New York, 1947), 3–50.

9. Sifra on Lev. 19:2. See John Bowker, *Jesus and the Pharisees* (Cambridge, 1973), 13–14, and his collection of texts which make this equation on 163–66.

10. Sifra on Lev. 20:26.

11. See, for example, the contents of the "articles of confederation" agreed to by the community under Ezra: Neh. 10:30–39.

counts for the increasing separation from the nations. Theologically, the calamity of 586 B.C.E. (the conquest of Judah and Jerusalem and the destruction of the Temple by the Babylonian empire) was seen as God's judgment upon Israel because of its corruption by the practices of the nations. Moreover, the emphasis on holiness served the very important function of separating Israel from and insulating it against the incursions of alien culture. Reasonable people in Judaism could agree that "segregation alone could preserve it from extinction" and that "a splendid isolation was the only policy possible," just as some form of monasticism was probably necessary for the survival of the Christian church after the fall of Rome.[12] Furthermore, the intent of the program of holiness was thoroughly noble. It sought "to save the tiny nation, the guardian of great ideals, from sinking into the broad sea of heathen culture," thereby preserving the possibility of realizing its ideals in its national life.[13] Thus the political program of postexilic Judaism was the permeation of national life by holiness, a program undergirded by the twin institutions of Torah and Temple.

Effects of the Maccabean Era

Beginning in the fourth century B.C.E., Alexander the Great and his Ptolemaic and Seleucid successors introduced the new cultural force of Hellenism into the ancient Near East and to the Jewish homeland in particular. Initially quite receptive, Judaism adapted and incorporated Hellenism within an essentially Jewish framework to such an extent that one may not speak of a non-Hellenized Judaism.[14] However, in 175 B.C.E., a Hellenistic reform party within Judaism, supported by the Seleucid monarch Antiochus Epiphanes, sought to replace Torah and Temple with syncretistic Hellenistic religion. Because of this attempt, the initial period of "reception" of Hellenism was replaced by "repudiation."[15]

---

12. W. D. Davies, *Paul and Rabbinic Judaism* (London, 1948), 61; cf. F. C. Grant, *Ancient Judaism and the New Testament* (London, 1960), 8; and H. H. Rowley, *Israel's Mission to the World* (London, 1939), 39, 42, 46, 71.

13. J. Klausner, *Jesus of Nazareth* (London, 1929), 376.

14. See especially Martin Hengel, *Judaism and Hellenism*, for the documentation of the effect of Hellenism on Judaism up to and including the Maccabean era. On 1:252, Hengel comments: "even Palestinian Judaism must be regarded as Hellenistic Judaism."

15. The quoted words are from a section heading in Hengel, *Judaism and Hellenism*, 1:247: "Palestinian Judaism between *Reception* and the *Repudiation* of Hellenism." See also his *Jews, Greeks and Barbarians*, trans. John Bowden (Philadelphia, 1980), 79, where he speaks of "the inner affinity of Judaism to the Greek world and also *its opposition*."

The Hellenistic onslaught against the two pillars of Jewish culture and the quite unexpected success of the Maccabean-led Jewish resistance against demonstrably superior power had a number of profound effects upon Judaism. Together, they gave "a new direction to the political and intellectual development of the Jewish people."[16]

Antiochus and the Hellenistic reform party made clear to the Jewish people as a whole what perceptive minds such as Ezra and Nehemiah had seen since the return from exile: the Jewish state could not survive without Temple and Torah.[17] With the proscription of Torah observance and appropriation of the Temple for the Olympian Zeus,[18] Antiochus and the reformers unwittingly elevated the status of Temple and Torah from taken-for-granted institutions to consciously held symbols of loyalty. Though institutions by themselves are powerful, when vested with symbolic significance, they not only regulate behavior, but for them people are willing to die. Any threat to them is seen not simply as a threat to the institution but to the survival of the culture and the identity of the people.

Torah and Temple thus became the distinctive symbols of the Jewish people. Zeal for the law and the sanctuary dominates the Maccabean literature.[19] Indeed, the twofold climax of 2 Maccabees was the establishment of Hanukkah and Nicanor's Day, both of which celebrated the deliverance of the Temple from actual or threatened desecration by the Gentiles.[20] Henceforth loyalty to Israel and Israel's God was to be expressed in terms of loyalty to Temple and Torah. There developed "an *extreme sensitivity* of Palestinian Judaism toward even an apparent usurpation of power over the law and the sanctuary."[21]

Second, by searing into Jewish consciousness a deep awareness of the peril posed by Gentile power, Antiochus intensified the already existing division between Jew and Gentile. Moreover, since Antiochus was aided initially by Hellenistically inclined Jews in prominent positions, distrust increased not only of foreign military power but also of more subtle Gentile cultural influence. The rejection of non-Jewish culture is illustrated both by the literature which emerges from the pe-

---

16. Hengel, *Judaism and Hellenism*, 1:306.

17. For the suggestion that Antiochus's policy was motivated by an astute realization that Judea could become a domesticated client state only through suppression of Torah and Temple, see Moore, *Judaism*, 1:51–52.

18. Proscription of Torah observance under penalty of death (1 Macc. 1:44–50) and the persecutions which followed (e.g., 1 Macc. 1:60–63; 2 Macc. 6:10–11, 18–31; 2 Macc. 7); his sacrilege of the Temple: 1 Macc. 1:54; 2 Macc. 6:2; Dan. 11:31.

19. 1 Macc. 2:27; 3:43, 58–59; 13:3; 2 Macc. 15:18.

20. J. C. Dancy, *A Commentary on 1 Maccabees* (Oxford, 1954), 14.

21. Hengel, *Judaism and Hellenism*, 1:306. Italics are in Hengel.

riod and by archaeological finds.[22] In the Jewish homeland, a brake was put on "manifest syncretistic tendencies."[23] The period of reaction and opposition to Hellenism began.

Third, the victories of the Maccabees revived the "activistic holy war theology which continued to be strong in New Testament times."[24] Their success provided empirical verification for the claim of the Book of Judith that Yahweh gives victory to the chosen people.[25] It demonstrated that resistance was reasonable, even when it seemed foolish on more pragmatic grounds: "It is not on the size of the army that victory in battle depends, but strength comes from heaven."[26] Thus realistic considerations such as the superior power of an opponent did not need to serve as a deterrent to active resistance.

Significantly, the memories of the Maccabean victories were alive and celebrated in the first century.[27] Each year in Jerusalem for eight days the Maccabean defense of Torah and Temple was commemorated at Hanukkah. Nicanor's Day, immediately preceding Purim, which recalled the triumphs of Esther and Mordecai over the enemies of Israel, provided another annual occasion for recalling Maccabean zeal for the Temple and victory over the Gentile oppressors.[28]

The story of seven Jewish martyrs killed in the persecution under Antiochus is found in differing forms in 2 and 4 Maccabees. The differing forms point to a popular oral tradition which remembered their heroic piety, not simply to two authors who recorded their deeds.[29] Finally, the role of the Maccabees as folk heroes in the first century is evidenced by the veneration of Maccabean tombs[30] and the popularity of Maccabean names.[31] Throughout the period of Roman domination, "there was a belief in a repetition of the 'Maccabean miracle.' "[32]

---

22. K. M. Kenyon, *Jerusalem* (London, 1967), 136–37, reports that whereas the pottery finds at Samaria consist largely of copies of Hellenistic vessels, pottery unearthed in Jerusalem is notable for the near absence of Hellenistic influence; "The contrast . . . is absolute."

23. Hengel, *Judaism and Hellenism*, 1:308.

24. Buchanan, *The Consequences of the Covenant*, 23.

25. Jud. 13:11–14.

26. 1 Macc. 3:19; cf. 2:61, 12:15, 16:3, and 2 Maccabees, which is dominated by this affirmation.

27. Demonstrated especially by W. R. Farmer, *Maccabees, Zealots, and Josephus*, 125–53.

28. As further evidence that the memory of the Maccabees was alive, Farmer cites the composition of 1 and 2 Maccabees, Jason's history, and Megillath Taanith.

29. 2 Macc. 6–7; 4 Macc. 8–14.

30. W. H. C. Frend, *Martyrdom and Persecution in the Early Church* (Oxford, 1965), 60 and 76, n. 159, citing 4 Macc. 17:8.

31. Farmer, "Judas, Simon and Athronges."

32. Hengel, *Judaism and Hellenism*, 1:307.

All of the above created an ethos of resistance to external power and influence grounded in the quest for holiness. The elevation of Torah and Temple to the status of life and death symbols, the increasing hostility toward non-Jewish practices and ideas, and the renaissance of holy war theology intensified "the tendency towards spiritual segregation from outsiders," and "the Hasidic ideal of piety became dominant for the majority of Palestinian Jews."[33] The primary vehicles for implementing the Hasidic ideal in the first century were two of the renewal movements active during the ministry of Jesus.

The Quest for Holiness in the First Century

The one hundred years of Jewish independence under the Maccabees and their successors came to an end when the Roman general Pompey occupied Jerusalem and the Temple in 63 B.C.E. and incorporated the Jewish homeland into the Roman empire. Jews were faced with the question, "What did it mean in these circumstances to be loyal to Yahweh?" The answer provided by the postexilic development was clear: be holy. But what did that mean?[34] A proliferation of groups and movements within Judaism gave their answers. Of most, only the name remains.[35]

Two of these movements, however, were important enough to leave significant literary deposits and to be described by Josephus as among the major "philosophies" of Judaism: the Essenes and the Pharisees.[36]

---

33. Ibid., 1:179.

34. See Bowker, *Jesus and the Pharisees,* 15–16: "Fundamental in the Hakamic movement (the sages of the post-Seleucid period) was a *vision of holiness* — a vision of implementing what God required of his people if they were to be his people. There is nothing surprising in the vision itself; it was shared by many other Jews. *The real issue was how to achieve it:* how is it possible for the command, Be holy as I am holy, to be implemented? Many of the divisions among Jews during the period of the second (16) commonwealth were in fact a consequence of different answers being given to that deeply basic question. On one point most would be agreed: that holiness requires separation from uncleanness and from anything which Torah defines as imparting impurity. But how is separation to be achieved?"

35. For the multiplicity and diversity of groups in first-century Judaism, see M. Smith, "Palestinian Judaism in the First Century," in M. Davis, ed., *Israel: Its Role in Civilization* (New York, 1956), 67–81; M. Black, *The Scrolls and Christian Origins* (London, 1961), 6–11. For the lists of Jewish sects according to the early church fathers, see M. Black, "The Patristic Accounts of Jewish Sectarianism," *BJRL* 41 (1958–59): 285–303.

36. Josephus also mentions the Sadducees and the otherwise unnamed "fourth philosophy." The Sadducees, however, were not a *renewal* movement, but a conservative aristocratic priestly party. Whether the "fourth philosophy" is to be viewed as a distinct renewal movement or as composed of radicalized elements of various segments of the population is unclear; see the discussion in the next section of this chapter.

Both represented a new form of "religious association" in Judaism — a voluntary association with its own communal identity and polity, with membership based on the decision or "conversion" of the individual.[37] Both emerged from the Hasidim of the Maccabean period,[38] both centered in Torah and Temple,[39] and both intensified the quest for holiness.

The Essenes intensified the quest for holiness so as to require separation from society.[40] Known to us most intimately through the discovery of the Dead Sea Scrolls near the middle of this century, the Essenes originated as a reaction to the Hellenistic practices adopted by the Maccabean dynasty in the decades after their successful expulsion of the Seleucids. Convinced that a life of holiness within society as presently constituted was impossible, they withdrew from mainstream society to the wilderness along the Dead Sea, living a highly disciplined monastic style of life, holding all things in common.

They referred to themselves as "the men of holiness" and "the men of perfect holiness," as a "House of Holiness" and a "Building of Holiness."[41] They intensified the commands of Torah, especially as they applied to purity and tithing. Their sanctions for enforcing their understanding were twofold. On the one hand, those outside of the community were viewed as apostate Jews. Especially marked was their hostility toward the present priesthood of the Temple. Within the community, violations of Torah were punished by expulsion for varying periods of time. Living in isolated self-sufficient communes, they avoided contact with the impurity of the *amme ha aretz* and Gentiles. As already noted, by the first century they harbored the expectation that Rome would soon be expelled from the land in the final apocalyptic battle between the children of light and the children of darkness. The expectation may have led them to join the great rebellion against Rome and demonstrates their hostility to Rome in the name of holiness.

---

37. Hengel, *Jews, Greeks and Barbarians*, 123; *Judaism and Hellenism*, 1:243–44.

38. Hengel, *Judaism and Hellenism*, 1:176: "The Hasidim are looked to as the common root of the two most significant religious groups of postbiblical Judaism, the Essenes . . . and the Pharisees."

39. See Hengel, *Jews, Greeks and Barbarians*, 124 and n. 71, 174, where he refers to "the fight of Hasidim, Essenes and Pharisees for the purity of the Temple and its worship."

40. For a compact presentation of the Essenes as known through the Dead Sea Scrolls, see G. Vermes, *The Dead Sea Scrolls* (London, 1977). For a careful comparison of the Essenes as known in Philo, Josephus, and Pliny with what is disclosed in the Dead Sea Scrolls, see Schürer-Vermes, *The History of the Jewish People in the Age of Jesus Christ*, 2:555–97.

41. Vermes, *The Dead Sea Scrolls*, 88, 168, 170.

The Pharisees intensified the quest for holiness so as to require a separation *within* society.[42] Their connection to holiness is clear. Their name was probably derived from the Greek transliteration of the Hebrew *parush* or Aramaic *perishaya*,[43] "separated," which, as we have already seen, was understood as the equivalent of *qadosh*, "holy."

The two identifying marks of the Pharisees, as defined by Jacob Neusner, also underline their connection to holiness. They ate unconsecrated food as if they were Temple priests, and they practiced meticulous tithing.[44] For the Pharisees, Israel was to be a "Kingdom of priests and a holy nation," following the same laws of purity that normally applied only to priests in the Temple.[45] Thus the Pharisees intensified the Torah by extending to the people as a whole the requirements of holiness that once applied only to the priesthood: Israel as a nation was to be holy. Consequently, as John Bowker observes, it is "entirely appropriate that the Tannaitic sources . . . should define *perushim* in terms of holiness."[46]

The Pharisaic program was intended for all of Israel. Rather than secede from society as did the men of Qumran, the Pharisees' brand of utopianism remained within society to be a leaven as an expansionist,

---

42. For the Pharisees, see especially the voluminous work of Jacob Neusner in the 1970s: *The Rabbinic Traditions about the Pharisees before 70*, 3 vols. (Leiden, 1970); *From Politics to Piety: The Emergence of Pharisaic Judaism* (Englewood Cliffs, N.J., 1973); also relevant are his *The Idea of Purity in Ancient Judaism* (Leiden, 1973), *Early Rabbinic Judaism* (Leiden, 1975), and *A Life of Yohanan ben Zakkai*, 2d ed. (Leiden, 1970). Neusner affirms that what the rabbinic literature says about the *perushim* can be used, cautiously and critically, to construct a picture of the Pharisees. Ellis Rivkin, *A Hidden Revolution* (Nashville, 1978), disagrees, arguing that the *perushim* are extreme separatists, and that the Pharisees are not to be defined by the *perushim's* concentration on tithing and purity; instead, they are "a scholar class dedicated to the supremacy of the twofold Law" (176). See Rivkin's article "Pharisees" in the supplemental volume (1976) to the *IDB*, 657–63. That the Pharisees were concerned about both the written and oral law is not to be denied, of course; but Neusner's critical use of some *perushim* texts in his description of pre-70 Pharisees remains convincing. For a careful analysis of how one might explain the diverse use of *perushim* in the rabbinic literature, see Bowker, *Jesus and the Pharisees*, 1–38. Bowker's conclusions are consistent with Neusner's.

43. So Baeck, *The Pharisees*, 3; see also Bowker, *Jesus and the Pharisees*, 4; and Schürer-Vermes, *The History of the Jewish People in the Age of Jesus Christ*, 2:395. Other etymologies have been suggested, but this one seems most probable.

44. J. Neusner, *The Idea of Purity in Ancient Judaism* (Leiden, 1973), 66, and *From Politics to Piety*, 83.

45. Neusner, *Early Rabbinic Judaism*, 51. The quoted words are from Ex. 19:6, which were sometimes combined with the opening words of Lev. 19:1–2, "you shall be holy," as in Midrash Tehillim on Ps. 10:1. See also Bowker, *Jesus and the Pharisees*, 17; K. Kohler, "Pharisees," *JE* 9:661; A. Finkel, *The Pharisees and the Teacher of Nazareth* (Leiden, 1964), 43; Baeck, *The Pharisees*, 41–42; A. Isaksson, *Marriage and Ministry in the New Testament* (Lund, 1965), 7–9.

46. Bowker, *Jesus and the Pharisees*, 18, 29.

not a secessionist movement.[47] They did not intend to be a party within Israel but intended to be Israel itself.[48] Moreover, they introduced structural reforms to further the achievement of holiness in the nation.[49] Thus the Pharisees became the bearers of the quest for holiness in public life, "the classic representatives of the course adopted by Judaism in its inner development during the postexilic epoch."[50] Though they were not very numerous (in the first century probably six thousand Pharisaic heads of families[51] out of a Jewish population of around six hundred thousand), their influence increased until many, perhaps most, of those outside the Pharisaic fellowships granted the validity of the Pharisaic vision of holiness for Israel,[52] even though they did not fulfill the Pharisaic regulations.

The Pharisaic intensification of purity laws and tithing not only flowed out of the quest for holiness, but sought to counter directly the corrosive effects of Roman political control and Gentile influence. Purity laws required separation from all that was unclean, including Gentiles and many Gentile practices. Socially, the emphasis upon purity was intended to insulate and isolate Israel from the practices of the heathen, to protect it against assimilation and corruption. Religiously, the emphasis flowed out of devotion to Yahweh as the holy one.

Meticulous tithing of all agricultural products addressed the greatest source of nonobservance, the double system of Jewish and Roman taxation.[53] All tithes (the Jewish "taxes") were to be paid, and a person who would be holy could not eat untithed food. Most apparently tolerated the payment of the Roman taxes as well, so long as one first gave to God what was God's (the tithes).[54]

Hence the Pharisees advocated an intensification of holiness precisely in the area in which the temptation to be nonobservant was the greatest. Yet to focus on that which distinguishes them from first-century Judaism leaves the picture incomplete. They also were devoted

---

47. For an excellent statement of the difference, see J. Neusner, "Qumran and Jerusalem: Two Jewish Roads to Utopia," *JBR* 27 (1959): 284–90.

48. Bowker, *Jesus and the Pharisees*, 21.

49. Pawlikowski, "On Renewing the Revolution of the Pharisees," esp. 418–23.

50. Schürer-Vermes, *The History of the Jewish People in the Age of Jesus Christ*, 2:389.

51. *Ant.* 17.42.

52. Jeremias, *Jerusalem*, 266; Finkel, *The Pharisees and the Teacher of Nazareth*, 81; Kohler, "Pharisees," 665; S. W. Baron, *A Social and Religious History of the Jews*, 2d ed. (New York, 1952), 2:36, 342–44; Reicke, *New Testament Era*, 156, 162; L. Ginzberg, "The Religion of the Jews at the time of Jesus," *HUCA* 1 (1924): 309: Pharisaism represented "the religious consciousness of the bulk of the nation or Catholic Israel."

53. See chapter 2 above.

54. Because the Pharisees may have been largely artisans, they may not have felt the economic burden of the double system of taxation as acutely as farmers did.

to all that was common to Judaism: absolute loyalty to God, love of neighbor, the joy of the sabbath, the richness of the Jewish festivals, religious disciplines such as prayer and fasting. Pharisaic circles produced some of the noblest "saints" in Judaism.[55] In the first century there was the peaceable and lovable Hillel. Slightly later in the same century, Yohanan ben Zakkai wrested from the ruins of the great rebellion the fundamental form of Jewish piety that persists to this day. In the second century, Akiba put loyalty to Torah above life. In his nineties, he was flayed alive by the Romans. His last words were, "Hear, O Israel, the Lord is our God, the Lord is One; and thou shalt love the Lord thy God with all thine heart, and with all thy soul, and with all thy might."[56]

Thus the religious dynamic of first-century Judaism, derived from the postexilic period, intensified in the Maccabean era, and incarnate in the two major renewal groups of the period, was the quest for holiness. To this religious dynamic must be added a conviction flowing out of the Hebrew Bible, so important that it was one of the "dogmas" of Judaism: the land of Israel was Yahweh's land and thus holy.[57] It was sacred space, not to be profaned: "You shall not defile the land in which you live, in the midst of which I dwell, for I the Lord dwell in the midst of the people of Israel."[58] Because the land was holy, its inhabitants were not to defile it, and if they did, the land would vomit them out.[59] Moreover, the command to preserve the holiness of the land applied to both Jews and Gentiles, to both "the native or the stranger who sojourns among you" (Lev. 18:26). Thus the condition for living in the holy land was obedience to the laws of holiness.

The conviction that the land was holy continued to develop in the postbiblical and rabbinic periods. According to the Mishnah, the land of Israel was the outermost of ten concentric circles or degrees of holiness.[60] The walled cities of Israel were within the next degree of ho-

---

55. Presumably Essene piety produced a number of "saints" as well, though we know very little about individual personalities from that community.

56. L. Finkelstein, *Akiba: Scholar, Saint and Martyr* (New York, 1975; originally published in 1936), 276–77.

57. See especially Davies, *The Gospel and the Land*, 24–35, 49–104. Davies is well aware that speaking of "dogma" or "doctrines" in Judaism is extraordinary, but actually uses the phrase "dogma of Judaism" to describe "the emphasis on the land..., one of the most persistent and passionately held doctrines... traceable throughout the Old Testament, the Apocrypha and Pseudepigrapha, the Qumran scrolls, and the Rabbinic and Hellenistic Jewish sources."

58. Num. 35:34, commented on by Davies, *The Gospel and the Land*, 29, 31.

59. Davies, *The Gospel and the Land*, 30–31, citing Lev. 20:22–26 and 18:24–30.

60. M. Kel. 1:6–9, commented on by Davies, *The Gospel and the Land*, 58–60. See also 4 Ez. 9:8, 13:48.

liness; next came the city of Jerusalem, followed by the Temple mount, the Temple rampart,[61] and then the various courts of the Temple, culminating in the innermost circle of holiness, the holy of holies, the focal dwelling place of "the holy," the navel of the earth connecting the holy to the profane.

Because the land was holy, it was to be kept clean or pure. And because of the close connection between purity and holiness,[62] the holiness of the land and Temple connected directly to the emphasis on purity among both Essenes and Pharisees. Preserving the holiness of the land, the condition for being permitted to live in it, required the observance of the Torah, especially its laws on purity and tithing.

The holiness of the Temple required meticulous observance of the Temple ritual,[63] protecting the Temple from uncleanness, and excluding Gentiles from its courts. According to an inscription which either separated the outer court from the court of the women, or divided the outer court of the Temple in two, "No alien may enter within the barrier and wall around the Temple. Whoever is caught is alone responsible for the death which follows."[64] In a passage which makes a generalized claim concerning Jewish willingness to defend the Temple, Philo cites this warning as conclusive evidence: "Still more abounding and peculiar is the zeal of them all for the Temple, and the strongest proof of this is that death without appeal is the sentence against those of other races who penetrate into its inner confines."[65]

Thus a confluence of currents combined to constitute the ideology of holiness. Yahweh was holy and Yahweh's people, living by an *imitatio dei*, were to be holy. The land itself was holy and was to be kept pure. Temple and Torah were both essential to holiness: the Temple was the center of holiness, and the holiness of Temple, land, and people depended upon the careful observance of Torah. Moreover, the two major renewal movements were both committed to an intensification of ho-

---

61. The rampart surrounds "the rectangular group of inner courts, containing the Temple structure to the west and the Court of the Women to the east." Davies, *The Gospel and the Land*, 59.

62. Neusner, *The Idea of Purity in Ancient Judaism*, 108.

63. The conviction that the Temple ritual was not being properly observed by the priests of the Maccabean era led to the formation of the Essenes. Their concern for the purity of the Temple was the motivating factor leading to their secession from society. See Neusner, *The Idea of Purity*, 50.

64. That it divided the outer court is persuasively argued by F. J. Hollis, *The Archaeology of Herod's Temple* (London, 1934), 153–59, and plate 10, 160–61.

65. Philo, *Legatio*, 211–12. Josephus refers to the exclusion as well (*B.J.* 5.194 and 6.124–25), and the accusation that Paul violated it was the cause of his arrest in Jerusalem (Acts 21:26ff., 24:6).

liness. Here, in the quest for holiness, we find the religious dynamic which was the ideological cause of Jewish resistance to Rome.

Holiness and Resistance

Holiness required not only that individual Jews should be free to observe the Torah and the Temple rituals, but ideally required that the Jews collectively be free to structure their corporate life. In addition, holiness demanded that the land itself should not be defiled by violations of Torah or interference with the Temple service, whether by Jews or Gentiles. Loyalty to Torah and Temple in the quest for holiness expressed itself in each of the above forms and accounts for most (and perhaps all) of the resistance to Gentile power.

Resistance to Proscription of Torah and Temple

Resistance occurred when there was a direct attack on Torah or Temple. Resistance could take the form of individual disobedience to proscription, as in the stories of Daniel and his friends disobeying a pagan king in order to be loyal to their traditions and in the stories of the martyrs in the early Maccabean period.[66] It could also lead to open armed revolt as in the Maccabean resistance, when zeal for Torah was the rallying cry: "'Follow me,' Mattathias shouted through the town, 'every one of you who is zealous for the Torah and strives to maintain the covenant!'" (1 Macc. 2:27).

Unlike the Seleucids, the Romans never sought to ban the Torah. But the emperor Caligula's plans around 40 C.E. to erect a statue of himself in the Jerusalem Temple constituted as major a threat to the Temple, as did the effort of Antiochus Epiphanes to transform the Temple into a sanctuary to the Olympian Zeus. Not surprisingly, it was on this occasion that the most massive outburst of anti-Roman activity occurred between the death of Herod and the great war of 66–70.

Though resorting to arms proved to be unnecessary because of Caligula's timely death and the withdrawal of the plan, large numbers of the Jewish people were ready to go to war.[67] Philo expresses well what was at stake in Caligula's threat (and that the "mystical Jew of the Diaspora" should say this is significant): the name Israel and the whole

---

66. Dan. 1–4; 1 Macc. 1:60–64, 2:37–38; 2 Macc. 6–7; 4 Macc. 8–14.
67. See above p. 61.

nation of the Jews "depends for its existence upon the existence of the Temple."[68]

Resistance to Practices Violating the Holiness of the Land

By far the greatest number of known protests against Rome were occasioned by practices of the ruling authorities which violated the Torah or threatened to defile the Temple, even though Torah observance by Jews was not thereby prohibited. At stake here was the holiness of the land. As noted earlier, even Gentiles were not to defile the holiness of the geographical limits of Israel by their actions. To the Gentiles applied the rules for "resident aliens," basically the Noachian laws: abstention from idolatry and idolatrous practices, from eating flesh with blood in it, and from serious crimes such as murder, robbery, theft, adultery, and fornication.[69] Though apparently enforced under Maccabean rule,[70] these regulations regarding the behavior of Gentiles could not be enforced under Gentile rule when the Jewish people found themselves legally impotent to insure the holiness of the land.

Numerous practices regarded as idolatrous were constantly performed by Gentile private persons.[71] Even more evident were the practices of public authorities. Idolatrous expressions of loyalty to the emperor undoubtedly occurred in the Roman governor's palace in Caesarea, historically part of Israel. The architectural endeavors of Herod included temples and edifices honoring the emperor and were cited as one cause of complaint when the Jewish delegation opposed the succession of Archelaus in 4 B.C.E.[72] Numerous instances from the case studies in the previous chapter fall into the category of defiling the holiness of the land by violating Torah: the Roman eagle on the Temple; the standards, votive shields and coinage introduced by Pilate and his attempted use of holy funds for profane purposes; and Caligula's proposed erection of an idolatrous object in the Temple.

Indeed, the holiness of the land was violated by Gentile ownership or even renting of portions of it.[73] This was so for two reasons. As notorious idolaters, Gentiles could be expected to practice idolatry in fields or houses occupied by them. Moreover, holiness required the payment

---

68. H. A. Wolfson, *Philo* (Cambridge, Mass., 1948), 2:397, referring to *Legatio*, 194.

69. Moore, *Judaism*, 1:339.

70. L. Finkelstein, "Some Examples of the Maccabean Halaka," *JBL* 49 (1930): 21–25.

71. For manifold examples, see M. Av. Zar.

72. *Ant.* 17.306–7; *B.J.* 2.85.

73. M. Av. Zar. 1:8.

of tithes from every field in Israel, which few if any Gentiles would do.[74] Schürer rightly discerns the potential source of unrest: "And what with such views must have been their feelings at finding the heathen really in possession — if not privately yet politically — of the whole land?"[75] Thus the land could not be kept free from idolatry and, conversely, could not be kept holy under Gentile rule, whether direct or indirect. However well intentioned the Romans, their typical and unexceptional activities render it possible to say "succinctly but truthfully, that the presence of Rome meant the dishonouring of Torah."[76]

Attempts to Acquire Requisite Freedom

Several times attempts were made to secure the freedom necessary for Israel to employ the Torah as its sole religio-political blueprint and thus to live according to holiness. The delegations to Rome in 4 B.C.E. and 6 C.E. which attempted to depose Herodian rule in favor of the San-hedrin (even if under a Roman governor) fall into this category, as do the armed phase of the Maccabean revolt and at least some of the armed insurrections of the first century. Perceptive minds could see that the Roman presence, especially the economic burden of double taxa-tion, encouraged nonobservance of the Torah by Jews. According to the holiness code, Israel could continue to live in the land only if it obeyed the commandments — and the Roman presence made that difficult.[77] Because of this indirect and constant threat to Torah observance, the yearning to be free from Roman rule must have been persistent.

Was there a group within Judaism organized for this purpose? That is, was there a resistance movement with a communal organization and identity, persisting in time, operative throughout the first century, anal-ogous to the Pharisees and Essenes, so that one should speak of the resistance as a renewal group within Judaism? As argued earlier, the common designation for such a group, "Zealots," was apparently not current until the 60s of the first century C.E.[78]

---

74. Neusner, *Yohanan ben Zakkai*, 15, citing L. Ginzberg, *On Jewish Law and Lore* (Philadelphia, 1945), 86ff.

75. Schürer, *The Jewish People in the Times of Jesus Christ*, 2:55–56.

76. Parkes, *Foundations of Judaism and Christianity*, 238.

77. See Davies, *The Gospel and the Land*, 95: "What was it that most threatened the loyalty due to Torah and Temple through which the covenant people could enjoy life in the promised land? It was the threat of an 'alien,' occupying power to both Torah and Temple ... History had taught the Jews in the Maccabean period, as in the Roman, that a foreign ruler could disrupt the conditions under which alone the covenant people could live in the promised land." Davies makes the above statements in a discussion of the holiness of the land.

78. See chapter 2 above, pp. 50–52.

Should we nevertheless imagine that there was such a group, either without a name or with a name lost to us? The evidence from Josephus is ambiguous. On the one hand, he provides no name for the group and mentions nothing of their activity until much later in the century. Moreover, after mentioning the "fourth philosophy" (which an earlier generation of scholars identified as "the Zealots"), he then says, "Jewish philosophy in fact takes *three* forms" (Pharisees, Sadducees, and Essenes) and omits Judas the Galilean's "sect" from his treatment.[79] Finally, he describes the "fourth philosophy" as agreeing "in all other respects with the opinions of the Pharisees, except that they have a passion for liberty that is almost unconquerable, since they are convinced that God alone is their leader and master."[80] That is, Josephus does not portray a movement with a comprehensive and distinctive set of practices and beliefs, as he does when he describes the Pharisees and Essenes.

Thus the "resistance fighters"[81] may simply have been radicalized elements from several segments of the population, coalescing from time to time in response to a particular crisis as the Hebrew tribes did during the time of the judges.[82] If they were a distinct movement, then their ideology was another form of the intensification of the quest for holiness: holiness required expulsion of Rome from the land. They intensified the first commandment especially, arguing that the lordship of Yahweh precluded acknowledging the lordship of Caesar. Presumably they opposed all Roman taxation on the grounds that all of the produce of the holy land belonged to Yahweh:[83] one must give to Yahweh what is Yahweh's and to Caesar what is Caesar's — namely, nothing. Even if a movement, their position is not that different from the Pharisees. Josephus's picture of them as agreeing "in all other respects with

---

79. *B.J.* 2.119.

80. *Ant.* 18.23. For a careful consideration of whether or not Judas actually founded a sect, see Rhoads, *Israel in Revolution*, 52–60. Rhoads concludes that such a sect, *if it existed at all*, was quiescent from its birth until at least forty years later (59).

81. Theissen's term in *Sociology of Early Palestinian Christianity*, 38, 50, etc.

82. Josephus does mention a continuity of leadership. Two of Judas's sons were crucified in 46–48 C.E. (*Ant.* 20.102), and other descendants of his were leaders in the war of 66–74 C.E. (*B.J.* 2.433, 7.253). Such continuity is consistent either with the notion that a renewal movement existed from the time of Judas onward, or with the suggestion that radicalized elements coalesced around a hereditary leadership from time to time.

83. See the story in Av. Zar 2b in which the Romans give their account to God of all that they have done for Palestine, to which God's reply is: "Imbeciles! Everything that you did, you did only for your own good. You established marketplaces to have your brothels, you built bathhouses to give pleasure to your bodies, and the gold and silver you stole from Me, for so it is written, the silver is Mine and the gold is Mine." Though the saying cannot be ascribed to a particular group within Judaism, it pointedly expresses the view that the produce of the holy land belongs to God, not Caesar.

the opinions of the Pharisees"[84] may be correct. The resistance fighters' ideology is a consistent deduction from the holiness of the land, a conviction which the Pharisees also held. The Pharisaic attempt to cope with the problem of nonobservance by stressing meticulous tithing could easily shade into opposition to that which was the chief obstacle to such tithing, the Roman taxes. That is, the ideology of holiness as purity and separation was common to both.[85] Perhaps the outbreaks of actual or threatened armed resistance throughout the first century are to be attributed to a persistent hostility to Roman rule which could be triggered by specific incidents rather than to a particular movement with its own identity and peculiar ideology.

Such is the impression created by the ancient sources. In all three categories of resistance above, the concern for holiness — and thus for Torah and Temple — is the ideological motivation. Moreover, according to the detailed case studies reported in chapter 2, in all three categories resistance took the forms of both active nonviolent protest and willingness to take up arms. Moreover, the resistance embraced cross-sections of the population, both in terms of party affiliation and geography. In short, resistance to Rome had its source in an ideology which permeated all groups rather than in the ideology of a particular movement. The quest for holiness was the cultural dynamic which largely accounted for the collision course with Rome.

Ideology, of course, can function either as legitimation or motivation. Resentment toward Rome could flow from many sources. For example, Roman rule indirectly forced many small landowners to lose their land and become day-laborers. For such individuals, the ideology of holiness may have served as legitimation for the hostility engendered by the deprivation of economic livelihood brought by Rome.

Yet religious ideology can also operate as motivation, perhaps more so in the ancient world than in the modern world. In the modern world, religion is typically one element among many in a pluralistic world-

---

84. *Ant.* 18.23.

85. See the treatment of the Pharisees' political attitude in Vermes-Schürer, 2:394–95. The Pharisees could view Roman control either from the standpoint of providence or divine election. Under the former, Gentile rule could be viewed as the will of God, perhaps as chastisement. Under the latter, Gentile control "would appear as an enormity to be purged. Israel was to acknowledge no other king but God alone, and the ruler appointed by him from the house of David. Gentile domination was contrary to Scripture." The latter view "may be presumed to have been the popular viewpoint among the people as well as among the Pharisees.... Thus, however indifferent to politics Pharisaism was to begin with, the revolutionary trend which gained increasing ground among the Jews in the first century A.D. is to be attributed, indirectly at least, to its influence." There is no perceptible difference between this viewpoint and the ideology often attributed to the resistance.

view and, operating weakly as an independent motive, often functions as legitimation for a course of action motivated by other reasons. In first-century Judaism however, religion was not simply one element in a worldview, but constituted their "social world," or "nomos,"[86] that way of looking at reality created by tradition and sustained by a community, within which one received one's identity. For them, Torah was "nomos" — the "sacred canopy" was still largely intact. But it was threatened and "all the old grounds of identity were imperiled by agglomeration."[87] In that situation religious ideology, still constituting their social world, would have been a powerful motivation for many.

Affirming that Jewish resistance was grounded in the quest for holiness does not mean that we are arguing for a uniform militarism, as if (for example) most or even a majority of the Pharisees were either covert members of the armed phase of the resistance or yearned to be such. Nor are we affirming that most Jews deliberately intended a final confrontation with Rome. No doubt many yearned for peace. But historical actors often produce unintended results. For example, one can hardly think that a larger number of individuals wanted war in the first half of the twentieth century than in the last three-quarters of the nineteenth century.[88] Or, to use the example of the Vietnam War, one cannot think that Presidents Kennedy, Johnson, and Nixon wanted war. All desired peace, at least so their statements indicated, and to doubt their good intentions would be less than charitable. But in their case, the accumulated momentum of loyalty to certain institutions and shibboleths produced and prolonged the conflict, despite their desire for peace. What was required to avoid or shorten the conflict was not simply a desire for peace or the quality of peaceableness, but insight and concrete actions to reverse or qualify the loyalties which created the struggle.

Such was the case in the first century. The conflict from the Jewish side stemmed from the accumulated momentum of loyalty to Torah and Temple understood under the paradigm of holiness. This is why the collection of pro-Roman Pharisaic statements amassed by H. Loewe and others misses the point.[89] Even if the statements were representative of opinion before 70 c.e. (which they probably are not),[90] they would

---

86. See Peter Berger, *The Sacred Canopy* (Garden City, N.Y., 1969). "Nomos" is Berger's term for the humanly created "ordering of experience" imposed upon reality; "society is a world-building enterprise," i.e., a means by which a "social world," or "nomos," is created.

87. Kee, *Christian Origins in Sociological Perspective*, 75.

88. E. H. Carr, *What Is History?* (Penguin Books, 1964), 50–52.

89. Loewe, *Render unto Caesar*, 20–33.

90. Most of the citations come from the third century c.e. or later when a *modus*

not change the fact that resistance was rooted in more fundamental loyalties which the Pharisees shared.

This religious dynamic explains the "politics" of a Diaspora mystical Jew such as Philo, often portrayed as an apolitical Jew who had divested himself of such feelings.[91] He shared the life-and-death loyalty to Torah and Temple which he reports to be characteristic of the Jews.[92] He too hoped for a messianic age which involved the return of the Diaspora, curses on the enemies of Israel, and the fall of Rome.[93] And there is some evidence that he not only awaited the messianic husbandman "but would swing an axe with him when he came,"[94] an axe directed at Rome. Such feelings may have been found in the Jewish community in Rome itself.[95] Thus loyalty to Torah and Temple in the quest for holiness, at a time when these central symbols and dynamic were repeatedly threatened from without and within, is the most adequate explanation for Jewish resistance to Rome.

Holiness and Internal Division

The quest for holiness affected not only Judaism's posture toward Rome, but also deeply affected Jewish society itself. Each of the renewal movements had its own program for the internal reform of Judaism, each centering in the intensification of Torah. The intention of the intensifications was to produce greater "intercultural segregation," i.e., greater Jewish solidarity in the face of corrosive forces. Ironically, the result was greater "intracultural differentiation," an increasing division within Jewish society.[96]

There were the various groups themselves, each claiming to be the true Israel. Moreover, the definition of a true Jew as one who lived by an intensified form of holiness created large groups of "second-rank" and

---

vivendi vis-à-vis Rome had been worked out, following the failures of the revolts of 66–70 and 132–35 C.E. For this modus vivendi as a second-century development at the earliest, see also R. S. Barbour, "Loyalty and Law in New Testament Times," SJT 11 (1958): 344. For another criticism of the alleged pacifism of the Pharisees, see Buchanan, The Consequences of the Covenant, 260–61, and notes 4 and 11, pp. 260, 262.

91. See, e.g., C. Guignebert, The Jewish World in the Time of Jesus (London, 1939), 227; cf. 155.

92. Philo, Legatio, 207–15.

93. Wolfson, Philo, 2:407–26.

94. E. R. Goodenough, The Politics of Philo Judaeus (New Haven, 1938); the quoted phrase is from p. 25. See also pp. 24–27, 113, 117.

95. See the present writer's "A New Context for Romans xiii," NTS 19 (1973): 205–19.

96. Theissen, Sociology of Palestinian Christianity, 84–85.

outcast Jews: "The more strictly the norms of a society are defined, the fewer people can observe them. The stricter the demands on the 'true Jews,' the smaller the group of 'true Jews' becomes."[97] Each movement, in effect, generated its own antithesis. For the Essenes, those outside of their movement were "sons of darkness," even if Jewish. Resistance fighters, as would be expected, were especially hostile to Jews who could be viewed as collaborators.

The policy of the Pharisees, simply because more is known about it, is especially instructive. Though the Romans could enforce payment of taxes levied by them with police power, the Pharisees had no police power to enforce the payment of the Jewish taxes. Their sanctions were of another kind. Some Pharisees appear to have boycotted the produce of the *amme ha aretz,* purchasing only from observant Jews. The effect of this economic boycott could not have been great, however, for their numbers were small. They had some influence over the priests, for they gave their tithes only to priests who followed the Pharisaic understanding of the Torah. But their major sanction was social and religious ostracism. The most offensive of the nonobservant, "the sinners," were declared to have lost all civil and religious rights. They were deprived of the right to sit on local councils and lost their place as children of Abraham in the life of the age to come. They became "as Gentiles," having forfeited their status as members of the holy people of God.[98]

To a considerable extent, "righteous" and "sinners" inhabited the same social world. That is, the social world, or nomos, of first-century Judaism was defined by the normative religion of the country which "consisted of reverence for the Temple cult and belief in the revelation of Moses"[99] and by the renewal movements which sought to intensify Jewish loyalties. Through the process of socialization, both "righteous" and "sinners" would have internalized similar understandings of what it meant to be a faithful Jew. For the sinners, the internalization of these norms meant that the judgment of them as outcasts operated within their own psyches. The intensification of norms produced not only divisions within society, but also a large number of people who felt profoundly alienated and worthless.[100]

97. Theissen, *Sociology of Early Palestinian Christianity,* 84.

98. For more detailed analysis and documentation, see the next chapter, pp. 98–99.

99. Neusner, *The Idea of Purity in Ancient Judaism,* 113.

100. See the comments of Robin Scroggs, "The Earliest Christian Communities as Sectarian Movement," in J. Neusner, ed., *Christianity, Judaism and Other Greco-Roman Cults* (Leiden, 1975), 2:10–11: the peasant's hostility to the Pharisees "would have ultimately been directed against God *and the peasant himself.* . . . To feel that he was violating God's decrees was an inevitable result of the Pharisaic exclusivism and the peasant could only

Prospectus

To the picture of the social matrix sketched at the beginning of chapter 2 must be added two elements. First, there operated within Jewish society a powerful cultural dynamic, the quest for holiness, which pushed Judaism increasingly toward a collision with Rome. Second, this same cultural dynamic produced a society increasingly marked by internal divisions. Each renewal group had its own interpretation of the Torah and, more specifically, of what holiness meant.

In this set of circumstances, another renewal movement emerged, the Jesus movement, which traced its origin back to its founder. Not only did a renewal movement spring up in Jesus' wake, but it was apparently his historical intention to bring one into existence. His deliberate calling of *twelve* disciples suggests that they were to be the nucleus of a community. The style of Jesus' public activity points to a concern to reach all of Israel: his life "on the road" as an itinerant preacher, the restriction of his activity to Israel, the urgent tone of his preaching, his selection of followers to be wandering charismatics and preachers like he himself was, and his deliberate decision to bring his ministry to Jerusalem and the Temple, the heart of his people's life. His movement attracted enough of a following for him to be considered a threat and thereby crucified. All of these specifics point to a renewal movement originating during the ministry itself, grounded in Jesus' intention "to constitute a community worthy of the name of a people of God."[101]

The claim that Jesus founded a renewal movement must be carefully distinguished from two other questions with which it is easily confused. Did Jesus intend to found a new religion? No. His sacred scriptures remained Jewish and he was loyal to the Torah throughout his life. His thought patterns and symbols remained Jewish. His concern was with Judaism. Did Jesus intend to found a church? If by this is meant an organization separate from Judaism, again the answer is no. The emergence of a church distinguishable from Judaism was a later development. Rather, his movement was a "voluntary association" within Judaism, a movement like that of the Pharisees and Essenes. Like the Pharisees, his voluntary association was intended to renew all of Judaism, to be a leaven just as the Pharisees sought to be.

These renewal movements competed with each other. Most obviously, they competed for the loyalty of the people. Beneath this

---

have felt locked out of religion, resentful toward God and more than ever convinced of his own worthlessness."

101. C. H. Dodd, *The Founder of Christianity* (London, 1971), 90.

competition, however, they competed with each other regarding the right interpretation of Torah. Jewish parties agreed on the fundamental importance of Torah, but "the question of its authoritative interpretation constantly gave rise to bitter disputes."[102] On this level, the struggle between the renewal movements was an exegetical or hermeneutical battle, a concern about the paradigm in light of which Torah was to be interpreted and applied.[103] The question of how one interpreted Torah had political implications in two different directions — toward the internal life of Judaism and toward Rome. On the one hand, given that the Torah was the "constitution" of the Jewish community, the question of its interpretation was really the question of how the historical community was to be structured so that its life manifested faithfulness to Yahweh, which was a political as well as religious issue. The clash was between alternative visions of what Israel should be.

On the other hand, the interpretation of Torah very much affected the posture taken toward Rome. The two dimensions of the political question were, of course, related: how the historical community was structured had implications for the relationship with Rome. Conversely, the stance taken toward Rome had implications for what was possible in the structuring of the community.

Recognizing these two dimensions, the key to understanding the politics of Jesus, dictates that Jesus' political stance cannot be examined simply by asking about his attitude toward Rome, but must be treated by inquiring about his stance vis-à-vis the quest for holiness. To state it differently, Jesus was related to more than one political entity: not simply to Rome, but also to that complex politico-religious phenomenon which was first-century Palestinian Judaism. Treatments of Jesus' political stance do not often recognize this twofold dimension, most commonly addressing only the question of Rome.[104]

This twofold dimension provides us with a prospectus for this study. First, what was the relationship between the teaching of Jesus and the quest for holiness? How did he respond to the cultural dynamic which

---

102. Hengel, *Judaism and Hellenism*, 1:252.

103. See Sheldon Isenberg, "Power through Temple and Torah in Greco-Roman Palestine," in Neusner, ed., *Christianity, Judaism and Other Greco-Roman Cults*, 2:24–52. Isenberg notes that the authority to interpret Torah meant power (32) and that the Pharisees and Essenes both sought hermeneutical supremacy: "control of redemptive media based on *a monopoly of exegetical authority*" (42; italics added).

104. See, e.g., O. Cullmann, *The State in the New Testament* (New York, 1956), one of the classic studies of the New Testament and politics. Throughout, only the Roman state is considered. The tendency is also illustrated by the large number of commentaries which entertain the question of Jesus and politics only in connection with the tribute question, where explicit reference to the emperor is made (Mark 12:13–17 par.).

so deeply flavored first-century Judaism? Did he affirm the ideology of holiness, or qualify it by interpreting it differently, or replace it with another ideology, also derivative from the Jewish tradition?

Second, I have argued that the quest for holiness was responsible for the collision course with Rome. Did Jesus see that connection? What did he say about the future of his people, Jerusalem, and the Temple? What did he say about the path of armed resistance to Rome? In particular, is the unmistakable urgency which marked his mission to be connected to the historical crisis which his people faced? Finally, in a concluding chapter, I will place Jesus' response to the quest for holiness and his articulation of an alternative within the framework of his teaching as a whole.

CHAPTER FOUR

Jesus and the Quest for Holiness: Opposition

Jesus appeared in history as a "holy man," or "Spirit person," to use the term I prefer. He was one of a number of Jewish "holy men," or "Spirit persons," roughly contemporary with him.[1] "Holy" is not being used here in a moral sense or in the sense of "separation," but in the sense argued by Rudolf Otto as a designation for the numinous, the awe-inspiring Mystery, the sacred "other" which is known in primal religious experience.[2] A "holy man," or "Spirit person," is one who is in touch with this power.

Like Jewish Spirit persons, and like Spirit persons in other cultures,[3] Jesus was known for his intimate communion with "the holy," or "the sacred," through such means as meditative prayer and fasting. Because of that communion, he (like them) was able to mediate the power of the sacred into this world in the form of miracles, especially healings and exorcisms. Spirit persons thus function as the "delegate of the tribe to the other realm,"[4] representing their people to the numinous and mediating the power of the numinous to the people. Experientially in contact with the sacred, Spirit persons frequently have a striking authority and presence: they speak from their experience and radiate a numinous presence.

Though Jesus was recognizably of this type, he also differed from contemporary Jewish Spirit persons in several important ways. First, much more of his teaching has been preserved. Second, he proclaimed the Kingdom of God and saw himself as mediator of its presence. Third, he

---

1. See esp. Geza Vermes, *Jesus the Jew* (New York, 1973), 65–78, 206–13. Also relevant are E. E. Urbach, *The Sages* (Jerusalem, 1975), 97–123; and A. Büchler, *Types of Jewish Palestinian Piety* (New York, 1968; first published in 1922), 87–107, 196–252.

2. Rudolf Otto, *The Idea of the Holy* (New York, 1958).

3. See, e.g., Stephen Larsen, *The Shaman's Doorway* (New York, 1976); I. M. Lewis, *Ecstatic Religion: An Anthropological Study of Spirit Possession* (Penguin, 1971); M. Eliade, *Shamanism: Archaic Techniques of Ecstasy* (Princeton, 1970).

4. Larsen, *The Shaman's Doorway*, 65–66.

was known for his association with the outcasts of his society. Fourth, he challenged the religious and collective direction of his people, climaxing in a series of dramatic encounters during the last week of his life. Fifth and finally, he was crucified and eventually became the central figure of a worldwide religion. All of these differences flowed from the fact that he, unlike other Jewish Spirit persons contemporary with him, founded a renewal movement.

The renewal movement initiated by Jesus found itself in conflict with other renewal movements. These conflicts are recorded in the Gospels, sometimes in the form of conflict stories,[5] but also in the form of parables and short sayings which explicitly or implicitly reflect a setting of controversy. By examining the points at which the Jesus movement in the Jewish homeland conflicted with other Jewish renewal movements, we can see more clearly the teaching of Jesus and the contours of the movement which he founded.

Most of these conflicts were with the Pharisees. Indeed, none of the other renewal movements is clearly mentioned at all.[6] The silence is not surprising, for neither the Essenes nor the resistance movement (if there was such a movement) was active in public life. The former had withdrawn to the wilderness, and the latter would have been by necessity a clandestine group. Thus the Jesus movement and the Pharisees competed for the same audience: both operated *within* society and sought to provide a way of faithfulness that did not require withdrawal.[7] Moreover, since the Pharisees were the bearers of the quest for holiness in public life, an examination of the conflicts with them should disclose much about the posture of the Jesus movement toward the quest for holiness, and thus about the attitude of Jesus himself.[8]

---

5. See the study by Arland Hultgren, *Jesus and His Adversaries: The Form and Function of the Conflict Stories in the Synoptic Tradition* (Minneapolis, 1979). Hultgren confines himself to how these stories functioned in the life of the early church and does not treat conflict as an aspect of the ministry itself.

6. Controversies with the Sadducees are mentioned (e.g., the question about the resurrection reported in Mark 12:18–27; interestingly, Jesus and the Pharisees would have been allies on this issue), but as already noted, they were not a renewal movement.

7. See Kee, *Christian Origins in Sociological Perspective,* 42. He identifies four options within first-century Judaism: (1) going along with the Romans and their culture; (2) withdrawing completely to a pure life of seclusion; (3) organizing a national revolt; (4) redefining God's purpose for the covenant people. He affirms that both the Pharisees and the early Christian movement took the last route, thus competing directly with each other.

8. See the methodological statement by Theissen, *Sociology of Early Palestinian Christianity,* 4: a sociology of the Jesus movement "suggests that we should assume a continuity between Jesus and the Jesus movement and in so doing opens up the possibility of transferring insights into the Jesus movement to Jesus himself." See also n. 4 on pp. 120–21 of his book.

The conflicts between Jesus and the Pharisees have often been understood as attacks upon legalism or ritualism or hypocrisy, perhaps in the name of an individualized internalized spirituality or liberal humanitarianism. But the conflicts were in fact based upon two competing visions of what Israel was to be, each of which had identifiable historical consequences for Israel's future. We shall discover that Jesus challenged the quest for holiness and replaced it with an alternative vision.

In this chapter, we shall examine the challenge as it came to expression in Jesus' table fellowship with outcasts, his teaching on purity and tithing, and his criticisms of the effects of the quest for holiness. In the next chapter we shall describe the alternative vision which he articulated.

Prolegomena

Since much of the treatment of the teaching of Jesus in this and subsequent chapters pertains to his departure from established patterns of behavior vis-à-vis table fellowship, sabbath, and the Temple, it is important to precede it with two general observations about actors in situations of social conflict.

Challenges to Culturally Sanctioned Norms: Strategic or Programmatic

Historical actors in a situation of conflict and crisis may challenge or override the claims of an authoritative norm for either of two fundamentally different reasons. On the one hand, they may claim that the demands of the norm must temporarily yield because of the urgency of the situation. In this case, the violation is *strategic*, momentary, intended only for the limited duration of the crisis, and done for the sake of achieving some end which does not involve the permanent abrogation or transformation of the norm.

Such strategic suspension of Torah is known in Judaism as two instances, one national and one individual, demonstrate. During the Maccabean conflict with the Seleucid forces, a group of Jews was massacred on the sabbath because resistance would have involved activities falling into the category of prohibited work. Shortly thereafter the Maccabean patriarch Mattathias ruled that defensive warfare was to be permitted on the sabbath (1 Macc. 2:29–41). In short, a religiously sanctioned norm was suspended temporarily for the sake of preserving the people of God.

So also in the case of danger to individual life on the sabbath. Work normally prohibited could always be done if an individual's life were in danger.[9] But such suspensions do not in any way indicate an attitude of opposition to the institution involved. Indeed, the emergency suspension of expected behavior is done to insure the continuing function of the institution. Simon ben Menasya, for example, justified saving life on the sabbath in order "to preserve a man for keeping many sabbaths."[10] This approach can be designated by the apt phrase "Torah expediency": "the principle of compromising one part of the Torah in order that the whole might be preserved,"[11] either by the individual or the nation. Such compromise of cultural norms is completely consistent with fundamental affirmation of the lasting importance of the norms.

On the other hand, a challenge may be rooted in opposition to the norm in its present form. Here the agent may claim that the norm in its present form is pernicious, perhaps partly responsible for the present crisis. Therefore, in order that the crisis may be resolved, the norm must be abrogated, transformed, or restored to its original purpose. Alternatively, the norm may be viewed not as positively pernicious, but simply as outdated and no longer relevant. In this case, as an anachronism it stands in the way of the achievement of some ideal. But in either case the intent of the teaching or action is *programmatic*, not strategic: the culturally sanctioned norm is opposed, not simply suspended temporarily because of an emergency.

A second major point must also be made. The Gospels report not only that Jesus was in conflict with religiously sanctioned norms, but also that he was in conflict with other persons about those norms. At once this means that he was not simply making the exceptions upon which there was common agreement. But the hostility is consistent with either of two explanations. First, his opponents may have perceived his nonconforming behavior as a temporary suspension of a particular stipulation, but disagreed that there was a crisis of sufficient magnitude to justify it. In this case, the conflict was due to their differing interpretations of the present.[12]

---

9. M. Yoma 8:6, Yoma 85b; see I. Abrahams, *Studies in Pharisaism and the Gospels* (Cambridge, 1917–24), 1:129–32. For a study of the compromising of institutional claims in emergency situations at a later date, see D. Daube, *Collaboration with Tyranny in Rabbinic Law* (London, 1965).

10. Abrahams, *Studies*, 1:136.

11. Farmer, *Maccabees, Zealots, and Josephus*, 77.

12. Modern examples illustrate this well. Most people agree that there are conceivable circumstances which justify martial law, or civil disobedience, or even tyrannicide; but there is likely to be bitter conflict about whether or not a particular set of circumstances is sufficiently grave to justify such actions.

Second, his opponents may have perceived the action or teaching as an attempt permanently to transform or abrogate a norm so that its present function was undermined. This usually involves, as in the first instance, a different interpretation of the present situation, but goes farther in that it sees the future as constituted by other or transformed norms. One party in the conflict perceives this as desirable, the other as a threat. Whether the opposition to Jesus consists of the first or the second or some combination thereof can be determined only in individual instances.

These distinctions have a twofold utility. First, we cannot assume that a challenge or violation means opposition to the norm; it can be consistent with fundamental affirmation of the norm in its present form. This realization permits greater analytical precision, for it forces one to ask why the challenge was made. Second, the distinctions provide us with a variety of questions to be asked about individual incidents in the Gospels. Is the intent of the teaching or action strategic or programmatic? Is the stance of the opponents due to their conviction that an emergency does not exist, or to the belief that a transformation is intended which would threaten the present function of the norm? We cannot expect to answer each question in connection with each incident because of the limited information available, but the limited information makes it advantageous to have a variety of questions to ask.

Challenges to a Paradigm: Replacement or Redefinition?

Agents of social change can follow either or both of two approaches when challenging the core paradigm or paradigms which have dominated the development of their society's life. They may argue that the paradigm must be replaced by another one. Or they may argue that the essential meaning of the dominant paradigm is different from what it is commonly taken to be, thus redefining the paradigm. To use a modern example, persons seeking to transform a society whose watchword is free-enterprise democracy to a system in which the means of production are controlled by the workers or the government on behalf of the people can (and do) opt for either of two terminological courses. They may change terms and argue that socialism is necessary because democracy has failed. On the other hand, they may argue that the true meaning of democracy includes economic democracy, entailing not only the preservation of traditional civil liberties and the electoral process, but also the direct control of economic affairs by the people as a whole. In this case, obviously, they have redefined democracy. Nor are they inconsistent if they pursue both terminological options.

So it is in the teaching of Jesus regarding the paradigm of holiness. In some texts, holiness is replaced by another core value or paradigm; in others, holiness is understood in a way different from the prevalent conception in first-century Judaism. With these considerations in mind, we can now begin to examine the teaching and actions of Jesus regarding the cultural dynamic which informed most of first-century Judaism.

Table Fellowship and Holiness

One of the most conspicuous and controversial aspects of the renewal movement founded by Jesus was its table fellowship, a practice that goes back to the public activity of Jesus himself. Jesus ate with "tax collectors and sinners," to use a frequent phrase from the Gospels. Norman Perrin called it "the central feature" of Jesus' ministry.[13] Moreover, according to the Jewish scholar Geza Vermes, it is the practice which differentiated Jesus "more than any other" from "both his contemporaries and even his prophetic predecessors." Jesus " . . . took his stand among the pariahs of his world, those despised by the respectable. Sinners were his table-companions and the ostracized tax collectors and prostitutes his friends."[14] Indeed, one of his disciples was a tax collector.

Strikingly, his table fellowship engendered sharp hostility between Jesus and his Jewish opponents. Three of the four strands of the synoptic tradition contain his opponents' explicit accusation:

Matt. 11:19=Luke 7:34 (Q): Look at him! A glutton and a drinker, a friend of tax gatherers and sinners!

Mark 2:15: So he eats and drinks with tax collectors and sinners?

Luke 19:7 (L): They all murmured, "He has gone in to be the guest of a man (a tax collector) who is a sinner."

Luke 15:1–2 (L): Another time the tax gatherers and other bad characters were all crowding in to listen to him; saying, "This fellow welcomes sinners and eats with them."

Furthermore, as we shall see, much of the teaching of Jesus in both parables and sayings focused on table fellowship and the issues intrinsically related to it. Here, we may be sure, we are not only in touch with

---

13. Perrin, *Rediscovering*, 107. W. G. Kümmel in his review article "Norman Perrin's *Rediscovering the Teaching of Jesus*," *JR* 49 (1969): 62, demurs. Perrin also notes that the importance of table fellowship is attested by the practice of the early church; he cites Acts, the epistles, and the *Didache*. The early Christian meals, he argues, are best explained as a continuation of the regular practice of Jesus (104–5).

14. Vermes, *Jesus the Jew*, 224.

the *ipsissima vox Jesu* (the voice of Jesus), but also with the *ipsissimae voces contradicentium* (the voices of his opponents).

The depth of this hostility has led two scholars to claim that Jesus' table fellowship was the sufficient cause of his being delivered up for execution to the Romans by some of the leaders of Israel.[15] Why was table fellowship such an inflammable issue, and what was at stake in challenging conventional practice? The source of this conflict will be adduced by explicating the threat perceived by the antagonists as well as the intent of Jesus. To achieve this end, I will describe the significance of table fellowship, in particular the way in which it became the focus of the cultural dynamic of holiness; the specific offense of association with sinners and tax collectors; and the intention of the teaching and behavior of Jesus.

The Meal and Holiness as a Goal for Society

Two factors contributed to the significance of table fellowship in first-century Judaism. The first was generally operative throughout the ancient Near East. Sitting at table with another was an expression of intimacy and fellowship;[16] to invite people to a meal honored them and expressed both trust and acceptance. In the Hebrew Bible, a place of honor at a meal given by Evil-merodach symbolized the rehabilitation of King Jehoiachin. At a much later date, Herod Agrippa similarly commemorated the restoration to favor of his military commander.[17] Contrariwise, refusal to share a meal symbolized disapproval and rejection. Such rejection was a form of social control whereby unseemly behavior was discouraged.[18] Thus sharing or refusing to share a table in antiquity had a social function, expressing approval or disapproval of different modes of behavior.

---

15. Perrin, *Rediscovering,* 103; W. R. Farmer, "An Historical Essay on the Humanity of Jesus Christ," in *Christian History and Interpretation,* ed. Farmer et al. (Cambridge, 1967), 103.

16. D. E. Nineham, *Saint Mark* (Penguin Books, 1969), 95; J. F. Ross, *IDB,* 2:306, 3:315; G. Bornkamm, *Jesus of Nazareth* (New York, 1960), 80.

17. 2 Kings 25:27–30=Jer. 52:31–34; *Ant.* 19.321; see Jeremias, *New Testament Theology,* 115. That it also had this meaning in everyday life is illustrated vividly by Luke 15:23–24.

18. See J. D. M. Derrett, *Law in the New Testament* (London, 1970), 282, who comments on the significance of refusing to eat with a man whose wealth was wrongfully attained: "Social ostracism has, or at least had, some chance of being an effective deterrent. And just as the hole is necessary to the rat, and the receiver of stolen goods to the thief, so people who will take his food are a necessity to the extortioner or corrupt politician. Unless these are deprived of their social potential there is, under normal eastern conditions, no hope of keeping them in check."

Within Judaism the significance of table fellowship was even greater. In it came to focus the cultural dynamic of holiness, of which the Pharisees were preeminently the bearers. For the Pharisees the meal had become a microcosm of Israel's intended historic structure as well as a model of Israel's destiny. In the meal converged the two streams of *halakhic* development which dominated the quest after holiness: tithing and purity.[19]

No fewer than 229 of the 341 rabbinic texts attributed to the Pharisaic schools of Shammai and Hillel pertain to table fellowship.[20] The Pharisees were thus "a table-fellowship sect."[21] Members of a Pharisaic fellowship (*havurah*)[22] were committed to the tithing of all food and to eating *every* meal in that degree of purity observed by officiating priests in the Temple.[23] Such purity included insuring that the food was not defiled during preparation or serving and the washing of hands before meals, to which a prospective member of a Pharisaic *havurah* committed himself during the initiatory period of his affiliation, a commitment which continued, of course, through the novitiate and after becoming a full member.[24]

---

19. Parkes, *Foundations of Judaism and Christianity,* 139: the three subjects which the Pharisees developed as specifically Pharisaic teaching were building a fence around the Torah, the absolute duty to pay tithes, and the necessity for all Jews to preserve a state of ritual purity, even outside of the Temple precincts.

20. J. Neusner, "Pharisaic Law in New Testament Times," *USQR* 26 (1971): 337. Compare his summary statement in *The Rabbinic Traditions about the Pharisees before 70,* 1:338: all legal sayings which contain a reference to both Hillel and Shammai "pertain to legal matters of cleanness and proper donation of agricultural taxes, the two matters of primary concern to the Pharisaic *havurah.*" See also his *From Politics to Piety,* 83–86.

21. Neusner, *From Politics to Piety,* 80.

22. Not all Pharisees were members of a *havurah,* though all members of a *havurah* were Pharisees. See Neusner, "The Fellowship," 125; "Qumran and Jerusalem," 285; Moore, *Judaism,* 3:26; Stephen Westerholm, *Jesus and Scribal Authority* (Lund, 1978), 15: "The terms Pharisee and *haver* are thus not synonymous; but the regulations of the *havurot* represent Pharisaic views on the subjects of tithing and ritual purity." He further notes that the *havurah* can be dated back to the beginning of the first century (134, n. 23).

23. See chapter 3 above, pp. 73–74. We should add that we are not referring to a special meal observed by the *havurah,* for which indeed there is no evidence (see J. Jeremias, *The Eucharistic Words of Jesus* [London, 1966], 29–31), but to the ordinary, everyday meals eaten by members whether with their own household or elsewhere (Neusner, "Pharisaic Law in New Testament Times," 337–40, and *The Idea of Purity,* 67).

24. See T. Dem. 2:11–12; Neusner, "The Fellowship," 132–34, and 124, n. 2, where he rejects A. Büchler's claim that hand washing applied only to priests. V. Taylor, *The Gospel according to St. Mark,* 2d ed. (London, 1966), 338–39, summarizes the debate between Büchler (*ET* 21 [1909–10]: 34–40) and G. Margoliouth (*ET* 22 [1910–11]: 261–63), and agrees with Margoliouth that the custom was current among the pious and not simply among the priests at the time of Jesus. For detailed argumentation and a similar conclusion, see B. H. Branscomb, *Jesus and the Law of Moses* (London, 1930), 158–60. The controversy is resolved by the recognition that regulations intended for the

This twofold emphasis on tithing and purity, the distinctive marks of a Pharisaic *havurah,* posed two practical limitations on table fellowship. First, one could not be the guest of a person who was untrustworthy with regard to payment of tithes or preparation of foods (though a Pharisee could *host* non-Pharisees if they were provided with clean garments upon entering the house and if they were not among that class of people whose presence would defile the house and all within it). Second, one could not share a table with people whose presence might defile the meal.[25]

Though this overarching concern with table fellowship was in one sense an innovation, it was also the crystallization of that development which became discernible during and after the exile: the quest for holiness, with holiness understood as separation.[26] Indeed, it is this development that enables us to see the societal dimension of table fellowship: it mirrored the structure which the Pharisees affirmed for Israel. Disputes about table fellowship were not matters of genteel etiquette, but about the shape of the community whose life truly manifested loyalty to Yahweh. Thus the meals of those belonging to the Pharisaic fellowships symbolized what was expected of the nation Israel: holiness, understood as separation.

Table fellowship not only symbolized Israel's proper present course. It also anticipated its destiny, which was often pictured with the image of a meal.[27] Israel as it ate that meal would be a kingdom of priests, holy as befits such a kingdom.[28] Table fellowship thus exemplified that holiness which, as both *praxis* and *telos,* was to characterize Israel. As such it was laden with symbolic significance. Moreover, as we argued earlier, holiness as separation served a survival function by separating Israel from elements subversive of its solidarity. Table fellowship as a public embodiment of holiness seemed to many a "survival symbol," which, if shattered or eroded, would threaten the cohesiveness of Israel, expose it to the disciplining judgment of God, and call into question the theological underpinning of society: the understanding of God as *qadosh/parush.*

---

priests (so far Büchler is right) were being extended to the laity through the *havurah.* See also Westerholm, *Jesus and Scribal Authority,* 73.

25. See M. Dem. 2:2–3; Neusner, "The Fellowship," 135, 129–40.

26. See chapter 3 above, passim.

27. E.g., Is. 25:6, Zeph. 3:13, Enoch 62:14, 2 Bar. 29:4, 4 Ezra 6:52; see S-B 4:1154–65.

28. Elliott, *The Elect and the Holy,* 103–5.

Revolutionary Action, Protest, and Response

Jesus' Employment of Table Fellowship. In his behavior, teaching, and pictorial representations of the destiny of the people of God, Jesus accepted the central role assigned by his contemporaries to table fellowship. As in Judaism,[29] sitting at table was an occasion for teaching (Mark 14:3–9 par.; Luke 7:36–50, 10:38–42, 11:37–52, 14:1–24, 22:14–38).[30] Table fellowship was often the subject of teaching, either directly or as an illustration of something else (Mark 7:1–23 par., 12:39 par., 14:22–25 par.; Matt. 8:11 par., 22:1–14, 23:23–26 par., 25:1–13; Luke 12:35–38, 14:7–24, 17:7–10, 22:27, 30). It was also a suitable picture of the future (Mark 14:25 par., Matt. 8:11 par., Luke 22:30).[31] But, as already mentioned, it was Jesus' practice of eating with "tax collectors and sinners" that drew attack from his opponents.

Jesus did not simply accept the central role of table fellowship, but used it as a weapon. From the fact that his teaching shows an awareness of the centrality of the meal, it is clear that his action was deliberately provocative. The synoptics have preserved this impression by presenting this behavior (as well as other incidents) in a tripartite literary form analyzed by David Daube as "revolutionary action, protest, silencing of opponents."[32]

Revolutionary Action. According to Daube's analysis, the action is novel, performed on a definite occasion, and is always an action in the narrow sense, not a statement; it concerns practice, not merely an academic debating point.[33] Furthermore, the terminology of the accusation suggests that Jesus was sometimes host of the meal,[34] so the charge was not simply that he indiscriminately accepted the hospitality of others. This implies that his table fellowship was deliberate, an "acted parable,"[35] a symbolic act, chosen as terrain on which to do battle.

But what did his table fellowship mean? What was intended by it? To

---

29. M. Aboth 3:3; Abrahams, *Studies*, 1:55–56.

30. Though many of the settings may be redactional, contemporary Jewish practice makes it a priori probable that the passages represent historical reality.

31. We leave undecided for now whether the feast of Luke 14:16–24=Matt. 22:1–14, was intended primarily as a picture of the future or as a pointer to the urgency of the present.

32. D. Daube, *The New Testament and Rabbinic Judaism* (London, 1956), 170–75.

33. Ibid., 172–74.

34. Luke 15:2; Jeremias, *Parables*, 227, n. 92, argues that this is probably the meaning of Mark 2:15. See also the meals in the desert where, whatever one does with the question of historicity, Jesus is host.

35. Perrin, *Rediscovering*, 102; Jeremias, *Parables*, 227.

address this question, we shall first examine his opponents' perception of it and then the intention implied by his teaching.

The Protest. The voices of the opponents consistently linked two groups: sinners and tax collectors. Because these terms had identifiable denotations in the first century, we can discern the offense as the opponents perceived it by examining each in turn.

To people raised in the Christian tradition, the charge that Jesus associated with sinners brands the plaintiffs at once as hypocrites, for subsequent Christian theological tradition has affirmed that all people are sinners. Indeed, Western religious thought during the Christian epoch has almost made "sinner" into an honorific term. But such was not the case in the first century. Then the term "sinners" carried the meaning of "outcasts," almost "untouchables," to suggest a not wholly inappropriate analogy.

To be sure, the status of "sinner" or "outcast" was not inherited and thus did not have the rigidity found in some caste systems. The term referred to an identifiable social group, just as the term "righteous" did. Moreover, the distinction should not be seen as hypocritical. That is, the charge cannot be thought of primarily as pointing to the shallowness of the opponents (who, only by the standards of a later theology, should have realized that they also were "sinners"), but as an objection to association with a particular group in society.

True, the term "sinners" was somewhat fluid, for it had four possible meanings. First, it could refer primarily to an occupational grouping: people who practiced one of the seven despised trades (including tax collecting) which deprived them de jure of all civil rights, deprivation of which made them "as a Gentile,"[36] or, by extension, members of the larger group of trades which were suspected of immorality and deprived them de facto (though not de jure) of civil rights.[37] Second, it could refer to those guilty of flagrant immorality, e.g., adulterers, prostitutes, extortioners, murderers, idolaters, etc. Third, it could designate all those who did not observe the Torah according to the Pharisaic understanding of it; on this definition, it embraced the majority of Is-

---

36. Gamblers with dice, usurers, organizers of games of chance, dealers in produce of the sabbatical year, shepherds, tax collectors, and revenue farmers. See Sanh. 25b; Jeremias, *Jerusalem*, 310–12.

37. Workers in the transport trades, herdsmen, shopkeepers, physicians, butchers, goldsmiths, flaxcombers, handmill cleaners, peddlers, weavers, barbers, launderers, bloodletters, bath attendants, tanners. See Kidd. 82a, M. Kidd. 4:14 (cf. J. Kidd. 4:11, 66b); Jeremias, *Jerusalem*, 303–9. There is another group of trades which, though not morally suspect, were aesthetically repugnant.

rael.[38] Fourth, it had become a technical term for Gentiles, who were excluded from the holiness which was Israel's alone.[39]

Which of the first three meanings was intended by the opponents is unclear, though the fourth can be eliminated because table fellowship with Gentiles was not a feature of Jesus' activity. Nor is it necessary to decide which of the three groupings was meant, for all three had one factor in common: they did not accept in practice the Pharisaic program of holiness for Israel and could not be trusted with regard to tithing and cleanness. And yet Jesus, in the name of the ultimate hope of Israel (the Kingdom of God), sat at table with sinners. To say, and to express in action, that the Kingdom of God included these meant to his opponents that he had rejected their understanding of Israel's holiness as separation, both as present practice and as final destiny. In short, to the extent that Jesus was a public figure,[40] his action was perceived as a serious challenge to the internal movement of reform which was intended to make Israel a holy community, a kingdom of priests, in the sense in which those expressions were then used. Such can be gleaned from the accusation that he ate with sinners.

But Jesus was also charged with eating with tax collectors, which suggests an added dimension to the threat perceived by the opponents. That they were singled out for special mention is striking, for it is a priori probable and confirmed by the synoptics that those who associated with Jesus included members of despised groups other than tax collectors.[41] Why then were they singled out by the opponents? We cannot simply answer that they were the most notorious of a despised class or that they were especially unclean,[42] or that repentance was nearly or

---

38. K. H. Rengstorf, *TDNT*, 1:323, n. 47; 328. John 7:49.

39. Rengstorf, *TDNT*, 1:324–26; it apparently has this meaning in Mark 14:41 par., Gal. 2:15.

40. That is, Jesus' behavior would not have been threatening or a cause of offense if he had been an obscure sinner associating with other sinners; that would only have been expected. Rather, the charge implies that he was recognized as a teacher with some public influence.

41. E.g., prostitutes, as is implied in Matt. 21:31–32 and Luke 7:36–50 (see Derrett, *Law in the New Testament*, 266–85, who notes that the legal background makes sense only if we presume that she was a prostitute). Though the Pharisee who was host was clearly shocked in the Lucan story (v. 39), Jesus' opponents never included the charge that Jesus associated with prostitutes. In passing, one can note that in a culture in which association with respectable women was regarded with suspicion (see Jeremias, *Jerusalem*, 359–76), Jesus included prostitutes among his contacts.

42. See M. Toh. 7:6: "If tax gatherers entered a house [all that is within it] becomes unclean." Thus it is not only the case that one could not accept the hospitality of a tax collector, but one also could not entertain him in one's own home without thereby defiling the food and everything else in the house. See O. Michel, *TWNT*, 8:101–2.

completely impossible for them,[43] for the question would still have to be asked why they were the most notorious, a most serious source of defilement, etc. In short, what differentiated them from other despised groups so that their presence as Jesus' table companions was regarded as especially noteworthy and alarming?

The differentiation lay in their obvious and continual contact with Gentiles, in a twofold sense. In both Herodian Galilee and Roman Judea, daily commercial intercourse with Gentile inhabitants and traders subjected tax collectors to grave risk of defilement. Beyond that, they were viewed as collaborators, quislings; they obviously had answered the question of whether it was lawful to pay taxes to Caesar.[44] This was most clear in Judea where the revenues they collected went into the coffers of the Roman provincial administration, but also in Galilee, for the Herods were viewed as non-Israelites and were not popular until at least the time of Herod Agrippa (41–44 c.e.). The collaboration of the tax collectors threatened the community goal of holiness which required separation from Gentile uncleanness and rule.

To the proponents of the holy community, Jesus' action implied an acceptance of quisling behavior and thereby threatened to shatter "the closed ranks of the community against their enemy"[45] and to break down the cohesiveness necessary to the survival of a society immersed in conflict. Thus nothing hypocritical must be read into the accusations. Instead, they reflected the fact that Jesus' association with sinners and tax collectors appeared to threaten both the internal reform of Judaism and its solidarity over against the Gentiles. Moreover, his table fellowship with outcasts challenged the understanding of God upon which that reform and solidarity were based. Such the *ipsissimae voces contradicentium* suggest.

"Silencing of Opponents": Jesus' Response. According to the synoptic tradition, Jesus responded relatively briefly to three of the four accusations reported above and more fulsomely to the fourth. Though all four of the responses are relevant to our treatment, the fourth contains the most substantial material.

The first is in a Q text reporting "this generation's" complaints about Jesus and John the Baptist. Here Jesus himself quoted the accusation:

43. B. K. 94b; Abrahams, *Studies*, 1:54, citing Behk. 31a; the restriction was later mitigated. See also Michel, *TWNT*, 8:102–3; Loewe, *Render unto Caesar*, 54–59.

44. Cf. Cohn, *The Trial and Death of Jesus*, 6: "even the members of his [a tax collector's] family would be suspect if they failed to prevent him from so degrading himself as to become a lackey of Rome." He cites Shebu. 39a.

45. Perrin, *Rediscovering*, 103.

To what then shall I compare the men of this generation and what are they like? They are like children sitting in the marketplace and calling to one another:

"We piped to you, and you did not dance;
We wailed, and you did not weep."

For John the Baptist has come eating no bread and drinking no wine; and you say, "He has a demon." The son of man has come eating and drinking; and you say, "Behold, a glutton and a drunkard, a friend of tax collectors and sinners!" Yet wisdom is justified by all her children. (Luke 7:31–35=Matt. 11:16–19)

In the accusation itself, the parallelism between "glutton and drunkard" and "friend of tax collectors and sinners" suggests that the offense was that such eating and drinking occurred in the company of tax collectors and sinners,[46] not the quantity of food eaten or the failure to observe fasts.[47] Jesus' response compared his opponents[48] to children playing in the marketplace, who complain that their friends won't play the games (weddings and funerals) that they suggest.[49] Like the children, "this generation" complained: John was an ascetic and Jesus was not. John was accused of having a demon[50] and Jesus was vilified because he ate with tax collectors and sinners. Like children in the marketplace expecting their peers to play their games, Jesus' opponents expected him (and John) to behave according to normal Jewish practices.[51] Implicitly they were saying about Jesus' table fellowship with sinners, "No legitimate Jewish holy man or teacher would behave like that."[52]

---

46. Perrin, *Rediscovering*, 105–6; Buchanan, *The Consequences of the Covenant*, 162–63, agrees that the reference cannot be to the quantity of food eaten, but must be either to the type of food he ate or the people with whom he ate, or both.

47. Because the charge against Jesus follows the complaint against John that he neither ate nor drank, some commentators suggest that what was at stake was Jesus' failure to observe fasts (cf. Mark 2:18): T. W. Manson in H. D. A. Major, T. W. Manson, and C. J. Wright, *The Mission and Message of Jesus* (London, 1929), 274–75; Bultmann, *Jesus*, 100. On this view, the charge is twofold: Jesus does not observe fasts as he ought, and he is a friend of undesirables. Such an interpretation is possible, though not as attractive as seeing a direct connection between the two halves of the charge.

48. In the Lucan context, his opponents are identified as "Pharisees and lawyers" (7:29–30); in Matthew, the opponents are simply "this generation."

49. Commentators have often seen the "piping" and "wailing" children as Jesus and John respectively, despite the fact that the words of the text explicitly say that "this generation" is like the children. For a convincing case that the children are to be identified with "this generation" and not with Jesus and John, see O. Linton, "The Parable of the Children's Game," *NTS* 22 (1976): 159–77, esp. 171–74.

50. The accusation was also directed against Jesus; see Mark 3:22 par., Matt. 9:34. The charge is repeated in the Johannine tradition: John 7:20, 8:48 and 52, 10:20.

51. Linton, "The Parable of the Children's Game," 174, 176, 177.

52. Interestingly, other Jewish holy men contemporary with Jesus were also criticized

Jesus responded by saying, in effect, "You are like complaining quarrelsome children, and you would complain no matter what we did, so
long as it differed from what you wanted." At one level, their complaint flowed out of the rivalry between competing renewal movements
and the attempt of one to discredit leading figures in another. Beneath
that rivalry, however, was a commitment to different understandings of
what Israel was to be. For his opponents, that understanding was Israel
as a holy community. Jesus' response suggests his awareness of his opponents' resolute unwillingness to permit deviation from the course they
thought should be followed. It yields no further information about what
he thought was at stake in table fellowship.[53]

The second response is found in Mark 2:15–17:

> And as Jesus sat at table in his house, many tax collectors and sinners
> were sitting with him and his disciples; for there were many who followed
> him. And the scribes of the Pharisees, when they saw that he was eating
> with sinners and tax collectors, said to his disciples, "Why does he eat
> with tax collectors and sinners?" And when Jesus heard it, he said to
> them, "Those who are well have no need of a physician, but those who
> are sick; I came not to call the righteous, but sinners."

Here the Pharisaic opponents addressed their complaint to his disciples,
perhaps implicitly inviting them to break their relationship with Jesus
over this issue,[54] presumably on the grounds that such behavior manifestly disclosed the illegitimacy of a Jewish teacher. Jesus justified his
behavior by appealing to the example of a doctor.[55] Accepting the view
that his table companions were "not well," he claimed that, just as doctors must come into contact with those whom they would treat, so also
religious teachers must come into contact with those whom they would
transform. The text ends with the opponents momentarily silenced by

---

by the orthodox; they were suspected of being indifferent or casual toward matters of the
law. See Vermes, *Jesus the Jew*, 77–82.

53. The pericope may end with a threat; Linton, "The Parable of the Children's
Game," 177–78, suggests that the last verse should be read, "Wisdom is justified *against*
her children." If so, the refusal of "this generation" to accept what was happening in Jesus
and John is seen as having dire consequences.

54. So Jeremias, *New Testament Theology* (London, 1971), 118, n. 2.

55. There is near unanimity that the first half of this saying is authentic. Opinion is
divided, however, on whether or not the application in the second half of the verse ("I
came not to call the righteous, but sinners") is original to Jesus. For a cogent presentation
of the problems and a persuasive case that 17b reflects the retrospective view of the early
community, most of whom were conscious of being "sinners" and who were aware that
the righteous had not responded to Jesus, see Nineham, *Mark*, 98; so also Dodd, *Parables*,
90–91; E. Haenchen, *Der Weg Jesu*, 2d ed. (Berlin, 1968), 111; for a contrary view, see
C. E. B. Cranfield, *The Gospel according to St. Mark*, 2d ed. (Cambridge, 1966), 106. In
any case, we do not need to resolve this question since our exposition depends upon the
doctor metaphor, not upon the application.

this commonsense observation: of course a doctor must have intimate contact with the sick. Jesus' response also hints that table fellowship with the unacceptables or outcasts was part of the restorative healing process.

The third protest and response are found in a passage attested by Luke alone which also reflects characteristic Lucan emphases[56] and whose authenticity to Jesus must therefore be viewed cautiously. Nevertheless, a few observations are worthwhile:

> And when they [the crowd] saw it [that Jesus was about to be the guest of Zacchaeus, a wealthy tax collector], they all murmured, "He has gone in to be the guest of a man who is a sinner." And Zacchaeus stood and said to the master, "Behold, master, the half of my goods I give to the poor; and if I have defrauded any one of anything, I restore it fourfold." And Jesus said to him, "Today salvation has come to this house, since he also is a son of Abraham. For the son of man came to seek and to save the lost." (Luke 19:7–10)

According to the Pharisees, Zacchaeus was no longer a son of Abraham. As a tax collector, he had forfeited that status and had become "as a Gentile." According to this text, Jesus rejected that notion and affirmed that those excluded by the quest for holiness remained children of Abraham. "Sinners" were not a permanently unacceptable class, but were among the lost whom Jesus sought to restore into a community more inclusive than that envisioned by the quest for holiness.

The fourth protest is also found in Luke alone, but a near consensus of scholarly opinion affirms the authenticity of the three parables[57] with which Jesus responded as well as the appropriateness of Luke's setting:[58] "This man receives sinners and eats with them."

---

56. Luke 18:1–10. The author of Luke-Acts emphasizes Jesus' relationship to the "unacceptables" (sinners, tax collectors, women, and, in Acts, Gentiles) more than the other Gospel writers; the closing verse of the pericope crystallizes this concern.

57. Throughout this study we shall often refer to parables of Jesus, sometimes making a passing reference and other times providing a quite detailed treatment. As recent studies have pointed out, the parables have many dimensions of meaning, including "transhistorical" dimensions, i.e., meanings not restricted to what the parables meant in a first-century setting. For a very useful survey of parable research, see Perrin, *Jesus and the Language of the Kingdom*, chapter 4. Recognizing these transhistorical dimensions does not change the fact that the parables were originally spoken in a first-century setting and often contain pointed references to that setting. Perrin, *Jesus and the Language of the Kingdom*, 143–44, also recognizes their "occasional" nature. Without implying that the first-century setting exhausts or restricts the meaning of the parables, we shall nevertheless confine ourselves to what they would have meant in the setting of the Jesus movement's appeal to Israel.

58. Jeremias, *Parables*, 132–33; Perrin, *Rediscovering*, 94–98, 107; E. Linnemann, *Parables of Jesus* (London, 1966), 69, 73; C. H. Dodd, *The Parables of the Kingdom* (London, 1961), 91–93; W. Tooley, "The Shepherd and Sheep Image in the Teaching of Jesus," *NovTest* 7 (1964–65): 22–23. The only Matthaean parallel, Matt. 18:12–14, is set within

The Lost Sheep: What man of you, having a hundred sheep, if he has lost one of them, does not leave the ninety-nine in the wilderness, and go after the one which is lost, until he finds it? And when he has found it, he lays it on his shoulders, rejoicing. And when he comes home, will he not call together his friends and his neighbors, saying to them, "Rejoice with me, for I have found my sheep which was lost"? (Luke 15:4–6)

The Lost Coin: Or what woman, having ten silver coins, if she loses one coin, does not light a lamp and sweep the house and seek diligently until she finds it? And when she has found it, will she not call together her friends and neighbors, saying, "Rejoice with me, for I have found the coin which I have lost?" (Luke 15:8–9)[59]

The Lost Son, Part One: There was a man who had two sons; and the younger of them said to his father, "Father, give me the share of property that falls to me." And he divided his living between them. Not many days later, the younger son gathered all he had and took his journey into a far country, and there he squandered his property in loose living. And when he had spent everything, a great famine arose in that country and he began to be in want. So he went and joined himself to one of the citizens of that country, who sent him into the fields to feed swine. And he would gladly have fed on the pods that the swine ate; and no one gave him anything. But when he came to himself, he said, "How many of my father's hired servants have bread enough and to spare, but I perish here with hunger! I will arise and go to my father, and I will say to him, 'Father, I have sinned against heaven and before you; I am no longer worthy to be called your son; treat me as one of your hired servants.'" And he arose and came to his father. But while he was yet at a distance, his father saw him and had compassion, and ran and embraced him and kissed him. And the son said to him, "Father, I have sinned against heaven and before you; I am no longer worthy to be called your son." But the father said to his servants, "Bring quickly the best robe, and put it on him; and put a ring on his hand, and shoes on his feet; and bring the fatted calf and kill it, and let us eat and make merry; for this my son was dead, and is alive again; he was lost and is found." And they began to make merry. (Luke 15:11–24)

The plot and climax of the first two parables are virtually identical. Both speak of persons who lost something and of their reaction when they recovered it. When a shepherd who lost one of his sheep in the

---

the context of ecclesiastical practice and, within that context, urges diligence in the pursuit of a straying brother. L. Schottroff, "Das Gleichnis vom verlorenen Sohn," *ZTK* 68 (1971): 27–52, an exception to the consensus, denies that the prodigal son goes back to Jesus.

59. As Jeremias, *Parables*, 133–34, points out, both parables are to be read as a question. The applications in vv. 7 and 10 are both secondary; see Perrin, *Rediscovering*, 99–101; Linnemann, *Parables*, 65–73, 146–50; Dodd, *Parables*, 91–92.

wilderness finds it, will he not call his neighbors together and celebrate the recovery of the lost? When a woman who lost one of her meager supply of coins finds it after a diligent search of her house, will she not call her neighbors together and say, "Rejoice with me"?

Though the parable of the lost son is much more detailed, the climax of its first half is the same as the two parables above. The son was genuinely prodigal: emigrating to a "far country," a Gentile land, he wasted his assets in loose living, ignoring the moral claim which his father still had on his property. When he had exhausted his resources, instead of seeking charity at a Diaspora synagogue, he worked for a Gentile, rendering impossible the observance of such Jewish ordinances as the sabbath. Not only did he become a despised herdsman, but a *swineherd.*[60] He lived in gross impurity and had become, according to the standards of the quest for holiness, a non-Jew, and his father's statement, "This my son *was dead,*" was correct in an important sense: his son had ceased to be a Jew.[61] Nevertheless, when the son returned, what did the father do? Like the shepherd and the woman, he celebrated his return and, significantly, arranged for a festive banquet.

As responses to the protest of his opponents, these parables were both a defense of Jesus' behavior and an invitation to his opponents to join in the celebration. Jesus defended his table fellowship as a festive celebration of the return of the outcasts (who were also children of Abraham).[62] The defense, however, was also an invitation to his opponents, as suggested by the parabolic form.

Unlike a straightforward defense or indictment, the parables of Jesus frequently functioned to lead people to see things differently by inviting them to make a judgment about an everyday situation and then to transfer that judgment to the situation at hand. The parables sought to bridge the gap between speaker and hearer, frequently accomplishing this by being cast in the form of a question, explicitly or implicitly: what will a shepherd do when he finds a lost sheep? Will he not celebrate? By appealing to the normal reactions of ordinary human beings when they recover something of value (whether a sheep, a coin, or a child), Jesus implicitly asked his hearers, "Do you not see that it makes sense to celebrate?"

The invitation became explicit in the second half of the parable of the lost son:

---

60. See B.K. 7:7.

61. See, above all, Linnemann, *Parables,* 73–81, 150–54; Derrett, *Law in the New Testament,* 100–125, esp. 104–16; Perrin, *Rediscovering,* 94–98; G. V. Jones, *The Art and Truth of the Parables* (London, 1964), 167–205; Manson, *Mission and Message,* 576–82.

62. See Luke 19:9, 13:16.

The Lost Son, Part Two: Now his elder son was in the field; and as he
came and drew near to the house, he heard music and dancing. And
he called one of the servants and asked what this meant. And he said
to him, "Your brother has come, and your father has killed the fatted
calf, because he has received him safe and sound." But he was angry and
refused to go in. His father came out and entreated him, but he answered
his father, "Lo, these many years I have served you, and I never disobeyed
your command; yet you never gave me a kid, that I might make merry
with my friends. But when this son of yours came, who has devoured
your living with harlots, you killed for him the fatted calf!" And he said
to him, "Son, you are always with me, and all that is mine is yours. It was
fitting to make merry and be glad, for this your brother was dead, and is
alive; he was lost, and is found." (Luke 15:25–32)

Just as the lost son in the first half of the parable has a historical equivalent (the outcasts who had become as non-Jews), so the elder son in
the second half has his equivalent: he represents the protesters.[63] Like
them, he had been dutiful, consistently obeying his father's commands;
like them, he was outraged by the acceptance of the wastrel.

The words spoken to the elder son were implicitly directed to Jesus'
opponents. They repeat, gently and imploringly, the justification for the
festive celebration: "Son, you are always with me, and all that is mine
is yours. It was fitting to make merry and be glad, for this your brother
was dead, and is alive; he was lost and is found." As the climax to a
spoken parable in a setting of actual controversy over table fellowship,
the final words hang in the air trailing an unexpressed question. Will
the elder son join the festivity? Or will he let his own standard of proper
behavior prevent him from joining the celebration? Will the protesters'
commitment to the quest for holiness make them adamant that outcasts
such as these cannot be part of the people of God? For them to have
accepted the invitation would have required a seismic change in their
understanding of what the people of God were intended to be, a radical
reorientation of both their perception and their animating vision, one
that would fundamentally transform their social world.

Thus Jesus responded to the protests about his revolutionary action
in three different ways. In one instance he attacked his opponents by
comparing them to quarrelsome children who insisted that their game
be played. At other times he sought to silence his opponents by defend-
ing the outcasts: they were sick, they were lost, and they were children

---

63. To speak of figures in a parable as having historical equivalents does not imply an
allegorical approach, but simply recognizes that the parables were spoken in highly specific
circumstances — i.e., in a particular cultural setting marked by particular issues. When
the correspondences are quite exact, we can be relatively sure that Jesus deliberately had
them in mind.

of Abraham, that is, part of the people of God. Finally, he explained
the behavior itself by speaking of the festive meals as celebrations of
the return of the lost.

The Meaning of the Action. There is much that we do not know
about the festive meals of Jesus. Was some form of ritual part of them
even before his death? Were they a regular part of the life of "communities of local sympathizers,"[64] even in his absence during his ministry?
Or did they occur only where he was? Were there "rules" governing
his festive meals, as there were for the Pharisees and Essenes? Or were
they completely inclusive, symbolizing an utterly egalitarian social vision? Did his meals celebrate a transformation or commitment already
begun? Or were they restorative meals, part of the healing process?
Perhaps too sharp a distinction should not be made.

Nevertheless, despite our lack of knowledge about many matters,
and quite apart from specific teaching associated with it, Jesus' table
fellowship had meaning *as an act:* it was a "parabolic action."[65] In their
treatment of Jesus' table fellowship, Joachim Jeremias and Norman Perrin speak of it as an acted parable of the forgiveness of sins, signifying
that "the age of forgiveness" had dawned.[66] Clearly, given that sharing a meal symbolized acceptance in that culture, eating with a Spirit
person with a powerful numinous presence could mediate a profound
sense of acceptance and be an instrumental part of the therapeutic process whereby the internalized alienation of the outcasts was overcome
and they would once again be able to see themselves as part of the
people of God.

Yet to stop there misses an important — indeed, crucial — dimension of meaning. To speak of Jesus' table practice as only or primarily an
acted parable of forgiveness makes it too narrowly religious. It over-
looks the particular meaning which table fellowship had in Judaism
as a symbol of Israel's pursuit of holiness as both historical path and
destiny. Moreover, to speak of it primarily as symbolizing forgiveness
makes it too theological, severing it from its meaning in the context of
competing renewal movements.

Was Jesus' table practice only an acted parable of acceptance, or also
(like the table fellowship of the Pharisees) an acted parable of what Israel should be, embodying a different understanding of Israel's nature

---

64. The phrase is Theissen's. It identifies people who were responsive to the ministry of Jesus but who did not become part of the itinerant ministry of the "wandering
charismatics." Whether such communities existed during the ministry itself is uncertain.

65. Jeremias, *Parables,* 227: "His most significant parabolic action was his extension
of hospitality to the outcasts."

66. Jeremias, *Parables,* 227; Perrin, *Rediscovering,* 107.

and purpose? Clearly his opponents perceived it as an alternative (and unacceptable) vision of what Israel should be, competing with their own sense of what loyalty to God entailed. But was this what Jesus intended? Or was it the case, as so often in conflict situations, that the antagonists misunderstood the intentions of each other? In short, did the table fellowship of Jesus point to an alternative course for Israel, distinct from the quest for holiness? Was his table fellowship with outcasts simply a celebration of the return of the lost, or was it also a contravention of the Pharisaic program for Israel?

Only one argument stands in the way of the claim that Jesus intended a contravention: the possibility that he intended only a strategic temporary suspension of the demands of holiness for the sake of mission. For this there is some (though not much) support. If the metaphors of the doctor and the sick, the shepherd and the lost sheep, and the woman and the lost coin are pressed, as perhaps the applications (Mark 2:17b, Luke 15:7, 10) already do, then the inference could be drawn that Jesus' association with sinners was strategic, necessitated only by their status as lost or ill.

Thus, one could argue, Jesus' table fellowship implied no programmatic contradiction of the holiness ideal. Rather, it was a temporary suspension of normal behavior in order to restore the lost sheep to the already existing fold, to make the sick healthy like those who were already healthy. Just as doctors continually suspend rules of noncontact with carriers of communicable diseases (rules which others are still to observe) in order to treat patients, so Jesus for the sake of restoring the lost and ill had to come into contact with them.[67] On this view, the objection of the opponents must have been based either on their failure to understand that this was Jesus' objective, or on their skepticism that treatment which required such means could succeed.

But the argument that Jesus' departure from convention was essentially strategic requires two unacceptable corollaries. First, it implies that he saw himself as having a mission to only a part of Israel, namely, the lost. But the evidence is overwhelming that he saw his task in national terms. It was Israel who was threatened with the loss of its status in the preaching of John the Baptist: "God is able from these stones

---

67. Nineham, *Mark*, 97–98n, draws out the metaphor of the doctor in the following way: "If a person is suffering from a dangerous infectious disease, the *general* rule is that other people ought to avoid contact. But when the doctor 'comes' to deal with the situation it is right for him to consort with the patient; indeed, he must, in order to do the job for which he 'came.' The same is true of the nurses he sends.... But the doctor and, to a lesser extent, the nurses are exceptional people, and *no doubt is cast on the wisdom of the general rule.*" However, it is not clear that he is arguing that this was the *historical* reason for Jesus' table fellowship.

to raise up children to Abraham" (Luke 3:8 par.). It was those who thought of themselves as Israel who risked exclusion from the great banquet with Abraham, Isaac, and Jacob (Luke 13:28–29 par.). It was "this generation" as a whole that faced a crisis, not discrete individuals within it.[68] Entire cities were urged to repent, not just "lost" individuals within them, and upon entire cities the warning of judgment fell (Luke 10:13–15 par.). Indeed, the fate of the center of national life, Jerusalem, was itself in question.[69]

Just as the crisis which Jesus announced concerned Israel as a whole, so too the criticisms which he made, as we shall see, concerned national shortcomings, not the shortcomings of a smaller group who could be designated "the lost." Moreover, to see his contravention of holiness as strategic implies that Jesus viewed the righteous as really righteous, the healthy as really healthy, so that what was needed was to restore the sick to that state of well-being. But much of the teaching of Jesus to be considered in this chapter suggests that the healthy were not healthy after all. Therefore, one cannot claim that the sick were to be made like them.[70] Instead, the genitive construction "lost sheep *of* the house of Israel" must be understood as an explanatory genitive, not as a partitive genitive.[71] Both the sayings of crisis and the criticisms directed against his contemporaries point to a mission of all of Israel, not simply to a part.

The Contravention of the Quest for Holiness

The subsequent sections of this chapter direct attention to those portions of Jesus' teaching which evidence a programmatic contravention of the ideal of holiness. This entails an examination, first, of texts directly connected to table fellowship and, beyond that, of parables and

---

68. Luke 7:31–32 par., 11:29–31 par., 11:49–51 par., 17:25; Matt. 12:45.

69. See chapter 7 below.

70. What then does one do with the verses that imply a limitation to the lost? First, they could reflect the church's awareness that response to Jesus came largely from the social group "sinners"; see above pp. 98–100. Second, references to the righteous may be ironic: Taylor, *Mark*, 207; G. Schrenk, *TDNT*, 2:189; see also D. R. Fletcher, "The Riddle of the Unjust Steward: Is Irony the Key?" *JBL* 82 (1963): 27–28; J. D. Smart, *The Quiet Revolution* (Philadelphia, 1969), 50; J. Jónsson, *Humor and Irony in the New Testament* (Reykjavik, 1965), 156–57, 186–87. Third, the emphasis in each saying may be on the first half, which justifies a concern for the lost, not on the second half, which implies the health of the righteous: Cranfield, *Mark*, 106.

71. See J. Jeremias, *Jesus' Promise to the Nations* (London, 1958), 26. Cf. H. J. Cadbury, *Jesus: What Manner of Man* (New York, 1948), 25: "For in spite of his words, 'I came not to call the righteous but sinners to repentance,' Jesus seems to have had a great deal to say to the righteous or self-righteous among his people."

sayings which imply a contradiction of the content of the Pharisaic ideal. Here we shall discover how a consideration of table fellowship leads into many facets of the teaching of Jesus, pointing to the centrality of this motif for an understanding of his mission.

Ritual Washing of Hands. As indicated earlier, one of the consequences of the Pharisaic extension of priestly regulations to nonpriests was the insistence that hands be washed before even ordinary meals. At issue here, of course, was not hygiene but holiness. According to both Mark and Q (or Luke),[72] Jesus and his disciples were charged with eating with unwashed hands. Both sources indicate deliberate nonobservance and give no reason to suggest that the behavior was necessitated by special circumstances.

To determine the response of Jesus to this accusation, the complexities of Mark 7:1–23 must serve as the point of departure. As it stands in Mark, it begins with the accusation regarding washing of hands and climaxes with v. 15:

> There is nothing outside of a person which by going into that person can defile; but the things which come out of a person are what defile.

There is virtual unanimity among all schools of criticism that this saying is authentic.[73] The major issue is the meaning of the saying. To what did it refer when Jesus spoke it? Since it was spoken to some concrete situation involving controversy with opponents, its primary thrust is to be determined by that controversy rather than in isolation.

In Mark, it has two different thrusts to two different audiences. In public (v. 14), it answered the Pharisaic charge that Jesus' disciples ate

---

72. Mark 7:1–2; Luke 11:37–38. The saying in Luke which answers the charge (Luke 11:39–41) is Q (cf. Matt. 23:25–26) though the accusation itself is not paralleled in Matthew. Thus either Matthew has dropped the accusation from Q, or Luke has added it — if the latter, he has done so independently of Mark. Mark's statement in 7:3 that *all* Jews washed their hands before eating is incorrect if intended as a description of what all first-century Jews did in fact do; however, it is true from the Pharisaic point of view that *all* Jews ought to be committed to priestly purity and therefore ought to wash ritually before meals. See n. 24 above.

73. E.g., H. F. Weisz, *TWNT*, 9:43; Taylor, *Mark*, 342; Haenchen, *Weg Jesu*, 265; Bultmann, *History of the Synoptic Tradition*, 105; C. G. Montefiore, *The Synoptic Gospels*, 2d ed. (London, 1927), 1:132–33; Cranfield, *Mark*, 240; Käsemann, *Essays*, 39; D. R. Catchpole in E. Bammel, ed., *The Trial of Jesus* (London, 1970), 49; H. Merkel, "Jesus und die Pharisäer," *NTS* 14 (1967–68): 205–6; Perrin, *Rediscovering*, 149–50; R. Banks, *Jesus and the Law in the Synoptic Tradition* (Cambridge, 1975), 138–39. The only semi-dissenting voice is C. E. Carlston, "The Things That Defile (Mark 7:14) and the Law in Matthew and Mark," *NTS* 15 (1968–69): 94–95. However, his hesitation is based on the unjustified assumption that the saying may be referring to food laws; moreover, he grants that the saying may be based on an authentic saying such as "what truly defiles a man comes from within, not without."

with unwashed hands. In private (vv. 17–23), to the disciples, it nulli-
fied the Mosaic laws on clean and unclean foods (Deut. 14:3–20; Lev.
11), most explicitly in v. 19b: "Thus he declared all foods clean."

That the second thrust is authentic is unlikely for several reasons.
First, there is no indication elsewhere that this was an issue during the
ministry.[74] Indeed, had Jesus rejected the food laws of the Pentateuch,
most likely an accusation to that effect would have been made and preserved, but no such accusation is reported. Though this is an argument
from silence, it has some force since accusations about sabbath observance, washing of hands, eating with tax collectors and sinners, etc.,
do appear. Of greater weight is a second reason: the indecision of the
early Jesus movement after Jesus' death over the continued validity of
the Mosaic laws on forbidden foods[75] is virtually inexplicable if Jesus
had unambiguously rejected the distinction between clean and unclean
foods.[76] Moreover, v. 19b, which is responsible for directing the saying
to the question of forbidden foods, is in a section (vv. 17–23) commonly
viewed as secondary, not only because of the previously mentioned difficulties but also on grounds of vocabulary.[77] Thus Mark 7:15 must be
interpreted apart from the context suggested by vv. 17–23, and there
is therefore no reason to refer it to an abrogation of the food laws. To
what then did it refer?

Two possibilities remain: it was addressed to a conflict which can
no longer with certainty be identified, or it was directed to the issue of
ritual purity of hands at meals. The first is certainly possible, though the
second is more probable for two reasons. Concern about ritual purity of
hands is a known controversy; and Luke independently of Mark reports
a Q saying with similar content as a reply to the same accusation:

> Luke 11:38–41: The Pharisee noticed with surprise that Jesus had not
> begun by washing before the meal. But the Lord said to him, "You Phar-
> isees! You clean the outside of cup and plate; but inside you there is
> nothing but greed and wickedness. You fools! Did not he who made the

---

74. The argument of S. Schulz, "Markus und das Alte Testament," ZTK 58 (1961):
190, that Jesus' table fellowship with sinners would have involved eating meats forbidden
by the Torah is unconvincing, for it is neither necessary nor likely to suppose that these
meals included pork or shellfish, etc.

75. Acts 10:9–16, 15:4–29; Gal. 2:11–14; Rom. 14:13–14.

76. Taylor, Mark, 343; Carlston, "The Things That Defile," 95; Montefiore, Synoptic
Gospels, 1:147; Branscomb, Jesus and the Law of Moses, 176; Banks, Jesus and the Law, 141.

77. So Taylor, Mark, 96, 342–45; Weisz, TWNT, 9:43; Haenchen, Weg Jesu, 265; Carlston, "The Things That Defile," 91–93; Branscomb, Jesus and the Law of Moses, 175;
Perrin, Rediscovering, 150; Cranfield, Mark, 243, grant their secondary status only as a
possibility.

outside make the inside too? But cleanse those things which are within; and behold, everything is clean for you."[78]

The corroboration provided by Luke 11:38–41 suggests that Mark has the saying in its most probable historical context: to the charge that the disciples of Jesus ate with unwashed hands, Jesus replied, "There is nothing outside a person which by going into that person can defile."

Taken together, the accusations and replies reported by Mark and Luke lead to two very important conclusions. First, the behavior against which the accusations were directed contravened an important aspect of the extension of priestly regulations to daily life: it denied the validity of one of the main requirements for membership in a Pharisaic *havurah*. Second, the warrant given for the contravention called into question and indeed negated the whole notion of how holiness was to be achieved. The equation between holiness and separation, *qadosh* and *parush*, was denied, for holiness had nothing to do with separation from external sources of defilement: "there is nothing outside of a person which by going into that person can defile." Thus Mark's understanding of the passage as an abrogation of the food laws is simultaneously too broad and too narrow: too broad in the sense that the saying had nothing directly to do with eating rabbit or pork; too narrow in the sense that Mark focuses attention on one part of the Mosaic law rather than seeing the issue as related to the earnest quest for an Israel whose behavior and institutions would manifest holiness.[79] Denying the equation of *qadosh* and *parush* constituted an eminently clear opposition to the main thrust of Pharisaic polity and indeed to much of the postexilic development of Judaism.

The historic meaning of this challenge can be refined by comparing it to two modern ways of stating the significance of Mark 7:15, both of which blunt the cultural and political edge of the controversy. Perrin

---

78. Verse 41 in Luke actually reads, "But *give for alms* those things which are within; and behold everything is clean for you." The reference to alms is odd, above all because it introduces an extraneous subject into the context, and is probably due to mistranslation of an underlying Aramaic expression which Matthew in his parallel account (Matt. 23:26) has rendered correctly. The suggestion goes back to Wellhausen; see M. Black, *An Aramaic Approach to the Gospels and Acts*, 3d ed. (Oxford, 1967), 2, 194. Neusner, "First Cleanse the Inside," *NTS* 22 (1975–76): 486–95, argues that the simplest and earliest version of the saying was, "First cleanse the inside, and then the outside will be clean."

79. This does not devalue Mark's redaction, for when he wrote Israel's quest for holiness was no longer an issue for his audience. Moreover, it can be argued that the abrogation of food laws is a logical (even if not necessarily intended by Jesus) extension of the words of Mark 7:15. Mark quite appropriately adapted the tradition to the theological and pastoral needs of a community that was beginning to expand beyond Palestine and Judaism.

and Käsemann, both of whom appreciate the radical nature of the saying, argue that here Jesus abolished the distinction between the sacred
and the secular.[80] Though this may finally be quite similar to what is
argued above, putting the issue in the form, "Jesus denied the equation
of holiness with separation," has the advantage of being cast in the form
of a cultural question of the day. Its historical bite as a challenge to the
Pharisaic program for Israel can thus better be appreciated. Its controversial setting is more seriously obscured by a second modern way of
stating the point: Jesus replaces the concern about external rectitude
with concern about the inner spiritual health of the individual. Though
this is a valid insight, it both generalizes and individualizes what was
originally a specific challenge to a collective model of behavior for a
society.

Here then, in the behavior of Jesus and his disciples, we have a specific contravention of a necessary prerequisite for table fellowship as
understood by the Pharisees, and of a major element in the program
to make of Israel a kingdom of priests. Moreover, the warrant which
Jesus articulated for such nonobservance denied not only the necessity
of ritual washing of hands, but also undercut the understanding of holiness as separation upon which hinged Israel's course in the present and
anticipation of the future.[81]

Tithing. The issue is the subject of a vituperative stricture di-

---

80. Perrin, *Rediscovering,* 150, and Käsemann, *Essays,* 39.

81. Mark 7:1–23 also contains two attacks (7:6–8, 9–13) on the *halakhic* tradition of
the Pharisees; some doubt attaches to the authenticity of both. Verses 6–8 in the opinion
of some scholars depend on the LXX for a point which the Masoretic text does not yield
(e.g., Haenchen, *Weg Jesu,* 262; A. E. J. Rawlinson, *The Gospel according to St. Mark*
[London, 1925], 94; K. Stendahl, *The School of St. Matthew,* 2d ed. [Philadelphia, 1968],
57–58. For a contrasting opinion, see Taylor, *Mark,* 337–38, and France, *Jesus and the
Old Testament,* 248–50). The *korban* controversy in vv. 9–13 is also differently evaluated;
some argue that Jesus' attack did not fairly represent the Pharisaic position on oaths
(see above all Montefiore, *The Synoptic Gospels,* 1:148–52). But J. D. M. Derrett has
demonstrated persuasively that the controversy does fit first-century Palestine ("Korban
Ho Estin Doron," *NTS* 16 [1969–70]: 364–68). So at least this incident may be regarded
as authentic. If it belonged historically to the controversy about washing of hands, then
it offered an additional reason for repudiating such washings: not only because holiness
was not a matter of separation (7:15), but also because the demand was based on oral
tradition which could in another instance be shown to be defective. If it did not belong
in this context, then all that can be said is that it countered a particular instance of oral
interpretation of Torah. In neither case could it mean that Jesus' repudiation of hand
washing was based upon a generalized opposition to all authoritative oral interpretation
of the Torah, thus making him akin to the Sadducees in this respect (as is done, e.g., by
Rawlinson, *Mark,* 92; R. Leszynsky, *Die Sadduzäer* [Berlin, 1912]), for he himself offered
an oral interpretation which had authority for his followers (see, e.g., Bornkamm, *Jesus,*
97). Thus it was opposition to a specific oral tradition which misunderstood the nature of
holiness, not a general opposition to all *halakhic* development.

rected by Jesus against the Pharisees[82] in Luke 11:42=Matt. 23:23. Set in a polemical context by both Matthew and Luke, the saying, whose variants constitute the beginning of our discussion, concerns the relationship of tithing to other aspects of loyalty to Yahweh:

> Luke 11:42: Alas for you Pharisees! You pay tithes of *mint* and *rue* and *every garden herb*, but have no care for *justice* and the *love of God*. It is these you should have practiced without neglecting the others!

> Matt. 23:23: Alas for you, scribes and Pharisees, hypocrites! You pay tithes of *mint* and *dill* and *cummin;* but you have overlooked the weightier demands of the Law, *justice, mercy,* and *faithfulness*. It is these you should have practiced without neglecting the others!

Two differences in wording call for initial attention. What was it that the Pharisees tithed, and what was it that they neglected?

First, if Luke's list of mint, rue, and garden herbs is authentic, then Jesus must have been speaking in hyperbole, for there is no evidence that these items were ever subject to tithe, even by the most scrupulous. The rabbinic literature is silent about mint, rue was definitely exempt (M. Shebi. 9:1), and not every garden herb was subject to tithe.[83] Matthew's list, on the other hand, more accurately reflects rabbinic practice: dill and cummin were both subject to tithe (M. Maas. 4:5, M. Dem. 2:1), leaving only mint, which may or may not have been. The problem is largely resolved by the recognition that the Hebrew words for rue and dill are very similar and that Luke has likely written "rue" where he should have written "dill."[84] If so, then Matthew's wording is to be preferred, and the saying assailed the Pharisees for observing as part of the quest for holiness the extension of tithing to items not covered in the Pentateuch.

Such observance had as its worst effect the neglect of the weightier matters of the Torah: according to Luke, "justice and the love of God"; according to Matthew, "justice, compassion, and faithfulness." Though

---

82. Matthew directs it indiscriminately against scribes and Pharisees, whereas Luke directs it against the Pharisees alone. By so doing, Luke preserves a distinction known to exist: the scribes were trained in Scripture, whereas the Pharisees included many who had no special scriptural training. Not all Pharisees were scribes, nor were all scribes Pharisees, though it is likely that most of the scribes in the Gospels were. For the distinction, see Jeremias, *Jerusalem*, 252–57. Luke observes the distinction throughout his sevenfold set of rebukes: the first four woes of Luke 11:39–52 are addressed to the Pharisees, the final three to the scribes, a distribution which fits what is known about each group.

83. See Manson, *Mission and Message*, 390. It is doubtful that the problem can be solved (as attempted by Manson) by arguing that the pious might tithe these, even though not required, in order to build a fence around the Torah, for the rabbinic literature (which excludes these) contains the content of that fence.

84. Black, *Aramaic Approach*, 194.

there is little difference in meaning, there is some evidence that Matthew's triad is more primitive. The combination "justice, compassion,
and faithfulness" is more Hebraic than Luke's "justice and the love of
God," which may reflect Luke's "accommodation of his 'Jewish' material
to Gentile ways of thought."[85] This is bolstered by the fact that "love"
and "compassion" could be used to render a common Semitic original;[86]
Matthew has chosen a Greek word with a slightly more Hebraic flavor,
Luke one with a nuance perhaps more appropriate to his audience.

If we then accept Matthew's version as more primitive, Jesus strongly
opposed the meticulous tithing which was prerequisite to table fellowship and to the ideal of a society characterized by holiness. Over against
this he juxtaposed justice, compassion, and faithfulness.

But the saying concludes in both Matthew and Luke with words
which, if taken literally, suggest not outright opposition but a shift
in emphasis: "these you ought to have done without neglecting the
others." There is no problem believing that Jesus endorsed tithing in
general, for the Pentateuch commanded it; the difficulty is that these
words seem to endorse the tithing of the previously mentioned items in
accordance with the *halakhic* development of the Pharisees. So startling
are these words that most scholars refuse to credit them to Jesus. Some
argue that they do not belong to the text of Luke on the grounds of
their omission by Codex Bezae and Marcion;[87] others claim that even
if they do belong to the text, it is psychologically impossible to believe
that Jesus said them.[88] On the whole, it seems best to regard them as
part of the text and as authentic and then to ask what they mean.[89]

If genuine, they could be meant either as an endorsement or in other
than a straightforward sense. For example, they could be interpreted as
an argument which momentarily granted the opponents' position, in
which case the meaning of the saying might be paraphrased, "Given

85. Ibid., 190.

86. As in Hos. 2:23 in the LXX. See M'Neile, *Matthew*, 335.

87. B. S. Easton, *The Gospel according to St. Luke* (Edinburgh, 1926), 189, who
also cites Wellhausen, Harnack, J. Weiss, Loisy; E. Klostermann, *Das Lukasevangelium*
(Tübingen, 1919), 131. More cautiously: Montefiore, *Synoptic Gospels*, 2:301, 482; Manson, *Mission and Message*, 390; J. M. Creed, *The Gospel according to St. Luke* (London,
1930), 166.

88. Branscomb, *Jesus and the Law of Moses*, 207–13; Manson, *Mission and Message*, 390; Easton, *Luke*, 189; Montefiore, *Synoptic Gospels*, 2:482. A dissenting voice is
A. Plummer, *The Gospel according to St. Luke* (Edinburgh, 1896), 311.

89. The textual authorities for omission are not strong. Moreover the words are Q
and cannot easily be ascribed to the interests of the early community since they are
found in a layer of tradition (Q) which is not "Judaizing." If they were found in Matthew
alone, then a strong case could be made that they reflect a Judaizing tradition discernible
elsewhere in his (or a predecessor's) redaction.

the obvious intent to be faithful to Yahweh and the Torah which your fastidious tithing evinces, you should have been concerned about the weightier matters, even if you would not neglect the others." There is much in favor of understanding the phrase as other than a straightforward endorsement of the Pharisaic elaboration of tithing: the sheer fact that Jesus ate with tax collectors and sinners; the indubitable denial of handwashing as a requirement; the obvious indignation of this saying itself.

But, simply because it would be easier to deny the force of the phrase through surgery or by insisting on a nonliteral interpretation, let us conclude by suggesting what the clause means if authentic and an endorsement of tithing.[90] If it fulfills both of these requirements, it still proclaimed a decisive shift in emphasis and perspective, a shift in the paradigm whereby God and Israel's response to God were to be understood. To the extent that the imitation of God as holy led to this meticulous concern to the neglect of the weightier matters of Torah, holiness was inappropriate as the dominant model for Israel's self-understanding and understanding of God. Instead such emphasis was subordinated to a concern pointing to a different dominant paradigm designated by the terms "justice," "compassion," and "faithfulness." These, like "holiness," were all characteristics of God and should on an *imitatio dei* model be characteristic of the community which would be faithful to Yahweh. This shift in paradigms, even if it did not entail a negation of tithing, constituted a sharp challenge to a program whose operative blueprint for society was holiness.

The examination of passages which explicitly challenged washing of hands and tithing is complete. Yet there are many more texts in which the holiness program of the Pharisees is the subject. In the parables of the good Samaritan, the Pharisee and the tax collector, and the two sons, the hearers of Jesus were invited to see that faithful fulfillment of the Pharisaic program was nonfulfillment of the will of God. In the sayings on leaven and unmarked graves, Pharisaic influence in Israel was declared to be deleterious, a criticism continued in the castigation of scribal teaching. In the parable of money in trust, the hearers were asked to consider that the quest for holiness as a means of preserving Israel was in fact irresponsible stewardship, and a motif present in many

---

90. Westerholm, *Jesus and Scribal Authority,* 58–59, argues similarly. Given the polemical context, Jesus might have granted tithing in order to make the larger point and "to prevent the objection that tithing, too, was a part of the Mosaic law.... Jesus assigned to tithing, despite its scriptural basis, a minor place in the will of God." See also Banks, *Jesus and the Law,* 179–80.

traditions characterized Israel's present state as one of unfruitfulness. To these traditions we now turn.

The Good Samaritan: But the lawyer, desiring to justify himself, said to Jesus, "And who is my neighbor?" Jesus replied, "A man was going down from Jerusalem to Jericho, and he fell among robbers, who stripped him and beat him, and departed, leaving him half dead. Now by chance a priest was going down that road; and when he saw him he passed by on the other side. So likewise a Levite, when he came to the place and saw him, passed by on the other side. But a Samaritan, as he journeyed, came to where he was; and when he saw him, he had compassion, and went to him and bound up his wounds, pouring on oil and wine; then he set him on his own beast and brought him to an inn, and took care of him. And the next day he took out two denarii and gave them to the innkeeper, saying, 'Take care of him; and whatever more you spend, I will repay you when I come back.' Which of these three, do you think, proved neighbor to the man who fell among the robbers?" He said, "The one who showed compassion on him." And Jesus said to him, "Go and do likewise." (Luke 10:29–37)

Though this parable makes more than one point, here the criticism of holiness contained within it will be elucidated. To do so a question must be asked: what would the original hearers have understood as the reason why the priest and Levite passed by? Two quite different answers are given by modern scholars.

One approach argues that the above question is not germane because of the bad reputation of priests and Levites: they behaved only as the hearers would have expected. Therefore, taking their behavior for granted, the hearers would not have bothered to reflect on the reasons.[91] Two problems arise. One is factual: were priests and Levites on such universal disrepute that this behavior would cause no comment? More serious is the question of what the parable meant within this view. The audience would have been very comfortable hearing that the priest and Levite passed by. Indeed, on this reading, the two had no significance at all except that they led to the expectation that the party necessary to complete the triad[92] would be an Israelite, i.e., a layman.[93]

---

91. Linnemann, *Parables,* 53, and especially notes 6 and 7, p. 139, citing *S-B* 2:182 and 4:334–53.

92. On the "law of three," see B. Reicke, "Der barmherzige Samariter," in O. Böcher and K. Haacker, ed., *Verborum Veritas: Festschrift für G. Stählin* (Wuppertal, 1970), 105. For the collocation of priest, Levite, and Israelite, see Abrahams, *Studies,* 2:35.

93. So strong is the expectation that J. Hálevy, *Revue des Études juives* 4 (1882): 249–55, followed by Montefiore, *Synoptic Gospels,* 2:466–67, maintains that the original parable must have contained an Israelite instead of a Samaritan. The suggestion is generally rejected; see Abrahams, *Studies,* 2:34; B. T. D. Smith, *The Parables of the Synop-*

On this view, the cutting edge of the parable rested in the substitution of the hated Samaritan for the expected Israelite, not in the contrast between priest-Levite and Samaritan. What contrast remained between priest-Levite and Samaritan was insipid: the hated Samaritan stopped to help whereas the representatives of the universally contemptible classes did not. At this point one wonders why the parable contained a reference to priest and Levite at all; it would have been more to the point to have an Israelite pass by, followed by the gracious Samaritan.

These difficulties render it probable that the presence of the priest and Levite was significant and that the audience was intended to reflect on the reasons for their failure to offer assistance. So maintains J. D. M. Derrett. He rigorously examines the legal situation of the priest and Levite and argues that the hearers would have understood the legal dilemma facing them, which centered around the possibility of incurring ritual defilement through proximity to a corpse.[94] If the wounded victim were dead (and since he was "half-dead," one could not tell without approaching closely), the situation posed three risks of defilement (which would also occur if the man, though alive, died in the presence of the priest or Levite): by coming within four cubits of the corpse;[95] by casting one's shadow over the corpse; or, if an overhanging rock overshadowed the corpse, by stepping within that shadow.

On the other hand, if the priest or Levite were certain that the person was a neighbor (a Jew), he had an obligation to help. But such certainty required close examination, which was precisely what the danger of defilement precluded. In a situation of doubt, preference was to be given to fulfilling that law which could be fulfilled with certainty (in this case, avoiding defilement), and the priest and Levite were thereby entitled to travel on.[96]

Yet there was legal justification for the priest and Levite to risk defilement, but only with the concomitant risk of the inconvenience and cost of subsequent purification and temporary loss of the right to re-

---

tic Gospels (Cambridge, 1937), 181; Derrett, Law in the New Testament, 211, n. 2; Manson, Mission and Message, 554.

94. Derrett, Law in the New Testament, 208–27, esp. 211–17. Other scholars have suggested that fear of ritual defilement is operative, though Derrett's work is most detailed: G. B. Caird, St. Luke (Penguin Books, 1963), 148; Reicke, "Der barmherzige Samariter," 104–5; less decisively E. E. Ellis, The Gospel of St. Luke (London, 1966), 159; Perrin, Rediscovering, 123; Jeremias, Parables, 203; K. Börnhauser, Studien zum Sondergut des Lukas (Gütersloh, 1934), 71.

95. This may be the significance of the unusual Greek verb "passed by on the other side," here (10:31–32) and in Wisd. 16:10, which may suggest a deliberate distancing: they passed on the opposite side to insure a distance of four cubits.

96. For this point, see Derrett, Law in the New Testament, 214.

ceive tithe.[97] The point, Derrett concludes, is that the ethics of the time gave no decisive guidance.[98] Either course of action was justifiable as a fulfillment of God's law, though stopping did entail risks. Such was the dilemma facing the priest and Levite, and so the hearers would have understood it;[99] the two chose to pass by, and by so doing fulfilled the Torah as then understood.[100] Manifestly, that which explained and justified their action was the quest for a holy community, understood as separation from that which defiles.

The parable concluded by eliciting the judgment that the Samaritan, not the priest or Levite, actually became a neighbor to the wounded man. Hence the parable judged negatively the action of priest and Levite, despite their legal rectitude.[101] Jesus claimed that their action, motivated by and consistent with the Pharisaic dynamic of holiness, really amounted to failure to be a neighbor. Over against such behavior in accordance with the demands of holiness was placed the behavior of the heretical half-breed Samaritan whose action was summed up not by the watchword holiness, but by compassion (vv. 33, 37).

Thus this most famous of parables was not simply a story about compassionate neighborliness, but also criticized the ideal which dominated the Pharisaic understanding of the community which would be faithful to Yahweh. It, like table fellowship with tax collectors and sinners, called into question the controlling idea in conformity with which the community was to be structured.

The Pharisee and the Tax Collector: Two men went up into the Temple to pray, one a Pharisee and the other a tax collector. The Pharisee stood and prayed thus with himself, "God, I thank thee that I am not like other men, extortioners, unjust, adulterers, or even like this tax collector. I fast twice a week, I give tithes of all that I get." But the tax collector, standing far off, would not even lift up his eyes to heaven, but beat his

---

97. The risk of loss was intensified by the pledge of the *haverim* to give tithe only to those priests and Levites who conformed to their standards of eating *every* meal in a state of ritual purity (T. Dem. 2:2; Neusner, "The Fellowship," 141). This means that the Levite and the priest, even though not headed for Jerusalem and Temple service, faced the risk equally.

98. Derrett, *Law in the New Testament*, 216.

99. Derrett, *Law in the New Testament*, 220–21, notes a humorous element which the crowd may also have appreciated: oil and wine from a Samaritan are forbidden (and are also *demai*), so the wounded man should have refused to benefit from them.

100. Reicke, "Der barmherzige Samariter," 104–5, also comments that the priest and Levite believed that they were fulfilling the Torah by their action.

101. Cf. Derrett's understanding of one of the principal points which the parable makes, 222: "If real life can find such defects in the Pharisees' ordinances it is high time that their fundamental structure was re-examined. Opponents of Pharisaism would enjoy the point, which is put as delicately as it is inescapable."

breast, saying "God, be merciful to me a sinner!" I tell you, this man went
down to his house justified rather than the other. (Luke 18:10–14a)

This parable is of obvious relevance because of the two main characters,
a Pharisee who epitomized the quest for holiness and a tax collector
who represented the most despised of the outcasts. Yet interpretations
of the parable, beginning with Luke himself, generally overlook the connection to the cultural dynamics of first-century Palestine. For Luke the
parable was a judgment on self-righteous prayer and praise of contrition:
he set it in a context of how to pray[102] and both the introduction (v. 9)
and the application (v. 14b) point to this meaning.[103] Usually the parable is given the same meaning by interpreters who seek its meaning in
the *Sitz im Leben Jesu*: it concerned the proper attitude toward God.[104]
But since the context, introduction, and conclusion are all secondary,
as is agreed by most commentators, we may ask whether it would or
could have had this meaning to the original hearers.

To us, as well as to the early Christian readers of Luke's Gospel, the
Pharisee's prayer marks him at once as self-righteous. Neither we nor
they need to hear the judgment of v. 14a, for we know what it will be,
not because we have heard the parable before, but because our redefini-
tion of "sinner" in a theological sense to embrace all persons means that
the Pharisee's attempt to distinguish himself from other people sounds
perverse at once, and because previous acquaintance with the Gospel
tradition has led us uncritically to identify the Pharisees as the villains,
as models of hypocrisy.

Just as we have virtually made "sinners" into an honorable term, so
we have made "Pharisees" into a term of abuse. But neither condition
prevailed for the first hearers of the parable. Does their "disadvantage"
mean simply that the conclusion of the parable would have come as
a surprise to them, or does it also mean that the parable would have

---

102. Note its juxtaposition to Luke 18:1–8, which for Luke teaches persistence in
prayer.

103. Verse 9: "He also told this parable to some who trusted in themselves that they
were righteous and despised others"; v. 14b: "for all who exalt themselves will be humbled, but all who humble themselves will be exalted." Thus commentators on Luke who
emphasize the contrast between pride and humility are correct that it had that meaning *for Luke*; e.g., Creed, *Luke*, 222–24; Plummer, *Luke*, 415–20; Caird, *Luke*, 202–3;
Klostermann, *Lukasevangelium*, 177–81; Ellis, *Luke*, 214–16.

104. B. T. D. Smith, *Parables*, 176–79; C. W. F. Smith, *The Jesus of the Parables*, 117–22:
the parable concerns right and wrong attitudes toward God. Jeremias, *Parables*, 139–44,
contrasts the despairing, hopeless sinner to the self-righteous Pharisee (144). Manson,
Mission and Message, 600–604. Montefiore, *Synoptic Gospels*, 2:555–58, cites the moral
as "humility is always more pleasing to God than confidence in one's own merits." For
further citations, see Linnemann, *Parables*, note 11, pp. 144–46, who dissociates herself
from this meaning.

meant something more or other than a story about proper attitudes toward God? To answer this question, we must put ourselves in their position as best we can.[105]

Nothing about the Pharisee in the parable would have struck the original audience as self-righteous. His prayer was a prayer of thanksgiving;[106] moreover, his claim to belong to the righteous and not to the sinners would have been accepted as accurate and not as hypocritical. The words quoted from his prayer cannot be considered to draw attention primarily to a superior attitude. As the parallels in Jewish literature show, statements such as that of this Pharisee are found in contexts which put them in a much more favorable light. The most frequently cited parallel, "I thank thee, O Lord my God, that thou hast given me my lot with those who sit in the seat of learning, and not with those who sit at the street-corners" (Ber. 28b), is closely adjacent to another prayer which favorably compares the lot of agricultural workers to the rabbis.[107] More illuminating yet is a prayer in the Dead Sea Scroll 1QH 7:34 which contains the petition, "I thank Thee, O God, for Thou hast not cast my lot in the congregation of vanity, nor hast Thou placed my portion in the council of the cunning." Thus far, this prayer sounds "arrogant," but it is immediately preceded by a petition thanking God for showing mercy to a *perverse* heart and is followed by the phrase, "Thou hast led me to Thy grace and forgiveness." Thus the words of the Pharisee's prayer could be accompanied by a quite appropriate attitude toward God.

So the quoted words should not be thought of as the sum total of the Pharisee's prayer. Rather, what the audience was given was a snippet, which they would have recognized as such, every bit of which focused attention not on a haughty attitude but on the separation between the Pharisee and others brought about by specific elements in the Pharisaic program. The two works which he explicitly cited, fasting twice a week and paying tithe on all that he bought, were identifying characteristics of the Pharisees and integral to the quest for holiness, not supererogatory works performed by him to "out-Pharisee" the Pharisees.

It is usual to view them as supererogatory works. In one sense they were, of course, since they were not commanded by the written Torah. But they were part of the Pharisaic program of holiness. This is most

---

105. Linnemann, *Parables*, 58, strongly and properly emphasizes the need to appreciate the difference between our perspective and theirs.

106. The sincerity of his thanksgiving is usually granted even by expositors who see him as a model of self-righteousness: Jeremias, *Parables*, 143; Manson, *Mission and Message*, 602; Creed, *Luke*, 224; B. T. D. Smith, *Parables*, 178.

107. See Montefiore, *Synoptic Gospels*, 2:557.

evident in the case of paying tithes "on all that I buy," which refers to the practice of tithing everything that was purchased in case the tithes had not been paid by the seller.[108] The twice weekly fast must have been quite widespread and not simply the idiosyncrasy of a few individuals, since at least one portion of the Christian community carried on the custom, explicitly mentioning its continuity with Judaism, though it distinguished itself from the Jewish practice by changing the days on which it was observed.[109] In short, the audience would have accepted the Pharisee, attitude and behavior as well, not as a type of arrogance, but as a model of piety. His prayer would not have struck them as haughty or self-righteous, and his works would have struck them as what all Israel should be doing: conforming to the program of holiness as an ideal to be approximated in history.[110]

To the Pharisee was contrasted the tax collector, whose social and religious position has already been described. The parable focused on his recognition that he stood in need of mercy and climaxed with the opening verse of Psalm 51, which was the content of his prayer: "God, be merciful to me, a sinner!" Then followed the shock: "I tell you, this man, not the other, went home as one whom God had declared to be in the right."[111]

How would the audience have understood this shocking verdict? As a judgment on the self-righteousness of the Pharisee? But this presupposes that they would have singled out one aspect of the picture of the Pharisee drawn by Jesus, namely, his attitude. As we have seen, there was nothing in the Pharisee's prayer which would lead them to isolate his attitude. Instead, they would have understood the judgment to be on the whole of the Pharisee's piety: the *content* of his piety, as well as his attitude.[112] In sum, the parable judged the Pharisaic program and

---

108. M. Dem. 2:2; Neusner, "The Fellowship," 132; Westerholm, *Jesus and Scribal Authority,* 56.

109. Did. 8:1.

110. Cf. Linnemann, *Parables,* 60: "The verdict of the listeners on this figure which Jesus sets before their eyes was bound to be: 'Here is a man after God's heart.'"

111. The meaning of *dedikaiómenos* as a judicial verdict is deliberately maintained, avoiding the translation "forgiven." As Linnemann points out, *Parables,* 144, it makes no sense to understand the verdict as meaning that the tax collector rather than the Pharisee was forgiven, for the Pharisee had not sought forgiveness nor, in the opinion of the audience, did he need it.

112. There is one further difficulty with the approach which emphasizes attitude as the essential point of the parable. If its point is essentially to teach humility, then Jesus in this instance is transformed into a teacher of generalized virtue; Linnemann, *Parables,* 145, appropriately asks, "...was Jesus really a teacher of virtue, who wanted to 'teach that in all circumstances humility is more welcome to God than self-righteousness'? Then he would have won the full approval of his opponents, and they would hardly have crucified him." See also C. W. F. Smith, *Jesus,* 17, who argues that the exegesis of the parables must

declared it to be in the wrong.[113] Contrasted to the quest for holiness was the picture of the despised tax collector who was declared to be in the right because of his appeal to the mercy of God.

> *The Parable of the Two Sons:* What do you think? A man had two sons; and he went to the first and said, "Son, go and work in the vineyard today." And he answered, "I will not." But afterward he repented and went. And he went to the second and said the same; and he answered, "I go, sir," but did not go. "Which of the two did the will of his father?" They said, "The first." Jesus said to them, "Truly, I say to you, the tax collectors and the harlots go into the Kingdom of God before you." (Matt. 21:28–31)

Similarly connected to the issues posed by table fellowship with sinners and tax collectors is this parable in which Jesus presented his hearers with a picture of two sons whom their father requested to work in his vineyard.[114] The first refused and then later went to work; the second agreed to work and then did not go.[115] Eliciting from his audience the response that the first had better followed the father's wish despite his initial refusal, Jesus then retorted, "Truly I say to you, tax collectors and harlots are entering the Kingdom of God ahead of you."

With this retort Jesus directed the audience to see in the tax collectors and harlots the historical equivalent of the first son. Jesus claimed that they, though apparently having refused the command of God, were now actually doing God's will. But how would the audience have understood the second son who said "Yes" and then did not work in the vineyard? It is clear that the audience was invited to see a historical equivalent here, too: the countertype of the tax collectors and sinners, the righteous or the Pharisees. They above all were those who were understood to have said "Yes" to God, just as the despised classes were understood to have said "No." But the audience was also invited to see

---

not be satisfied with generalized virtues, no matter how noble: "Jesus used parables and Jesus was put to death. The two facts are related....No one would crucify a teacher who told pleasant stories to enforce prudential morality."

113. See also E. Haenchen, "Matthäus 23," *ZTK* 48 (1951): 51–52: "This false understanding earnestly pursued, not a false front hypocritically projected, is what Jesus opposed in the Pharisees."

114. Verse 32, which connects the parable to the activity of John the Baptist, is a floating logion also found in Luke 7:29–30, which Matthew or a predecessor has attached to the parable. See Jeremias, *Parables*, 80; Perrin, *Rediscovering*, 119; Dodd, *Parables*, 93; B. T. D. Smith, *Parables*, 209; J. A. Baird, *The Justice of God in the Teaching of Jesus* (London, 1963), 126.

115. The difficult textual problem in this parable does not seem to affect the meaning. For a thorough description of it (and a suggestion that various stages in the redaction of the parable are reflected in it), see J. R. Michaels, "The Parable of the Regretful Son," *HTR* 61 (1968): 15–26.

a discrepancy between that "Yes" and actual performance of the will of God. Of what did this discrepancy consist?

As in the parable of the Pharisee and the tax collector, interpreters have been inclined to understand the discrepancy as summed up by hypocrisy: in this case, discrepancy between verbal obedience and behavioral nonperformance, between word and deed.[116] Two logically possible understandings of the discrepancy understood in this way emerge: a verbal "Yes" to Jesus and a repudiation of that "Yes" in their behavior; or a "Yes" to their own understanding of God's command and nonobservance of it in practice.

But the audience could not have understood it in either of these ways. That there is no indication that the opponents of Jesus agreed verbally to what he was doing, and much evidence to the contrary, excludes the first possibility. That their nonperformance consisted of failing to live out in behavior the "Yes" which they gave to their understanding of the command of God is excluded by two considerations. First, there is the overwhelming evidence that the Pharisees took practice very seriously;[117] with good reason, their concern has been described as *orthopraxis* instead of orthodoxy. Criticism of the Pharisees for failure to practice that to which they gave verbal assent would not only be unfair, but the implication of such a criticism is that Jesus wanted them to conform even more stringently to their understanding of God's command. Second, the parable makes it clear that their nonperformance did not consist of failure to live up to their under-

---

116. For example, B. T. D. Smith, *Parables*, 209: the person who in practice fails to carry out the profession of obedience; Manson, *Mission and Message*, 515: those who "maintained the outward appearance of piety without any real devotion to the will of God"; P. Fiebig, *Die Gleichnisreden Jesu* (Tübingen, 1912), 199–200. C. W. F. Smith, *Jesus*, 144–45, vacillates between this interpretation and one more akin to the one that will be offered here. That Jesus on occasion attacked inconsistency between word and deed, as in Matt. 7:21, is not denied; what is being questioned is whether Matt. 7:21 is a parallel to this parable.

117. Matt. 23:3 is an exception in that it reports that Jesus criticized the Pharisees for not practicing what they preached and urged the disciples to observe all that the Pharisees preach. But this is not a serious exception for two reasons. First, it is impossible that the Jesus of the sabbath controversies, of Mark 7, etc., could have urged his disciples to practice *everything* which the Pharisees preached. See Branscomb, *Jesus and the Law of Moses*, 231–33; Manson, *Mission and Message*, 521; Weiss, *TWNT*, 9:44–45; Jeremias, *New Testament Theology*, 145; Banks, *Jesus and the Law*, 175–77; see also Westerholm, *Jesus and Scribal Authority*, 126–27, who argues that the saying may be "a concession granted for the sake of argument (rather) than an objective assessment of the legitimacy of scribal teaching." Second, the criticism of the Pharisees which is based on discrepancy between their words and deeds seems due to the redaction of Matthew as a predecessor, not to Jesus himself. See Merkel, "Jesus und die Pharisäer," 200–201; Carlston, "The Things That Defile," 90–91; E. P. Blair, *Jesus in the Gospel of Matthew* (New York, 1960), 112–13; R. S. McConnell, *Law and Prophecy in Matthew's Gospel* (Basel, 1969), 82–83.

standing of their obligation. Since their nonperformance is contrasted
to the acceptance by sinners of that which Jesus has initiated, their
nonperformance must be nonacceptance of that which has begun with
Jesus; it had nothing to do with a discrepancy between what they said
and did.

Thus it seems best to discard the interpretations which depend upon
a contrast between word and deed. When this is done, the nature
of their "Yes" becomes clear: their "Yes" included both allegiance to
and fulfillment of their understanding of the will of God; so the audience would have understood it, even though they might not have
agreed that it constituted nonperformance of God's will. The parable
claims that their "Yes" in both word and deed really amounted to nonperformance of the will of God — not because they failed to perform
that to which they had committed themselves, but because that to
which they had committed themselves was not the will of God. Thus,
insofar as hypocrisy means either insincerity or discrepancy between
words and practice, the parable had nothing to do with hypocrisy. Instead, it invited Jesus' listeners to consider that the verbal "Yes" and the
practical embodiment of that "Yes" really amounted to a refusal to work
in the vineyard. Like the parable of the Pharisee and the tax collector,
it attacked the content of the Pharisaic program.

The same judgment emerges when we consider sayings which speak
of Pharisaic influence in first-century Judaism.

The Pharisees as Leaven. All three synoptic Gospels preserve in
varying forms the warning, "Beware of the leaven of the Pharisees."
Luke 12:1, almost certainly independent of Mark, warns of the Pharisees alone and interprets the leaven as hypocrisy. Mark 8:15, apparently under the influence of Mark 3:6, adds "the leaven of Herod," but
offers no interpretation; indeed, the Marcan context yields no clue as
to what was meant by either the leaven of the Pharisees or the leaven
of Herod.[118] The Matthaean parallel to Mark replaces "Herod" with

---

118. Most commentators view it is an isolated saying which has not been integrated
fully into its Marcan context. See esp. Nineham, *Mark*, 214–15; Montefiore, *Synoptic
Gospels*, 1:176–78; more cautiously, Taylor, *Mark*, 363–65. C. H. Turner, "Marcan Usage:
Notes, Critical and Exegetical, on the Second Gospel," *JTS* 26 (1925): 150–51 (cited with
approval by Nineham and Montefiore), argues that 8:15 is really a parenthesis which a
modern writer would have put in a footnote and introduced with the word "compare ... ";
the context of bread led Mark to insert it here. For a contrary view, see J. Bowman, *The
Gospel of Mark* (Leiden, 1965), 180–82, who affirms (though without much argumentation) that 8:15 is the raison d'être of the whole passage: those participating in the new
exodus are to leave behind the leaven of the Pharisees and Herod. Cranfield, *Mark*, 259–
60, thinks that 8:15 is in its true historical setting. The difficulty in accepting Mark's
context is seen in Cranfield's attempted explanation of why the saying is not taken up
in succeeding verses: because the disciples were so preoccupied with their problem that

"Sadducees" and interprets the leaven as the teaching of the Pharisees and the Sadducees (16:6, 11–12). Because of this diversity, it seems best to regard the tradition as an isolated saying warning against the Pharisees alone, which each evangelist has handled in his own way.[119] Accordingly we must seek the meaning of the saying by examining the meaning of leaven in the Jewish background.

Leaven as a metaphor in Judaism had three different associations. First, it was used in a neutral sense as a metaphor for permeation of the whole by a small amount. In this neutral sense, no value judgment was implied on the process, which may be either to good or bad effect. Obviously this use was drawn from observation of leaven as an agent in baking, as in the parable of leaven (Matt. 13:33=Luke 13:32). Though Paul applied it in a negative sense, the natural function of leaven is clear in his twofold quotation of a proverbial saying: "A little leaven leavens all the dough" (1 Cor. 5:6, Gal. 5:9).[120] Second, reflected in the custom of ridding the house of leaven before Passover began, it was used as a metaphor for that which was corrupt.[121] Here the emphasis was not so much on its spreading qualities, but on its character as a corrupt substance. Finally, there is some indication that it had become a metaphor for the rabbinic notion of the *yetzer ha-ra*, the evil inclination which in every person wars with the good inclination.[122]

To speak of the leaven of the Pharisees was probably to allude to one of these three meanings. The third, however, is unlikely. Not only

---

they failed to pay attention to what Jesus was saying, Jesus dropped the subject. On this view, we would have to suppose that the oral tradition faithfully preserved an "interrupted lecture," despite its total lack of impact on the disciples who, according to the narrative, were the only audience.

119. So also B. W. Bacon, *Studies in Matthew* (New York, 1930) in his appended note on the leaven of the Pharisees, 511–17; Manson, *Mission and Message*, 562. Hoehner, *Herod Antipas*, 202–13, retains the reference to Herod.

120. See also Abrahams, *Studies*, 1:51, who notes the ambiguity of the leaven image. On the one hand, in all antiquity "panary fermentation" was understood as a process of corruption. On the other hand, since leavened bread was more palatable, leavening came to be known as an improving process. This ambiguity means that the metaphor is neutral with the context determining the meaning. The attempt to deny that the oriental mind comprehended leavening as a process but thought only of the contrasts of unleavened and leavened (e.g., Jeremias, *Parables*, 148–49) is unconvincing; see N. A. Dahl, "The Parables of Growth," *StTh* 5 (1952): 132–66, esp. 140–45. He comments that modern scholars who will not credit the ancients with an understanding of growth fail to distinguish between the idea of growth itself and the biological-scientific explanation of it. The ancients certainly understood the former, as his examination of pagan, Jewish, and Christian literature shows.

121. Ex. 12:15, 19; 13:7; Deut. 16:4. For the regulations on *hametz* in the Mishnah, see M. Pes. 1:1–2, 3:1–8, 9:3. Paul combines this use with the previous one, as in 1 Cor. 5:7–8.

122. Abrahams, *Studies*, 1:52, citing Ber. 17a; C. G. Montefiore and H. Loewe, eds., *A Rabbinic Anthology* (London, 1938), 300, 301, 362, 578.

is the evidence for this at least two centuries later than the New Testament,[123] but, since the *yetzer ha-ra* was found in every person, it makes no real sense to warn somebody about the *yetzer ha-ra* of a particular group. It would be more to the point to warn a person of his or her own *yetzer ha-ra*.[124] If the second meaning was intended, then the saying was a scathing criticism of the Pharisees: they, like leaven in a house at Passover, were viewed as a corrupt substance that ought not to be in Israel.[125] If the first sense of the metaphor was dominant, it was used *in malam partem* ("Beware...") with an equally scathing meaning, but with a subtle difference. Attention was drawn to the expansive, influential characteristic of Pharisaism as a program intended for all of Israel; it was not so much that Pharisaism was corrupt, but corrupting. Like leaven which permeates the lump, Pharisaism sought to bring all of Israel to holiness as they understood it, and the audience was warned against this penetrating influence.[126]

Choosing between these last two meanings is unnecessary, for both imply a judgment consistent with the thesis that Jesus intended a contravention of the Pharisaic ideal: the group preeminently committed to the extension of holiness was, like leaven, corrupt or corrupting. But there are indications that the expansive characteristic of Pharisaism was intended,[127] notably in another synoptic saying which speaks of Pharisaism as a contagion which spread its influence.

---

123. The five rabbis cited by Abrahams and Montefiore-Loewe are all third century or later; this by itself is not decisive, of course.

124. On the evil inclination, see W. D. Davies, *Paul and Rabbinic Judaism* (London, 1948), 20–23; Moore, *Judaism*, 1:479–93; Montefiore-Loewe, *A Rabbinic Anthology*, 295–314. In all the passages cited from the rabbinic literature, not one could be found in which a person is told to beware of the danger of somebody else's evil inclination; stories are often told about somebody else's battle with the *yetzer ha-ra*, but in each case as a warning to beware of similar tendencies in one's self.

125. See Ex. 13:7 and Deut. 16:4 where the prohibition of leaven at Passover extended to "all your territory," not just to houses.

126. Hoehner, *Herod Antipas*, 202–13, also understands the metaphor in terms of influence: beware of the influence of the Pharisees. He does not, however, connect it explicitly to holiness as a cultural ideal, but to the hope for "a purely external nationalistic political kingdom."

127. Such an allusion may be found in a woe to the Pharisees reported by Matthew alone: "Woe...for you traverse sea and land to make one convert" (23:15). This may refer to the attempt of Pharisees to lead other Jews to Pharisaism, though usually it is interpreted to refer to Pharisaic proselytizing of Gentiles, presumably because of the words "you traverse land and sea." The latter has some infrequently noticed difficulties. Are we to think of Pharisaism as sponsoring foreign missions to distant places à la nineteenth-century Christianity? That Jews in the Diaspora converted Gentiles is, of course, true, and that Palestinian Jews converted Palestinian Gentiles is also true. But evidence of a mission by Palestinian Jews to overseas Gentiles, sufficiently widespread to call forth this criticism, is lacking. It seems more likely that the words "traverse land and sea" are not intended literally, but refer to the vigor of the effort. If this is the case, then the reason

Unmarked Graves. Luke and Matthew report variants of what appears to be the same saying:

> Luke 11:44: Woe to you [Pharisees]: for you are like unmarked graves over which people may walk without knowing it!

> Matt. 23:27–28: Woe to you, scribes and Pharisees, hypocrites! You are like tombs covered with whitewash, which outwardly appear beautiful, but inside they are filled with dead men's bones and all uncleanness. So it is with you: outside you look righteous, but inside you are brim full of hypocrisy and iniquity.

Both sayings reflect the annual custom of whitewashing burial places with chalk or lime prior to Passover[128] to warn people not to come in contact with them and thereby become defiled by proximity to a corpse.[129] But though the variants reflect the same custom, they differ in their use of it as an image. In Matthew, the Pharisees are likened to tombs which have been whitewashed; in Luke they are like graves which have *not* been. This leads to a difference in the application of the metaphor: for Matthew, the point of comparison is that the Pharisees appear righteous ("beautiful"), but inside they are full of hypocrisy and iniquity. For Luke, on the other hand, the point is that the Pharisees, like a grave, are a source of defilement, but people are not aware of that, for the Pharisees are like unmarked graves. Thus Matthew reproves the Pharisees for the contradiction within themselves of external propriety and internal wickedness; Luke speaks, not of something within the Pharisees, but of their effect on other people.

There are both general and specific reasons for preferring Luke's version. The section of Luke in which this indictment appears shows fewer signs of intensive redaction than the corresponding section in Matthew.[130] Moreover, Luke preserves a known distinction which Matthew obliterates.[131] More specifically, Matthew's version does not reflect an understanding of the Jewish purpose of whitewashing graves: the purpose is to warn people away from the graves, not to make the tombs or graves beautiful.[132] Indeed, Matthew's use of the saying as a castigation of hypocrisy requires a non-Jewish understanding of the purposes

---

for referring it to a Gentile mission overseas evaporates, and it is equally possible that we have a reference to the attempt to lead other Jews to Pharisaism.

128. M. Shek. 1:1; B. Kat. 1a, 5a.

129. Num. 19:16.

130. For the overall effect which Matthew's redaction achieves see E. Haenchen, "Matthäus 23, *ZTK* 48 (1951): 38–63, summary on 61.

131. See above n. 82.

132. Caird, *Luke*, 158. Montefiore, *Synoptic Gospels*, 2:482–83, very strangely argues that Luke is secondary on the grounds that his version is an attempt to make the saying intelligible to readers unacquainted with Jewish customs. On the contrary, Luke's version

of whitewashing burial places, for if the custom is understood from a Palestinian point of view, then whitewashed graves do not provide a good picture of hypocrisy: whitewashed graves proclaim their pollution rather than concealing it.[133] Only when the custom is sequestered from its Jewish rationale does Matthew's version make any sense.[134]

The more primitive tradition, represented by Luke, credits Jesus with comparing the Pharisees to unmarked graves: like graves, they emanate defilement. From Jesus' point of view, the Pharisees, far from being a social religious group bringing Israel to holiness, were the very opposite. He characterized their influence on those around them as pernicious, as a defiling rather than hallowing contagion, as one about which Israel needed to be warned in the strongest terms.

Interestingly, the two variants offer explicit evidence of the process for which we have argued in the parables of the two sons and the Pharisee and the tax collector. Criticisms originally directed at the content of the Pharisaic ideal for Israel have been transformed into criticisms of individual piety. For Matthew the fault of the Pharisees in this saying was their hypocrisy, the discrepancy between external appearance and inward reality. Presumably he intended his readers to avoid such hypocrisy in their own lives and to discern that true piety entails a correspondence between external behavior and inner wholeness. The emphasis is on the individual. But Luke's version had nothing to do with hypocrisy; no emphasis was placed on a contrast between external rectitude and internal rot. Indeed, such a contrast was not even mentioned. Instead, all the emphasis in Luke was on the influence of Pharisaism in Israel, an influence which must be their teaching, their conception of the course which Israel was to follow.[135] Like contact with a corpse, that course, the metaphor implies, far from producing holiness, produced alienation from God.

To return momentarily to the saying on leaven, this exegesis confirms that the association intended is not the corruptness of leaven in a static

---

positively requires an understanding of the Jewish tabu on contact with death. Matthew's contrast between beautiful tombs/rotting bodies within could be understood by anybody in the Greco-Roman world.

133. See M'Neile, *Matthew*, 337.

134. See Abrahams, *Studies*, 2:29–30, who affirms that Matthew's variant may reflect an acquaintance with Roman sepulchral monuments. G. Schwarz, "Unkenntiche Gräber?" *NTS* 23 (1976–77): 345–46, prefers Matthew's reading, but misunderstands the connection between the Jewish custom and Matthew's version.

135. If this seems too abrupt, one must ask, "What else could it be?" It cannot mean that they, like a corpse, are literally a source of ritual impurity, for within the presuppositions of that system they were undoubtedly clean. Rather, that which they radiate is their vision for Israel.

sense. Like a corpse as a source of defilement, leaven permeates that
which surrounds it.

On Scribal Teaching. The criticism of Jesus' opponents continues in
two Q sayings. The first is Luke 6:39=Matt. 15:14:

> He also told them a parable: "Can a blind person guide a blind person?
> Will not both fall into a pit?"

The folly of following a blind guide is a common proverb.[136] But to
whom was it applied in this particular case?[137] Matt. 23:16 and 24 apply
the phrase "blind guides" to the Pharisees and scribes but, since this
is probably due to his redaction, it cannot be used as evidence here.
However, a clue is provided by Paul in Rom. 2:19, where he refers to
his fellow Jews who are trained in the law as "guides of the blind,"
suggesting that this was a common (and positive) description of the
learned in Judaism.[138] Thus it is likely that Jesus applied the proverb to
those charged with a teaching responsibility in Judaism. Accepting the
appellation "guides of the blind," he then characterized these guides as
blind themselves. The concluding rhetorical question declared that the
course advocated by such guides could lead to only one consequence for
themselves and their followers: "Will they not both fall into a pit?"[139]

The same note is struck in Luke 11:52, paralleled in Matt. 23:13:

---

136. W. Michaelis, *TDNT,* 5:99, n. 14. Bultmann, *History of the Synoptic Tradition,* 102,
regards it as a profane proverb added to the sayings of Jesus.

137. One cannot believe that Jesus intended the saying in a literal sense as a piece
of advice to a literally blind man, as Michaelis, *TDNT,* 5:99–100, seems to imply. He
insists that "lead" in Luke 6:39 is used in the literal sense of leading or guiding the blind,
not in the figurative sense of instruction or teaching. If he simply means that the proverb
requires the meaning "guide" and not "teacher," he is correct. However, he does not seem
to consider the possibility of a shift of meaning in the application of the proverb.

138. So Easton, *Luke,* 91; M'Neile, *Matthew,* 228; Haenchen, "Matthäus 23," 47.
Michaelis, *TDNT,* 5:99, disagrees, arguing that there is no parallel in Jewish literature.
Instead, he claims, Paul must have known the tradition now preserved in Matt. 23:16–
24. It seems unnecessary to see this as the source of Paul's terminology, not because
there are any difficulties in supposing that Paul was familiar with elements of the synoptic
tradition, but because Paul uses the term initially in a favorable sense, apparently as a
description that his real or imaginary interlocutor would accept. On the other hand, if
Michaelis is right, then Rom. 2:19 provides us with evidence that "guides of the blind" as
a reference to those skilled in the Torah is not due to Matthaean redaction, but was part
of the synoptic tradition by the 50s (at the latest) of the first century.

139. The subsequent sayings about someone with a log in the eye continue the theme
of blindness and were probably also originally anti-Pharisaic polemic. This creates the
possibility of integrating Luke 6:40 into the same framework: "A disciple is not above the
teacher, but every one when fully taught will be like the teacher." If this does belong to
the context of blind guides, then it affirms that the disciples of the Pharisaic scribes cannot be any more sighted than their teachers. The possibility is raised by H. Schürmann,
Das Lukasevangelium 1 (Freiburg, 1969), 369–70.

Woe to you lawyers! for you have taken away the key of knowledge; you did not enter yourselves, and you hindered those who were entering.

The metaphor behind both Luke's and Matthew's versions is that of the Kingdom of God as having a door through which one enters.[140] Thus, despite the differences in wording, the versions of both evangelists are very similar: for Matthew, the charge is that those trained in the Law ("lawyers") have shut the door to the Kingdom. For Luke, the charge is that they have taken away or hidden the key to the door. The key, which the scribes above all should have possessed, was the knowledge of God's will in the Torah.[141] Here Jesus claimed that the experts in Torah had an incorrect hermeneutic; it was not that they were negligent in their teaching,[142] but that the content or emphasis of their teaching was inappropriate. As is the case with blind guides and their followers falling into a pit, neither they nor their followers could enter the door without the key. Once again, the direction which Israel was to follow according to the hermeneutics of the scribes was contravened.

Money in Trust. Finally, the parable of money in trust (Matt. 25:14–30=Luke 19:12–27) brings together two lines of criticism: criticism of the preservative aspect of the holiness program and of the scribal interpreters responsible for it. The persuasiveness of the interpretation offered by Dodd and Jeremias has not been superseded.[143] Both agree that the parousia setting provided by Matthew and Luke, in which the departing master is Jesus, the return is the second coming, and those called to account to account for their stewardship are the leaders (or members) of the church, must be viewed as secondary. Both also note that the agreement between the Matthaean and Lucan versions is greatest in the reckoning scene with the third servant: everything else in the parable is subordinated to it.

The servant, entrusted with something of value by his master, upon which the master expected a return, was fearful of losing that with

---

140. Jeremias, *TDNT*, 3:747: "entry into the royal dominion of God" is a specifically Palestinian image; Aalen, " 'Reign' and 'House' in the Kingdom of God in the Gospels," 215–40; see pp. 233–40 for the Jewish background and 220–23, 228–29, for its use in the Gospels; Gaston, *No Stone on Another*, 229–40.

141. Jeremias, *TDNT*, 3:747; Manson, *Mission and Message*, 395; Caird, *Luke*, 159.

142. A possibility raised by Plummer, *Luke*, 314, who suggests that the fault may have been their failure to teach the common folk. But this is ruled out by the evidence that the scribes were willing to receive as pupils people of the most humble origin. Moreover, the saying declares not only that they did not give the key to others, but also that they did not possess the key themselves: "you did not enter yourselves."

143. Dodd, *Parables*, 114–21; Jeremias, *Parables*, 58–63, and his preceding exegesis of the "Servant entrusted with supervision" (Matt. 24:45–51=Luke 12:41–46), 55–58, to which this parable has affinities. J. Dupont, "La parabole des talents ou des mines," *RTPhil* 19 (1969): 376–91, largely follows Dodd's line of exegesis.

which he had been entrusted — so he buried it (Matthew) or wrapped it in a napkin (Luke). Now he is called to account for it: he has preserved it and hands it back to his master. But far from approving his act of preservation, the master reproves him severely and deprives him of what he has. Both Dodd and Jeremias then ask what the original audience would have understood by a servant entrusted with special responsibility, and both point to the understanding of God's relationship to Israel and its leaders as one of master to servant. At this point their interpretations diverge slightly: Dodd argues that the cautious servant would have been understood as the type of pious Jew represented by the Pharisees, whose policy of exclusion meant that God received no interest on the wealth with which they had been entrusted. Jeremias sees it as directed against the religious leaders, especially the scribes, who had withheld from people their share in God's gifts.

The interpretation which points to the role of the scribes as caretakers of the Torah may well be correct, for among the three things given as a deposit by God in Jewish thought was the Torah.[144] Here the great care which the servant exercised in preserving the entrusted deposit, a perfect image of the survival intention of the quest after holiness, was judged to be irresponsible. Both the concern for preservation and those responsible for it were pictured as carelessness masquerading as care. Implicit in this was an invitation to the hearers to make their own judgment that another course was more fitting. Something other than preservation was called for.

The Motif of Unproductivity. My final point concerning the contravention of the Pharisaic ideal does not require the exegesis of individual texts so much as it calls for observation of a theme which is common to several sayings and parables: unproductivity where something was expected. An absentee landlord expected a return from the tenants of his vineyard, but received none (Mark 12:1–9 par.); a vineyard owner looked repeatedly for figs on an unproductive fig tree (Luke 13:6–9; cf. Mark 11:12–14 par.); a master anticipated a profit from money entrusted to his servants (Matt. 25:14–30; Luke 19:11–27); another master expected his servant to discharge his responsibilities faithfully (Luke 12:42–46; Matt. 24:45–51); a sovereign found his forgiven steward acting in an unforgiving manner (Matt. 18:23–35); a father expected his son to work in the vineyard, but discovered that he had not (Matt. 21:28–32). Salt had lost its salinity (Matt. 5:13; Luke

---

144. Derrett, *Law in the New Testament,* 26–27. The other two are the soul and the riches of the world, neither of which seems appropriate to this parable. See M. Ab. 2:14–16.

14:34–35; Mark 9:50); light was not giving light but had been hidden (Matt. 5:15; Luke 11:33; Mark 4:21). In some cases the central point of the parable or saying may have been other than nonproductivity,[145] but the repeated presence of the motif in all the strands of the synoptic tradition calls for explanation. How are these recurrent figures and images to be understood? To whom do they apply?

For the most part, the Gospels apply them as warnings to the followers of Jesus in the post-Easter situation or, less commonly, to Israel's failure to respond to Jesus. But as Jeremias and Dodd above all have demonstrated, most originally applied to Israel or to those responsible for Israel's course.[146] Moreover, Israel's nonproductivity was not simply related to nonresponse to Jesus, though this was sometimes viewed as the culmination of unfruitfulness. Rather, the motif points to a situation of nonproductivity antedating the ministry of Jesus. Jesus' ministry did not initiate the crisis of unproductivity; his ministry was a response to the unfruitfulness that had characterized Israel for some indefinite period prior to the ministry. Furthermore, in some cases the criticism was specifically directed to the leadership of Israel,[147] presumably including the Temple hierarchy and scribal interpreters. Thus the motif of unproductivity points in the same direction as the texts on blind guides and the key of knowledge: a judgment upon those who had set Israel upon a course which, even if dominated by the quest for holiness, did not produce that which Yahweh desired.

Summary

The preceding material justifies the claim that Jesus' table fellowship was a protest against the Pharisaic understanding of Israel's historical character and destiny. It called into question the Pharisaic program of internal reform which, as one would expect, had implications for Israel's

---

145. For example, the element of crisis is often present and sometimes dominant. But there is still a difference between these texts and those parables dominated primarily by the motifs of crisis and unpreparedness, for these offer nonproductivity as the reason for the crisis.

146. Jeremias, *Parables*, 48–66; Dodd, *Parables*, 85ff. Exegeses of the above traditions are found on the following pages: Dodd, 93, 96–102, 108–21, 125–27; Jeremias, 55–58, 70–77, 120–21, 127, 168–71. C. W. F. Smith, *Jesus*, 157–64, 218–27, also shows a strong appreciation of the national application of many of these parables.

147. In addition to texts in which unproductivity appears, see also the intimations that Israel is leaderless, like sheep without a shepherd. See Mark 6:34, Matt. 9:36; cf. Matt. 9:24, 10:6; John 10:1–5 and the analysis thereof by J. A. T. Robinson, "The Parable of the Shepherd," *Twelve New Testament Studies* (London, 1962), 67–75. For shepherds as leaders of Israel, see Ezek. 34, Zech. 11, Num. 27:17, 1 Kings 22:17.

relation to the nations as well, which shall be dealt with later. Concerning the two practices which were qualifications for membership in a
Pharisaic *havurah*, Jesus denied the necessity of ritual washing of hands,
offering as justification the claim that holiness was not a matter of separation, and subordinated tithing to explicitly articulated concerns which
required a different dominant paradigm for understanding Yahweh and
the community that would be loyal to God.

The critique of holiness as the dominant paradigm of the people of
God continues throughout much of the teaching of Jesus. One cutting
edge of the story of the good Samaritan was that the quest for holiness could obstruct the exercise of compassion. Jesus pronounced in the
wrong the Pharisee at prayer who typified the quest, and the tax collector who appealed to the mercy of God was said to be in the right.
The "yes" which the righteous gave with both their voice and behavior
was understood as a failure to work in the vineyard. Jesus stigmatized as
leaven the teaching responsible for this understanding of Israel's task,
having a defiling effect, just as did unmarked graves. Scribal teachers
were pilloried as blind guides who did not have the key to the Kingdom
of God, and as having hidden that which had been entrusted to them
in order to preserve it. Not surprisingly, under this influence the fruit
which Israel was to yield to Yahweh was not forthcoming.

In short, Jesus' practice of table fellowship and his teaching concerning issues related to table fellowship contravened the understanding
of Israel as a holy, separated community. In this context, table fellowship cannot be described simply as festive celebration and acceptance.
Rather, it was a political act of national significance: to advocate and
practice a different form of table fellowship was to protest against the
present structures of Israel. Moreover, there was more than protest:
an alternative program was advocated for the people of God in their
historical existence. To this we turn in the next chapter.

CHAPTER FIVE

Jesus and the Quest for Holiness: The Alternative Paradigm

Though Jesus did not formulate a detailed program for Israel's life, his teaching did include a paradigm, or core value, for the construction of such a program, and broad indications of its effects on Israel's historical structures and future. In his challenge to the quest for holiness and his articulation of an alternative paradigm, Jesus followed both of the approaches open to an agent who challenges a dominant paradigm. On the one hand, he advocated a different paradigm, replacing holiness with compassion as the core value of Israel's life. On the other hand, he redefined holiness, transforming its meaning.

Substitution: Compassion Replaces Holiness

In our analysis of Jesus' criticism of the quest for holiness, we have already seen glimpses of the alternative paradigm. Consistently, "compassion" appears in opposition to holiness or to behavior mandated by holiness. To the meticulous tithing which derived from the paradigm of holiness, Jesus contrasted the triad compassion, faithfulness, and justice (Matt. 23:23). In the parable of the good Samaritan, the Samaritan's behavior was distinguished from that of priest and Levite by its quality of compassion: the Samaritan was the one who "had compassion" (Luke 10:33, 37). The father of the prodigal responded to his son's plight with compassion: "while the son was yet at a distance, his father saw him and had compassion and ran and embraced him and kissed him" (Luke 15:20). Implicitly, the question addressed to the elder son was, "Do you begrudge the fact that I have acted compassionately?"[1]

---

1. The parable of the workers in the vineyard (Matt. 20:1–15) makes a similar point. Spoken in all likelihood as part of Jesus' defense of his association with tax collectors and sinners (see Jeremias, *Parables*, 36–38, 136–39), the parable described a situation in which workers who had toiled all day complained because those who worked only an hour were

On two occasions attested by Matthew alone, Jesus contrasted holiness with compassion, citing Hos. 6:6 both times.[2] In the context
of Pharisaic criticism of Jesus' table fellowship with outcasts, Jesus retorted: "Go and learn what this means. 'I desire compassion and not
sacrifice'" (Matt. 9:13). The same verse is cited in the context of Pharisaic criticism of his disciples for breaking the sabbath, the maintenance
of which was absolutely central to the quest for holiness.[3]

> If you had known what this means, "I desire mercy [compassion] and not
> sacrifice," you would not have condemned the guiltless." (Matt. 12:7)

Since both of these are Matthaean additions to Marcan texts, they
have little claim to authenticity, though they do provide evidence that
the early community in Palestine (the Jesus movement itself) saw the
conflict in these terms.

The reference to compassion in the quotation from Hos. 6:6 reminds
us that the Hebrew Bible speaks very often about God as compassionate, as well as about human compassion.[4] Thus it was not new for Jesus
to emphasize compassion. What was remarkable is that he often spoke
of compassion in contexts where it was opposed to concerns mandated
by holiness as then understood.

The contrast continues in two important texts in which Jesus explicitly spoke of an *imitatio dei* whose content was compassion and which
specify with considerable precision the sense in which compassion
was meant.

Compassion as the Content of the *Imitatio Dei*

The heart of Jesus' ethic is the imitation of God. Observing that scholars have often treated Jesus' ethical teaching under the two rubrics of
love of God and love of neighbor (the "Great Commandment"), C. H.
Dodd notes that this was not Jesus' way of summing up his teaching. Instead, Jesus "when he is speaking in language of his own choice...says
(in effect) 'God is your Father; become what you are, his child.'" To be

---

paid the same as they were. The parable ends with the words of the employer to the
complainers: "Am I not allowed to do what I choose with what belongs to me? Or do you
begrudge my generosity?" (Matt. 20:15). As Jeremias notes, 37: "This is what God is like."

2. See David Hill, "On the Use and Meaning of Hosea vi. 6 in Matthew's Gospel,"
NTS 24 (1977): 107–19.

3. See chapter 6 below.

4. N. Snaith, *The Distinctive Ideas of the Old Testament* (London, 1944), 94–130;
A. Schulz, *Nachfolgen und Nachahmen* (Munich, 1962), 234–37; Bultmann, *TDNT*,
2:479–82.

God's child is to act on the maxim "Like father, like child ... to live as a child of God is to treat your neighbor as God treats you," to imitate in one's own behavior the "quality" and "direction" of God's activity.[5]

Jesus' ethic, in short, was based on an *imitatio dei*, just as the quest for holiness was based on an *imitatio dei*. Moreover, just as the Pharisaic *imitatio dei* was intended as a program for Israel's life, so it is reasonable to assume that the alternative *imitatio dei* of Jesus was intended as the guiding paradigm for Israel as a social reality.

This assumption is confirmed by two texts which speak of the alternative paradigm, the second of which most clearly provides specific application to Israel's life.

> *The Unmerciful Servant:* Therefore the Kingdom of heaven may be compared to a king who wished to settle accounts with his servants. When he began the reckoning, one was brought to him who owed him ten thousand talents; and as he could not pay, his lord ordered him to be sold, with his wife and children and all that he had, and payment to be made. So the servant fell on his knees, imploring him, "Lord, have patience with me, and I will pay you everything." And out of pity for him the lord of that servant released him and forgave him the debt. But that same servant, as he went out, came upon one of his fellow servants who owed him a hundred denarii, and seizing him by the throat he said, "Pay what you owe." So his fellow servant fell down and besought him, "Have patience with me, and I will pay you." He refused and put him in prison till he should pay the debt. When his fellow servants saw what had taken place, they were greatly distressed, and they went and reported to their lord all that had taken place. Then his lord summoned him and said to him, "You wicked servant! I forgave you all that debt because you besought me; and should not you have had mercy on your fellow servant, as I had mercy on you?" And in his anger his lord delivered him to the jailers, till he should pay all his debt. So also my heavenly Father will do to every one of you, if you do not forgive your brother from your heart. (Matt. 18:23–35)

In Matthew, the parable is set in the context of church practice. It is addressed to the disciples to stress the importance of their being willing to forgive. The fate of the unmerciful servant will be theirs also "if you do not forgive your brother from your heart."

Though this setting is recognized as secondary by almost every commentator, what Jesus meant when he spoke this parable is still most frequently stated as if Matthew's setting were original. The parable was, it is affirmed, addressed to those who knew the forgiveness of sins

---

5. Dodd, *Founder of Christianity,* 63–65.

through Jesus (i.e., to followers of Jesus, as in Matthew).[6] On this interpretation the historical parallel to the rescinding of the debt by the king was the forgiveness of sins bestowed by God through Jesus. But this interpretation is doubtful, both because it depends on the secondary context and because another interpretation is more natural.

The parable tells the story of a hopelessly indebted high official who, though he had been shown mercy[7] by his king, seized a fellow official by the throat and demanded repayment of a comparatively small sum owed to him. The colleague was unable to pay and the first official had him imprisoned. The king angrily recalled the first official and asked him the question which is the climax of the parable (v. 33): "should you not have had *mercy* on your fellow servant as I had *mercy* on you?"[8]

The point of the parable can be stated simply: mercy given is to have its consequences.[9] The mercy shown to the first servant should have had as its consequence the governance of his life by mercy.

This simple and very obvious reading means that we need not think of the audience as those who had experienced God's forgiveness through Jesus. Rather, it was a long-standing Jewish tradition that *Israel* lived under the mercy of God.[10] The parable suggests that taking seriously the mercy/compassion of God would mean embodying mercy/compassion.

Thus the parable invited the reflection that the fitting response of the people who lived under the compassion of God was compassion. Simultaneously, it warned of the threatening consequences of the failure to make compassion normative. Israel, who in its history knew God as compassionate, was to be a compassionate community. Indeed there is here an *imitatio dei,* the content of which is compassion.

---

6. E.g., Jeremias, *Parables,* 210–14, includes it in the section titled "Realized Discipleship"; that it is directed as a warning to those who have heard the offer of forgiveness *from Jesus* is clear especially on pp. 211 and 213. Perrin, *Rediscovering,* 126, states that it is addressed to those who know the Kingdom of God in terms of the forgiveness of sins; so also Manson, *Mission and Message,* 505–6.

7. *Note added in 1998:* In this parable, I am uncertain whether to use the word "mercy" or "compassion." The parable may be read to indicate that the king *felt* the steward's plight, and then "compassion" would be the better word. But if the language of forgiveness is metaphorized into a legal context, then "mercy" (with its connotation of letting somebody off the hook in spite of wrongdoing) may be the better word. Though a reasonable case can be made for both options, I decided to leave the English text as "mercy," primarily because the parable is commonly known as "The Unmerciful Servant."

8. For illumination of the customs reflected in the detail of the parable, see esp. Jeremias, *Parables,* 210–14, and Linnemann, *Parables,* 108–11, 175–77.

9. Linnemann, *Parables,* 111–12; 177, n. 17.

10. Cf. Linnemann, *Parables,* 178, n. 17: "If the parable was to be at all effective, it had to presuppose a knowledge of mercy received. Because Jesus' listeners were Jews, there were no difficulties in this."

The "Compassion Code"

The imperative to replace holiness as the content of the *imitatio dei* with compassion and the consequence of this substitution for the historical life of Israel are most clear in Luke 6:27–36=Matt. 5:38–48. This block of teaching echoes and modifies the Holiness Code of Leviticus 19 at crucial points.

The unmistakably Q portion reads:

> But I say to you, Love your enemies and pray for those who abuse you. To him who strikes you on the cheek, offer the other also; and from him who takes away your cloak do not withhold your undergarment as well. Give to everyone who begs from you. If you love only those who love you, what credit is that to you? For even the sinners [or "tax collectors"] love those who love them. But love your enemies and you will be sons of the Most High; for God is kind to the ungrateful and the selfish. *Be compassionate as God is compassionate.*

Both terminology and content point to the status of this section as articulating an alternative to the quest for holiness. The concluding saying of this block is strikingly parallel to the summation of the Holiness Code in Lev. 19:2, but with a decisive difference. "You shall be *holy* because I am *holy*" becomes "Be *compassionate* as God is *compassionate*."[11] That this saying echoed Lev. 19:2 is apparent,[12] and thus the replacement of holiness with compassion as the content of the *imitatio dei* was deliberate. Where the tradition of the scribes spoke of holiness as the paradigm for the community's life, Jesus spoke of compassion.

This conclusion is supported by the near silence of the synoptic tradition in applying the term "holy" to God or the community.[13] Even though one could argue that the holiness of God was presumed (and we shall see that it was, in modified form), the silence contrasts starkly

---

11. Luke 6:36. Matt. 5:48 has, "You therefore must be perfect as your heavenly Father is perfect." The difference between Luke's "compassionate" and Matthew's "perfect" is not crucial since the meaning is largely determined by the context which they share. Nevertheless, with the majority of commentators, I think Luke's reading is most likely that of Q: J. Piper, *"Love Your Enemies"* (Cambridge, 1979), 63, 146; Manson, *Mission and Message*, 347; Davies, *Setting of the Sermon on the Mount*, 209–10; Schürmann, *Das Lukasevangelium*, 1:360 and n. 119 with citation of literature; Schulz, *Nachfolgen*, 231–34; R. Schnackenburg, *The Moral Teaching of the New Testament* (London, 1965), 108; Barth, *Tradition and Interpretation in Matthew*, 97; against this is Black, *Aramaic Approach*, 181.

12. So Branscomb, *Jesus and the Law of Moses*, 249; H. J. Schoeps, *Aus frühchristlicher Zeit* (Tübingen, 1950), 290; Stendahl, *School of St. Matthew*, 134; McConnell, *Law and Prophecy*, 38–39; Schulz, *Nachfolgen*, 234; Wilder, *Eschatology and Ethics*, 120–21.

13. Only once: the first petition of the Lord's Prayer, where the passive voice indicates that it is God who is being asked to hallow the divine name. Thus even here it does not explicitly commend holiness in the community; indeed, it is significant that the only mention of human response in that prayer is tied to God's activity in forgiveness.

with the common expression of the rabbinic tradition, "The Holy One, blessed is he. . . . " How does one account for the double phenomenon: the replacement of holiness with compassion, and the absence of "holiness"?[14] The obvious suggestion is that it reflects a shift in dominant paradigms.

What is meant by the compassion of God is clarified by the verse immediately preceding the *imitatio dei*. Luke has, "God makes the sun rise on the evil and on the good, and sends rain on the just and the unjust." The thought is the same: the compassion of God is an *inclusive* compassion, embracing the selfish and the unselfish, the just and the unjust.

Though compassion as a quality of God is a major emphasis of the Hebrew Bible, both Christians and Jews have commonly limited the radical inclusiveness of compassion as we see it in Jesus. In the Hebrew Bible, "compassion" designated both a quality of God as well as an attribute of human behavior. The "compassion of God" established and sustained the covenant with Israel. *Hesed* — most commonly rendered by *eleos* in the LXX,[15] by "mercy" in the King James Version, and by "steadfast love" in the RSV — was a covenant word and emphasized steadfastness to a covenant and to those within it. From the same notion derived the postexilic *hasidim*,[16] marked by their steadfast loyalty to the Torah, including the separating function of the Torah.

Just as God's *hesed* established the covenant, so the covenant established the realm within which compassion operated. God's compassion was not granted to those outside the covenant relationship.[17] Similarly, human compassion is intrinsically tied to the community, moving outward in concentric circles from family to tribe to the people as a whole, but not to those outside the covenant.[18] The tendency to limit compassion primarily to one's own community is not, of course, a tendency peculiar to Judaism. It has been a persistent tendency within Christianity as well. Indeed, it is probably typical of most human groups. The in-group/out-group distinction is deeply embedded in culture.

But in the text we are looking at, God's compassion is not limited to

---

14. The reserve of the synoptic tradition is matched by the New Testament generally; though the holiness of God is everywhere presumed, it is seldom stated: John 17:11; 1 Pet. 1:15–16; Rev. 4:8, 6:10. See O. Procksch, *TDNT*, 1:101. On the other hand, "compassion" applied to God is common.

15. Bultmann, *TDNT*, 2:479–80.

16. See especially Snaith, *Distinctive Ideas*, 94–130, esp. 122–30; and W. Lofthouse, "*Chen* and *Chesed* in the Old Testament," *ZAW* 20 (1933): 29–35.

17. E. R. Achtemeier, *IDB*, 3:352: "Not once is God's mercy granted to those outside the covenant relationship."

18. *IDB*, 3:353.

those within the covenant. Instead, God's compassion is seen in the fact that the sun and the rain come to both the just and the unjust, i.e., to everybody, and not just to those with whom a special relationship exists.

Similarly, specific behavioral applications in the extended text point to the inclusiveness of compassion as a quality of human behavior. The practice of compassion was not to be limited by the expectation of reciprocity: do good even to those who abuse you, lend without expectation of return.

Even more strikingly, in a saying which also echoed the Holiness Code of Leviticus 19 even as it transformed it, what it meant to be compassionate not only transcended the covenant relationship, but also pertained directly to the conflict with Rome which flowed out of the quest for holiness.

In a saying derived from Q, Luke 6:27 implicitly refers to Lev. 19:18, and Matt. 5:43 explicitly quotes it: "Love your neighbor." But "neighbor" in the Holiness Code, consistent with the understanding of holiness as separation and of compassion as covenant loyalty, included only fellow Israelites and converts. "Neighbor" in Lev. 19:18 is parallel to "sons of your own people," and was thus often (and naturally) read as "fellow Israelite."[19] Nor was it expanded by the subsequent directive to love the sojourner in Israel (Lev. 19:34), for "sojourner" had come to mean convert or proselyte and did not embrace the non-Jew.[20] Thus "Love your neighbor" in the Holiness Code (at least by the time of the first century) meant "Love your compatriot," your fellow-member of the covenant.

But this understanding was contravened in the "compassion code" we are examining. Jesus said, in deliberate contrast to the limitation of love to one's compatriot, "Love your enemies." The antithesis is explicit in Matthew: "You have heard that it was said, 'You shall love your neighbor and hate your enemy,'[21] but I say to you, Love your en-

---

19. So also M'Neile, *Matthew,* 71; H. Marriott, *The Sermon on the Mount* (London, 1925), 192; Manson, *Mission and Message,* 453; O. Linton, "St. Matthew 5:43," *StTh* (1964): 69.

20. So it is rendered in the LXX of Lev. 19:33–34 and Deut. 10:18–19; see also O. J. F. Seitz, "Love Your Enemies," *NTS* 16 (1969–70): 48; Piper, *"Love Your Enemies,"* 30–32, 47–48, 91.

21. Since it is unlikely that Matthew's "hate your enemy" was part of the original saying, its specific origin need not detain us, though suggestions abound. That it refers to the teaching of Qumran, passages of which enjoin hatred of the enemy: Ellis, *Luke,* 115; Davies, *Setting of the Sermon on the Mount,* 213, 427; Merkel, "Jesus und die Pharisäer," 200, n. 4; Dodd, *Founder of Christianity,* 66, grants that Qumran may be in mind; Seitz, "Love Your Enemies," 49–51; Rowley, "The Qumran Sect and Christian Origins," 130. That it refers to a Targum or synagogue teaching which added hatred of enemies: Seitz, "Love Your Enemies," 42, 52; M. Smith, "Mt. 5:43: 'Hate Thine Enemy,'" *HTR* 45

emies." It is implicit in Luke: "*But* I say to you that hear, Love your enemies."[22]

"Love your enemies" thus had the connotation of "Love your non-compatriots." What would this have meant in teaching directed to Israel in the late twenties of the first century? It had an inescapable and identifiable political implication: the non-Jewish enemy was, above all, Rome. To say "Love your enemy" would have meant, "Love the Romans; do not join the resistance movement," whatever other implications it might also have had.[23] That it would carry this meaning in a milieu of political conflict is illustrated by what the saying would be understood to mean when uttered in a modern situation of conflict, whether in Northern Ireland or Central America or elsewhere. To say "Love your enemies" would have a concrete as opposed to generalized meaning. It would not simply inculcate a discarnate attitude of benevolence, but would mean to eschew acts of terrorism and revenge.[24]

The political implications of this saying are frequently denied. Sometimes it is claimed that the saying concerned the personal enemy within Israel, not the national enemy, and appeal is made to the use of *echthros* (personal enemy) rather than *polemios* (enemy in wartime) in Luke 6:27=Matt. 5:43–44.[25] But this distinction is impossible to maintain

(1952): 72. That it is a logical corollary of the biblical "to love," which means first of all "to favor, to select, to prefer"; to favor the neighbor entails to disfavor the other: Linton, "St. Matthew 5:43," 67–69. That it is intended in a comparative rather than antithetical sense: Banks, *Law in the Synoptic Tradition*, 200.

22. Luke has the strong adversative *alla*; and the expression *tois akouousin* may imply that the audience has heard something from elsewhere to which the word of Jesus is contrasted; see Seitz, "Love Your Enemies," 40–41; Piper, *"Love Your Enemies,"* 55.

23. Piper, *"Love Your Enemies,"* 98–99, agrees that it would have had this meaning, though he argues that the issue of national resistance is not the crucial context. M. Hengel, *Victory over Violence: Jesus and the Revolutionists* (Philadelphia, 1973), 49–50, also argues that "love of enemies" was spoken in *conscious* contrast to the "Zealot" option; to the resistance movement Jesus appeared simultaneously as both competitor and traitor (54).

24. The broader context of this block of material in Q may also be significant, where it is likely to have followed the Beatitudes (and "woes to the rich," if Q included them). So Luke has it, and Matthew preserves the same sequence, even though he separates love of enemies from the Beatitudes by the insertion of special material and Q material found elsewhere in Luke. The Beatitudes are addressed to the poor, the hungry, the sorrowing — roughly the same groups to which the resistance movement directed its message. See P. Hoffman, "Die Versuchungsgeschichte in der Logienquelle," *BZ* 13 (1969): 221; for the socio-economic concerns of the resistance movement, see *B.J.* 2.427; Hengel, *Die Zeloten*, 368–69; S. Applebaum, "The Zealots: The Case for Revaluation," *JRS* 61 (1971): 158–59, 167–68. If this connection also reflects the ministry, then to the same classes from which the freedom movement recruited adherents, Jesus urged, "Love your enemies."

25. Marshall, *Challenge of New Testament Ethics*, 119–20; Jeremias, *New Testament*

in the biblical tradition.[26] *Polemios* simply does not appear in the New Testament, and *echthros* therefore serves to denote both personal and national enemies (e.g., in Luke 1:71, 74). The rarity of *polemios* in the canonical LXX (three occurrences[27]) is striking compared to the over five hundred appearances of *echthros*, used for both personal and national enemies. Hence no significance can be assigned to the use of *echthros* rather than *polemios* in this saying. Moreover, as already noted, since *echthros* here stands in antithesis to "compatriot," it must mean non-Israelite, not the personal enemy within Israel.[28]

Perhaps more often it is claimed that the saying was not to be taken specifically or literally. Attention is drawn to the absurd consequence of understanding literally the adjacent command to yield to the one who steals the outer garment the inner one as well (the only two garments normally worn in first-century Palestine): nakedness. Instead, it is argued, the whole section illustrates the radically new approach to life which abandons natural pride, standing on one's own rights, and prudential considerations. Nowhere, it is claimed, is it more evident than here that Jesus' teaching "is spectacularly devoid of specific commandments."[29]

Yet the section itself calls this conclusion into question. Though hyperbole is present, the specificity of the illustrations is, if anything, even more apparent. This is especially clear in the related verse in Matt. 5:41 (M): "if anyone forces you to go one mile, go with him two miles." For decades it has been recognized that this referred explicitly to the right of a Roman legionnaire to require a civilian to carry his gear for one mile.[30] Though a slavish following of this command was not necessarily intended, the fact that it employed as an illustration the practice of Roman troops is surely significant.

Moreover, it is possible that the saying about the inner and outer garment also pointed to a practice of the occupation forces. If so, it in-

---

Theology, 213, n. 3; Montefiore, *Synoptic Gospels*, 2:71, 79, 85; Branscomb, *Jesus and the Law of Moses*, 247.

26. And elsewhere as well; W. Foerster, *TDNT*, 2:811, notes that Plutarch uses *echthros* to refer to the enemy in war.

27. 1 Chr. 18:10; Esther 9:16; 2 Esdr. 8:31.

28. Marriott, *Sermon on the Mount*, 191, offers additional support. "Love your enemy" *presented in antithesis* to what the hearers have heard cannot refer to a fellow Jew who has a personal enemy, for the Hebrew Bible already restricted hatred toward them: Ex. 23:4–5; Job 31:29–30; Prov. 20:22, 24:29, 25:21–22; Ecclus. 10:6; and, of course, Lev. 19:17–18.

29. Perrin, *Rediscovering*, 147–49; the quoted words are from p. 147.

30. L. Dougall, "The Salvation of the Nations," *Hibbert Journal* 20 (1921): 114; Montefiore, *Synoptic Gospels*, 2:74; Manson, *Mission and Message*, 452; Seitz, "Love Your Enemies," 52, n. 2; and Perrin himself, *Rediscovering*, 146.

vited a spirit toward the occupation forces which consented not only to deprivation of the outer garment, but "to be stripped to the skin."[31] Of course a literal fulfillment still issues in nakedness and it therefore may not be taken literally, but the specificity of the illustrations suggests that the commands were to be taken specifically. They did not refer simply to a style of life which did not insist on its own rights, but specifically to the issue of resistance to Rome. Indeed, could their point be missed in the historical situation of first-century Palestine?

To this command and the emulation of God's compassion from which it derived, the highest priority was attached. To fail to observe it was to become as a "tax collector" (Matt. 5:46) or a "sinner" (Luke 6:32). It was to become "one who has made himself a Gentile," and to forfeit one's standing as an Israelite. Conversely, those who observed it would be called "sons of God" (Matt. 5:45=Luke 6:35),[32] i.e., Israel.[33] Sonship in this text consists of being like the "Father" who is compassionate. The path of those who were truly Israel was to love the Roman enemy, in imitation of God the compassionate one who "makes the sun rise on the evil and on the good, and sends rain on the just and the unjust" (Matt. 5:45). To do otherwise was to sink to the level of the enemy: "for even the Gentiles love those who love them."

To the emphasis on love of enemies in the "compassion code" should be added several other synoptic passages. Two are peculiar to Matthew. The highest status is assigned to "peacemakers": "Blessed are the peacemakers, for they shall be called sons of God" (Matt. 5:9).[34] It is the same promise extended to those who show compassion by loving their enemies. According to Matthew, when one of those with Jesus as he was arrested struck the high priest's servant with a sword, Jesus said: "Put

---

31. J. S. Kennard, *Render to God* (New York, 1950), 36–37. In Matthew the saying envisions a lawsuit in which a person loses his undershirt (!); Luke, on the other hand, implies an unlawful seizure of the outer garment, the cloak. Citing Egyptian papyri (P. Oxy. 285, 394; B. G. U. 515), Kennard claims that when the manufacture of clothing ceased to be a government monopoly, Roman legions were empowered to requisition clothing from provincial civilians. Dougall, "The Salvation of the Nations," 114, connects the seizure to the activity of tax collectors, which gives to the illustration a similar import.

32. See the comment by Piper, *"Love Your Enemies,"* 62, which nicely links sonship, *imitatio dei,* and love of enemies: "sonship of God depends on acting like God: God is kind to his enemies; therefore anyone who wants to be a son of God must do the same."

33. See, e.g., Deut. 14:1, Hos. 1:19, Ps. Sol. 17:30, M. Aboth 3:15.

34. That this is not a spiritualized understanding of peace is indicated by Foerster, *TDNT,* 2:419: peacemaking "...denotes the establishment of peace and concord between men. It is thus a mistake to refer with Dausch to those who promote happiness and well-being. Nor is it a matter of helping others to peace with God, as Brouwer suggests. The reference is to those who disinterestedly come between two contending parties and try to make peace."

your sword back into its place; for all who take the sword will perish by the sword" (Matt. 26:52).[35]

Because these sayings are found in Matthew alone, they cannot with confidence be attributed to Jesus. But at the very least they are evidence of the early community's convictions, consistent with and most likely derived from Jesus' teaching on love of enemies. In traditions recorded in Luke alone, Jesus used the enigmatic phrase "sons of peace"[36] and in a passage which clearly speaks of war, lamented that Jerusalem did not know "the things that make for peace."[37] Finally, in a dramatic action reported by all three synoptic authors, Jesus entered Jerusalem on an animal which symbolized the way of peace instead of the way of war (Mark 11:1–10 par.).

All these traditions were directly pertinent to one of the central issues facing Israel and the renewal movements operating within it. These traditions flow out of compassion understood in an inclusive sense. Contrary to the "holiness code" which undergirded resistance, the "compassion code" urged love of enemies and the way of peace. Thus the "compassion code" strikes a new but complementary note. Whereas the other substitutions of compassion for holiness were concerned primarily with shaping the internal corporate life of Israel in the direction of greater inclusiveness, this material points specifically to the consequences of the shift of paradigms for Israel's relationship to Rome.

Thus Jesus' understanding of God as compassionate implied showing compassion to those outside the covenant and to those considered to have forfeited their status within the covenant (the outcasts). Though the understanding of *hesed* in the Hebrew Bible may stand behind the synoptic use of "compassion," *rahamim* and/or *chen* are more appropriate to the contexts in which "compassion" appears in the teaching of Jesus. *Rahamim* is the plural of a noun which in its singular form means

---

35. Why the disciples were armed is a puzzle. Luke even reports that Jesus at the end of his ministry ordered his disciples to purchase swords and that they already had two (Luke 22:35–38). Brandon, *Jesus and the Zealots*, repeatedly cites this incident as an indication that Jesus was sympathetic to the Zealots. Too much should not be made of this, however, as we do not know very much about the use of swords in first-century Palestine to warrant such a definite conclusion. Was it, for example, the custom of men leading an itinerant life to carry a sword, just as backpackers typically carry a hunting knife today? Did possessing a sword intrinsically imply the willingness to use it on a human, even if only in self-defense, or did swords have other important uses?

36. Luke 10:5–6. See William Klassen, "'A Child of Peace' (Luke 10:6) in First Century Context," *NTS* 27 (1981): 488–506, esp. 497–502.

37. Luke 19:42–44. For detailed exegesis and an argument that it is authentic to Jesus, see below pp. 199–201.

"womb."[38] To the extent that the plural form resonated with associations derived from the singular, one may speak (if it is not too daring) of God's compassion as God's *womblikeness* — life-giving, nourishing, perhaps embracing. When this understanding of compassion is also seen as the norm for human behavior, then the meaning of compassion has shifted from steadfast loyalty within a covenant, with its concomitant dimensions of reciprocity and exclusiveness, to a compassion which is inclusive and not limited.

This emphasis exploded the boundaries established by the quest for holiness understood as separation.[39] Based like the Pharisaic program on an *imitatio dei*, Jesus' paradigm pointed to a different aspect of God for primary emulation and thus to a different historical course for the people of God.[40]

The contrasting paradigms "holiness" and "compassion" did not, it must be stressed, point to an absolute difference between Jesus and his opponents. For first-century Judaism the claim that God was holy involved no denial that God was compassionate, loving, etc.,[41] though it did circumscribe the sphere within which people were to imitate the compassion and love of God. Similarly, for Jesus the claim that God was compassionate involved no denial that God was also holy. But it did involve both a shift in paradigms, already argued, and a corresponding modification of holiness, to which we now turn.

---

38. See esp. Phyllis Trible, *God and the Rhetoric of Sexuality* (Philadelphia, 1978), 31–59, esp. 33, 38–53.

39. Perhaps this expansive understanding of compassion is the new wine that threatens to break the old wineskins (Mark 2:21–22 par.).

40. Matt. 5:20 reports that Jesus spoke of the differentiation between his followers and the Pharisees not in terms of compassion versus holiness, but in terms of a "righteousness which exceeds that of the scribes and Pharisees." Since this saying is reported by Matthew alone, his context (which is obviously redactional) is the only guide we have for interpreting it. McConnell, *Law and Prophecy*, 37–38, argues convincingly that "you shall be perfect" in Matt. 5:48 defines the righteousness which *exceeds* that of the scribes and Pharisees: (a) both 5:20 and 5:48 give summaries of the life that corresponds to God's will; (b) just as 5:20 introduces the antitheses of the Sermon on the Mount, 5:48 concludes them; (c) forms of *perisseuein* are found in both 5:20 and 5:47. This permits McConnell to write, 37: "A perfection that corresponds to God's perfection is the righteousness that far exceeds that of the scribes and Pharisees." Barth, *Tradition and Interpretation*, 97, also argues that 5:48 defines 5:20: "perfect" in v. 48 "denotes the 'more' which distinguishes the doers of the teaching of Jesus from others"; moreover, it is not denied that the Pharisees are righteous, but the righteousness of the congregation of Matthew's day is to exceed that. The degree to which Matthew here also represents the original import of Jesus' word in 5:20 cannot be determined. But it is significant that the "more" expected from those who respond to Jesus is expressed in terms of perfect/compassion in a saying which echoes the summary of the "holiness code." Hill, "On the Use and Meaning of Hosea vi. 6 in Matthew's Gospel," 117, also suggests that the "higher righteousness" of Matt. 5:20 is compassion.

41. See also Schulz, *Nachfolgen*, 237.

Modification: Holiness as Transforming Power

Sayings *explicitly* modifying holiness are not to be found, since, as already noted, there is only one occasion upon which Jesus spoke of God as holy. What is to be found are sayings and narratives which implicitly presupposed a different understanding of holiness.

The criticisms of the Pharisees as leaven and as unmarked graves[42] implied that Israel was indeed intended to be the holy people of God. Only if this was so did it make sense to criticize the Pharisees as defiling and corrupting. The criticism also implied, of course, that holiness was to be understood differently than in the postexilic quest after holiness. There the holiness of God was understood to require protection, insulation from sources of defilement. Thus for Israel to be holy necessitated separation from the contagion of uncleanness. For uncleanness was not simply a lack of cleanness, but a power which positively defiled.[43]

But in the teaching of Jesus, holiness, not uncleanness, was understood to be contagious. Holiness — the power of the holy, of the sacred — was understood as a transforming power, not as a power that needed protection through rigorous separation. Such is implied in the metaphor of the physician in Mark 2:17 par., set in the context of table fellowship. Physicians are not overcome by those who were ill, but rather overcome the illness.

An understanding of holiness as a contagious power also lies behind several miracle stories. These cannot be used as direct evidence for the teaching of Jesus, since the relevant data lie in the narrative description of what happened, not in reported words of Jesus. Thus they provide evidence for the early community's understanding of the shift occasioned by Jesus' ministry. For the same reason, the question of the historicity of the miracles need not concern us, since our interest lies in the beliefs of the community to which the narrative accounts give expression.

In the healing of the leper in Mark 1:40–45, Mark reports that Jesus "stretched out his hand and *touched him* and said, 'Be clean.' " Leprosy excluded one from human community because it rendered one unclean, and everything touched by a leper became unclean.[44] For Jesus to touch a leper ought to have involved defilement, just as in touching a corpse.[45]

---

42. Mark 8:15; Luke 12:1; Matt. 16:6, 11–12; Luke 11:44; Matt. 23:27–28; see above pp. 125–30.

43. See, e.g., F. Hauck and R. Meyer, *TDNT*, 3:416, 418.

44. See Lev. 13:45–46; Num. 5:1–4; *S-B* 4:751–57. On holiness and leprosy, see H. van der Loos, *The Miracles of Jesus* (Leiden, 1968), 471–74.

45. Rawlinson, *Mark*, 21, n. 1; noted also by Cranfield, *Mark*, 92–93; Nineham, *Mark*, 87–88; Montefiore, *The Synoptic Gospels*, 1:39; A. Richardson, *The Miracle Sto-*

Yet the narrative reverses this: it was not Jesus who was made unclean by touching the leper. Rather, the leper was made clean. The viewpoint of the Jesus movement in Palestine[46] is clear: holiness was understood to overpower uncleanness rather than the converse.

Exactly the same transformation in the understanding of holiness underlies the account of the healing of the woman with a discharge in Mark 5:25–34. Her condition rendered her and all that she touched unclean (Lev. 15:25–30). Yet when she touched Jesus' garment, it was not uncleanness that was transferred, but rather "power went forth" from Jesus (5:30) and she was healed.

To these two narratives involving touch[47] should also be added narratives in which uncleanness is emphasized. The background detail of the story of the Gerasene demoniac (Mark 5:1–20) is a picture of absolute uncleanness: a man living among tombs, in Gentile territory, in proximity to swine, possessed by an unclean spirit — but all of this was overcome (including the destruction of the unclean swine!).[48] The exorcism accounts frequently portray Jesus in triumphant conflict with unclean spirits.[49] These stories, most or all current in a Palestinian milieu in which the significance of uncleanness was well understood, reflect the Jesus movement's affirmation that holiness, far from needing protection, was an active dynamic power that overcame uncleanness.

This dramatic reversal also lies behind Paul's words of advice to Christians in Corinth whose spouses were nonbelievers. Do not leave them, he writes in 1 Cor. 7:12–14 (unless the unbelieving partner wished a separation), "for the unbelieving husband is *sanctified* by the wife, and the unbelieving wife is *sanctified* by the husband; if this were not the case, your children would be *unclean*, whereas they are in

---

ries of the Gospels (London, 1941), 60–61; McConnell, *Law and Prophecy,* 81–82; van der Loos, *Miracles of Jesus,* 485. Because of the issue of defilement involved, F. Mussner, *The Miracles of Jesus* (Shannon, 1970), 28–37, understands this miracle as one of several with an "anti-Pharisaic front."

46. Bultmann, *History of the Synoptic Tradition,* 240, points out that the detail about showing one's self to the priest could hardly originate in a non-Palestinian milieu; Jeremias, *New Testament Theology,* 92, also notes marks of primitiveness.

47. Cf. the comment of M. D. Hooker, "Interchange in Christ," *JTS* 22 (1971): 351n: in certain miracle stories, "Jesus touches (or is touched by) those who, according to Jewish law, are unclean, which should make him unclean also. Instead of becoming unclean, however, or perhaps in spite of it, he is able to overcome the power of defilement, and to make those with whom he comes in contact clean."

48. Cf. the comment of Nineham, *Mark,* 151: "This is the first time in the Gospel that Jesus has been in Gentile territory, so it is noteworthy that his holy presence routs and banishes the uncleanness."

49. Mark 1:23–27 (note that the unclean spirit addresses Jesus as "the *Holy* One of God"); 7:24–30; 9:14–27; summary accounts in 3:11, 6:7.

fact *holy*." Here the "clinging and infectious force"[50] of impurity was replaced by an understanding of holiness as infectious.

This prodigious modification of holiness in both Paul and the Palestinian church is best explicable as derivative from (and evidence for) the practice of Jesus. He implicitly modified the understanding of holiness. No longer was holiness understood to need protection, but as an active force which overcame uncleanness. The people of God had no need to worry about God's holiness being contaminated. In any confrontation it would triumph.

The Consequences of Compassion

Jesus' understanding of God as compassionate and of the norm for Israel's development as compassion accounted for his opposition to the quest for holiness. The shift in paradigms was directly responsible for the two highly specific yet centrally important applications treated in the last two chapters: table fellowship with outcasts and love of enemies. The first was possible because God was compassionate — that is, forgiving, accepting, nourishing of righteous and sinner alike. Because God accepted such as these, God's children — Israel — were to do so as well. For Israel's internal life, this understanding pointed toward greater inclusiveness, toward an overcoming of the "intracultural segregation" which increasingly marked its life. The second was possible and necessary for the same reason, but with primary implications for Israel's "external" life, its relationship to Rome. To be compassionate meant to eschew the path of violence.

Strikingly, these two applications are the two chief marks of the Jesus movement itself. Operating in Palestine in the crucial generation between 30 and 70 c.e., it was, according to Gerd Theissen's study, the inclusive movement and the "peace party" among the renewal groups. It intensified the Torah in such a way as to render meaningless the distinction between righteous and sinner,[51] and it renounced the path of national resistance as well as providing multiple means of overcoming aggressive impulses.[52]

For Israel this shift in paradigms created new possibilities both for its internal reform and relationship to the world, possibilities effectively

---

50. Hauck, *TDNT*, 3:429; for the intriguing suggestion that the question concerns a Jewish-Christian *haver* married to a Jewish-Christian *am ha-aretz*, see J. M. Ford, "'Hast Thou Tithed Thy Meal?' and 'Is Thy Child Kosher?'" *JTS* 16 (1966): 71–79.

51. Theissen, *Sociology of Early Palestinian Christianity*, esp. 78–80, 103–7.

52. Ibid., esp. 64–65, 99–110, 114.

closed by the postexilic quest for holiness. The same understanding of compassion and reinterpretation of holiness which made it possible for the table fellowship of Jesus to embrace tax collectors and sinners made possible an abandonment of the policy of isolation from the larger world, a possibility which the post-Easter Gentile mission realized.

Yet it was first of all a possibility for Israel, not only because Jesus restricted his mission to Israel, but because the evidence is overwhelming that he intended this policy as a corporate (i.e., national) course for the people of God, not simply as a means of reconciling otherwise lost individuals to God. Only if this is true does his choice of table fellowship, that microcosm of Israel's collective life, as the arena in which to do battle, make sense. Only so does his criticism of Pharisaism, based not upon their alleged hypocrisy but upon their program for the people of God, become meaningful.

Would following the paradigm of compassion have meant the loss of a distinctive identity and thus have posed a threat to the survival of the Jewish tradition, as Jesus' opponents apparently feared? To attempt to answer is to speculate. One can say that to live with compassion as one's overarching norm does not necessarily involve the loss of a distinctive identity that persists through time, as religious orders throughout the world have sometimes demonstrated through lives dedicated to compassion even though marked by highly specific practices. Indeed, the capacity to be compassionate probably flows out of the distinctive lifestyle and identity.

Moreover, Jesus himself did not oppose the distinctiveness of the Jewish tradition. So far as we know, he never set aside the written Torah. Consistently, his disputes with his opponents concerned the *interpretation* of the Torah, not the validity of the Torah itself. The Matthaean passage on the eternal validity of the Torah reflects the posture of the Jesus movement and probably the attitude of Jesus himself: "Think not that I have come to abolish the Torah and the prophets; I have come not to abolish them but to fulfill them. For truly, I say to you, till heaven and earth pass away, not an iota, not a dot, will pass from the Torah until all is accomplished."[53] The Jesus movement also continued to worship in the Temple and follow religious practices such

---

53. Matt. 5:17–18. Whether authentic to Jesus or the product of the Jesus movement, the passage suggests that the issue is the *interpretation* of the Torah, not whether loyalty to Torah is essential (though it makes that claim). The introductory words ("*Think not that I have come to abolish the Torah . . .*") suggest that Jesus (or his movement) had been saying things which somebody thought to be a denial of Torah. Since the following affirmation denies this, it is likely that the suspicion and response were based on different interpretations of Torah, not on whether or not Torah as a whole was valid.

as prayer and fasting. In short, the substitution of compassion for holiness need not have meant the dissolution of Israel, even though it burst the limitations of holiness as a corporate ideal.

Just as orthodox Judaism today may be thought of as a religious order within society, a religious community with a very distinctive identity and life-style, so also the Pharisees (the ancestors of orthodox Judaism) and Jesus movement may be thought of as religious orders living within first-century Jewish society. The first, committed to the actualization of holiness, had narrow and sharp boundaries. The second, animated by the vision of compassion, had broad and very indistinct boundaries. Though it maintained its own identity, it sought, on the one hand, not to judge that some were beyond God's compassion and, on the other hand, to embrace all, even the outcasts, seeing them as also affirmed by the compassion of God.

Epilogue: Jesus and the Pharisees

The Gospel portrait of the Pharisees as the antitype of true piety has posed a problem since the modern rediscovery of the genuine devotion and piety of the Pharisees. About the earnestness of their concern, the integrity of their intent, and their loyalty to Yahweh, there can be little doubt. "It was not a sinning generation," writes Jacob Neusner about the generation living before the war of 66–70, "but one deeply faithful to the covenant and the Scripture that set forth its terms, perhaps more so than many who have since condemned it."[54]

It has seemed that either one must deny the validity of modern scholarship's picture of the Pharisees in order to save the honor of Jesus[55] or, more commonly, save the honor of both Jesus and the Pharisees by explaining away the Gospel picture of conflict. Sometimes it is affirmed that Jesus criticized only some of the Pharisees, just as the rabbinic literature itself records criticisms of five classes of Pharisees.[56] For this view, Jesus criticized only those who were "fraudulent";[57] indeed,

---

54. Neusner, *Yohanan ben Zakkai*, 11.

55. The more unflattering portions of the Gospel portrait were still repeated well into this century. For example, Schnackenburg, *Moral Teaching of the New Testament*, 66–73, speaks of the "false piety and vanity," "mendacity and hypocrisy" of the Pharisees. Marshall, *Challenge*, 10, 42, 54, 66–67, speaks of their "ostentatious piety," "punctiliar regard for ceremonial law combined with the frequent monstrous neglect of the moral law," "harshness in judgment of others," "contempt for the masses," "self-satisfied cocksureness," etc.

56. Sot. 22b; Jer. Ber. 9:14b; cf. M. Sot. 3:4.

57. Manson, *Mission and Message*, 391.

he levelled the same indictments which any authentic Pharisee would have made, and thus the honor of both Jesus and *authentic* Pharisaism is saved.[58] Or a radical change in Pharisaism is posited after 70 C.E. under the guidance of Yohanan ben Zakkai, and it is this mature and truly pious Pharisaism that has been rediscovered by modern scholarship. Prior to 70, some affirm, Pharisaism was inchoate and probably included elements which wholly merited the castigations recorded in the Gospels.[59] Here the honor of Jesus and *post*-70 Pharisaism is saved. Alternatively, the hostile passages are explained as the retrojection of the early Christian movement's growing conflict with the synagogue into the ministry itself. Here the honor of both Jesus and the Pharisees is saved by attributing the most unflattering strokes of the portrait to a harassed Christian movement whose distress understandably produced virtually unrestrained abuse.[60]

It has even been claimed that the mutual hostility was due to a communication problem and personality clash. Jesus saw the Pharisees only from the outside, and they never could understand him.[61] And so the honor of both is saved by attributing a certain dullness of mind to each.

Each of the above explanations accepts the Gospel picture of the conflict as one between individual styles of piety and then seeks either to find Pharisees who deserve the epithets or some situation in the early Christian movement in the decades after Easter that explains the indictments in their present form. The effect of this is to minimize the conflict between Jesus and the Pharisees.

True, there is some validity in many of the above claims.[62] Yet a close

---

58. K. Kohler, "Pharisees," *JE* 9:665; J. Z. Lauterbach, "The Pharisees and Their Teachings," *HUCA* 6 (1929): 139; H. Loewe, "Pharisaism," in W. O. E. Oesterley, ed., *Judaism and Christianity: The Age of Transition* (London, 1937), 1:179–88; Manson, *Mission and Message*, 391; Pawlikowski, "On Renewing the Revolution of the Pharisees," 425–27.

59. F. C. Burkitt, "Jesus and the Pharisees," *JTS* 28 (1927): 392–97. Finkel, *The Pharisees*, 133–42, emphasizes that the woes were addressed to the school of Shammai, which largely disappeared after 70.

60. Most thoroughly by Winter, *On the Trial of Jesus*, 111–35.

61. R. T. Herford, *The Pharisees* (London, 1924), 202; *Judaism in the New Testament Period* (London, 1928), 200–201. Noting that Jesus allegedly met few Pharisees in Galilee, he continues: "Each was seen by the other in the least favorable aspect. The Pharisees never saw him, and never could see him, as his friends of the multitude saw him. And he never saw the Pharisees with any sympathetic discernment of what they really meant by their religion. He saw, as an outsider could only see, what they did; and like any outsider, he had no clue to understand why they did it."

62. For example, undoubtedly there were some Pharisees whose integrity was questionable, just as there were such Christians; there were some significant differences between pre- and post-70 Pharisaism; the developing synoptic tradition did at times insert "Pharisees" into contexts where the opponents of Jesus were either unidentified or otherwise identified; some of the sayings do reflect the conflict between church and synagogue.

examination of the tradition demonstrates that the conflict was real, though not fundamentally about whether Pharisaic piety was genuine or sham, subjectively considered. Rather, the conflict had a pointed historical reference to the issue facing the nation: the validity of the quest for holiness as the vocation of Israel, and whether that quest was to dominate both the internal reform of Judaism and its relation to the Gentile world.

In his practice of table fellowship and in his spoken defense of this practice, Jesus answered with an unmistakable "no." Instead he called Israel to imitate the compassion of God, to affirm holiness as a power active in the world which, far from needing protection, hallowed that which it touched.

Yet even while challenging the religio-cultural program of the Pharisees, he showed himself to be like the Pharisees in a crucial respect. He too was concerned with the purpose of the people of God in the world, with their collective historical life and the structures thereof. For he did not challenge Pharisaism in the name of a religious individualism separated from a historical community, but in the name of a different paradigm for and vision of the people of God.

Indeed, the *ideological* nature of the conflict between Jesus and the Pharisees accounts for the intensity. According to studies of social conflict, conflict reaches "its most intense level" when it concerns "competing views of the same ideology," for what is at stake for the antagonists "is a matter of one's entire universe," of the "social world" in which one lives. Moreover, "the closer the relationship" between the antagonists, "the more intense the conflict."[63] Thus the similarity between Jesus and the Pharisees — sharing the same tradition, struggling with the same questions, competing for the allegiance of the same people — accounts for the depth of the conflict between them.

In the same manner, the enmity of the Pharisees was not because they were "evil men," resentful that the teacher from Nazareth exposed their "hypocrisy" and "mendacity." Rather, they perceived the program of Jesus as a threat to the symbols and institutions which provided the cohesiveness necessary for the continued existence of the people of God in a world in which the winds of change threatened that existence. Their intent was altogether noble and admirable: to preserve a people who would worship and serve Yahweh.[64] They understandably viewed

---

63. The quoted phrases are from Gager, *Kingdom and Community*, 82–83. Gager draws the propositions about conflict from Lewis Coser, *The Function of Social Conflict* (New York, 1956); he does not apply them to Jews and Pharisees, but to conflict between Judaism and early Christianity and within early Christianity itself.

64. Klausner, *Jesus of Nazareth*, 369ff., similarly argues that the opponents of Jesus

the teaching of Jesus as "the breaking down of the fence around the garden, instead of the bursting of the shell for the release of the living power."[65]

Most frequently the Gospels do present the hostility between Jesus and the Pharisees in other terms, as one between genuine and false piety. Whereas the Pharisees were hypocrites, Christians were to be sincere; whereas the Pharisees were ostentatious, Christians were to be humble; whereas the Pharisees were arrogant, Christians were to be gracious; whereas the Pharisees concerned themselves about external rectitude, Christians were to recognize that true goodness is a matter of the heart. It is altogether understandable that the evangelists should often cast the conflict in these terms. To some extent writing for Christians geographically and culturally distant from the conflict, they sought to give the controversy an immediate and permanent edifying content, and they did so by transforming it into a struggle over types of individual piety.

Yet it is equally clear that this was not the original substance of the conflict. Sometimes the tradition has preserved variants of the same saying whose differences point to the original national thrust. In other instances it is clear that the original hearers could only have derived a meaning quite different from that possible for later Christians. This is a result of primary significance for method: behind the present references to more or less permanent spiritual issues facing the individual, often the tradition originally had a pointed reference to specific identifiable cultural-religious issues.

Ultimately, the conflict between Jesus and the Pharisees was a hermeneutical battle between compassion and holiness, a struggle concerning the correct interpretation of Torah.[66] To call it a hermeneutical battle may seem too theological or intellectual, given the complex social matrix of economic/political/cultural factors. But because of the central role which religion played in structuring their social world, it was a hermeneutical battle with historical-political consequences, of which both Jesus and his opponents seemed to be aware.

---

feared that his teaching would dissolve the cords which bound the nation together; however, he sees Jesus as offering only a program for individuals, not for Israel.

65. H. H. Rowley, *Israel's Mission to the World* (London, 1939), 76. His judgment on 77–78 has affinities to the above: "The attitude of the Pharisees to the new offshoot of Judaism was wrong, but it was wrong not because Pharisaism was evil through and through, a sham and a snare, but because Pharisaism contained so much that was good and great, because the life that had been fostered under its protecting care was now ready to burst forth, and they knew it not." C. H. Dodd has consistently understood the conflict in these terms: see, e.g., *More New Testament Studies*, 92–96; *Founder of Christianity*, 77.

66. See above p. 86 and n. 103.

We shall explore Jesus' perception of the consequences of the hermeneutic of holiness for Israel's historical course in chapters on the Temple
and the future. But first we will examine the other major controversy
between Jesus and the Pharisees, second only to table fellowship: the
conflict over the sabbath, an institution essential to Israel's holiness.

CHAPTER SIX

Jesus and the Quest for Holiness: The Sabbath

No aspect of the quest for holiness was so publicly visible to the non-Jewish world as the observance of the sabbath.[1] By the first century it had become one of the hallmarks of Judaism, widely commented upon by writers in the Greco-Roman world[2] and exploited by Gentiles when attacking or persecuting Israel.[3] Their perception of its importance was accurate. Within Judaism, proper observance of the sabbath was not only a central religious practice, but integral to the quest for holiness, and an increasingly important symbol of loyalty to the covenant and hence of Israel's solidarity.

The command to observe the sabbath was the only one of the Ten Commandments explicitly linked to holiness:

> Remember the sabbath day, to keep it *holy*. Six days you shall labor, and do all your work; but the seventh day is a sabbath to the LORD your God; in it you shall do no work . . . for in six days the LORD made heaven and earth, the sea, and all that is in them, and rested the seventh day; therefore the LORD blessed the sabbath day and *hallowed* it. (Ex. 20:8–11; cf. Deut. 5:12–15)

Mythically and psychologically, sabbath observance functioned to create one day of "sacred time" each week: a day in which the world reverted to the time before human work on and in the world began, to the "time" before time, the time of the beginning. Thus it was one of the central religious practices of ancient Israel, one of the chief instrumental means for providing an awareness of the holy.

---

1. See the comment of Safrai, *Compendia* I.2:804. The sabbath was "so characteristic that hardly any text, Jewish or non-Jewish, omits to mention it when speaking of the Jews of [this] period."

2. Juvenal, *Satires*, 14.96–106; Tacitus, *Hist.* 5.4; Persius, 5.179–84; Martial, 4.4.7; Seneca, quoted by Augustine, *City of God*, 6.11; Agatharcides, quoted by Josephus, *Ap.* 1.209–10.

3. 1 Macc. 1:45–56; 2:32–38; 2 Macc. 5:25–26; 6:6, 11; *Ant.* 14.63–64; 18.319–22, 354.

Because of the sabbath's explicit connection to holiness, the post-exilic quest for holiness naturally emphasized it. The small size of the Jewish community after the return from exile intensified the need for distinctive symbols of loyalty. The sabbath was an eternal sign of Yahweh's covenant with Israel, to be observed forever.[4] Violation of it was not simply a personal matter, but a national concern: its disregard was understood to be a major cause of the calamity which crushed Judah in 586 B.C.E.[5] Indeed, it has been claimed that the sabbath was "the most important part of the divine Law" for the postexilic community: "That Yahweh gave the Law and that he commanded the sanctifying of the Sabbath mean much the same thing."[6]

The persecutions, martyrdoms, and threat to Israel's corporate existence under Antiochus Epiphanes in the second century B.C.E. made the symbolic significance of loyalty to the sabbath even greater.[7] The explication of what was permitted and forbidden became more precise, a development that culminated in the rabbinic tractates Shabbath, Erubin, and Betzah. Throughout the period, the rabbinic schools devoted much attention to sabbath statutes. Thirty-nine categories of work were prohibited, and each of these categories was eventually subdivided into six and then thirty-nine prohibitions in a process that continued well into the present era.[8] Sabbath law became "one of the most developed fields of rabbinic law"; and for Pharisees, the party in public life most rigorously committed to holiness, "precise observance" of it was "among the more important matters which separated the Pharisees from ordinary Jews."[9]

Yet this did not transform the sabbath into a burden, for clearly it was a joyful occasion.[10] Indeed, much of the legislation explicated what was permitted, thereby easing the restrictive character of the prohibitions.[11] The penalty for transgression was death, though it is doubtful

---

4. Ex. 31:13, 16; Ezek. 20:12, 20; Jub. 2:19, 31; 50:9–10.

5. Jer. 17:19–27; Ezek. 20:13, 16, 21, 24; 22:8, 26; 23:38.

6. E. Lohse, *TDNT*, 7:5.

7. E. G. Hirsch, "Sabbath," *JE* 10:558.

8. Jer. Shab. 9b–c; Moore, *Judaism*, 2:28; cf. E. Stauffer, *Jerusalem und Rom im Zeitalter Jesu Christi* (Bern, 1957), 64: "Die grosze Spezialität der rabbinischen Thoraexegese und pharisäischen Thorapraxis ist das Sabbathgebot."

9. M. Smith, "The Dead Sea Sect in Relation to Ancient Judaism," *NTS* 7 (1960–61), 354.

10. J. Morgenstern, *IDB*, 4:140; Montefiore, *The Synoptic Gospels*, 1:63–64; Hirsch, "Sabbath," 590, 597–98; Moore, *Judaism*, 2:34–38; Manson, *Mission and Message*, 481.

11. Moore, *Judaism*, 2:30–31; Bowman, *Mark*, 119, contrasts the delight of a sabbath spent with a strict rabbinic family to the somber *au pied de la lettre* observance of the Samaritans and Qaraites.

that this was often enforced;[12] it is most likely an expression of the centrality of the institution. In similar fashion, the great accolades to the sabbath should be understood as expressions using metaphysical and cosmological language to articulate the importance of sabbath observance.[13]

All of this points to the paramount significance of this institution which was also a symbol. Jews had died rather than desecrate it. Loyalty to it was the "touchstone of allegiance" to Israel and Yahweh, distinguishing the "true Jew from the cosmopolite or the apostate"[14] and guaranteeing the survival of Israel in a hostile world. Thus for Israel, threatened both by persecution and assimilation, and in particular for those committed to holiness understood as separation, sabbath observance became "the chief way of preserving Jewish communal identity and the Jewish vocation."[15]

Confirmation of the life-and-death significance of loyalty to the sabbath is found in the New Testament. Mark and John *independently* attribute the initial movement to put Jesus to death to the hostility aroused by his violation of the sabbath.[16] This charge reflects either the bitter controversy between the Jesus movement and the synagogue over sabbath observance, or it is accurate historical recollection of fatal hostility between Jesus and his opponents (or both). In either case, it indicates that sabbath violation by a teacher and/or the community around him exceeded the limits of tolerance of first-century Judaism and further demonstrates the central symbolic significance of sabbath fidelity.

Thus modern criticism of first-century sabbath legislation as irksome, burdensome, tyrannical, or casuistical misses the point.[17] Not only does such criticism imply that any relatively enlightened person could have recognized it as foolishness, which demeans both Jesus and his opponents, but it ignores the three central points in which the preceding can be summarized: the sabbath provided a joyful entry into "sacred time"; it seemed necessary for the survival of the people of God, a bul-

---

12. Ex. 31:14–15; Num. 15:32–36; Jub. 2:25, 27; 50:8, 13. An execution is referred to in Yeb. 90b, Sanh. 46a. A lightening of penalties is observable in M. Shab. 7:1–4.

13. For example: God created the sabbath before the creation of the world; people become co-creators of the world through sabbath observance; Israel brings redemption to the world by observing the sabbath. See Abrahams, *Studies*, 1:129; E. Lohmeyer, *Das Evangelium des Markus* 15 (Göttingen, 1959), 63.

14. Moore, *Judaism*, 2:26; cf. Parkes, *Foundations of Judaism and Christianity*, 175–76.

15. Pawlikowski, "On Renewing the Revolution of the Pharisees," 425.

16. Mark 3:6; John 5:16, 7:19–23.

17. For all of these charges, see, e.g., Major, *Mission and Message*, 57–58.

wark against Hellenistic homogenization; and it was understood as one
means par excellence by which Yahweh's holiness was honored.

Jesus and the Sabbath

Controversy between Jesus and his opponents concerning the sabbath
is one of the best attested features in the Gospels. It is found in three
of the four traditions behind the synoptics[18] and absent only from Q,
which is hardly surprising since Q contained but one narrative. Moreover, the independent tradition behind the fourth Gospel contained two
sabbath controversy stories.[19] Thus, though individual details in the stories may be products of the primitive community or evangelists, there
can be little doubt that this multiple attestation certifies the presence
of sabbath controversy in the ministry of Jesus.[20]

Furthermore, the tradition strongly suggests that Jesus deliberately
chose the sabbath as an issue over which to do battle. The synoptics (and John) consistently affirm that Jesus, not the afflicted, took
the initiative in healings *on the sabbath.*[21] Indeed, the afflicted, according to the Marcan narrative, expected to wait until the sabbath was
over: "That evening, at sundown (i.e., when sabbath had ended), they

---

18. In Mark: 2:23–28, 3:1–6; in L: Luke 13:10–17, 14:1–5; in M: the independent
saying Matt. 12:11–12, and the perhaps Matthaean construction Matt. 12:5–7.

19. John 5:1–18, 9:1–17; cf. 7:19–24. Dodd, *Historical Tradition*, 178, 185, affirms
that mention of the sabbath in 5:1–18 may have been part of the tradition which John
received, though he doubts that it was integral to the narrative behind 9:1–17.

20. Cf. E. Lohse, "Jesu Worte über den Sabbat," in *Judentum, Urchristentum, Kirche:
Festschrift für Joachim Jeremias* (Berlin, 1964), 84. D. Flusser, *Jesus* (New York, 1969), 49–
50, has challenged this conclusion by arguing that healing by word (as distinct from using
physical means) was always permitted on the sabbath, even when there was no danger to
life, and that Jesus' sabbath healings in the synoptics (though not in John) thus conform
to Jewish law. The implication is that there can have been no controversy over Jesus'
sabbath healing; the anger of his opponents was due instead to their *inability* to catch him
violating the law (50). Yet the sabbath controversies are so deeply embedded in the tradition that they must be granted evidential value. Explanations are possible which grant
the validity of Flusser's point though not his inference. Perhaps the healings *did* involve
physical means, the details of which were not retained because they were considered irrelevant or irreverent (note that both Matthew and Luke omit the two Marcan healings
[7:32–35, 8:23–26] which involved the use of spittle). Or perhaps there was a prohibition
of healings by word even though extant Jewish sources do not preserve it. Westerholm,
Jesus and Scribal Authority, 149, n. 18, rejects Flusser's claim that healings by word were
permitted.

21. Mark 3:3; Luke 13:12, 14:1–6; John 5:1–18, 9:1–17. the question of initiative is
slightly obscured in Mark 1:21–28 since the demon initiates the conversation; even so,
it can be said that the demon fears that Jesus will take the initiative. In John, it is Jesus
who gives the command to violate the sabbath in 5:8: "Rise to your feet, *take up your bed
and walk.*"

brought to him all who were sick..." (Mark 1:32–34). On the other hand, the afflicted always took the initiative in healings performed on days other than the sabbath.[22] From this remarkably consistent pattern emerges the conclusion that Jesus' healings on the sabbath, as in the case of table fellowship, were deliberate revolutionary gestures — perhaps done for the sake of teaching, or for demonstrating the purpose of the sabbath. That this was so is supported also by the fact that Jesus' sabbath healings never involved cases in which there was danger to life. That he did not wait until the day after sabbath suggests deliberate provocation. Jesus, not his opponents, chose to make the sabbath an issue.

But why? Various answers are given. Sometimes the sabbath controversies are seen as a conflict between humanitarian concerns versus law, or even as one between permissiveness and restrictiveness, as if, for example, the real issue in plucking corn on the sabbath were one of convenience versus inconvenience. My claim is twofold: that the sabbath controversies are best understood as another manifestation of the conflict between holiness and compassion, and that both the opposition to and the actions of Jesus reflected an awareness of the politico-religious situation of first-century Palestine.

The Non-Marcan Sabbath Controversies

The non-Marcan sabbath conflict stories all follow a common pattern. Jesus, taking the initiative, healed a person in the presence of opponents and then legitimated his action with a rhetorical question that referred to common human behavior. Two are peculiar to Luke:

> Luke 13:15–16: Does not each of you on the sabbath untie his ox or his ass from the manger and lead it away to water it? Then ought not this woman, a daughter of Abraham whom Satan bound for eighteen years, be loosed from her bond on the sabbath?

> Luke 14:5: Which of you having a son[23] or an ox that has fallen into a well will not immediately pull him out on a sabbath day?

---

22. Mark 1:32–34, 40–45; 2:1–12; 5:21–43 (two healings); 6:53–56; 7:24–30, 31–37; 8:22–26, 9:14–29; 10:46–52. Luke 7:1–10=Matt. 8:5–13. Luke 7:11–17; 17:11–19. In Mark 5:1–20, the question of initiative is again obscured by a conversation with a demon.

23. The textual variant "son" is probably to be preferred to the RSV's "ass" and NEB's "donkey." See Banks, *Jesus and the Law*, 128, n. 1.

In neither case did the opponents reply; they were put to silence. The same style of argument is found in the saying which Matthew added to the Marcan story of the man with the withered hand:

> Matt. 12:11-12: What man of you, if he has one sheep and it falls into a pit on the sabbath, will not lay hold of it and pull it out? Of how much more value is a man than a sheep!

In each case, Jesus invited them to consider what they naturally did when they saw an animal[24] in need (thirsty) or suffering (fallen into a pit) on the sabbath.

Interestingly, Jesus' argument was not *halakhic*, that is, not based on appeal to legal deduction or precedent.[25] In all likelihood, there was no legal ruling on the matter within the mainstream of Judaism.[26] In the absence of a legal ruling, commonsense compassion would naturally determine the course. Compassion — the movement within humans (within the bowels or womb in Hebrew thought) in the presence of creature-suffering — would lead to attending to the animal's needs. Thus compassion in the presence of human suffering became the implicit criterion for exceptions to sabbath law. The movements of compassion took precedence over the requirements of holiness.

Luke's account of Jesus' response in the story of the crippled woman adds two further details. The explicit identification of the woman as a "daughter of Abraham" did not mean simply that she was Jewish, as if that needed underlining. Rather, it may point to the inclusiveness of Jesus' concern, just as the explicit identification of the tax collector Zacchaeus as a "son of Abraham" did.[27] Describing the woman's healing as an untying from Satan's bondage (besides being parallel to untying an animal so that it might drink) links her healing to the plundering of Satan's kingdom, which elsewhere in the synoptics is associated with the power of holiness understood as a transforming energy, notably in the confrontations between the "holy one" and the unclean spirits.[28]

---

24. Or son, if the textual variant in Luke is accepted; see n. 23 above.

25. Westerholm, *Jesus and Scribal Authority*, 101–2. See also Banks, *Jesus and the Law*, 126, 128, 130: the appeal was not to scribal tradition, but to common practice.

26. There was no settled opinion on whether it was lawful to pull an animal out of a pit on the sabbath. The community which produced the Zadokite document, now also known from Qumran, prohibited it (CD 11:16; cf. R. H. Charles, ed., *Apocrypha and Pseudepigrapha of the Old Testament*, 2 vols. [Oxford, 1913], Zad. Fr. 13:23, Ap. Ps. 2:827). But the argument of Jesus assumed that he was speaking to those who permitted such an action. See S. T. Kimbrough, Jr., "The Concept of Sabbath at Qumran," *RQ* 5 (1966): 487–98, who displays the sabbath teachings of the Damascus Document, the Hebrew Bible, intertestamental literature, and rabbinical literature in eleven pages of parallel columns.

27. Luke 19:9; see above p. 103.

28. See pp. 147–49 above and Mark 1:21–28, 3:22–30.

Though one must be careful not to press the detail, perhaps the sabbath is seen as an especially appropriate day for the holiness of God to be active.

In none of these cases did the healing seem to be a strategic suspension of sabbath law, as neither danger to life nor particular exigencies of the mission were involved. Instead, these violations of sabbath law as then understood seem to be programmatic, flowing out of the alternative paradigm which Jesus taught: the sabbath was a day for works of compassion. This change did not mean that the sabbath was abrogated; rather, it was subordinated to deeds of compassion rather than to the quest for holiness.

The Marcan Sabbath Controversies

Mark's two sabbath conflict stories are more complex and raise a number of additional issues. The first story concerns the disciples' behavior on the sabbath as they pluck grain from a field while on a journey:

> Mark 2:23–28: [23]One sabbath he was going through the grainfields; and as they made their way his disciples began to pluck heads of grain. [24]And the Pharisees said to him, "Look, why are they doing what is not lawful on the sabbath?" [25]And he said to them, "Have you never read what David did, when he was in need and was hungry, he and those who were with him: [26]how he entered the house of God, when Abiathar was high priest, and ate the bread of the Presence, which it is not lawful for any but the priests to eat? [27]And he said to them, "The sabbath was made for humankind, and not humankind for the sabbath; [28]so the son of man is lord even of the sabbath."

We must first determine the limits and authenticity of the pericope. The problem lies initially in the fact that v. 27 is introduced by "and he said to them," an introductory formula which suggests that vv. 27 and 28 may not have been part of the controversy over plucking corn on the sabbath.[29] More complex is the problem posed by v. 28. The presence of the phrase "son of man" has led commentators to pronounce the verse to be authentic or unauthentic on the basis of whether or not "son of man" is used in a special sense here and, if so, whether or not Jesus used it in a special sense to refer to present activity.[30] Because of

---

29. So most commentators: Taylor, *Mark*, 218; Cranfield, *Mark*, 116–17 (cautiously); Nineham, *Mark*, 106–7; Bultmann, *History of the Synoptic Tradition*, 16; Lohmeyer, *Markus*, 63, 65.

30. Most interpret it as a Christian comment: Taylor, *Mark*, 220; Cranfield, *Mark*, 118; Nineham, *Mark*, 106; F. W. Beare, "The Sabbath Was Made for Man?" *JBL* 79

these problems, Mark 2:23–26 will be treated first. Verse 27 will then be examined to see if it is consistent with the picture that emerges from vv. 23–26. Verse 28 will not now be examined, primarily because this would require a premature decision about "son of man."

What was unlawful was not plucking corn from a stranger's field. This was permitted so long as a sickle was not used (Deut. 23:25). But doing so *on the sabbath* involved the prohibited work of harvesting. Because the charge was directed against the disciples and not Jesus ("Why are *they* doing what is not lawful on the sabbath?"), several commentators argue that vv. 23–26 were created by the community as a justification for the sabbath freedom of the early church.[31] But it is odd that such an extraordinary scene (plucking and harvesting corn in a stranger's field) would be created to justify general abrogation of the sabbath.[32] More likely, the special situation points to an actual historical occurrence rather than to the imaginative faculty of the community.[33] Moreover, a teacher was accountable for the behavior of his disciples. Hence it is not odd that here, as elsewhere,[34] Jesus was questioned about the actions of his followers. The scene, in short, has good claims to authenticity.

The answer of Jesus appealed to the example of David. While King Saul sought his life, David was given the bread of the presence by the priest Ahimilech for him and his companions to eat, bread which only priests could lawfully eat (1 Sam. 21:1–6). This appeal, though broadly consistent with the appeals to precedent in the rabbinic tradition, has some difficulties,[35] two of which are most important. First, the argument of Jesus appealed to example, not precept, thus depending upon

---

(1960): 135; E. Klostermann, *Das Markusevangelium*, 3d ed. (Tübingen, 1936), 31; Lohmeyer, *Markus*, 66; Haenchen, *Weg Jesu*, 121. See M. D. Hooker, *The Son of Man in Mark* (London, 1967), 94, 175–77, for a summary of the case for unauthenticity (of which she is critical).

31. Bultmann, *History of the Synoptic Tradition*, 16; Lohse, "Jesu Worte über den Sabbat"; Beare, "The Sabbath Was Made for Man?" 133; Lohmeyer, *Markus*, 165, and n. 2; Winter, *On the Trial of Jesus*, 118–20, 125.

32. Haenchen, *Weg Jesu*, 122–23. His question on p. 122, n. 4, is apt: was it the practice of the community to go through fields plucking corn on the sabbath?

33. Haenchen, *Weg Jesu*, 122, argues that it is an actual scene from the ministry; so also Merkel, "Jesus und die Pharisäer," 204; cf. the general comment of W. Grundmann, *TLZ* 83 (1958): 839: "die Erkenntnis spezieller und nicht typischer Situationen in der Ramung der Berichte, in denen historischen Erinnerung enthalten ist."

34. E.g., Mark 2:18. See D. Daube, "Responsibilities of Master and Disciples in the Gospels," *NTS* 19 (1972): 1–15. For the claim that the criticism originally included both Jesus and his disciples, see the plausible explanation of Haenchen, *Weg Jesu*, 122, n. 4.

35. For summaries, see Daube, *New Testament and Rabbinic Judaism*, 68–71; Lohmeyer, *Markus*, 64–65; Hooker, *Son of Man in Mark*, 97; Haenchen, *Weg Jesu*, 120–21.

haggadha, not *halakha,* which would render it invalid to his opponents.[36] Second, the action of David had nothing to do with sabbath violation,[37] but with eating that which was forbidden. These difficulties have led some scholars to pronounce the verdict of unauthenticity.[38]

But the difficulties may be read another way. They plausibly suggest that it was important to refer to the incident involving *David,* even though the argument was thereby not as legally precise as it might otherwise have been. Moreover, though the analogy to David's action was not exact, there was nevertheless a real parallel: regulations meant to safeguard something holy were set aside for David and his companions, just as regulations meant to safeguard something holy (the sabbath) are now set aside for Jesus and those with him.[39]

Thus emphasis is to be placed on the appeal to *David,*[40] the significance of whom may be understood here in one of two complementary ways. In the biblical and postbiblical tradition, David and his career were the subject of continuing reflection.[41] The picture which emerged was of the supremely pious king[42] whose two most important works were the molding of the nation Israel and the planning of the Temple.[43] Thus, when David was pursued by Saul in 1 Samuel 21, he and his companions were not simply hungry, but the future of Israel was at stake: the

---

36. Daube, *New Testament and Rabbinic Judaism,* 68–71. Matthew recognizes the weakness and compensates by adding the technically correct argument from the priests' "work" in the Temple on the sabbath (Matt. 12:5–7).

37. The rabbinic tradition states that David's act did occur on the sabbath (see Abrahams, *Studies,* 1:134). However it is not certain that this tradition existed in the first century. In any case, Jesus' reference to David's act did not mention the sabbath.

38. E.g., Haenchen, *Weg Jesu,* 120–21, argues that such a misunderstanding cannot be attributed to Jesus. Instead, the reference to David was added by somebody who erroneously thought that the illegality of the disciples' act consisted of eating that which was not theirs. Thus, with the appeal to David (vv. 25–26) declared to be unauthentic, he accepts v. 27 as the original and authentic answer to the charge of vv. 23–24.

39. Hooker, *Son of Man in Mark,* 97–98.

40. Of course this suggestion is not new. Older commentators saw the reference to David as messianic. Banks, *Jesus and the Law,* 116, argues that the reference to David is authentic and christological. Most commentators have argued (quite rightly) that a messianic reference is "oversubtle" and improbable (e.g., Cranfield, *Mark,* 115; Taylor, *Mark,* 216; Rawlinson, *Mark,* 34). But to dismiss for that reason any significance to the reference to David is premature. One may still ask, why this justification rather than some other?

41. See L. Ginzberg, "David in Rabbinical Literature," *JE* 4:453–57.

42. For example, so pious was David that his father was affirmed to be sinless (Shab. 55b). He was the writer and collector of the Psalms. He was such an industrious student of the Torah that he was satisfied with sixty breaths of sleep (Suk. 26b). See Ginzberg, "David in Rabbinical Literature," 453–55.

43. In the revision of David's role in Israel's history in Chronicles, David is primarily preoccupied with the organization of the Temple service. He gathered the materials, made the plans, arranged the ritual, and organized the priests into twenty-four lots.

life of David, the nation-builder and Temple-planner, was in peril.[44] The urgency which justified his action was the future of Israel.

Alternatively and more specifically, perhaps David's particular situation in 1 Samuel 21 was in mind. There David and his companions had "kept themselves from women." That is, they were in that state of purity incumbent upon soldiers in a holy war. As holy warriors, they were not only on a mission of God, but on one in which, again, the future of Israel was at stake, as was the case with holy war. In both cases, the emergency which justified his action was the future of Israel.

The point of comparison between the action of the disciples and the action of David seems therefore to be that an equally urgent situation existed: the future of Israel was now, too, at stake. That Jesus and his disciples were on a mission of some urgency is implicit in the scene of the pericope.[45] Normally the sabbath would be spent in one's place of residence where the necessary food would have been prepared the day before. That they found it necessary to pick grain shows that they were in fact some distance from home on the sabbath, evidently for the purpose of their mission to Israel. The urgency of their mission, which also led to suspending food laws and conventional obligations,[46] here led to suspension of the sabbath.

The incident may thus suggest that Jesus believed that a state of emergency existed for Israel, and, moreover, that the activity of him and his disciples was organically connected to the resolution of the crisis. They, like David and those with him, were on a mission of God directly related to the future of Israel. The reaction of the opponents to his reply is not given. But one can say that they could have accepted his reply only if they agreed that Israel faced a crisis and that Jesus and those with him were engaged in a mission to resolve the crisis. That they would have accepted this explanation may be regarded as doubtful. Finally, the coherence of this interpretation of the pericope with the general crisis situation of the ministry leaves no objection to accepting it as authentic.[47]

---

44. Cf. 2 Sam. 21:17. There, in another context, David and Israel are closely identified: his men forbid him to go out to war "for fear that the lamp of Israel might be extinguished."

45. Note that the following observation does not depend upon Marcan chronology or geography, but is directly derived from the text as an isolated unit.

46. Luke 9:60; 10:4, 7. Presumably it means not to bother about whether the food has been tithed, and does not refer to eating foods forbidden by the Pentateuch.

47. To which can be added the consideration that the pericope belongs to an early pre-Marcan controversy collection, as first argued by M. Albertz, Die synoptischen Streitgespräche (Berlin, 1921), 5–16, and now generally accepted.

Mark follows this incident with the saying, "The sabbath was made for humankind, and not humankind for the sabbath."[48] Two interpretations of the Greek word *anthropos* in this verse are possible. Most interpret it as "humankind." Jesus (or the community) asserted that the sabbath was created for humanity in general so that individuals may dispense with sabbath regulations which interfere with the fulfillment of legitimate human need. Though there was at least a formal parallel in the rabbinic literature, as will soon be noted, commentators usually emphasize that Jesus here implied much more than what Judaism could endorse,[49] namely, that humankind is lord of the sabbath. Indeed, the saying was even too radical for the early church, it is claimed. Matthew and Luke omit it, and Mark qualifies it by restricting freedom over the sabbath to Jesus as "son of man" in the following (unauthentic) verse, refusing such freedom to people in general.[50]

If the above interpretation is correct, then the saying is radical, almost audaciously so. Yet it is also curiously modern, for it means that whenever people find a sabbath restriction legitimately inconvenient, they are free to dispense with it. Moreover, since we may fairly assume a connection between a general statement such as this and incidents in the ministry, even though we cannot say with certainty that the verse belongs to the grain-picking episode, the above interpretation justifies the action of the disciples in the cornfield not because something important was at stake, as in the case of David, but simply because they were hungry (not starving). The inconvenience of the sabbath restriction is criticized.

---

48. Some have noted that the Aramaic *bar nasha* could (though not necessarily does) lie behind the Greek *anthropos* in v. 27. If so, then it could be translated "humankind" (as is done by Mark or a predecessor), or as "son of man" in a special sense, or as a circumlocution for "I." However, the possibility seems unlikely, for Mark or a predecessor has undoubtedly rendered *bar nasha* in v. 28 with *ho huios tou anthropou* ("son of man"). If he also was thinking of *bar nasha* in v. 27, it is not at all clear why he should render it simply *anthropos*.

49. Merkel, "Jesus und die Pharisäer," 205: "Jesus dispensiert nicht nur in äuszersten Notfällen von der strengen Sabbat-observanz, sondern meint eine grundsätzliche, bedingungslose Freiheit gegenüber dem Sabbatgebot." Lohse, "Jesu Worte über den Sabbat," 85; Lohmeyer, *Markus*, 65–66: determination of sabbath behavior is given to individuals, not to "das Volk"; Haenchen, *Weg Jesu*, 121; Bornkamm, *Jesus of Nazareth*, 97: "For this to come from the lips of an ordinary rabbi is quite without parallel." Käsemann, *Essays*, 38. All of the above consider it to be authentic.

50. Because of its radical nature, many commentators accept is as authentic, appealing to the criterion of dissimilarity: because the saying disagrees both with Judaism and the church, it must be authentic. Yet it also illustrates a difficulty with this criterion, for at what point does a saying become too "un-Jewish" to be accepted as authentic? Cf. Beare, "The Sabbath Was Made for Man?" 132, 135, who concludes that the saying is unauthentic because the assertion of the lordship of humanity over the sabbath is inconceivable on the lips of Jesus.

But an alternative understanding of the word for "humankind" in this verse is more likely: namely, "humankind" would mean "Israel." Both before and after the beginning of the current era, Judaism understood the sabbath (and Torah as a whole) to be created for Israel,[51] not for humankind in general.[52] Therefore whatever was said about the sabbath was directed to Israel. The most frequently cited rabbinic expression is from Simeon ben Menasya: "The sabbath is delivered unto you, and you are not delivered to the sabbath,"[53] where it is clear that the indefinite "you" meant "Israel." So too to Jesus' hearers, the indefinite "humankind" in Mark 2:27 would have meant "Israel."[54] If the saying belonged to the corn-picking episode, then it repeated what was already accepted ("The sabbath was made for Israel, not Israel for the sabbath"), but used it to justify what in the eyes of Jesus' opponents was unjustified behavior. It then, like the corn-picking episode itself, pointed to the crisis which Israel faced (sabbath can be violated, because the future of Israel, as in the time of David, was at stake), and contained an implicit claim for the significance of Jesus and his disciples: upon their mission hinged the future of Israel. If, on the other hand, it is to be interpreted as an originally separate saying, it is difficult without a specific context to settle on one meaning, and an opinion can be ventured only after all of the sabbath teaching has been examined.

To summarize, the sabbath controversy in 2:23–26 and the adjoining statement in v. 27 need not imply, by themselves, a programmatic break with the sabbath. Rather, it is a strategic one, grounded in the conviction that Israel, for whom the sabbath was created, faced a crisis, the resolution of which was connected to the activity of Jesus and those with him. The attitude of the opponents means either that they did not perceive the crisis, or that they did not agree that that which Jesus and his disciples advocated was relevant to the resolution of the crisis.

Mark 3:1–6: [1]Again he entered the synagogue and a man was there who had a withered hand. [2]And they watched him, to see whether he would heal him on the sabbath, so that they might accuse him. [3]And he said to the man who had the withered hand, "Come here." [4]And he said to them, "Is it lawful on the sabbath to do good or to do harm, to save life or to kill?" But they were silent. [5]And he looked around

---

51. Jub. 2:30–31; Sanh. 58b; Ex. R. 25:11. For a collection of the data, see above all T. W. Manson, "Mark ii. 27f.," in *Coniectanea Neotestamentica* 11 (1947): 140–42, 145.

52. Though Is. 66:23 does anticipate the observance of the sabbath by all humankind.

53. Mek. 109b on Ex. 31:14.

54. So also Hooker, *Son of Man in Mark,* 95–96, who, in addition to the data cited above, adds as evidence her own well-documented case that Israel was spoken of as "humankind."

at them with anger, grieved at their hardness of heart, and said to the man, "Stretch out your hand." He stretched it out, and his hand was restored. [6]The Pharisees went out, and immediately held counsel with the Herodians against him, how to destroy him.

The limits and authenticity of this second Marcan sabbath controversy can be determined more succinctly than in the case of the previous text. Verse 6 is redactional. It is germane to the text only when set in a connected sequence of stories designed to account for the growing hostility between Jesus and his opponents, culminating in his death. It may have been added either as the climax to a connected group of conflict stories in the pre-Marcan tradition, or by the evangelist himself.[55]

Verses 1 through 5 have a reasonably strong claim to authenticity. They are part of a pre-Marcan controversy collection.[56] They are unlikely to be a community creation, since healings on the sabbath had no place in the primitive community's activity.[57] Moreover, v. 4, which shall receive primary attention, contains a sharp antithesis which is characteristic of much of the Jesus tradition.[58]

Commentators have devoted most attention to v. 4. Its two contrasts are the key to the pericope: "Is it lawful on the sabbath to do good or to do harm, to save life or to kill?" The two contrasts are in parallelism. Obviously the parallelism "do good/save life" referred to the act of healing; but to what did the parallelism "do harm/kill" refer?

One group of commentators refers "do harm/kill" to the nefarious plotting of the opponents who, according to v. 6, decided to destroy Jesus.[59] The contrast, then, was between Jesus who did good on the sabbath, and his opponents with their murderous intention. It might be paraphrased, "If you fine law-abiding folk can plot to kill on the sabbath, how much more ought doing good be permitted!" But, clever and biting as this interpretation is, this meaning is doubtful in the ministry.

---

55. So Nineham, Mark, 110; Bultmann, History of the Synoptic Tradition, 12; Klostermann, Markusevangelium, 31; Lohmeyer, Markus, 67. Taylor, Mark, 220, says that verse 6 is redactional but in the next paragraph contradicts this by claiming that it is integral to the pericope.

56. Albertz, Streitgespräche, 5–16.

57. Lohse, "Jesu Worte über den Sabbat," 85.

58. All commentaries consulted treat it as authentic with the exception of Haenchen, Weg Jesu, who finds the scene improbable. Bultmann, History of the Synoptic Tradition, 147, argues that v. 4 is a saying of Jesus in both form and content. Lohse, "Jesu Worte über den Sabbat," 84, lists it among the three sabbath sayings which definitely belong to the Jesus tradition.

59. So Taylor, Mark, 222; Major, Mission and Message, 58; Bowman, Mark, 120; Lohmeyer, Markus, 68–69.

Quite possibly, Mark intended this, or at least a *double entendre*.[60] But as already noted, v. 6, upon which this interpretation depends, is unlikely to have been part of the original pericope. Moreover, the question of Jesus becomes an *ad hominem* argument — certainly not impossible, but a departure from the style of argument that otherwise characterized the sabbath controversies.

Two options remain. One is commonly advanced, and a second seems to have been overlooked. For the first, the question was rhetorical. The implicit answer is that it is never lawful to do harm, and the doing of good is limited. Behind the rhetorical question lies, as it were, reflective musing on the purpose of the sabbath: was the sabbath an occasion for doing a service, or for doing an injury? The healing implied, just as in the Lucan pericopes, that restrictions on sabbath activity were to be subordinated to acts of compassion.[61] On this view, "do harm" referred to the failure to heal; the claim is that "not to heal" is equivalent to "doing harm." But this is also the major defect of this interpretation, for it virtually ignores the parallel between "to do harm" and "to kill." Though not healing could perhaps be viewed as "doing harm" or even as "letting life be destroyed," one can hardly view it as killing, particularly when this man was in no danger of death.[62]

The remaining option, however, does justice to the word "kill." Moreover, it recognizes that Jesus here used the traditional argument by precedent, and sets the controversy firmly within the historical context of Israel's survival in a hostile world. The key lies in the recognition that here, as in the other sabbath sayings, the words of Jesus do appeal to an activity that is permitted on the sabbath: warfare (and hence killing) for the sake of preserving the people of God from annihilation.

As briefly mentioned earlier, this exception was first made during the Maccabean period after a group of Jews refused to defend themselves on the sabbath and were thereby slaughtered by the forces of Antiochus (1 Macc. 2:29–41). The reason for the exception is clear enough. Without it, Israel would have been fatally vulnerable to attack during wartime by foreign commanders who knew of the sabbath re-

---

60. Haenchen, *Weg Jesu*, 124, cogently argues that the story as it stands in Mark has affinities to the Johannine theme that the opponents kill Jesus because he gives life.

61. So Cranfield, *Mark*, 120; Nineham, *Mark*, 109; Klostermann, *Markusevangelium*, 32; J. Schmid, *The Gospel according to Mark* (Staten Island, 1968), 75, though he grants that the reference to plotting is also possible.

62. Finkel, *The Pharisees*, 171, thinks that Jesus is referring to the accepted ruling of the school of Shemayah and Abtalion preserved in Yoma 35b: "Is it lawful to save life or let it die on the sabbath day?" But this ignores the two points which make it inappropriate to Mark 3:4: "kill" is much stronger than "let die," and the saying is irrelevant to a case where there was no danger to life.

strictions. In short, killing on the sabbath was occasionally necessary for the survival of Israel as the Torah community.

If this is the relevant background for Jesus' response, then his question was not rhetorical, for there was an answer. It was lawful (under certain circumstances) for the sake of Israel to kill on the sabbath, and "to kill" referred to this exception. The implied argument of Jesus was thus, "If it is lawful on the sabbath for the sake of Israel and the Torah to kill, how much more ought it be permitted to heal this man, who is an Israelite,[63] on the sabbath!" The question of Jesus was both ironic and polemical. It was not simply a defense of his action, but an attack on the sabbath institution *in its present form*. For the concern to preserve Israel had led the piety of the time, first, to permit killing on the sabbath in national self-defense but, second, to prohibit doing good (except where there was danger to life, of course). Both the permission and the prohibition served the cause of preserving the people of God; the sabbath had been subordinated to the need for collective self-preservation. That, Jesus' reply claimed, was not the purpose of the sabbath.[64]

The cogency of this option depends largely upon whether or not the reference to "to kill" would have called to mind the Maccabean exception. Some doubt must remain, but the following can be argued. The Maccabean exception was in fact the first exception to the sabbath prohibition of work.[65] Thus the precedent par excellence concerned warfare on the sabbath. Not only did the validity of the exception continue into and through the first century,[66] but it was the subject of reflection and debate in rabbinic circles and was extended to permit the continuation of *offensive* warfare begun before the sabbath,[67] a provision which the resistance fighters may have extended yet further.[68] The topic of warfare on the sabbath was "in the air."

Thus "to kill" on the sabbath may well have called to mind the exception necessitated by Israel's complex political situation in a hostile

---

63. Not explicitly said here, but certainly he was Jewish. Cf. the explicit reference in the sabbath healing in Luke 13:16: "Here is this woman, *a daughter of Abraham* . . . " and our comments on Mark 2:27: the sabbath was made for Israel.

64. To accept the claim that the sabbath was made for Israel, as our exegesis of Mark 2:27 indicates that Jesus did, does not mean that the sabbath was made for the self-preservation of Israel. That is, there is no inconsistency between our interpretation of 2:27 and the polemical interpretation of this pericope.

65. Schmid, *Mark*, 73.

66. *Ant.* 12.275–77; 14.63. For the apparent contradiction in *Vita*, 161, see Farmer, *Maccabees, Zealots, and Josephus*, 75.

67. Shab. 19a; Abrahams, *Studies*, 1:130–31. For more detailed treatments of the Maccabean exception, see Farmer, 72–81; Finkel, *The Pharisees*, 75–76; Barth, *Tradition and Interpretation in Matthew*, 91–92; Safrai, *Compendia*, I.2:805.

68. *B.J.* 2.517–18.

world. If so, then not only was Jesus cognizant of the suspension of the sabbath because of military-political exigency, but he also criticized this subordination of the sabbath to the necessities of national life. Rather, the sabbath was to be subordinated to acts of compassion, not to the quest for national survival.

Whichever of these last two options is most nearly correct, one point is constant. Healing — which was commonly understood as an act of compassion — was to be permitted on the sabbath, as in the non-Marcan sabbath controversies. And, if Mark 2:27 is to be interpreted as a general statement rather than as specifically connected to Mark 2:23–26, then it meant that, since the sabbath was made for Israel (and not Israel for the sabbath), the sabbath was an especially appropriate day for God's compassionate activity toward Israel.

To the opponents in the sabbath controversies, in most cases named as Pharisees,[69] this threatened to dissolve the sabbath institution as a distinctive mark of Israel, and thus threatened Israel's existence[70] — the very threat which the exception to which Jesus may have appealed in Mark 3:4 had been designed to combat. Jesus, on the other hand, argued that the thorough-going attempt to preserve a Torah people was defeating the purpose of Torah. To use modern terms, for Jesus the sabbath in its present form was dysfunctional to the purpose of Israel rather than functional. From the point of view of the opponents, what was at stake was the survival of Israel.[71] From the point of view of Jesus, what

---

69. Luke 13:14: the ruler of the synagogue. Luke 14:1–5: lawyers and Pharisees. Mark 2:24: Pharisees. Herodians along with Pharisees appear only in Mark 3:6, which we have understood to be redactional. The reference to Herodians is puzzling. Since they were almost certainly partisans of the Herodian dynasty (see H. H. Rowley, "The Herodians in the Gospels," *JTS* 41 [1940]: 14–27, and Hoehner, *Herod Antipas*, 331–42), it is difficult to imagine an alliance between them and the Pharisees at any time prior to the reign of Herod Agrippa (41–44 C.E.), who appears to have been sympathetic to them and they to him, and both were hostile to the church at that time (see Acts 12:1–19). The difficulty lies not in the fact that there were no Herodians ca. 30 (for there were in Galilee), but in imagining an alliance between them and the generally anti-Herod Pharisees. Could the alliance of 3:6 (and also of 12:13, cf. 8:15) be a retrojection of the relationship between Herod Agrippa and the Pharisees into the ministry of Jesus at the time when the collection of controversy stories was made?

70. Klausner, *Jesus of Nazareth*, 279, appreciates the national threat implied by Jesus' violation of the sabbath. He was not simply a rabbi with views of his own, like Hillel or Shammai, but "a danger to religion and ancestral traditions.... Whatever was opposed to the accepted opinion of the nation was, therefore, opposed also to the civil order."

71. This seems more complete than Nineham's description, *Mark*, 110: the opposition "rested on a fundamental misunderstanding — an inability, or refusal, to see that Jesus was God's eschatological agent and that his sovereign freedom with regard to law and custom sprang from that fact." That is well said and appropriate in that it recognizes that the opposition did rest on a different interpretation of what was happening, but it is

was at stake was the purpose for which the institutions of Israel had been given.

Several themes which appeared in the conflict over table fellowship reappear here. A behavioral pattern central to Israel's quest for holiness and to its survival was called into question. Moreover, it was in the name of compassion that modes of behavior mandated by holiness as separation were superseded. Nor did compassion here refer to an abstract theological principle but, on the one hand, to a powerful human emotion and, on the other hand, to God's compassionate activity in deeds of healing mediated by Jesus.

In John's Gospel, Jesus defended his sabbath healings by appeal to an *imitatio dei:* "My father has never ceased his work, and I am working too" (John 5:17). Though this must be regarded as reflective of Johannine theology, it is consistent with the synoptic theme described earlier: the characteristic of God which is to be imitated is not holiness, understood as separation from the world, but compassion, which continued even on the sabbath. The community which would be faithful was, like God, to subordinate the sabbath to compassion.

•

In chapter 3, the Torah and the Temple were designated as the two central pillars of the society which quested after holiness. Yet in subsequent chapters there has been no section bearing the title "Jesus and the Torah." Instead, the material itself drew our attention to the themes of tithing, purity, and the sabbath; to criticisms of actions mandated by holiness; to castigations of Israel's guides; and to indictments of Israel's unproductivity. An important implication follows. The conflict between Jesus and his opponents was not about whether or not the Torah deserved one's loyalty. Nor was it really about the Torah as a theological problem (that is, whether it was an adequate or inadequate revelation of God's purpose, or whether there should be an oral tradition, etc.).

Rather, what has been discovered is a different interpretation of Torah, notably of those provisions most responsible for the shape of the people of God in the first century and most related to the quest for holiness: tithing, purity, and sabbath.[72] On these issues, whether by

---

also virtually self-evident. That is, if they *had* recognized that Jesus was God's final agent, of course they would not have opposed him. But their opposition was rooted in their conviction that the survival of the people of God required these marks of distinctiveness; anybody who threatened them must be a destroyer, not the savior, of the people of God.

72. Strikingly, these are the three areas identified as the three most important concerns of the postexilic emphasis on holiness; see M. Smith, *Palestinian Parties and Politics That Shaped the Old Testament* (New York, 1971), 175–76.

provocative action or teaching, Jesus took the initiative. When he did speak on issues not notably related to the quest for holiness, it was usually because others initiated the discussion.[73] This concentration of his teaching suggests that his ministry was related most particularly to those provisions most responsible for Israel's present historical structures.

Thus, again, the question was not whether one should be loyal to Torah, but a question of hermeneutics. How was the Torah to be interpreted? Instead of a hermeneutic based on the quest for holiness, Jesus advocated a hermeneutic based on the conviction that God's primary attribute for human emulation was compassion. Compassion as the core value for interpreting the Torah stretched and at times burst the boundaries set by the quest for holiness. This was the paradigm in conformity with which the people of God were now to structure their existence.

---

73. For example, on divorce, Mark 10:1–12; on the resurrection, Mark 12:18–27.

CHAPTER SEVEN

Jesus and the Quest for Holiness: The Temple

The quest for holiness had identifiable political consequences not only for the internal life of Israel but also for its relationship to Rome, functioning as the cultural dynamic undergirding resistance. It was the ideological cause and legitimation of the suspicion and hostility which, when coupled with Rome's insensitivity, entangled the two nations in a course culminating in a confrontation catastrophic for the Jewish people, their capital, and the Temple.

Jesus, I have argued, challenged the quest for holiness as the program of internal reform and criticized its effects on Israel's life. In addition, did he also see its effects on Israel's relationship to the external world? A large body of material in the synoptics suggests an affirmative answer, indicating that Jesus warned of the historical and political consequences of following the path of holiness. Much of this material focuses on Jerusalem and the Temple. To see this teaching in its proper context, we must first sketch the convictions of first-century Judaism regarding the Temple.

The centrality of the Temple as one of the two pillars of the post-exilic quest for holiness has already been developed. As the place of God's presence, a sign of Israel's election, and the sole locus of sacrifice where atonement was made for sins and impurity, it was an institution substantive to the definition and existence of Israel. Representing for most Jews "the nexus between heaven and earth,"[1] the *axis mundi* by which the holy was connected to the earth, its proper operation was essential for the holiness of the land.

Much has already been said about the Temple in chapter 3 of this book. As the center of holiness, the Temple needed to be protected from defilement. Gentiles were excluded from much of its area. Its

---

1. J. Neusner, *From Politics to Piety: The Emergence of Pharisaic Judaism* (Englewood Cliffs, N.J., 1973), 3.

well-being was important to all the renewal movements. The Essenes came into existence because of their conviction that the present Temple service was improper. The Pharisees were strongly concerned that their interpretation of Temple regulations be followed by the priests. Moreover, their program was modelled on the Temple: to extend to every Israelite that degree of holiness required of officiating priests in the Temple. Jesus and his movement were also concerned about its well-being, as we shall see.

The Temple, Holiness, and Resistance

Because the Temple was one of the two pillars of the quest for holiness, threats to it were often the explicit cause of resistance to both Herod and Rome and, earlier, to the Seleucids.[2] In addition, surrounding the Temple itself was an ideology which affirmed that resistance in defense of holiness would be successful. So long as Israel was faithful to holiness, Yahweh would protect the divine dwelling place, the Temple, from harm. Grounded in a theology of Zion which affirmed its inviolability, reflected in an exegetical tradition alive in the intertestamental period, and fortified by the living memory of an incident prior to the exile, the belief operated as an ideology of resistance against foreign power and influence in the holy land.

The inviolability of the Temple was closely connected to the affirmation that there Yahweh, or the divine name or glory,[3] dwelled.[4] The conviction that Yahweh had chosen Zion as the divine dwelling place led to the corollary that Zion was impregnable, for there God had promised to dwell *forever.*

> For the LORD has chosen Zion;
> God has desired it for God's own habitation:
> "This is my resting place for ever;
> here I will dwell, for I have desired it."[5]

From there God would give aid to Israel, confounding its enemies:

> Hark, an uproar from the city!
> A voice from the Temple!

---

2. See chapter 3.

3. R. E. Clements, *God and Temple* (Oxford, 1965), 137. For a summary of Old Testament beliefs regarding Yahweh's presence, see K. Baltzer, "The Meaning of the Temple in the Lukan Writings," *HTR* (1965): 265–67.

4. For example, Ps. 20:2, 26:8, 78:68–69, 128:5, 132:13–14, 134:3, 135:21; Is. 6:1; Jer. 31:6; Amos 1:2; Ecclus. 36:13; Tob. 1:4; Jub. 1:28.

5. Ps. 132:13–14. See also, for example, Ps. 78:68–69; Tob. 1:4; Jub. 1:28.

> The voice of the Lord,
> rendering recompense to God's enemies![6]

Thus for many, the integrity of the Temple and the concomitant presence of God in it meant security and salvation for Israel.[7]

Consistent with this generally held conviction, there was near the beginning of the current era an exegetical tradition which affirmed that though the nations might attack and indeed occupy much of Israel, their forces would finally be routed by Yahweh when they threatened Jerusalem or the Temple. Probably inspired by the Gog/Magog tradition of Ezekiel 38–39, this tradition drew to itself echoes of many Hebrew Bible passages. A passage in the Sibylline Oracles[8] (second or first century B.C.E.) envisions an onslaught of the kings of the nations against Israel. When they seek *to ravage the shrine of God,* Yahweh will speak and destroy them.[9] That the attack upon the sanctuary is the turning point is clear: the nations fall because "with witless mind, with one united onslaught, ye cast your spears against *the Temple.*"[10]

The same motif is found in 1 Enoch 56:5–8. After the nations "tread under foot the land of God's elect ones," they approach Jerusalem, at which point "the city of my righteous" confounds them and they are defeated and slaughtered.[11] The modest hints of this exegetical tradition suggest that the Zion ideology was not only accepted, but continued to develop.

The notion that Yahweh would fight to defend Jerusalem and the Temple did not mean that Israel would therefore remain passively inactive, trusting to the unmediated activity of God. Rather, it was characteristic of holy war theology that earthly warriors fought, even though one spoke primarily of the divine warrior. Such is clear from the Dead Sea Scrolls as well as from the terse Hebrew Bible recitations of Yahweh's activity as divine warrior in the conquest of Canaan. No human heroes are mentioned, even though Israel was quite aware of the

---

6. Is. 66:6. See also, for example, Ps. 20:2.

7. Baltzer, "The Meaning of the Temple," 267–68.

8. Or. Sib. 3:663–97.

9. Ibid., 3:665–72.

10. Ibid., 3:688. H. C. O. Lanchester in Charles, *Ap. and Ps.*, 2:390, translates *eph hieron* with "the Holy One." The above translation accepts the note of L. Hartman, *Prophecy Interpreted* (Lund, 1966), 93, n. 29, that the natural translation of *hieron* is "Temple"; so also H. N. Bate, *The Sibylline Oracles* (London, 1918), 77, and A. Kurfess, *Sibyllinische Weissagungen* (Munich, 1951), both cited by Hartman.

11. These two passages are from a larger group which Hartman gathers under the rubric the "last assault of the Gentiles" (p. 47), including 1 En. 90:13ff., 4 Ez. 13:5, Test. Jos. 19:8. For his more detailed analysis, see his pp. 88–94.

role they played.[12] Hence divine warrior theology was often combined with an activist human response.

The Zion ideology and exegetical tradition were fortified by the memory of Jerusalem's miraculous deliverance in 701 B.C.E. from the encroaching armies of the Assyrian Sennacherib:

> That night the angel of Yahweh went out and struck down a hundred and eighty-five thousand men in the Assyrian camp. When morning dawned, they all lay dead. So Sennacherib king of Assyria broke camp and went back to Nineveh and stayed there.[13]

The memory of Sennacherib's rout lived on. It was recalled in Ecclus. 48:17–22. More significantly, on three different occasions the leaders of the Maccabean wars of liberation explicitly invoked the Sennacherib tradition and in each case divine assistance was given.[14] Yahweh had defended his city and Temple against aliens in the past — could divine help not be expected again?

Other selected incidents from Israel's recent past could be adduced to support the ideology. When the Seleucid general Nicanor threatened the Temple, had not Yahweh through the Maccabean warriors executed appropriate judgment?[15] And when Heliodorus sought to plunder the Temple treasury some years earlier, had not Yahweh miraculously prevented him from doing so? (2 Macc. 3:14–30). Similarly, when the infidel high priest Alcimus attempted to demolish the wall of the inner court in 159 B.C.E., had not he mysteriously suffered a stroke and died in great torment? (1 Macc. 9:54–56). In a later century, was not Caligula providentially murdered before he could consummate his designs on the Temple?[16]

Moreover, the size and location of the Temple gave it immense utility as a fortress and contributed to the belief that it was impregnable. The exclamation of the unnamed disciple, "Look, what huge stones!" (Mark 13:1) must have been echoed many times by other pilgrims, for some of the stones of the Temple erected by Herod measured (in cubits) perhaps

---

12. For example, Josh. 24:8–13; Ps. 78:53–55, 80:8–9; Amos 2:9; it also appears in the New Testament in Acts 7:45, 13:18 20. On Yahweh as divine warrior, see G. E. Wright, *The Old Testament and Theology* (New York, 1969), 121–50; and H. Fredriksson, *Jahwe als Krieger* (Lund, 1945).

13. 2 Kings 18:13–19:36; cf. Is. 36:1–37:37.

14. 1 Macc. 7:39–42; 2 Macc. 8:19–24, 15:20–27.

15. 1 Macc. 7:35ff.; esp. 2 Macc. 14:33 and 15:32–35. When Nicanor's severed head and hand are shown to the people, they exclaim, "Praise to God who has preserved the sanctuary from defilement!"

16. Josephus affirms God's providence in Caligula's death: *Ant.* 18.305–9.

as much as 45 by 6 by 5 and certainly as much as 25 by 12 by 8.[17] Surely no power on earth could overcome the house of Yahweh.

In each of the cases cited above, Yahweh intervened before the foe molested the sanctuary. In three other cases individuals who offended the Temple were struck down after their desecrating acts, with the fate of each understood as Yahweh's judgment: Antiochus Epiphanes, the collaborationist high priest Menelaus, and the Roman general Pompey.[18] At first glance these last three incidents seem to offer little support for the ideology, for Yahweh avenged the desecration of the sanctuary rather than protecting the sanctuary itself. But it is not so simple to dismiss them, for one must recognize that the offensive acts toward the Temple of each of these men were viewed as judgment on Israel for its sins, including illegitimate cultic practices.[19]

Two inferences can be drawn. First, even those who acted temporarily as Yahweh's ministers of judgment on Israel were eventually recompensed. One did not defile God's sanctuary with impunity. Indeed, Paul spoke of this ideology as common knowledge in 1 Cor. 3:16–17. Introducing the passage which includes the statement "Anyone who destroys God's Temple will be destroyed by God," he used the expression, "You know well," a formula commonly used to recall generally known facts. Paul recalled the ideology surrounding the actual Temple in Jerusalem, even though he applied it to the new Temple, the community.[20] The second inference, equally important, is that the Temple would not have been violated had not Israel's life and worship become impure.[21] This increased the urgency of holiness: Yahweh's protection could be assured if Israel lived in holiness, including the purity of Temple worship itself.

Finally, the reinforcement of the ideology provided by the annual festivals must not be ignored. The observance of Hanukkah and Nicanor's Day, both recalling the divine concern for the integrity of the Temple,

---

17. The former figure is found in *B.J.* 5.224. Thackeray in his note on the passage comments: "almost incredible . . . must have been exceptional." Jeremias, *Jerusalem*, 22, notes that these dimensions "need not be taken too seriously." The latter figure is found in *Ant.* 15.392, about which there is no skepticism.

18. 2 Macc. 1:13–17, 9:5–12, 28; 2 Macc. 13:8; Ps. Sol. 2.

19. 2 Macc. 5:17–20, 6:12–17; Ps. Sol. 2:3, 8:9–14.

20. Paul "spiritualizes" the notion of Temple here. The Temple consists of those to whom he is writing. The argument proceeds: just as you know that anybody who destroys the *literal* Temple will be destroyed, so anyone who destroys the Christian community in Corinth (Temple in a spiritualized sense) will be destroyed.

21. Explicitly so in Ps. Sol. The author confesses his astonishment that Pompey was able to enter Jerusalem and the Temple (1:7, 8:5–6), suggesting that he expected Yahweh to defend the city. Only after the *secret* sins of the cult are revealed to him does he grant that it was a righteous judgment on Israel.

has already been noted.[22] In addition, the Feast of Tabernacles included the daily singing of the Hallel (Pss. 113–18). Passages particularly supportive of an ideology of resistance include the celebration of deliverance from Egypt (114), ridicule of the gods of the nations as impotent (115), and Yahweh as the helper and shield of Israel (115:9–13). The Hallel also includes the affirmations, "Yahweh is on my side, I have no fear; what can any one do to me? ... I shall gloat over my enemies" (118:6–7), "All nations surround me, but in Yahweh's name I will drive them away" (118:25). The reminder of present pagan rule provided by the Roman sentries posted on the roof of the Temple during such festivals insured that the national significance of these celebrations would not be lost.

To be sure, the ideology of divine protection depended upon a selective reading of Israel's history. After all, there was the equally prominent tradition that Yahweh abandoned the Temple in Israel's past and fought on the side of its enemies.[23]

But precisely such a selective reading of the evidence was occurring in the first century, as suggested by events during and following the war of 66–70 C.E. Josephus reports the generalized conviction.[24] According to rabbinic tradition, when the Romans broke into the Temple, the Levites were singing Psalm 114 with its affirmation, "Yahweh will not abandon God's people nor forsake God's chosen nation."[25] Presumably they were looking for divine help in that exigency.

More specifically, the defenders of the city were explicitly depending upon an exegesis of the Sennacherib narrative. When Josephus sought to persuade them to surrender, he said, in effect, "Do not expect Yahweh to come to your aid as in the days of Sennacherib."[26] The reference suggests that they were basing the expectation of divine help in part on what had happened some 770 years before. The concern to insure the protection of Yahweh explains the restoration of the Zadokite priesthood in the course of the war and perhaps some of the internecine warfare as well.[27]

It also explains the curious behavior of the Jewish forces after they

---

22. See above p. 70.

23. For example, Jer. 21:5; Ezek. 11:22–23; and the frequent prophetic announcements of the impending destruction of the Temple by a foreign power.

24. B.J. 5.459; 6.98, 283–86.

25. Taan. 29a. The historical value of the tradition is questionable.

26. B.J. 5.387–88. The present writer is indebted especially to Farmer, *Maccabees, Zealots, and Josephus*, 97–111, for his valuable treatment of the Sennacherib incident.

27. C. Roth, "The Zealots in the War of 66–73," *JJS* 4 (1959): 341–42, and *The Historical Background of the Dead Sea Scrolls* (Oxford, 1958), 5. His point is valid even though one rejects his identification of the Zealots with Qumran.

had been driven out of the Temple. Rather than continuing to defend the most invulnerable parts of the city (which they still held, and which Josephus and Titus claim neither human power nor siege engines could have conquered[28]), they asked Titus for permission to leave the city. Why? The most satisfactory answer is that they were now convinced that Yahweh would not save the city. Yahweh had not intervened even at the decisive moment when the Roman soldiers committed idolatry in the courts of the Temple.[29] Until then they had believed that God would finally save Zion — but now, with that hope dashed, they sought to go to the desert where a new beginning with Yahweh might be made.[30] Such behavior is compelling evidence that they had assumed Yahweh's protection of the Temple.

Finally, departing from its usual custom, Rome deliberately destroyed the Temple after the conquest. In the judgment of the Romans, the religion centered in it "fomented or promoted nationalist feeling and led to revolts."[31] Thus the Romans themselves provide evidence that the Temple was instrumental to Jewish resistance to imperial rule.

The confirmation provided by events during and after the war warrants the conclusion that in the great revolt and in the decades preceding it there was operative an ideology of resistance based on the Temple. The belief that Yahweh was present on Zion, the exegetical tradition which affirmed that God would destroy those who struck at the holy place, the explicit recollection of Sennacherib, the great festivals — all combined to provide an ideological underpinning for the already present willingness to defend the Temple, an institution indispensable for both practical and symbolic reasons.

Only a few voices are known to have dissented from the ideology in the first century. Josephus in retrospect did,[32] though it is extremely unlikely that he did so while fighting on the Jewish side. An otherwise unknown Jesus ben Ananias roamed through Jerusalem crying "Woe" to the city in the decade preceding the destruction. For this, he was

---

28. *B.J.* 6.399–400, 409–10.

29. Ibid., 6.316.

30. For a similar, more detailed analysis, see Farmer, *Maccabees, Zealots, and Josephus*, 114–20.

31. M. P. Charlesworth, *The Roman Empire* (New York, 1968), 100. Neusner, *Yohanan ben Zakkai*, 170–71, notes that the evidence on responsibility for the burning of the Temple is ambiguous (though it is clear that the Romans *deliberately razed* it; see *B.J.* 7.1–2), but concludes that for Rome both to destroy the Temple and disclaim responsibility constituted a "wise and shrewd policy."

32. Yahweh abandoned the city because of its impiety: *Ant.* 20.166–67; *B.J.* 2.539; 4.323; 5.19; 6.110, 299–300.

arrested and judged insane.[33] There remain in the Jewish tradition only two known exceptions. The great rabbi Yohanan ben Zakkai had premonitions of the city's destruction and abandoned it during the siege.[34] The other was Jesus.

Jesus and the Temple

The reported teaching and behavior of Jesus regarding the Temple is copious and complex. It has been interpreted diversely, and the authenticity of much of it denied. Accordingly, we must move carefully through the major passages, notably Jesus' expulsion of the merchants from the Temple and the numerous warnings of catastrophe facing the Temple and Jerusalem. As we do so, we shall see the issues of holiness, inclusiveness and peace emerging once again.

The Disruption in the Temple[35]

The expulsion of the merchants from the Temple, recounted in Mark 11:15a–17 par. and John 2:13–19, was one of the most famous episodes in the ministry. Indeed, Joseph Klausner called it Jesus' "greatest public deed."[36]

According to Mark:

> And Jesus entered the Temple and began to drive out those who sold and those who bought in the Temple. He overturned the tables of the money-changers and the seats of those who sold pigeons; and he would not allow anyone to carry anything through the Temple. And he taught and said to them, "Is it not written, 'My house shall be called a house of prayer for all the nations'? But you have made it a den of robbers."

Those whom Jesus drove out included the sellers of sacrificial birds as well as those who operated the *bureau de change* where pilgrims

---

33. *B.J.* 6.300–9.

34. Yoma 39b, Git. 56a; Neusner, *Yohanan ben Zakkai*, 64–65, 157–66.

35. Though commonly designated the *cleansing* of the Temple, there is no basis for this word in the text, and it was introduced only by later exegesis. Moreover, since "cleansing" implies a concern for purification, the term prematurely and misleadingly points to a certain understanding of the incident. See Haenchen, *Weg Jesu*, 388, and Gaston, *No Stone*, 81–82.

36. Klausner, *Jesus of Nazareth*, 312. Compare the title of the book which Scott devotes totally to the incident: *The Crisis in the Life of Jesus*. E. Trocmé, "L'expulsion des marchands du Temple," *NTS* 15 (1968–69): 22, comments that it marked the frontier between two different parts of the ministry and the emergence of Jesus as a national figure.

could exchange their diverse currencies for acceptable coinage with which to pay the Temple tax. The merchants occupied a fairly large area, either in the massive outer court or possibly under the Royal Portico.[37] Through this area, Mark reports, Jesus would not permit anyone to carry anything. The incident concluded with the pronouncement of v. 17 with its strong contrast:

> My house shall be called a house of prayer for all the nations — but you have made it a den of robbers.

The diverse interpretations of this superficially straightforward narrative — as protest against commercial activity, creation of historical or eschatological space for the Gentiles, eschatological purification, revolutionary putsch — support the claim that it was among "the most puzzling" of Jesus' actions.[38]

However, initial insight is provided by the perception that it was a prophetic or symbolic act, limited in area, intent, and duration. This conclusion flows directly from a consideration of the large area involved. Controlling such a large area would have required a paramilitary or mob action involving scores of followers (possibly more) using force. Some have sought to escape this fact by speaking, not very convincingly, of Jesus' moral authority. His opponents "simply quailed before His holy indignation";[39] Jesus "gave his order and all who heard him were conscious at once that this was their Master."[40]

If Jesus did mount an operation designed to secure complete even if temporary control of such a large area, the nonintervention of the Roman troops and the Temple police is incomprehensible. The fortress of the Roman garrison overlooked the Temple court. Moreover, during Passover, Roman soldiers reinforced by troops from Caesarea for the express purpose of coping with disturbances among the pilgrims were stationed on the Temple porticos. Both they and the Temple police intervened to maintain order on other occasions,[41] and one can

---

37. The outer court measured 500 by 365 cubits; see Danby, *Mishnah*, 589, n. 11 on M. Mid. 1.1. For the cubit as 21 inches, see Jeremias, *Jerusalem*, 11, n. 20; as 18 inches, see Hollis, *The Archaeology of Herod's Temple*, 113, 349. For the suggestion that the merchants were located under the Royal Portico, which stretched for several hundred feet inside the Temple court along the southern wall, see M. BenDov, *IDB*, 5 (supplement), 871.

38. R. H. Hiers, "Purification of the Temple: Preparation for the Kingdom of God," *JBL* 90 (1971): 82.

39. Rawlinson, *Mark*, 156.

40. Scott, *Crisis*, 19; cf. 83. So also G. H. C. Macgregor, *The New Testament Basis of Pacifism* (London, 1953), 17–18: "it was the compelling 'authority' of His words which overawed His opponents." Nineham's understated comment on Rawlinson is altogether appropriate: "This does not seem very convincing" (*Mark*, 301n).

41. *B.J.* 2.223–27; *Ant.* 20.105–12; Acts 4:1–4, 21:30–36; Luke 13:1–3, which locates Pilate's punitive action in the Temple.

hardly believe that they would have refrained from doing so during the provocative administration of Pilate.[42] Both an ancient and a modern commentator have felt the force of this problem and resolved it in strikingly similar fashions. Origen called the occupation of the Temple a miracle greater than the transformation of water into wine at Cana.[43] Early in this century, B. W. Bacon, who assumed that Jesus was able to obtain control nonviolently, neither offending the Romans nor permitting his more militant followers to exercise violence, commented: this is almost miraculous.[44]

The fact of nonintervention has been evaluated differently. For some scholars, it has led to the conclusion that the Temple incident is nonhistorical, or that it is so shrouded in obscurity that even the evangelists could only guess at its significance.[45] But against the verdict of nonhistorical is the fact that John independently attests the incident. Instead, the conclusion to be drawn from the fact of nonintervention[46] is that the action of Jesus was sufficiently limited so as not to incite

---

42. As Wilson suggests, *Execution of Jesus*, 100. Cranfield, *Mark*, 359, observes that the Romans would surely have intervened if the action had been openly messianic (which is true enough) and concludes thereby that it was not openly messianic. But this makes the odd assumption that the Romans and Temple police were willing to tolerate large-scale disturbances at Passover so long as they were not messianic.

43. *Comm. in Joann.* 10.

44. B. W. Bacon, *The Beginnings of Gospel Story* (New Haven, 1909), 161. Cohn, *The Trial and Death of Jesus*, 54–55, is so impressed with the nonintervention of the authorities that he concludes that they must have approved of Jesus' action.

45. C. Guignebert, *Jesus* (London, 1935), 418–19, and M. Goguel, *The Life of Jesus* (London, 1933), 414–15, deny that it happened, though Goguel grants that it may have been an oral protest transformed into an action by the tradition. Lohmeyer, *Markus*, 237, comments that the Marcan pericope can hardly be called a historical report. Haenchen, *Weg Jesu*, 388, affirms the historicity but says that we can know nothing of Jesus' intent because of the attendant difficulties; so also A. Loisy, *L'Evangile selon Marc* (Paris, 1912), 322–25; more cautiously, Nineham, *Mark*, 301–2. Bultmann, *History of the Synoptic Tradition*, 36; W. E. Bundy, *Jesus and the First Three Gospels* (Cambridge, Mass., 1955), 427; and Trocmé, "L'expulsion," 13–15, all affirm that v. 17 was appended to the incident only later. Trocmé does affirm that v. 17 is an authentic saying, but that it was spoken on another occasion.

46. This same fact eliminates the possibility that the action was a revolutionary putsch accompanied by large scale violence, designed to seize control of the Temple or Temple treasury as the first stage of a massive rebellion. Affirming variants of this view are J. S. Kennard, " 'Hosanna' and the Purpose of Jesus," *JBL* 67 (1948): 171–76, and *Jesus in the Temple* (Tokyo, 1935); Carmichael, *Death of Jesus*, 133–41, 159–62; Eisler, *Messiah Jesus*, 480–510; Brandon, *Jesus and the Zealots*, 331–43. Moreover, this view creates a picture of Jesus incompatible with the rest of the synoptic tradition, sustainable only by crediting the evangelists with tendentiousness bordering on mendacity. See Haenchen's comment, *Weg Jesu*, 387: "Zwischen diesem Jesus, der mit seinem Anhängern gewaltsam in Tempel eine 'neue Ordnung' einführt, und dem Jesus der Gleichnisse und der Sprüche besteht eine tiefe Kluft."

intervention.[47] It was not intended to be directly efficacious, but was a symbolic act.[48]

That it was a prophetic act has an important consequence for assessing the unity of the action and teaching. Prophetic acts, reported frequently in the Hebrew Bible,[49] were usually accompanied by explanatory teaching (most often, a terse pronouncement). The tradition of prophetic acts continued in the rabbinic milieu contemporary to Jesus, commonly expressed in a three-part form consisting of "odd gesture — question — pronouncement."[50] A mystifying action generated a question leading to an explanation of significance. Appropriately, such gestures had their setting in a circle of disciples surrounding a master.

The narrative of Jesus' action in the Temple resembles the rabbinic three-part form. The middle element (the question) is either assumed or has dropped out.[51] Since "odd gestures" had as their raison d'être the pronouncement which followed, the immediate inference is that the action of Jesus was probably never without an interpretation — it would have been interpreted by Jesus himself. Thus, unless we imagine that the early Christian movement found that pronouncement totally puzzling and hence unworthy of preservation, there is a strong prima facie case for affirming that v. 17 preserves the interpretation given by Jesus. The burden of proof therefore rests with those who deny that v. 17 is an integral part of the incident. The burden can be shifted only by showing that the pronouncement makes no coherent sense of the situation.[52] Conversely, a demonstration of

---

47. This is affirmed not to save Jesus from the charge of unseemly behavior, as Rawlinson, Scott, and Macgregor are perhaps concerned to do (cited earlier), but because the nonintervention requires it. To say that it was a symbolic act need not imply that no force was used, only that it was limited compared to what would have been required to control the whole court.

48. So also R. J. McKelvey, *The New Temple* (London, 1969), 66; Dodd, *History and the Gospel* (New York, 1938), 132–33. Gaston, *No Stone*, 86: it is "an acted parable, a symbolic action which is important not in itself but in what it signifies and which collects an audience for the following interpretation." D. Daube, *Civil Disobedience in Antiquity* (Edinburgh, 1972), agrees that it was a prophetic act (p. 103), but affirms that violence was nevertheless involved; for his account, see pp. 101–9.

49. For example, Is. 8:1–4, 20; Jer. 13, 19, 27, 32; Ezek. 4, 12.

50. Daube, *New Testament and Rabbinic Judaism*, 175–81.

51. Though Daube himself does not include the Temple incident in his discussion of this particular form, he later says of it: "Mark informs us expressly not only that Jesus accompanied his action by teaching, but also that it was the teaching implied in and accompanying the action which astonished the crowd; it was not the external disturbance as such" (220). Thus he rather nicely makes the point that Mark understood the act to be subordinate to the ensuing teaching.

52. It is illuminating to consider two reasons given by commentators who separate

its appropriateness would confirm the prima facie case in favor of its authenticity.

Because the pronouncement is the key to understanding a prophetic act or "odd gesture," the interpretation must begin with it rather than with the (sometimes mystifying) action itself. Attention must be paid to both halves of the pronouncement, which strongly contrasted "My house shall be called a house of prayer for all the nations" with "But you have made it a den of robbers."

"Den of robbers." Contrary to the most common interpretation, "robbers" almost certainly cannot refer to economic dishonesty on the part of the merchants, or to the inappropriateness of commercial activity in the Temple precincts.[53] Throughout the Septuagint, apocrypha, New Testament, and Josephus, the Greek word translated as "robbers" (*lestes* singular, *lestai* plural) meant people who killed and destroyed while plundering, not simply those who stole without violence. For the latter, all of the sources knew and used cognates of *kleptes*.[54] Indeed, as noted earlier, *lestai* is Josephus's favorite designation for the armed resistance movement. Thus *lestai* cannot mean "robbers" (certainly not in the sense of clerks charging a high rate of exchange!), but is more appropriately translated as "violent ones," or "brigands."

Moreover, the phrase "den of robbers" is from Jer. 7:11. There the Hebrew word *parisim* does not mean "robbers," but rather "violent ones," and it refers to those who blissfully trusted that the Temple provided security against Babylon despite their violation of the covenant. One thus might translate "den of robbers" as "den of vio-

---

v. 17 from the incident. Trocmé, "L'expulsion," 14–15, doubts that it could have been pronounced "dans le grand désordre causé par l'expulsion des marchands." But it is surely unnecessary to think of the words simultaneously accompanying, e.g., the overturning of the tables: as teaching deriving from a symbolic act, the words follow the action. Bundy, *Jesus*, 427, writes of v. 17: "Such a calm, almost academic comment does not fit the radical nature of the action." But following a symbolic act, it is precisely an "academic" comment that is in order.

53. Urging this as the major or a major motive are Scott, *Crisis in the Life of Jesus*, 16–17, 49–50, 58, 66, 72–73; Marshall, *Challenge of New Testament Ethics*, 59; Wilson, *Execution of Jesus*, 98; Cullmann, *Jesus and the Revolutionaries*, 20; Bacon, *Beginnings of Gospel Story*, 161–62; Cranfield, *Mark*, 358; Taylor, *Mark*, 463; K. H. Rengstorf, *TDNT*, 4:260; G. Schrenk, *TDNT*, 3:243; A. T. Olmstead, *Jesus in the Light of History* (New York, 1942), 92–93; Hengel, *Die Zeloten*, 221, Jeremias, *New Testament Theology*, 145; Trocmé, "L'expulsion," 1–22; Schmid, *Mark*, 209.

54. See esp. G. W. Buchanan, "Mark 11:15–19: Brigands in the Temple," *HUCA* 30 (1959): 169–77. The one biblical exception to the distinction between *lestes* and *kleptes* is John 10:10, though even there *kleptes* may be "shorthand" for the *lestes* and *kleptes* mentioned two verses earlier. Buchanan's conclusion is emphatic: there is no linguistic basis for the use of *lestes* to describe "graft, greed, fraudulent, or unfair commercial practices" (p. 175). Rengstorf, *TDNT*, 4:257–62, also recognizes the linguistic meaning of *lestes*, but strangely does not affect his understanding of the incident.

lent ones." Hence the language excludes the unfair business practice interpretation.[55]

Instead, the remarkable convergence in meaning of *lestai* in the first century and *parisim* in Jer. 7 points decisively to the role of the Temple in resistance toward Rome.[56] The description of the Temple as a "den of violent ones" can be understood in either a specific or general sense. If the former, the reference might be to the Temple as the scene of actual military violence during the life of Jesus[57] and/or to the warning notice which promised a violent death to any Gentile who crossed into forbidden territory.[58] Probably, though, the greater emphasis should be placed on the general: the role of the Temple ideology in the quest for holiness with its corollary of resistance to foreign rule.[59] As the *parisim* in 586 B.C.E. trusted the Temple to guarantee their impunity vis-à-vis Babylon, so for many elements in first-century Judaism the Temple was both a guarantor of security and a focal point of liberation hopes.[60]

"House of prayer for all the nations." Over against this state of affairs, Jesus articulated the role which the Temple ought to play: Yahweh's house shall be "a house of prayer for all the nations." The line is a quotation from Is. 56:7. Though the parallels in Matthew and Luke

---

55. Moreover, in the performance of their largely necessary services, there is little evidence that inflated prices were charged or that pilgrims were fleeced, and a fair amount of evidence that profits were controlled. Further, the profits that did accrue did not fill private purses, but were put to public use. See T. Shek. 1:8; M. Shek. 1:7; above all, Abrahams, *Studies,* 1:82–89, esp. 85–86; concurring opinions in Nineham, *Mark,* 301, 303–4; Gaston, *No Stone,* 85; V. Eppstein, "The Historicity of the Gospel Account of the Cleansing of the Temple," *ZNW* 55 (1964): 43.

56. *Note added in 1998:* For an important way in which my understanding of this incident has changed, see the introduction to this revised edition.

57. For example, in 4 B.C.E. (see chapter 2). Violence in the Temple seems also to have happened during the ministry itself, for Luke 13:1–3 points to military action in the Temple, though whether those killed by Pilate's forces had engaged in a provocative act within the Temple precincts is indeterminate.

58. See chapter 3 above, p. 76.

59. For example, Buchanan, "Mark 11:15–19," 176–77; Gaston, *No Stone,* 85, 474; and C. Roth, "The Cleansing of the Temple and Zechariah," *NovTest* 4 (1960): 176–77. All argue that *spelaion leston* must refer to militant nationalist activity, and all three then seek an incident which justifies the charge. The first two, translating the phrase as "Zealot stronghold," argue that this part of the contrast is a Marcan creation since the Temple was not such until its occupation by the Zealots in the war of 66–70. Roth suggests that Jesus must have addressed the charge to his *followers* who, misinterpreting his act, now tried to make the Temple into a locus of rebellion (p. 176; on p. 181, he seems to contradict this). All three attempts overlook the fact that the charge is appropriate at any time in the first century, given the ideological and actual role of the Temple in Jewish resistance to Rome.

60. It is possible (though only that) that there is an interesting though unexpressed play on words between *parisim* and the word which had come to mean "separated ones," "holy ones": *perushim.* If so, Jesus indicts the present quest after holiness through separation as having made of the Temple a "cave of *parisim/perushim.*"

omit "for all the nations," the phrase should be regarded as original to Mark.[61] Moreover, it goes well with the contrast "den of violent ones." Instead of being a fountain of resistance, Jerusalem with its Temple was meant to be the city set on a hill whose light would reach the nations.[62] Thus those commentators who stress a connection to the issue of the Gentiles are correct, though the usual concomitant emphasis that Jesus expelled the merchants from the "Court of the Gentiles" so that Gentiles could pray in "their" court is probably incorrect.[63] For the designation "Court of the Gentiles" is modern, unknown in antiquity,[64] even though the outer court was the only area to which Gentiles were permitted access. But this court was neither named after them nor meant for them. Moreover, the claim that Jesus cleared space (historical or eschatological) for the Gentiles in the outer court implies that that was where they belonged, while Israel would continue to enjoy a fuller service within the inner courts. But there was no intimation of this in the Hebrew Bible when it anticipated Gentiles worshiping in the Temple; they would have the same privileges as Israel.[65] So the indict-

---

61. *Contra* Hiers, "Purification of the Temple," 89, and Gärtner, *Temple and Community*, 110–11, who suggest it may be a later gloss in Mark. If an explanation must be offered for its admittedly puzzling absence from Matthew and especially Luke, Manson's suggestion is feasible: writing after the destruction of the Temple, both evangelists omit it because it was now impossible for the Temple to be a house of prayer for the nations (*Jesus and the Non-Jews* [London, 1955], 12). So also Schmid, *Mark*, 210.

62. Matt. 5:14. For the Hebrew Bible background which makes it probable that this saying refers to Jerusalem and the Gentiles, see G. von Rad, "The City on the Hill," in *The Problem of the Hexateuch* (Edinburgh, 1966), 232–42: Jerusalem as the city of light on the hill "will be seen in all its glory *by the whole world*, with the result that it will be the centre of a universal pilgrimage *for all nations*" (234; italics added).

63. A. Menzies, *The Earliest Gospel* (London, 1901), 209, wrote of the outer court and the Gentiles: "meant for them, and called after them, yet how impossible is it for the pious Gentile to carry out there the object of his journey to Jerusalem." Other interpreters who place major (though not necessarily exclusive) emphasis on this aspect include S. Liberty, *The Political Relations of Christ's Ministry* (London, 1916); R. H. Lightfoot, *The Gospel Message of St. Mark* (Oxford, 1950), 62–68; Manson, *Jesus and the Non-Jews*, 12; Caird, *Luke*, 217; F. Filson, *A New Testament History* (Philadelphia, 1964), 129; Dodd, *Founder of Christianity*, 147; Bowman, *Which Jesus?* 152–53. Allusions to it in Scott, *Crisis*, 23–24, 142–43; Cranfield, *Mark*, 358. Emphasizing that Jesus creates *eschatological* space for the Gentiles are, above all, Jeremias, *Promise*, 65–66, and *New Testament Theology*, 245–47; Hahn, *Mission*, 36–38; Hiers, "Purification of the Temple," 89; Lohmeyer, *Lord of the Temple*, 39–42 (apparently on the level of Mark's redaction, for he is elsewhere skeptical of the historicity: *Markus*, 237).

64. See vol. 8 of the Loeb edition of Josephus, 202, n.b.; Gaston, *No Stone*, 87; S. Perowne, *The Life and Times of Herod the Great* (London, 1956), 138; Kennard, *Jesus in the Temple*, 23–24.

65. For example, Is. 56:7 refers to the sacrifices and offerings of the Gentiles as well as to their prayers. "House of prayer" there is an inclusive term embracing the manifold activities of Temple worship. In 1 Kings 8:41–43, where the preceding verses (e.g., 30, 33, 35, 38) make clear that the Temple is thought of preeminently as a place of prayer,

ment was not of the merchants (who in any case could not be called "violent ones," either linguistically or in terms of their integrity) who allegedly prevented Gentiles from praying, but of the quest for separation expressed in the Temple ideology which excluded Gentiles generally.

The words of interpretation contrasted the intended universal role of the Temple with its present role as a pillar of chauvinism. But what is to be made of the action itself? Why were the merchants expelled? The key lies in recognizing the reason for their presence on the Temple mount in the first century: to protect the holiness of the Temple. They did this by exchanging profane coinage for "holy" coinage, by providing sacrificial doves (and, as in John, animals) guaranteed free from blemish. Manifesting the clear-cut distinction between holy/profane, holy nation/profane nations, their activity served and symbolized the quest for holiness understood as separation, a quest at the root of resistance to Rome. The act of expelling them, consistent with the words of interpretation, affirmed that understanding of holiness to be in error. And thus the "odd gesture" and the words of interpretation cohere: the quest for a holy, separated nation had made of the Temple a "den of violent ones." The merchants, typifying that separation by their activity, were expelled because "My house shall be called a house of prayer for all the nations," not a center of resistance to the nations.

Corroboration of the Temple action as a protest against the quest for holiness is provided by its close connection to the entry into Jerusalem. As a deliberate acted fulfillment of Zech. 9:9[66] (both in Mark 11:1–10 and John 12:12–15) it combined the motifs of universalism and anti-resistance. The coming king mounted on the foal of an ass was to be a king of peace who would banish the war horse and the warrior's bow from Jerusalem and speak peace to the nations,[67] a function completely consistent with the indictment of the Temple as a center of nationalist resistance.

Moreover, both it and the Temple incident, occurring as they most probably did during Passover, were deliberately public acts. Indeed, if

---

even when the supplicants are Israelites, the coming of the Gentiles to Yahweh's house for prayer implies that they are on equal footing.

66. The influence of Zech. 9–14 on Mark 11 is admirably demonstrated by R. M. Grant, "The Coming of the Kingdom," *JBL* 67 (1948): 297–303; and F. F. Bruce, "The Book of Zechariah and the Passion Narrative," *BJRL* 43 (1960–61): 336–53, and *This Is That* (Exeter, 1968), 101–14. Both attribute the influence largely to Jesus himself.

67. J. Blenkinsopp's argument, "The Oracle of Judah and the Messianic Entry," *JBL* 80 (1961): 55–64, that Gen. 49:10 lies in the background of the entry does not compete with the use of Zech. 9:9 but, as he recognizes, supplements it. As a fulfillment of Gen. 49:10, the act points to the "expectation of the nations" and "repudiates once and for all the current solution to Israel's dire need" (64).

the language is not too modern, both were staged "political demonstrations" at the time of year when the Jewish nation was most
comprehensively gathered in Jerusalem. That they thus were a dramatic
appeal to the nation to abandon the quest for holiness and follow a
different politico-religious policy seems clear. Could the "mundane" political implications of the king of peace of Zech. 9:9 and the words of
the Temple indictment be missed in that situation?[68] It would seem not,
and both the protagonist and those who saw and heard him must have
realized this. The combination of the entry with the prophetic act in
the Temple offers strong confirmation that the latter was an indictment
of the ideology which came to expression in militant separation from
and resistance to the Gentiles.[69]

As an indictment, it also included an implicit threat. Namely, as
in the time of Jeremiah, the consequence (though perhaps not yet inevitable) of uncritical trust in the Temple would be destruction.[70] Very
importantly, the reason it offered for the impending judgment — "You
have made it a 'den of violent ones' " — provides an essential link between the movement of resistance against Rome and the warning of
catastrophe.

The Threat of Destruction

The Words against the Temple. The implicit though clear threat of destruction in Mark 11:15b–17 is matched by several explicit warnings
of the destruction of the Temple or Jerusalem, widely attested in the
tradition. Explicit references are found in Q (Luke 13:34–35=Matt.
23:37–39), Mark (13:2, 14:58, 15:29), L (Luke 19:42–44, 21:20–24),
Acts (6:14), and John (2:19). Not only did Jesus speak of it, but his
opponents charged him with having made such a threat (Mark 14:58,
15:29, cf. Acts 6:14). To these eight explicit references should also be
added those passages which threatened military action against the land

---

68. To add to the drama, it is probable that the "political demonstration" of Jesus' entry was matched on the same day by the entry of Pilate, with his cohort of troops, arriving
in Jerusalem from Caesarea for their regular "peace-keeping" attendance at Passover.

69. Though without following the same specific lines of exegesis, the general conclu-
sion is shared by G. B. Caird, "The Mind of Christ; Christ's Attitude to Institutions,"
ET 62 (1950–51): 259–60: "Instead of being the center of a world religion, the Temple
had become the symbol of nationalism and division"; and Schulz, "Markus und das Alte
Testament," 193: "Gerade mit ihrem Exklusivitätsdogma haben Israeliten und Juden aus
Gottes Haus eine 'Räuberhöhle' gemacht."

70. So too McKelvey, *The New Temple*, 66–67, who argues that both Mark and John
(and Jesus) understood it to contain a threat of destruction, "except that the contingency
present in the case of Jesus is absent in Mark."

in general.[71] Finally there is the difficult reference to the "desolating sacrilege" in Mark 13:14.

Upon inspection, the eight explicit references above divide themselves into two groups. The first groups speaks not only of a destruction of the Temple, but also of its replacement:

Mark 14:58: We heard him say, "I will destroy [kataluso] this Temple [naon] that is made with hands and after three days I will build another, not made with hands."

Mark 15:29–30: Those who passed by hurled abuse at him: "Aha!" they cried, wagging their heads, 'You who would destroy [kataluon] the Temple [naon] and build it in three days, save yourself!'

John 2:19: "Destroy [lusate] this Temple [naon]" Jesus replied, "and in three days I will raise it again."

Besides the common motif of destruction and rebuilding, all three use forms of luo/kataluo; all refer to the Temple as naon rather than hieron; all refer to the rebuilding as occurring in three days. In the two passages from Mark, the agent of destruction is Jesus. John's interpretation of naos as the body of Jesus required that he attribute the destruction to an agent other than Jesus, whatever the tradition which he received said. Finally, in the two passages from Mark, the tradition is found on the lips of people hostile to Jesus (false witnesses, mockers). To this tradition should also be added Acts 6:14, which, though it does not speak of the replacement of the Temple, uses kataluo, speaks of Jesus as the agent of destruction, and attributes the accusation to false witnesses.

The second group, on the other hand, does not speak of Jesus as the agent of destruction. Two (Luke 19:42–44, 21:20–24) explicitly identify the destroyer as a foreign army. A third speaks of an abandonment of the city by the divine presence, leaving it defenseless (Luke 13:34–35 par.). A fourth (Mark 13:2) speaks of a destruction in which "not one stone will be left on another," a fate which in Luke 19:44 is the result of military conquest. Nor does the second group use naos to refer to that which will be destroyed. Instead it is Jerusalem (Luke 13:34–35 par., 19:42–44, 21:20–24), hieron (Mark 13:1), "these great buildings" (Mark 13:2).[72] Unlike the first group, kataluo/luo do not appear, except in the concluding phrase in Mark 13:2, where kataluthe may be derived from the tradition preserved in Mark 14:58. Finally, there is no attribution to false witnesses.

71. Mark 13:14b–18; Luke 13:1–5, 17:31–37, 23:28–31.

72. It should be noted, however, that whereas Jerusalem is integral to the first three warnings, hieron and "these great buildings" are part of the setting for the pronouncement in 13:2b, not part of the warning itself.

Attempts have been made to reduce these two traditions to one. Usually this is done by arguing that Mark 14:58 et al. contain the more primitive tradition, with Mark 13:2 et al. understood as later community formulations.[73] On this view, Jesus (or the community at a very early date) originally spoke of Jesus building a new Temple. The motif of destruction (whether by Jesus, as a false accusation, or by an agent other than Jesus, as a "historicizing" of the tradition) entered the tradition later.

The German scholar Rudolf Pesch has made a thorough case for this view. According to Pesch, Mark 13:1–4 (and with it 13:2b) stem totally from Marcan composition. Mark 13:2b in particular has been formulated on the basis of 14:58.[74] However, as Jacques Dupont convincingly pointed out, the only word common to both Mark 14:58 and Mark 13:2 is *kataluo*. It occurs in the final phrase of 13:2b and may well be adventitious. The words that form the nucleus of the warning (*aphiemi, lithos epi lithon*) are absent from 14:58.[75] Rather, if Mark 13:2b is linguistically linked to another synoptic passage, it is not to Mark 14:58, but to Luke 19:44, which contains a form of *aphiemi* as well as the phrase *lithon epi lithon*.[76]

Yet the relationship here cannot be literary. For example, if Luke is thought to have copied it from Mark, one would have to imagine him, after using Mark 11:10 in 19:38, turning forward to Mark 13:2 for this phrase and then using it again in Luke 21:6.[77] More likely, its presence in Luke is due to his use of another source for which, as we shall soon see, there is corroboratory evidence. But this means that the primitive tradition contained *two independent* witnesses to a logion which said, "There shall not be left one stone on another." Thus the attempt to account for Mark 13:2 et al. as derivative from Mark 14:58 et al. must be regarded as unsuccessful. We should therefore avoid an initial reduction of the two traditions to one.[78] Both are attested by a multiplicity of witnesses.

---

73. E.g., R. Pesch, *Naherwartungen: Tradition und Redaktion in Mk 13* (Düsseldorf, 1968), 83–96; Brandon, *Jesus and the Zealots*, 233–36; Marxsen, *Mark*, 167–68. They argue that Mark 14:58, which reflects the primitive community's contrast of the Temple to the risen lord and originally said nothing about a destruction, is modified by Mark in 13:2 so that "Mark is the first to speak of an actual destruction"; G. R. Beasley-Murray, *Jesus and the Future* (London, 1954), 251 (though he disagrees), cites Loisy, Colani, and Wellhausen, as well as Dodd, who does not seem to the present writer to hold this view.

74. Pesch, *Naherwartungen*, 91–92.

75. J. Dupont, "Il n'en sera pas laissé pierre sur pierre (Marc 13:2; Luc 19:44)," *Biblica* 52 (1971): 307–8.

76. Gaston, *No Stone*, 12, 66, 244; Hartman, *Prophecy Interpreted*, 220; Dupont, "Il n'en sera pas laissé pierre sur pierre," 304, 309–14.

77. Dupont, "Il n'en sera pas laissé pierre sur pierre," 313–14.

78. So also Hartman, *Prophecy Interpreted*, 219–20; Beasley-Murray, *Jesus and the Future*, 251–52.

Yet if one is to be chosen as the firmer point of departure, Mark 13:2 et al. are to be preferred, for several reasons. First, Jesus is unlikely ever to have said, "*I* will destroy this Temple," as almost all commentators agree.[79] Second, even if this difficulty is removed by converting the statement to the passive voice (the Temple will be destroyed) or ironic imperative ("Destroy this Temple," as it appears in John 2:19), difficulties remain. If "Temple" is used simply in the transferred sense given to it by John's interpretation in John 2:20–22, then the saying did not refer to the Jerusalem Temple at all, but to the body of Jesus. If on the other hand "Temple" refers to the literal Temple in the first half and the spiritual Temple in the second, the saying seems to predicate the building of the spiritual Temple upon the destruction of the old literal Temple, which makes no sense.[80] It is therefore difficult to believe that Jesus spoke of the destruction and rebuilding of the Temple in the same saying in this terse fashion, though he could have spoken of each in different sayings. Third, Mark 14:58 contains phrases characteristic of the church's theology: "in three days" and "made with hands/not made with hands."[81] Finally, for whatever reason, this form of the saying is always attributed to opponents. All of this renders the extraction of an authentic nucleus from Mark 14:58 problematic.[82]

---

79. Only a very few have urged that he did; among them is Lohmeyer, *Lord of the Temple*, 67–68. Against this affirmation may be cited: (1) How would Jesus have arrived at such an idea? Even if one affirms that Jesus thought of himself as the Messiah, there is very little evidence that the Messiah was expected to destroy the Temple; see Gaston, *No Stone*, 102–61, esp. 147–54. (2) It makes nonsense of the warnings concerning its destruction *by others*, which are better attested (Mark, Q, L, John). (3) It occurs only in statements attributed to hostile parties.

80. See Kümmel, *Promise and Fulfillment*, 101, n. 46. On the other hand, perhaps "Destroy this Temple, and I will build another" need not refer to a temporal sequence of literal destruction followed then (and only then) by a "new building." It would then mean, roughly, "Take the decision which will result in its destruction and I will build another."

81. "Not made with hands": Mark 14:58; 2 Cor. 5:1; Col. 2:11. "Made with hands": Mark 14:58; Acts 7:48, 17:24; Eph. 2:11; Heb. 9:11, 24. See especially C. F. D. Moule, "Sanctuary and Sacrifice in the Church of the New Testament," *JTS* 1 (1950): 29–41, who argues that the contrast was part of early Christian catechetical training, designed to give Christians an answer to opponents or inquirers who asked, "Where is your Temple?"

82. This is not to discard completely the tradition in Mark 14:58 et al., or to argue that it can be shown to have its origin in Mark 13:2 et al. Though there is not here the space to offer a complete argument, it is possible to account for Mark 14:58 in the following manner. It is possible that Jesus spoke of building another Temple (equals "community"), and certain that he spoke of the destruction of the Jerusalem Temple by others. Some of his opponents, knowing this, either honestly or maliciously did two things: (1) They combined the "destruction by others"/"building by Jesus" motifs into one saying; (2) And put it all into the first person. This accounts for their accusation and the characterization of it as false. On this view, Mark 14:58 offers evidence for the building of a new Temple by Jesus, but not for the destruction of the old by Jesus. Alternatively, if the

We therefore begin with the tradition preserved in Mark 13:2 et al.

1. *Mark 13:2:* And Jesus said to him, "Do you see these great buildings? There will not be left here one stone upon another that will not be
thrown down."

Formally the saying is a pronouncement story, with the nucleus in 2b.[83]
About the authenticity of 2b there need be little doubt.[84] Yet something
very much like 2a must have circulated with the warning from the beginning in order to give it a setting, even though the rest (vv. 1, 3, and
4) may be Marcan.[85]

As a saying of Jesus, the warning repudiated the belief in the inde-
structibility of the Temple, a belief here manifested in an exclamation
about the massiveness of the structure. Just as Jeremiah six centuries
before indicted those who expressed their trust in the Temple with the
threefold refrain, "This place is the Temple of the Lord,"[86] so Jesus in
the first century warned that "these great buildings" were not inviolable.

No indictment (a reason or warrant for the threat) is explicitly attached to this threat. But in the Marcan narrative the text is connected
to the rejection of the course which Jesus advocated in Mark 11–
12. This link suggests that Mark understood the threat in prophetic
rather than apocalyptic terms. The warning was not issued to conform
to a predetermined apocalyptic scheme, but was a consequence of the
failure of Jesus' mission as a renewal movement within Israel.[87] It conforms to the classic prophetic pattern of the Hebrew Bible, "Because...
therefore." Even though the Marcan setting is redactional, what was
true for Mark here was also likely to have been the case for Jesus. It is
inherently possible (and probably likely) that Jesus spoke of the fate of
Jerusalem during a visit to the city which he deliberately intended.

2. *Luke 13:34–35=Matt. 23:37–39.* O Jerusalem, the city that murders
the prophets and stones the messengers sent to her! How often have I
longed to gather your children, as a hen gathers her brood under her

---

suggested interpretation of John 2:19 in note 80 above be allowed, it could represent the
authentic core.

83. Bultmann, *History of the Synoptic Tradition*, 36.

84. See authorities cited by Gaston, *No Stone*, 65, n. 1: Bultmann, Goguel, Klostermann, Lohmeyer, Taylor, Schniewind, Wellhausen, Kümmel, Simon, Cullmann, R. A.
Hoffmann, Jeremias, Michel, A. Oepke, Flew, Delling, Cole.

85. Against the claim that 13:1, 3–4 are Marcan is Beasley-Murray, *A Commentary
on Mark Thirteen*, 19–29.

86. Jer. 7:4. For an impressive citation of the conceptual links between this section of
Mark and Jer. 7, see Hooker, *Son of Man in Mark*, 153–54.

87. Hooker, *Son of Man in Mark*, 150–55.

wings; but you would not let me. Look, look! There is your house, abandoned. And I tell you, you will not see me until the time comes when
you say, "Blessed is the one who comes in the name of the Lord!"

This passage from Q is cast in the form of a dirge.[88] As such, it not only
lamented the unresponsiveness of Jerusalem, but warned of destruction:
"There is your house, abandoned." "House" in this passage almost certainly means "the Temple."[89] The Temple has been abandoned. The
language echoes what happened when the previous Temple was destroyed by the army of Babylon in 586 B.C.E. in the time of Jeremiah
and Ezekiel. The Shekinah — the divine presence — left the Temple,
exposing the city and sanctuary, bereft of the divine protection, to
destruction.[90] Something similar was at stake in his generation, Jesus'
words implied.

But an additional motif flows from a consideration of the closing
half of Luke 13:35 (=Matt. 23:39). The words have often seemed puzzling: "I tell you, you will not see me until the time comes when you
say, 'Blessed is the one who comes in the name of the Lord!'" Most
commentators have assumed that the first-person pronoun here means
Jesus. On this view, Jesus (or the post-Easter tradition) promised somebody that they would not see Jesus again until the time came when they
used the acclamation "Blessed is the one who comes in the name of the
Lord!" The quoted words are from Ps. 118:26 and are part of the liturgy
for the Jewish festivals of Tabernacles, Passover, and Pentecost.

Two interpretations seem possible when the "I" is thus identified with
Jesus. A few scholars suppose that Jesus was designating the time when
he would next go to Jerusalem. He would go there at a time when the
people of Jerusalem (or the followers of Jesus, as in the entry into Jerusalem narrative) next used this acclamation, presumably at a festival.[91]

---

88. C. F. Burney, *The Poetry of Our Lord* (Oxford, 1925), 146.

89. The Greek word translated as "house" is *oikos*. The New English Bible renders it
as "Temple," as do, among others, C. H. Dodd, *Parables*, 44–45, and Baltzer, "The Meaning of the Temple in the Lukan Writings," 272. Strack-Billerbeck, 1:943–44, disagree,
claiming that *oikos* can never mean "Temple" when used with "your." However, there is
an exception in Is. 64:10. But since it is a solitary exception, perhaps *oikos* should be
translated as "commonwealth" (cf. Jer. 12:7) or "city." But the sense of the passage is not
substantially altered, since Temple, city, and commonwealth stand or fall together. See
H. van der Kwaak, "Die Klage über Jerusalem," *NovTest* 8 (1966): 163: "Auf jeden Fall
ist die Suggestion des Wortes deutlich: die Gegenwart Gottes, die 'Shekinah,' zieht sich
zurück."

90. Cf. Jer. 12:7: "I have forsaken my house, I have abandoned my heritage, I have
given the beloved of my soul into the hands of her enemies."

91. T. F. Glasson, *The Second Advent*, 3d ed. (London, 1963), 3:96, 98–99, but only
after separating the last sentence from the lament; M. Goguel, *La Vie de Jésus* (Paris,
1932), 408–9; R. Otto, *The Kingdom of God and the Son of Man* (London, 1938), 172,
cites Goguel's view with approval.

T. W. Manson's comment is appropriate: "it seems a very high-falutin' way of conveying a very prosaic piece of information."[92]

More scholars favor the meaning implied by Matthew's setting, where it may point forward to the parousia. But this is also awkward, for it not only supposes that Jesus spoke of his own parousia,[93] but that the people of Jerusalem would greet his parousia with the words, "Blessed is the one who comes in the name of the Lord." It seems exceedingly unlikely that the synoptic writers (or Jesus himself, if he spoke of his own parousia) thought that the inhabitants of the city would greet the parousia in such fashion.[94]

But another identity for the first person pronoun is possible. Indeed, because of the allusions to the Hebrew Bible and because it makes sense of the passage, it seems more probable. Namely, the "I" refers to God, not to Jesus. As is very common in prophetic oracles in the Hebrew Bible, the "I" is "God," even though the actual speaker is the prophet (in this case, Jesus.)[95] The suggestion is supported by the image of a bird sheltering or gathering its offspring under its wings; in the Hebrew Bible, this is a common metaphor for Yahweh sheltering the people of Israel.[96]

On this interpretation, it is Yahweh who sent the prophets, who longed to gather Jerusalem's citizens, who was refused, who now abandoned the city. If we continue to substitute "Yahweh" for "I" in the rest of the passage, it reads:

---

92. Manson, *Mission and Message*, 420. So also Kümmel, *Promise and Fulfillment*, 81n, and Plummer, *Luke*, 353. Manson, however, later withdrew his remark and argued, "All that is necessarily implied is a definition of the time of the next meeting...," which, according to Manson, was probably intended to be at Tabernacles; see "The Cleansing of the Temple," *BJRL* 33 (1950–51): 279n. His earlier judgment seems more sound.

93. See below pp. 231–33.

94. Van der Kwaak, "Die Klage über Jerusalem," 165–66, cites W. Trilling and G. Strecker as affirming that it does refer to a *terrified* greeting by the unrepentant inhabitants at Jesus' return as judge. After examining the uses of "blessed" in the LXX and the New Testament, van der Kwaak concludes that it cannot bear that meaning. Plummer, *Luke*, 353, also properly dismisses the view that it refers to the parousia: "where are we told that the unbelieving Jews will welcome the returning Christ with hymns of praise?" Having dismissed both of the common interpretations, Plummer then spiritualizes the saying and refers it to the conversion of Jews throughout all time when Jesus comes to them spiritually. This interpretation seems insufficiently historical.

95. Q may also support this. In Matthew the dirge is connected to the saying about the blood of the prophets being required of this generation (Matt. 23:34–36), a Q saying which in its Lucan form (11:49–50) identifies the "I" with God or the Wisdom of God. Thus if Q connected the sayings as Matthew does, the "I" of the lament must be God (or the Wisdom of God). See also Creed, *Luke*, 187.

96. Deut. 32:11; Ps. 17:8, 36:7, 57:1, 61:4, 91:4; Ruth 2:12; Is. 31:5. For a post–New Testament parallel to the whole passage in which the first person is clearly God, see 4 Ezra 1:28–33.

And I [Yahweh] tell you, you shall never see me [Yahweh] until the time comes when you say, "Blessed is the one [Jesus (?)][97] who comes in the name of the Lord!"

Seen this way, the passage contains a promise as well as a threat. Though the Shekinah had left the Temple, it would return (you will see *me*) if Jerusalem recognized Jesus, the one who came in Yahweh's name. Moreover, like many prophetic threats in the Hebrew Bible, the threat was contingent: the divine presence (and the divine protection) would return if Israel recognized the one who now came in the name of Yahweh. But if not, ahead lay destruction.

Against the above interpretation is the oddity within the Jewish tradition of speaking of "seeing" God. However, such language is not unparalleled. The New Testament uses the expression at least three times.[98] It is more frequent in the Hebrew Bible. Moreover, the contexts in which it occurs commonly associate it with God's presence in Israel,[99] precisely the context in which it occurs here.

Most illuminating is Is. 52:8, a section of Isaiah frequently cited in the New Testament: "for with their own eyes they shall *see Yahweh returning* in pity *to Zion*." Of course the historic reference is to the return of Yahweh to Jerusalem during the return from exile in Babylon. But what is significant is that "seeing Yahweh" is spoken of in the context of the divine return to Jerusalem for deliverance, which is identical to the conditional promise offered in this passage.

As part of Q, this passage as a whole cannot be a *vaticinium ex eventu*. There seems to be no sufficient reason to deny it to Jesus.[100] The saying characterized his generation as standing at the climax of a series of

---

97. So also B. Lindars, *New Testament Apologetic* (London, 1961), 172–73, who argues that "the one who comes" must refer to a different person from the speaker, whom he identifies as Yahweh throughout: "it seems to be a prophecy in which the speaker is God himself."

98. Matt. 5:8; Rev. 22:4; 1 John 3:22; implicitly in Heb. 12:14. Matt. 5:8 is especially striking: "How blest are those whose hearts are pure; they shall see God."

99. Ex. 24:10; Num. 14:14; 1 Kings 22:19=2 Chr. 18:18; Job 42:5; Ps. 17:5, 63:2; Is. 6:1, 52:8; Amos 9:1. Buchanan, *The Consequences of the Covenant*, 74, n. 10, observes that though the expression is strange, it does cohere with Hebrew Bible thought and relates to the Temple.

100. The alternative is to attribute it to a prophet of the early church. However, very little is actually known about the extent to which such prophets attributed their own prophecies to Jesus, despite the confident assignment of various sayings to them by some scholars. See the reservations of Downing, *The Church and Jesus*, 120–21. Moreover, unless we attribute their inspiration to a starkly unmediated activity of the Spirit, it is difficult to see why early Christian prophets would concern themselves with the impending destruction of Jerusalem unless there had been some impetus for this in the teaching of Jesus.

futile attempts by Yahweh to gather the people. Like preceding generations, that generation did not respond. The oracle spoke directly to the
ideology of resistance founded on the Temple. Jerusalem, confident that
Yahweh's presence meant security, was warned that the Shekinah had
abandoned Zion. One of the pillars of resistance was undercut. But the
threat was contingent: the Shekinah would return if Israel responded
to the way of compassion. The saying thus presumed the possibility
of a historical future for Jerusalem, for it makes no sense to speak of
the return of the Shekinah if the impending destruction was seen as
inevitable and final.

Besides these two warnings in Mark and Q, two more warnings are
found in material peculiar to Luke: 19:41–44, 21:20–24. For the most
part, these two Lucan texts have not counted for much in historical reconstructions of Jesus. Because they are singly attested in a work whose
final redaction occurred after 70 c.e., they are most frequently set aside
by scholars as *vaticinia ex eventu* (that is, as "predictions" created after
the event). Consequently, a case must be made for their authenticity.
I aim to establish with a reasonable degree of probability that they are
pre-70 Palestinian tradition (the tradition of the Jesus movement) and
not simply post-70 *vaticinia ex eventu*. Before considering the two texts
individually, I make two comments applicable to both.

The first concerns the way these two texts from Luke were seen
by Hans Conzelmann, one of the most influential Lucan scholars in
the middle of this century. He attributed both to Luke's "historicizing" of what was originally an eschatological expectation. According
to this view, Jesus expected the destruction of the Temple as part of the
"end-time" events to be brought about directly by God. Because "the
end" hadn't happened by the time Luke wrote (even though Jerusalem
and the Temple had been destroyed), Luke separated the expectation of
the Temple's destruction from "the end" and attributed it to historical
causes.[101] But his argument does not in itself entail that the warnings
are *ex eventu*. Indeed, it presumes the opposite, namely, the existence of
traditions prior to 70 c.e. which threatened the fall of Jerusalem (otherwise Luke would not have needed to historicize them, if that is what
he has done). Moreover, the claim that an eschatological expectation
excludes historical causes is indefensible.[102] The two, consistently inter-

---

101. H. Conzelmann, *The Theology of St. Luke* (New York, 1961), 113–35, esp. 125–
35.

102. As Kümmel, *Promise and Fulfillment*, strongly insists. That Jesus saw the fate of
Jerusalem in "a strictly eschatological sense" (99) eliminates the political and historical.
He claims (48), "that there can be no question of Jesus having expected a national catas-
trophe which he deduced from the political situation" and adds (101), "the theory that

twined in both the Hebrew Bible and intertestamental literature, are not to be sequestered[103] unless there are compelling reasons for doing so. Marxsen's question, originally addressed to Lohmeyer, is appropriate: "must the two contradict each other? Are not apocalyptic events always considered in their relation to political turmoil?"[104] So *even if* the tradition prior to Luke expected the fall of Jerusalem to usher in the cosmic dissolution and renewal of all things, there is no reason to say that Luke is the first to attribute the destruction to historical causes.[105]

Second, there is nothing in the language of the two Lucan oracles which requires the supposition that he created them out of a knowledge of what happened in 70 c.e. C. H. Dodd has demonstrated, first, that those details which do reflect the Roman conquest are ones which would be found in the siege of most walled cities in ancient times and would therefore be present in any threat, whether *ex eventu* or not.[106] Further, Dodd notes, Luke includes a detail which may not have happened (dashing children to the ground) and omits many of the distinctive features which caught the attention of Josephus: famine, factionalism, disease, and fire, to which should be added the appalling act in which Titus's troops sacrificed to their standards in the Temple.[107] Finally, the language which Luke does use is "entirely" the language of the Hebrew Bible. Dodd concludes, "So far as any historical event has coloured the picture, it is not Titus's capture of Jerusalem in a.d. 70, but Nebuchadnezzar's capture in 586 b.c."[108]

Jesus predicted the destruction of Jerusalem as a historical event because of the growing tension between the Jews and the Romans would not only take Mark 13:2 out of its connexion with Mark 14:58; Matt. 23:38, but would also ascribe to Jesus a prediction about the future course of earthly history without any parallel in the Jesus tradition."

103. The following passages in the Hebrew Bible associate a military assault on Jerusalem or Israel with the end of the age: Zech. 12:2–3; 14; Joel 3; Is. 29; Dan. 12. Harman, *Prophecy Interpreted*, 80–100, finds that an assault on the city is one item in the pattern of end-time expectations: 1 En. 90:13–19, 66:5–8; Or. Sib. 3:663–97; 2 Bar. 48:37, 70:7–71:1; 4 Ez. 13:5–11, 34–38; Ps. Sol. 17:23–27; Jub. 23:23.

104. Marxsen, *Mark*, 181. He asks the same question when discussing Schniewind's claim that the flight motif of Mark 13:15–16 belongs to the last things, not to a historical event: "Why not? These need not be contradictory!" (183n).

105. This is not to deny, of course, that he saw the judging activity of God in these historical events.

106. Brandon, *Jesus and the Zealots*, 318, and *The Fall of Jerusalem and the Christian Church*, 207, points to the circumvallation (Luke 19:43) as a decisive correspondence between Luke's warning and what actually happened. However, circumvallation was a common feature of ancient sieges; most notably, Nebuchadnezzar raised a siege wall around Jerusalem: 2 Kings 25:1–2; Jer. 52:4–5; see also Ezek. 4:1–3, 21:11, 26:8. See L. Gaston, "Sondergut und Markusstoff in Luk. 21," *ThZ* 16 (1960): 163.

107. *B.J.* 6.316. Titus and his staff also entered the holy of holies (*B.J.* 6.260). As Brandon, *Jesus and the Zealots*, 231, points out, here is the son of one blasphemously worshiped as a god standing in the Temple.

108. C. H. Dodd, "The Fall of Jerusalem and the 'Abomination of Desolation,'" *JRS*

In short, the two Lucan oracles lack the characteristics whereby *vaticinia ex eventu* are identified.[109] They could have been composed or uttered by anyone (Jesus, or somebody within the early Christian community) who anticipated the fall of Jerusalem, and knew the Hebrew Bible well. All that remains in favor of the argument *ex eventu* is that they are found in a work whose final redaction is *post eventum*. But one must beware of the fallacy *post eventum ergo propter eventum*, especially where there is, as shall soon be seen, evidence of a positive kind that the oracles are primitive.

3. *Luke 19:42–44.* [42]Would that even today you knew the things that make for peace! But now they are hid from your eyes. [43]For the days shall come upon you, when your enemies will cast up a bank about you and surround you, and hem you in on every side, [44]and dash you to the ground, you and your children within you, and they will not leave one stone upon another in you; because you did not know the time of your visitation.

Positive evidence that this is not a Lucan composition *ex eventu* is the presence of Aramaisms. Jacques Dupont notes especially that vv. 43–44b contain five short phrases introduced by five consecutive "and"s, and nine possessives, very common in Aramaic, and which, moreover, Luke normally seeks to eliminate.[110] Bultmann also grants that the logion is perhaps quite old and Aramaic in origin,[111] and Matthew Black suggests that v. 44c shows signs of translation from Aramaic.[112] Dupont, however, limits the assuredly pre-Lucan oracle to vv. 43–44b (omitting

---

37 (1947): 47–54, reprinted in Dodd's *More New Testament Studies* (Manchester, 1968), 69–83; quoted words are from the latter, 79.

109. Though Dodd's argument has not had an impact in all quarters, this is more because it is overlooked than countered. The only rejection of it known to this writer is that of S. G. Wilson, "Lukan Eschatology," *NTS* 16 (1970): 339, who comments on Dodd's analysis: "It is, however, an improbable explanation of their origin, mainly because one has to imagine a hotchpotch oracle being composed with one word from one Old Testament verse and two from another, etc. — scarcely a conceivable process." Wilson's description of the process as "hotchpotch" is needlessly pejorative, for it is in fact the method used by a person deeply immersed in the thought of the Hebrew Bible; see, for example, the use of the Hebrew Bible in Luke 1–2 and Revelation. Furthermore, his objection is irrelevant, for the echoes of language from the Hebrew Bible are in fact there, and the process of composition is equally easy or difficult to imagine whether they were composed prior to or after 70 C.E.

110. Dupont, "Il n'en sera pas laissé pierre sur pierre," 312 and notes. He also cites Wellhausen, Bultmann, Grundmann, Burney, and Bundy.

111. Bultmann, *History of the Synoptic Tradition*, 123. On the same page he inconsistently affirms that it is *ex eventu*; how it can be quite old, perhaps Aramaic, and yet post-70 is mystifying.

112. Black, *Aramaic Approach*, 115. The evidence lies in the difficult D reading: *eis kairon* instead of *ton kairon*, which can be explained either as dittography (from *eiselthon* in v. 45) or as an Aramaism. Since v. 44 is Semitic Greek and a saying of Jesus, *eis kairon*

"because you did not know the time of your visitation" from v. 44) on the grounds that vv. 42, 44c contain characteristically Lucan vocabulary and motifs.[113] Certainty is not possible, but it is clear that many of these "Lucan" characteristics in fact characterize the pre-Lucan tradition. Thus, though peculiar to Luke, they are not necessarily Lucan in origin.[114]

Even if the pre-Lucan oracle is limited to vv. 43–44b, then it adds to the threat tradition by making explicit what was implicit in the Q and Marcan threats. The coming destruction was to be at the hands of an enemy army, which in the first century could only mean Rome. The events of 586 B.C.E. threatened to repeat themselves; only the identity of the oppressor had changed. The future did not hold the prospect of triumph for the movement of liberation. That generation would not see Israel's enemies repulsed in the last assault on the city, but its own devastation by those enemies, so thorough that not one stone would be left on another.

If vv. 42 and 44b are also included in the pre-Lucan tradition, then a warrant is added to the threat. Because Israel did not know the things that made for *shalom*,[115] war now threatened. Nor did Israel realize that this was the time of God's visitation. With the term "visitation," the passage characterized that time as a decisive time for Israel: the time in which God visited Israel, for judgment or blessing, with the result dependent upon Israel's response.[116] The implicit parallelism between the contrasts blessing/judgment, *shalom*/war, implied that Israel's failure to understand that this was the decisive time brought on the alternative

---

may be a "translation version of an Aramaic saying." For the Aramaic construction, see his 80, n. 2.

113. Dupont, "Il n'en sera pas laissé pierre sur pierre," 310–11. On v. 42: *ta pros eirenen* occurs elsewhere only in Luke 14:32; the adverb *nun* occurs four times in Matthew, three times in Mark, fourteen times in Luke and twenty-five times in Acts; the motif of ignorance is Lucan.

114. For example, the other occurrence of *ta pros eirenen* (14:32) is in a parable, and there the phrase is found in an Aramaic construction (Jeremias, *Parables*, 196, n. 20). Though the "ignorance motif" is prominent in the Lucan writings, it seems to be part of the pre-Lucan tradition as well: implicit in all of the primitive kerygmatic speeches in Acts, it is explicit in two (Acts 3:17, 13:27). The theme of visitation, as well as being strongly biblical, is found in other passages not commonly attributed to Luke's editorial activity: 1:68, 78. Moreover, v. 42 may contain a word play on Aramaic "peace" (*shelama*) and the popular etymology of Jerusalem as "vision of Peace" (see Mansion, *Mission and Message*, 612).

115. *Shalom*, of course, does not mean simply spiritual peace, but wholeness of life both for the individual and the community. It is a political as well as religious concept. See Gaston, *No Stone*, 334–35.

116. For "visitation" as the coming of God, either in judgment or blessing, see Robinson, *Jesus and His Coming*, 59–82; Gaston, *No Stone*, 335–39.

of judgment/war. Recognition would have brought on the alternative of blessing/*shalom*.

> 4. *Luke 21:20, 21b–22, 23b–24.* But when you see Jerusalem encircled by armies, then you may be sure that her destruction is near. [21b]Those who are in the city must leave it, and those who are out in the country must not enter; [22]because this is the time of retribution, when all that stands written is to be fulfilled. [23b]For there will be great distress in the land and a terrible judgment upon this people. [24]They will fall at the sword's point; they will be carried into all countries; and Jerusalem will be trampled down by foreigners until their day has run its course.

In its present form in Luke, this text has been combined with Marcan material. Mark 13:14b ("then let those who are in Judea flee to the mountains") appears in v. 21a, and Mark 13:17 ("Alas for those who are with child and for those who give suck in those days!") appears in v. 23a. The remaining verses are completely independent from Mark. Of the alternatives of viewing 21:20, 21b–22, 23b–24 as freely created by Luke in his rewriting of Mark or as a pre-Lucan oracle, the case for the latter is reasonably strong.

First, these verses are not only completely independent from Mark, but constitute a formal homogeneous whole with both rhythm and parallelism.[117] Second, as it now stands, *autes* and *eis auten* in 21b must refer to Judea in 21a and should be translated:

> [21a]let those who are in Judea flee to the mountains, [21b] and let those who are in the midst of *Judea* [*en meso autes*, with Judea as the antecedent] depart, and let not those who are out in the country enter *Judea* [*eis auten*, again with Judea as the antecedent].

But that makes no sense. If, however, 21a is removed, then *autes/auten* have as a perfectly sensible antecedent "Jerusalem" in v. 20.[118] This creates a strong presumption in favor of an original connection between vv. 20 and 21b.[119] Third, if Luke here is freely rewriting Mark as opposed to using a separate source, he departs notably from his usual procedure of using Mark, both in this immediate context and in general.[120] Thus the oracle most probably stems from a pre-Lucan tradition.[121]

---

117. Dodd, "The Fall of Jerusalem," 71–72. Also stressed by P. Winter, "The Treatment of His Sources by the Third Evangelist in Luke xxi–xxiv," *StTh* 8 (1954): 145–46; Gaston, "Sondergut und Markusstoff in Luk. 21," 161–72; Hartman, *Prophecy Interpreted*, 227–28, attaches secondary importance to the homogeneity.

118. As, in fact, the NEB and RSV translate it.

119. So also Dodd, "The Fall of Jerusalem," 72; Gaston, "Sondergut und Markusstoff in Luk. 21," 165.

120. Stressed by Hartman, *Prophecy Interpreted*, 227–28.

121. Sharing this conclusion in addition to Dodd, Gaston, Hartman, and Winter

As already noted, Dodd has demonstrated that the language of this warning does not presuppose knowledge of the Roman siege but is drawn from the Hebrew Bible. However, Dodd deliberately limited his investigation to links with the Septuagint, though without presupposing that the links exist only in Greek.[122] Lars Hartman has carried the argument further and has shown that the association of certain motifs through key words in Luke 21:20–24, 25–28, can be explained only on the basis of the Masoretic text, not on the basis of the LXX.[123] Not only is this additional evidence for the existence of a source which Luke used in addition to Mark, but it also points to the antiquity of the tradition.

The content of the threat pointedly reversed the ideology of resistance rooted in the Temple. "When you see Jerusalem surrounded by armies" should have been the sign that Yahweh's intervention in behalf of Israel was imminent; the assault on the city by Israel's enemies should presage their defeat and Israel's exaltation.[124] But the expectation was reversed: the assault would be a sign "that its desolation has come near." Nor was the encirclement of the city to be a sign that faithful Jews should join the defense. Instead, "Let those who are in the city depart,[125] and let not those who are out in the country enter in." The reversal of contemporary expectation and the counsel to leave the city are followed in vv. 22, 23b–24 by more echoes of the Hebrew Bible, particularly day-of-Yahweh passages. These make it clear that the fall of Jerusalem was understood as the judgment of God:[126] these are

are Hahn, *Mission*, 128n; M. Goguel, "Luke and Mark: With a Discussion of Streeter's Theory," *NTR* 26 (1933): 28; T. Schramm, *Markuss-stoff bei Lukas* (Cambridge, 1971), 178–80; and most advocates of Proto-Luke. Hartman, *Prophecy Interpreted*, 227, also cites B. Weiss, Bacon, A. Schlatter, F. Busch, Manson, J. A. T. Robinson, Taylor, Beasley-Murray, and K. H. Rengstorf.

122. It is important to note that agreement with the LXX in itself is no indication that the oracles were composed by somebody using the LXX, nor is it an objection to authenticity. The "translators" of Jesus' Aramaic speech into Greek could be expected to use LXX words familiar to them, and even upon occasion to look up a passage in the LXX. Only when the citation depends upon the LXX against known Hebrew versions is the use of the LXX a factor in the question of authenticity. See France, *Jesus and the Old Testament*, 25–37, 240–58, esp. 25–26 and literature there cited.

123. Hartman, *Prophecy Interpreted*, 229–34, esp. 230–33. His conclusion is on p. 234: "The fact that the OT motifs were, to all appearances, linked together in the narrative on the basis of the TM and not of the LXX is surely an analytical result that is worthy of serious consideration."

124. See above pp. 175–80. Of the eight texts from the apocrypha and pseudepigrapha cited by Hartman (*Prophecy Interpreted*, 80–100), which refer to the assault of the heathen upon Israel, seven include the *defeat* of the heathen. The exception is Jub. 23:23, and even here the defeat of Israel is but a prelude to the intervention of God. Such is also the case in the Qumran war scroll.

125. Cf. Jeremiah 38, where Jeremiah's advice is to desert the beleaguered city and surrender to the Babylonians.

126. This leads Hartman, *Prophecy Interpreted*, 230–32 to qualify Dodd's argument: the

days of retribution,[127] of great distress,[128] and wrath upon this people.[129] Moreover, falling to the sword (v. 24) was consistently associated in the Hebrew Bible with Yahweh's judgment through warfare.[130]

The claim that the fall of the city would be divine discipline has a twofold significance. First, whether or not Luke thought of the destruction as part of the "last things," he certainly did not view it *simply* as an event of secular history; it was divine wrath. Second, the motif of retribution suggests an implicit warrant which sets this oracle into the prophetic pattern: it was because of present or past behavior (pursuit of the quest for holiness, or its corollary of the rejection of Jesus?) that the "retribution" came, not out of conformity to an end-time schema. Finally, v. 24 in its present form presupposes the continuation of history: after the destruction, the "day of the Gentiles" must run its course.

At the conclusion of this analysis of the two threats to Jerusalem peculiar to Luke, the question of authenticity again arises. Since they are not *ex eventu,* two possibilities remain. Either they do reflect the teaching of Jesus, or they were created by the Jesus movement prior to 70. If the latter, then one has to imagine a Jesus unconcerned about the Roman threat to Jerusalem, and his movement very shortly thereafter concerned about it. But why should that be? To put it differently, if Jesus did not prophesy about Jerusalem, then who was the insightful prophet in that generation who was responsible both for this concern and this use of the Hebrew Bible? Of course, the rhetorical question does not imply that the oracles contain the *ipsissima verba* Jesus, but it does imply that they reflect the *ipsissima vox* Jesus. Quite probably the Jesus movement and perhaps the evangelist reworked the language of the threats, but without an initial impulse from Jesus, it is difficult to account for their presence in the primitive tradition.[131]

Hebrew Bible texts echoed here show that the emphasis is not simply upon the destruction of the city, but "on the assertion that the destruction will be a divine punishment." See his citation of texts, n. 29, 230–31.

127. Cf. Deut. 32:35; Is. 10:3, 34:8, 61:2, 63:4; Jer. 46:10, 50:27, 31, 51:6; Hos. 9:7.

128. Cf. Deut. 28:52, 55, 57; Is. 8:22, 30:6; Amos 3:11; Zeph. 1:15.

129. Cf. Is. 10:4, 6; 13:9, 13; Zeph. 1:15.

130. See the present writer's "A New Context for Romans xiii," *NTS* 19 (1973).

131. See my earlier comment about prophets in the New Testament, n. 100. On this view, the function played by New Testament prophets was not the attribution to Jesus of new prophecies created out of study of the Hebrew Bible by itself, but rather meditation on and development of the Jesus tradition. That is, the primary object of study was the words of Jesus in conjunction with the Hebrew Bible, not the Hebrew Bible by itself. For a development of this view, see Hartman, *Prophecy Interpreted, passim.* Cf. E. E. Ellis, "Luke xi. 49–51: An Oracle of a Christian Prophet?" *ET* 74 (1962–63): 157–58, who suggests that early Christian prophets may have "peshered" sayings of Jesus.

5. *Mark 13:14.* But when you see the desolating sacrilege set up where it ought not to be (let the reader understand), then let those who are in Judea flee to the mountains....

Finally, this very difficult saying must be added to the explicit synoptic warnings of the fall of Jerusalem and the Temple. Examination of the various problems concerning Mark 13 in general is beyond the scope of this study,[132] as is a verdict on the authenticity of Mark 13:14. What can be said, however, is that the verse anticipates an event in the Temple inconceivable to adherents of the Temple ideology.[133] Mark's phrase "let the reader understand" indicates that the enigmatic reference to the "desolating sacrilege" could be understood if the reader attended sufficiently to it. The phrase echoes Dan. 9:27, 11:31, and 12:11, where it referred to the desolating act committed in the Temple by the Seleucid emperor Antiochus Epiphanes around 165 B.C.E. It suggests that Jesus and/or the early Christian community either saw the act of Antiochus Epiphanes as a type of what was soon to happen or interpreted these verses of Daniel as unfulfilled prophecy. In either case, it is fair to assume that the happenings associated with the phrase in its immediate Danielic contexts were expected to recur in the near future: invasion, war, cessation of sacrifice,[134] and the "appalling abomination." What exactly Jesus and/or the community expected the "desolating sacrilege" to be is an open question.[135] But that it entailed the events of invasion war and occupation of the Temple seems incontestable, given the Danielic contexts. The Marcan context confirms this, for the verses which follow immediately (esp. 14b–18) speak of hasty flight such as is appropriate in time of invasion, and not appropriate to the apocalyptic end of the present order. Thus Mark 13:14 assumes its place in the threats to Jerusalem spoken by Jesus and/or the early community.

---

132. Among detailed analyses of the problems, each offering a solution, are Gaston, *No Stone,* 8–64; Hartman, *Prophecy Interpreted;* Marxsen, *Mark,* 151–206; Beasley-Murray, *Jesus and the Future,* and *A Commentary on Mark Thirteen;* Pesch, *Naherwartungen;* Kümmel, *Promise and Fulfillment,* 95–104.

133. Cf. Jeremias, *New Testament Theology,* 125: Jewish apocalyptic commonly interpreted the desolation of the Temple as *fulfilled* prophecy and expected the Temple to flourish from now on.

134. Dan. 9:26–27 and 11:31 refer to all of these phenomena. 12:11 refers (apparently in summary form) only to the cessation of sacrifice and the abomination.

135. For an excellent survey of the attempted identifications see Beasley-Murray, *A Commentary on Mark Thirteen,* 59–72. His preference (56–58, 69–72) for understanding the anticipated abomination as the Roman army with its heathen insignia and worship has much to commend it; any conquest of Jerusalem by Rome could be expected to bring with it heathen idolatrous practice in the Temple itself. For either Jesus or the early church, Pilate's attempt to introduce standards onto the Temple mount (see above pp. 59–60) would have been sufficient warning as to what would occur if Rome ever had to suppress a massive war of liberation.

The Threat of War. Some of the threats of historical catastrophe
did not speak explicitly of the destruction of the Temple, but alluded
unmistakably to destruction by Roman power.

> 1. *Luke 13:1–5.* There were some present at that very time who told
> Jesus of the Galileans whose blood Pilate had mingled with their sacri-
> fices. And he answered them, "Do you think that these Galileans were
> worse sinners than all the other Galileans, because they suffered thus?
> I tell you, No; but unless you repent you will all likewise perish. Or
> those eighteen upon whom the tower in Siloam fell and killed them, do
> you think that they were worse offenders than all the others who dwelt
> in Jerusalem? I tell you, No; but unless you repent you will all likewise
> perish."

Unidentified people brought to Jesus the news of Roman action in the
Temple against Galilean Passover pilgrims, presumably guilty or suspected of sedition.[136] To this news, Jesus replied with two questions. In
the first (v. 2), he used the data which the questioners brought. In the
second (v. 4), he himself added the Siloam incident, which, it seems
probable, also involved Roman action.[137] Both questions end with an
identical warning which draws a correspondence between the fate of the
Galileans and Jerusalemites and the threatened fate of *all* his hearers:
"Unless you repent, you will all *likewise* perish."

Of what did this correspondence consist? In what sense would they
all "likewise" perish? Possibilities range from absolute precision of correspondence (you will perish at your sacrifices, you will be killed by
a falling tower) to a somewhat more generalized correspondence (by
Roman forces) to the most general kind — perhaps simply "suddenly,
unexpectedly." The clue to choosing from this range lies in the warning: it was the kind of death which they would *not* die if they repented.
This rules out the most generalized correspondence, for sudden unexpected death is not notably prevented by repentance. Rather, the
warning points to death at the hands of Roman forces as the content

---

136. See Blinzler, "Die Niedermetzelung von Galiläern."
137. The evidence for this lies solely in the fact that it is treated as a case parallel
to the Roman assault on the Galileans suspected or guilty of sedition in v. 1; there is
nothing in the wording of v. 4 itself which connects the incident to the suppression of
anti-Roman activity. So also Wood, "Interpreting This Time," 263. Attempts have been
made to identify it with the protests against Pilate's appropriation of Temple funds for
the building of an aqueduct; and Eisler, *Messiah Jesus,* 480–606, imaginatively argues
that it was a tower destroyed by Pilate's forces while combatting the armed followers
of Jesus. The former at least shows that it is feasible to give an anti-Roman setting to
the incident. Creed, *Luke,* 180–81, without attributing the fall to military activity, yet
offers an interpretation which warns against resistance to Rome: "The fall of the tower of
Siloam is an anticipation of the greater destruction which threatens the whole city."

of the threat. If you do not repent (i.e., change your course by respond-
ing to the teaching of Jesus), you, like the Galileans, will be slain by
the sword of Rome.[138] Significantly, the incident which Jesus added at
his initiative involved Jerusalemites: Jerusalem and Galilee, the whole
nation, was included in the warning.

This threat also contained a warrant. It is important to note Jesus'
response. His questioners, bringing the news of a Roman atrocity —
Galileans butchered in the act of worship — and perhaps expecting
to elicit anti-Roman indignation, were told instead that these people
were no worse than other Galileans: "Do you think that these Galileans
were worse sinners than[139] all the other Galileans, because they suffered
thus?" This could mean either that they were innocent; or that they
(though not worse sinners) shared commitments in common with other
Galileans (and indeed Jerusalemites) which would lead to disaster.[140]
Given the conviction of Jesus in other contexts that the nation was
heading toward catastrophe, the latter is more probable.[141] This common commitment was allegiance to the quest for holiness as the central
dynamic of post-Maccabean Judaism.[142] Unless that dynamic were dis-
avowed, the future would be filled with death. The warning counseled
both separation from the liberation movement and a repentance which
qualified the loyalties responsible for the coming collision with Rome.[143]
Moreover, to the extent that the falling tower of Siloam was seen as an

---

138. That the warning pertains to national disaster is affirmed by Creed, *Luke*, 180–81;
Wood, "Interpreting This Time," 263; Plummer, *Luke*, 338; Caird, *Luke*, 169–70; Cadoux,
Historic Mission, 270–71; Gaston, *No Stone*, 341–42. Brandon, *Jesus and the Zealots*, 316
and n. 6, agrees that it has this meaning in its present form and context, but suspects
its authenticity on the grounds that it conforms to the early community's portrait of the
pacific Christ.

139. The comparison (here and in v. 4) uses *para*, which, according to Black, *Aramaic
Approach*, 117, is a Semitism.

140. Cf. Blinzler, "Die Niedermetzelung," 39, n. 3: "Ausserdem sagt Jesus ja nicht,
dass die Getöteten ganz unschuldig gewesen seien, sondern nur, dass sie keine grösseren
Sünder waren als die sonstigen Galiläer."

141. Thus this text does not pertain to the question of innocent suffering or to
the question of whether there is an exact correspondence between individual guilt and
individual calamity.

142. See chapter 3 above, passim.

143. The parable fragment contained in Luke 19:12, 14–15a, 27 (see Robinson, *Jesus
and His Coming*, 67–68; Jeremias, *Parables*, 58–59) may also belong in this context, since
one possible interpretation of it is completely consistent with the meaning of Luke 13:1–
5. The fragment seems to allude to the unrest of 4 B.C.E., including the dispatch of an
embassy to Rome to protest the accession of Archelaus and to the punitive action taken
by the Romans and Archelaus thereafter (v. 27: "As for these enemies of mine, who did
not want me to reign over them, bring them here and slay them before me"). As such, it
was a warning of a similar fate facing those who continued actively to resist Roman rule.

antecedent of the falling buildings of Jerusalem,[144] the saying warned not only of war but of the destruction of the city.

2. *Luke 23:27–31.* And there followed him a great multitude of the people, and of women who bewailed and lamented him. But Jesus turning to them said, "Daughters of Jerusalem, do not weep for me, but weep for yourselves and for your children. For behold, the days are coming when they will say, 'Blessed are the barren, and the wombs that never bore, and the breasts that never gave suck!' Then they will begin to say to the mountains, 'Fall on us'; and to the hills, 'Cover us.' For if they do this when the wood is green, what will happen when it is dry?"

The same deduction from present happening to future disaster is found in the verse with which this text ends. But this time (in its present context) the object lesson was the fate of Jesus himself: "If they do this when the wood is green, what will happen when it is dry?" If Jesus, though not allied with the militant resistance movement, had just been sentenced to death as a resister by the Romans,[145] what would the Romans do when the whole nation fought a war of liberation?[146] That the Romans were meant by "they" is supported not only by the context, but also by the metaphor of wood about to be consumed by fire, which in the Hebrew Bible was used of Israel as it faced destruction by an invading army.[147] Therefore the daughters of Jerusalem ought to weep for themselves and their children: the future holds a threat so menacing that the curse of barrenness would be instead a blessing.[148] Here

---

144. See above nn. 137 and 138.

145. Whatever roles the Roman and Jewish administrations played in the trial, and whether or not Pilate found any fault in Jesus, both the mode of death and the titulus on the cross ("King of the Jews") indicate that Jesus was executed as a "brigand chief" on the charge of sedition.

146. See, above all, Cullmann, *State in the New Testament*, 48–49, and *Jesus and the Revolutionaries*, 49–50; so also Cadoux, *Historic Mission*, 277; Creed, *Luke*, 286; Caird, *Luke*, 249–50; Robinson, *Jesus and His Coming*, 77, 92; Gaston, *No Stone*, 364–65.

147. Ezek. 15:6–8; Jer. 21:14; Is. 9:18–19; and Ezek. 20:47, where the phrases "green wood" and "dry wood" actually occur. The latter is cited by Caird, *Luke*, 249, who comments: "a nation's manpower is compared to a great forest, about to be consumed by the forest fire of the divine judgment. Israel's intransigence has already kindled the flames of Roman impatience, and if the fire is now hot enough to destroy one whom Roman justice has pronounced innocent, what must the guilty expect?" Caird also cites Is. 10:16–19 where the wood metaphor is used, not of Israel, but Assyria.

148. There is good evidence that the heart of this passage, vv. 29–31, is pre-Lucan; see Dupont, "Il n'en sera pas laissé pierre sur pierre," 314–19. Bultmann, *History of the Synoptic Tradition*, 37, 116, classifies it as a pronouncement story of Aramaic origin; and Black, *Aramaic Approach*, 126–27, finds an Aramaism in v. 31. Verse 27 may well be a Lucan redactional link; whether v. 28 belonged to 29–31 prior to Luke is more difficult to determine. Dupont rejects such a connection, whereas W. Käser, "Exegetische und theologische Erwägungen zur Seligpreisung der Kinderlosen Lk. 23:29b," *ZNW* 54 (1963): 240–54, finds the primitive tradition to consist of vv. 27–28, 31. If 28 is integral to the

again is a threat in which Roman military power was the agent, with an implicit warrant as well: the present course of Israel would lead to a disastrous insurrection.

> 3. *Luke 17:31.* On that day, anyone on the housetop who has belongings in the house must not come down to take them away; and likewise, anyone in the field must not turn back.

> *Mark 13:14b–16.* Let those who are in Judea flee to the mountains; the one on the housetop must not go down or enter the house to take anything away; the one who is in the field must not turn back to get a coat.

Both sayings speak of the same two instances. If persons are on their rooftop when danger approaches, they are to go down the outside stairway and not even go inside to gather belongings; similarly, anyone in the field is not to return home to fetch travel provisions. The need for haste is too great.

Since Luke does not seem to be dependent upon Mark here,[149] this advice has double attestation (Mark and probably Q, though possibly L). Two considerations require notice. First, the advice to flee with haste makes no sense if the impending event is the last judgment.[150] Instead, the verses suit a localized judgment from which escape would be possible, most probably invasion by a foreign army. In that context, "emergency evacuation"[151] makes sense. Second, both the Marcan and Lucan contexts link the advice to the episode of Lot in Genesis 19. This is most obvious in the case of Luke, where 17:28–29 refer to the days of Lot and 17:32 states tersely: "Remember Lot's wife."[152] But Hartman

---

saying, then it does have the meaning given above: the fate of Jesus himself is the object lesson. If not, then there is no reason to connect it to the Passion, and it could refer to any incident in which the Romans had taken action, using that incident as a warning of what will happen when the wood is dry.

149. *Contra* Creed, *Luke*, 218. Such dependence requires that Luke extracted only these two verses from Mark 13 in this context, quite unlike his usual method of using Mark. Moreover, of Luke 17:22–37, Matthew uses vv. 23–24, 26–27, 34–35, and 37 (in Matt. 24:26–28, 37–41), which establishes the likelihood of a connected Q set of sayings from which Luke 17:31 may well be derived. See Jeremias, *New Testament Theology*, 122–26, who speaks of *two* "synoptic apocalypses": Mark 13 and Luke 17:20–37.

150. Cf. Beasley-Murray, *Jesus and the Future*, 202: "flee to the mountains" does not suggest that they are about to collapse!

151. Caird, *Luke*, 198. See also, among others, Glasson, *Second Advent*, 78; Manson, *Mission and Message*, 436–37; Taylor, *Mark*, 641–42; Beasley-Murray, *A Commentary on Mark Thirteen*, 73; Robinson, *Jesus and His Coming*, 75; Cadoux, *Historic Mission*, 274; Dodd, *Parables*, 47.

152. This also points to a localized judgment. As Glasson, *Second Advent*, 79, comments: if it were the end of the world that were in view, "of what use would it be to remember Lot's wife?"

has demonstrated that Mark 13:14b–16 allude to Gen. 19:17 as well.[153] This association indicates that what was at stake is flight from a city facing destruction. It points once again to the motif of judgment on Jerusalem.[154]

4. *Matt. 26:52b.* All who take the sword will perish by the sword.

The final nominee for this category suffers from two problems which render its successful candidacy questionable. As a saying peculiar to Matthew among the synoptics and as a retort to the perhaps embarrassing act of armed resistance in Gethsemane, the verse must be suspect as a piece of Christian apologetic. Yet since it also appears in Rev. 13:10, it is almost certainly not a Matthaean creation, but an isolated saying, used by both Matthew and John of Patmos, which Matthew has added to his passion narrative. As an isolated saying, it must therefore be quite early and current in widely separated geographical locales. However, even if early, it may be a piece of folk wisdom[155] applied in a purely individualistic sense: those who resort to violence usually meet a violent end. But perhaps one is to see in "perish by the sword" an allusion to the most familiar use of sword in the Hebrew Bible, which removes it from the category of individualistic folk wisdom: the sword wielded by the nations as the judging activity of God. If so, the saying (like Luke 13:1–5) threatened those who took up the sword of resistance against Rome with the sword of Rome as the present instrument of Yahweh's role as judge.

Results. At almost every point the Temple ideology was overturned by Jesus' warnings. The immediate future would not bring the exclusion of the Gentiles, but judgment upon the Temple because it had become a center of exclusiveness. The size of those great buildings meant nothing. The assault on the city by the heathen would not foreshadow their final defeat, but their triumph. The Shekinah was gone. The time was coming when one should flee the city of Jerusalem, not defend it. The commitments which led to resistance would lead to disaster.

At the heart of this reversal was a different interpretation of "this time." The historical paradigm to which appeal was made was not the miraculous protection of the sanctuary in 701 B.C.E. nor the triumphs of the Maccabees, but the destruction of Jerusalem by Yahweh through

---

153. Hartman, *Prophecy Interpreted,* 152–53.

154. And thus the suggestion of Brandon, *Jesus and the Zealots,* 55, 88–91, that the advice originally meant to flee to the mountains for the sake of offering guerilla resistance, as in the days of the Maccabees, is inappropriate. The flight is *from* defense of a city facing judgment, not a flight for the sake of offering resistance.

155. Though *S-B* cite no parallels.

Babylon in 586 B.C.E. Like the unfortunate and solitary Jesus ben Ananias, who beginning in 62 C.E. prophesied that Jerusalem would be
destroyed and whose reward for diverging from the Temple ideology
was arrest, floggings, and release as a maniac,[156] Jesus of Nazareth also
undercut one of the primary pillars of Jewish resistance to Rome.

Notably, the warnings most commonly follow the prophetic pattern
of warrant/threat, a "because/therefore" pattern, rather than an apocalyptic schema of prediction of a foreordained future. These warrants fall
into two related categories. One cites the pursuit of policies consistent
with the quest after holiness: Mark 11:15–17; Luke 13:1–5; perhaps
Matt. 26:52. The second cites the rejection of God's repeated attempts
to redirect the nation's course, frequently connected to the rejection
of Jesus: Luke 13:34–35 par., 19:42–44; Mark 13:2 (in context); Luke
23:28–31, perhaps.

As the studies of table fellowship and the sabbath demonstrated, the
rejection of Jesus by his opponents was due neither to spiritual torpor
nor malevolence, but to commitment to an alternative program for Israel: the quest for holiness. Thus the two warrants are but two sides
of the same coin: commitment to the quest entails the rejection of the
paradigm which Jesus taught and vice versa.

From this prophetic pattern of warrant/threat, and from the content
of the warrants, several implications follow. First, the pattern of warrant/
threat (rather than apocalyptic prevision based on claimed foreknowl-
edge) implied at least the possibility, however remote, that the future
could be filled with life rather than death. If Israel repented (Luke
13:1–5), if Jerusalem could realize the things that made for peace (Luke
19:42), if it said, "Blessings on him who comes in the name of Yahweh"
(Luke 13:35 par.), then the future could be otherwise.

Second, the content of the warrants indicates that the threatened
destruction was not seen as the vindictive act of an outraged deity,
avenging the mistreatment of an only son, but as the consequence of a
historical choice: continued commitment to the quest for holiness. Of
course, the threatened destruction was also seen as Yahweh's judgment,
but in a way that conformed to the most profound Hebraic insights into
the relationship between history and the judging activity of God. This
also means that the threats were not issued simply out of a perception
that Israel's present course would lead to a collision with Rome (which
would make Jesus primarily a political analyst, at least at this point)
but out of a conviction that Israel's present course did not conform to
Yahweh's intent for the people of God.

---

156. *B.J.* 6.300–309.

Third, the destruction was not threatened because of an in-principled objection to Temple worship, of which the warrants make no mention. Indeed, about the role of the Temple in Jewish worship (including sacrifice), Jesus did not say much. There is only the vague notion of "another Temple" coming from the mouths of accusers and mockers. Though the early Christian movement rapidly spiritualized the understanding of the Temple,[157] necessitated to a large extent by the conversion of Samaritans and Gentiles who were excluded from the Jerusalem Temple,[158] there is little evidence for this in the synoptics. They never report that Jesus opposed the Temple on the grounds that it was obsolete, or that he objected to sacrifice in principle. Indeed, about the Temple as *cult* there is silence.[159]

His silence about the Temple in general highlights by contrast the clarity with which he warned of its destruction and is consistent with the context of conflict which we have been developing as a frame-work within which to view the ministry of Jesus. The questions treated most by Jesus concerned the dynamics of the conflict situation rather than more abstract questions of principle. *Contra* the quest for holiness understood as separation, the present Temple was meant to be a house of prayer for all the nations. And if Israel persisted in the quest for holi-ness, he warned, the Temple would be destroyed by the imperial power which it was already confronting.

The material treated in this chapter places Jesus firmly in the pro-phetic tradition of Israel. He appeared in history not only as a Spirit person with numinous powers who undertook a mission of renewal in the name of compassion, but also as a prophet who spoke of the con-sequences of his people's present course. The categories "Spirit person" and "prophet" within the Jewish tradition share much in common. Like a Spirit person, the prophets were overwhelmed by the experience of the

157. John 2:19–21, 4:20–24, 7:37–38; 1 Cor. 3:16–17, 6:19–20; 2 Cor. 6:14–7:1; Eph. 2:18–22; 1 Pet. 2:4–10, perhaps 4:17; perhaps Heb. 3:1–6; perhaps Gal. 2:9; perhaps 1 Tim. 3:15. Though the notion of another Temple is not so clearly present Hebrews and Acts 7 agree that the present Temple has been superseded. See McKelvey, *The New Temple*; Gärtner, *Temple and Community*; Gaston, *No Stone*, 161–241; Moule, "Sanctu-ary and Sacrifice." "Temple" was also spiritualized within Judaism, beginning after the destruction of the Temple in 70 c.e.

158. McKelvey, *The New Temple*, 88.

159. The twofold Matthaean citation (9:13, 12:7) of Hos. 6:6, "I desire compassion and not sacrifice," does not presuppose an objection to Temple worship in general any more than do similar contrasts elsewhere. See 1 Sam. 15:22; Ps. 50:7–15, 51:15–17, 69:30–31, 141:2; Prov. 15:8, 21:27; Is. 1:12–17, 66:1–4; Hos. 6:6 itself; Amos 5:21–24; Mic. 6:6–8; Ecclus. 35:1–3. The same contrast is cited by a scribe in Mark 12:32–33, without implying that he was anti-Temple worship. As noted in chapter 5 above, the contrast does emphasize compassion rather than the demands of Temple holiness, even though it is not an absolute opposition.

numinous, entered "the other realm" ("the council of Yahweh"), experienced visions, and spoke of knowing God. Unlike Spirit persons, however, the prophets of the Hebrew Bible were intrinsically connected to a
crisis in the life of the people of God. On the basis of their understanding
of covenantal traditions and the immediacy of their own experience of
God, they spoke with the authority of the divine "I," imploring Israel to
see both the causes and consequences of its present course.

With his intimate connection to a crisis in Israel's history, Jesus stood
in this tradition. Perceived as a prophet by his contemporaries, he also
spoke of himself as one (Mark 6:4, 8:28; Luke 4:24, 13:33). Like the
prophets of the Hebrew Bible, he apparently experienced a call, the
echo of which may remain in the baptism narrative (Mark 1:9–11).
Like the prophets, he called Israel to be faithful to the Torah, but in
a manner differing from present practice: the word "repent" had both
an individual and national dimension. He even used one of their most
characteristic means, the prophetic act. Clearly fitting into this category are his disruption of the Temple, his entry into Jerusalem, his table
fellowship with outcasts, and perhaps also his deliberate initiation of
sabbath healings.

Like Amos, Hosea, and Isaiah in the eighth century warning the
Hebrew kingdoms of the Assyrian menace, and Jeremiah and Ezekiel
warning of the destruction of Jerusalem by the Babylonians in the sixth
century, Jesus warned that Israel's course would lead to the destruction of Jerusalem and the Temple by the Romans. Like them (especially
Jeremiah) he was filled with sorrow about the suffering which he fore-
saw for his people. The tone of several of the warnings is unmistakably
mournful and compassionate, not angry or judgmental. Indeed, Luke relates that he wept as he looked at the holy city, grieving that his people
could not see the catastrophe to which their misplaced commitments
would lead.

The traditions attributed to Jesus concerning the Temple fit the pattern which emerged in our treatment of table fellowship and sabbath.
Jesus criticized the quest for holiness and warned of the consequences of
continuing to follow that path. Instead, he proposed an alternative path
grounded in the nature of God as compassionate, gathered a community based on that paradigm, and sought to lead his people in the way
of peace, a way that flowed intrinsically from the paradigm of inclusive
compassion. But how does this essentially prophetic understanding of
the future as contingent consequence of the present relate to the rest
of Jesus' teaching about the future, especially to those traditions which
seem to speak of the end of history? To this question we turn in the
next chapter.

CHAPTER EIGHT
Jesus and the Future

The bell of crisis peals throughout the synoptic tradition. The axe is at the root of the tree. The vultures are gathering over the corpse. The fire licks even now at the chaff. The insolvent debtor has only moments before he faces the court. The time for building barns is past. Upon this generation would come all the blood of the prophets.

But for whom does it toll? The usual answer, given by the majority of scholars in this century, is "Everybody." The bell announces the imminent arrival of the end-time events. According to this view, Jesus and the early Christian movement expected the imminent supernatural coming of the messianic age, involving the resurrection of the dead, the last judgment, the dawn of the age of bliss for those worthy to inherit it, and perhaps even the destruction and renewal of the cosmos.

The previous chapters, however, argue that the teaching and actions of Jesus connected at very central points to the historical direction of his own people in the first century. Jesus criticized in particular those elements of Israel's corporate life in which the quest for holiness was most patent and articulated an alternative paradigm as the content of the *imitatio dei,* with specifiable consequences for both Israel's internal life and its relationship to the nations. Moreover, he warned of the destruction of Jerusalem and the Temple as the consequence of Israel's present course.

What is the connection between Jesus' concern about the present direction and historical future of Israel, on the one hand, and the rest of his teaching about the future? In particular, how is this concern about Israel to be related to what has been virtually an assumption among scholars through most of this century, namely, that Jesus' proclamation of the Kingdom of God is to be understood within the framework of apocalyptic eschatology, including resurrection, judgment, and Paradise Restored?

Most commonly, the threat of historical destruction is subordinated to the expectation of the end of the world. Either it is affirmed that the anticipations of historical catastrophe are post-Easter creations by the

213

community,[1] or that the end of the created order includes, of course, the end of Jerusalem and the Temple as well. In either case the conviction dominates that Jesus warned of imminent, inevitable, worldwide destruction, judgment, and renewal, brought about by an unmediated act of God, and that this expectation was the content of the crisis which resonated throughout his teaching.

But an examination of the whole threat tradition of the synoptic Gospels suggests a different picture of the future. What faced the hearers of Jesus was not the imminent and inevitable eschaton, but imminent and yet contingent catastrophe for Jerusalem and the Temple. Moreover, this threatened destruction was understood as the consequence of the quest for holiness as the blueprint for the people of God.

The data which justify the above position are found in the threats contained within the synoptic tradition, tabulated in an appendix.[2] There are sixty-seven such threats, discounting parallels, found in a variety of forms throughout the tradition. The forms include parables, pronouncement stories, comparisons, laments, and aphorisms. Ten are found in Mark, twenty-five in Q, twelve in L and twenty in M. What they have in common is a warning of a future consequence that flows out of present behavior. Thus they are more properly called threats or warnings rather than predictions. Of the sixty-seven threats, sixty-two have a "warrant" attached: an indication of the action that will lead to the actualization of the threat.[3]

Two basic questions require treatment. First, are the threats really seen as consequences of the quest for holiness, or are they the consequences of something else, e.g., individual transgressions or sinfulness? For this question, the contents of the *warrants* are crucial. The second question is the major one: what is the nature of the threatened consequences? Here primary attention centers on the contents of the *threats*.

---

1. See chapter 7, passim, esp. pp. 191, 196–99.
2. See below pp. 273–80.
3. "Warrant" here, as in the previous chapter, has affinities to the prophetic "indictment"; but insofar as "indictment" is narrowly understood as a citation of an action already completed, it is not identical to "warrant." Indictments so understood are to be found among the synoptic warrants, but the warrants in many cases point to a course of action in process or yet to be undertaken which entails threatening consequences, or sometimes take the form of an invitation to a course of action, refusal of which entails a threatening consequence. "Warrant" simply answers the question, "What is it that will actualize the threat?"

The Threat-Warrant Tradition
Peculiar to Matthew

If Matthew's special material alone served as the basis for making a judgment, the answers to both of the above questions would be straightforward: individual sinfulness warrants the threat of eternal condemnation.[4] Matthew's *warrants* consistently point to generalized sinfulness (entering the broad gate, bearing bad fruit, "all causes of sin and evildoers," "evil people"), or specific sins (relaxing a commandment, anger, insults, saying "You fool!" ostentatious piety, failing to forgive, careless words, refusing community discipline). Most frequently the *threats* peculiar to Matthew point to the eternal fate of the individual: such persons are liable to judgment, liable to hell, sentenced to hell; they will receive no forgiveness from God; they will be condemned on the day of judgment, thrown into the furnace of fire where people will weep and gnash their teeth, or cast into the outer darkness where similar weeping and gnashing will occur. In two cases, the threat consists of community discipline: persons will be liable to the council and shall be as a Gentile or tax collector (that is, expelled from the community). The exceptions to this pattern in Matthew are found, strikingly, in the parables peculiar to Matthew. But the Matthaean pattern in general, as regards both threats and warrants, diverges remarkably from that found in the rest of the synoptic tradition, as will soon be seen. For this reason, special Matthew will not be included in the following analysis, though the Matthaean parables (Mp) will.

The Warrant Tradition in Mark, Q, L, and Mp

Of the fifty-three threats found in the rest of the synoptic tradition, forty-eight have warrants attached to them.[5] In contrast to special Matthew, very few pertain to general sinfulness or specific sins, either in the sense of transgressing commandments of Torah or in the sense of violating generalized moral principles. Only four are candidates for this category: failure to cut off or pluck out the offending hand, foot, eye (Mark 9:43–48); failing to feed the hungry, etc. (Matt. 25:31–46); perhaps seeking the highest place at a banquet, if the point here is to teach that pride is a vice (Luke 14:8–11); and causing a "little one" to stumble (Mark 9:42).

---

4. See appendix, table 1, p. 274.
5. See appendix, tables 2 through 5, pp. 276–280 below.

But this last one more appropriately belongs to another category, for it has nothing to do with leading children astray. Instead, as Jeremias has suggestively argued, "little ones" here was probably a term of derision used by Jesus' opponents to characterize his followers. As a term of contempt, "little ones" meant people who were simple, uneducated, ignorant, poor, and without standing. Jesus accepted this designation but then used it in a positive sense.[6] The meaning of the saying then becomes, "Whoever causes Jesus' followers to stumble (on their chosen path), it would be better if a millstone were hung around their neck...." The saying thus fits the conflict context admirably and alludes to attempts to dissuade those who have chosen to follow Jesus. Thus of the warrants attached to threats, three at most refer to general moral failures.[7]

Seven warrants point to things or persons not performing a function for which they were intended: salt which had lost its taste (Luke 14:34–35 par.); trees not bearing fruit (Luke 13:6–9 par., 3:9 par.); a steward who betrayed his stewardship (Luke 12:41–46 par.); a servant who did not embody the compassion shown to him by his master (Matt. 18:23–35); a servant who produced no return on his master's deposit (Matt. 25:14–30 par.); workers who did not work in the vineyard (Matt. 21:28–32). These bear an obvious similarity to what was earlier called the motif of unproductivity and which was related to the quest for holiness: Israel's previous and present course had failed to produce when something was expected and had been marked by irresponsible stewardship rather than responsible stewardship.

Nine warrants point to the failure to perceive the urgency of the times. Here it was not behavior itself which was reprehensible, but the failure to perceive that the times called for drastic decisive action.[8] This too is consistent with the claim that Israel's present course, unless altered radically, would bring disaster. The largest group of warrants (twenty) cites the rejection of Jesus, his message, or his messengers. This charge, as noted earlier, is not a charge distinct from the quest for holi-

---

6. Jeremias, *New Testament Theology,* 111–12.

7. Moreover, just as it is not common sins or sinfulness that are indicted, so also it is not common morality that is enjoined. Exemplary here is the rich man who approaches Jesus in Mark 10:17–22 par. No doubt was cast on the veracity of his claim that he had observed all the commandments from his youth, but that was regarded as not really relevant to the situation. As Amos Wilder, *Eschatology and Ethics,* 166–67, comments, normal obedience to the Decalogue missed the point because it overlooked the supreme issue of history then present.

8. Luke 12:13–21 (this is no time for building barns); Luke 12:39–40 par., 12:57–59 par., 13:25–27 par., 17:26–27 par., 17:28–30, 19:42–44; Mark 13:33–37; Matt. 25:1–13 (the foolish maidens were absent when the bridegroom arrived).

ness, but the logical corollary of the quest for holiness: his rejection was due to commitment to an alternative program.[9]

The first question is therefore answered. The warrants connected to the threats of the synoptic tradition (apart from those peculiar to Matthew) justify the claim that what was indicted was not individual wickedness, but the continuation of the quest for holiness at a time when that quest would bring about disaster. The threats, therefore, are to be viewed as the consequences of the quest for holiness in Israel's corporate life.

The Synoptic Threat Tradition

I turn to the second primary question. What do the threats disclose about the future which Jesus perceived for his contemporaries? There are fifty-three threats, which can be divided into two major groupings. Twenty-one of them do not provide any clear clues to the nature of the threat. I call these *threats of unidentifiable content.* The other thirty-two contain *threats of identifiable content.*

The first group — threats of unidentifiable content — speaks of judgment in general terms, or leaves the threat in the imagery of the parable or metaphor.[10] People are warned of the wrath to come and of the possibility of not being forgiven. The chaff will be burned, the ruin of the house will be great, salt will be thrown out, the defendant will be delivered to the jailers, the fig tree will be cut down, people will be excluded from the wedding feast, and so forth. In each case the language describing the impending fate is dependent upon the imagery with which the metaphor or parable began. What they have in common is an unmistakable reference to urgency, but by themselves they do not indicate whether the source of urgency was *the* final judgment, historical disaster, or some other possibility (for example, the need for existential decision now). Assigning a specific reference to them depends upon the overall framework within which the teaching of Jesus is to be explicated, which can be determined only on other grounds.[11]

---

9. See above pp. 152–55. The remaining ten warrants divide themselves into warrants with unidentifiable reference (seven) and pursuit of a militant nationalist policy (Luke 13:1–5, Mark 11:15–17, Luke 23:28–31).

10. See appendix, table 2, p. 276 below.

11. Illustrations are manifold, but one will make the point. The parable of the defendant (Luke 12:58–59 par.) is interpreted by Jeremias, *Parables,* 180, to refer to the last judgment; and by Caird to refer to a historical catastrophe for the nation: "The Defendant (Matthew 5:25f.; Luke 12:58f.)," *ET* (1965–66): 36–39. Either is possible, depending upon the overall context.

Thus the thirty-two threats with identifiable content must provide the data for an answer. They are distributed approximately equally among three categories. Nine exhibit a "taken away/given to others" pattern,[12] eleven speak of destruction in historical terms,[13] and twelve apparently speak of a final judgment.[14] Each category must be examined and then the relationship among the three categories explored.

"Taken Away/Given to Others"[15]

Two elements are common to this category of threats. On the one hand, there is the warning that the priority of Israel was at stake, and, on the other hand, the intimation that priority would be given to others if Israel refused its opportunity. The purposes and promises of God would be fulfilled, but if not through and for those who by the standards of the day merited the eponym Israel, then through and for others. This does not necessarily imply Gentiles, but it would at least imply Jews who, from the vantage point of the pure, had become marginalized. Doubts about the authenticity of one or another of these nine threats may arise, but the multiple attestation of this theme, both by source and form, can leave no doubt that it belonged to the authentic themes of the ministry.

The theme is sounded immediately in the preaching of John the Baptist:

Matt. 3:9 par. "Do not presume to say to yourselves, 'We have Abraham as our father'; for I tell you, God is able from these stones to raise up children to Abraham."

Because of the merits of the patriarchs in general and Abraham in particular, descendants of Abraham were supposedly guaranteed a share in the messianic salvation.[16] The threat of John, which in Aramaic contained a word play on "stones/children,"[17] removed this support, and was itself a threat.[18] It also intimated that God would raise up from

---

12. Appendix, table 3, p. 278 below.
13. Appendix, table 4, p. 279 below.
14. Appendix, table 5, p. 280 below.
15. Appendix, table 3, p. 278 below.
16. Jeremias, *Jerusalem*, 300–302. On 270–300, Jeremias treats the emphasis upon legitimacy of ancestry in first-century Judaism and the rights that belonged to full Israelites alone, including important civil rights. See also Buchanan, *Consequences of the Covenant*, 34–35; S-B 1:116–20; Davies, *Paul and Rabbinic Judaism*, 268–73. The significance attached to descent from Abraham is in the background of several New Testament passages: John 8:31–59; Rom. 4, 9:4–8, 11:1–2; 2 Cor. 11:22; Gal. 4:21–31.
17. See, among others, Plummer, *Luke*, 90; Klausner, *Jesus of Nazareth*, 246.
18. Cf. the imaginative reconstruction of J. R. Coates, *The Christ of Revolution* (London, 1920), 35: to John's announcement that judgment is at hand, the people reply, "And we are the children of Abraham," to which John answers, "Do not say to yourselves...."

these stones others who would truly be children to Abraham.[19] The prerogatives and priority of those who thought of themselves as Israel may go to others.

The motif of children to Abraham is treated similarly in Luke 13:28–29=Matt. 8:11–12. Those who heard the words of Jesus would discover that the banquet with the patriarchs in the Kingdom of God *does* include the "many" from east and west, north and south, and *may* exclude them, who thought of themselves as assuredly belonging there. The banquet, which was beginning even then in the table fellowship of the ministry, was one in which people's participation was not guaranteed by descent from the fathers. They may discover their entry ticket taken away and given to others.[20]

In both the Marcan and Q mission charges, Israelites who did not respond were threatened with forfeiture of their status as Israelites.[21] The instructions to the disciples to "shake off the dust from your feet as a testimony" against the town or house that did not receive them, a custom followed when leaving Gentile territory, meant that they were to be reckoned as Gentiles.[22] In the context of mission, it is clear that the mission was to go on to others. This is made explicit in Luke 4:24–27, where the rejection was not of the twelve, but of Jesus himself. After quoting the proverb, "No prophet is acceptable in his own country" (also found in Mark 6:4), the Jesus of Luke spoke of Elijah and Elisha going to those outside of Israel.[23] The point is transparent: if Israel did not respond, the activity of God would be directed to others.

---

19. For the suggestion that John may have referred to actual stones, namely, the twelve memorial stones of Joshua 4 which stood near the Jordan east of Jericho, see O. J. F. Seitz, "What Do These Stones Mean?" *JBL* 79 (1960): 247–54.

20. Ideas surrounding children to Abraham may also explain Matt. 23:9: "Call no man your father on earth...," especially if it may be treated as an isolated saying, as its present context suggests. Verses 8 and 10 specify what the disciples may not be called, whereas this verse speaks of what Jesus' hearers are to call others. As an isolated saying, it may mean, "Do not boast that you are descended from Abraham," especially since a *baraita* states, "One calls 'father' none but three," namely, Abraham, Isaac and Jacob (Ber. 16b). For the suggestion, see J. T. Townsend, "Matthew 23:9," *JTS* 12 (1961): 56–59; and Dodd, *Historical Tradition*, 331–32.

21. Mark 6:11; Luke 10:11; the Matthaean parallel, Matt. 10:14, appears to be a conflation of the two.

22. See, among others, Taylor, *Mark*, 305; Nineham, *Mark*, 170.

23. Though the reference to Elijah and Elisha is peculiar to Luke, there are indicators that 4:25–27 reflect an Aramaic stratum. The evidence is collected by Jeremias, *Promise*, 51 and n. 1. Besides Aramaisms, he notes that the reference to a three *and one-half* year drought is not found in the biblical tradition, but only in a Palestinian rabbinic tradition. The criticism of Jeremias's interpretation of Luke 4:16–30 (esp. v. 22) by H. Anderson, "Broadening Horizons: The Rejection at Nazareth Pericope of Luke 4:16–30 in Light of Recent Critical Trends," *Int* 18 (1964): 259–75, does not seem to affect our use of the pericope.

The four remaining threats in this category are all contained in parables. All four conclude not only with the threat that those who had had priority might find it taken from them, but also that their prerogatives would be given to others. In the parable of the great supper (Luke 14:15–24=Matt. 22:1–14), not only might those originally invited find themselves shut out, but they might also find their seats at the banquet occupied by others.[24] Concluding the parable of the two sons (Matt. 21:28–31) was the exclusion/replacement threat: "Truly I say to you, the tax collectors and harlots are entering the Kingdom of God before you."[25] The cautious servant who failed to exercise his stewardship was not only chastised (Matt. 25:14–30=Luke 19:12–27), but he was deprived of his trust which was then given to others.[26] The parable of the wicked tenants (Mark 12:1–9) who receive the emissaries of the absent landlord with great hostility concludes with the question and answer:

> What will the owner of the vineyard do? He will come and destroy the tenants and give the vineyard to others.[27]

If a correspondence was intended between Israel and vineyard, tenants and leadership, then it was the care of Israel that would go to others.[28] If, however, the terms were to be understood less precisely, then it gave notice that those to whom the purposes and promises had been entrusted would find their possession given to others if they refused to produce fruit. In either case, the pattern of "taken away/given to others" is again present.

The second half of the motif, "given to others," makes it most natural to think of a continuing historical order. If it were the last judgment that were in mind, then only the "taken away" half of the motif is

---

24. Though their detailed exegeses differ, the following agree that the original parable contained both the threat of exclusion and the invitation to others: Hahn, "Das Gleichnis von der Einladung zum Festmahl," 64–66; Linnemann, *Parables*, 88–97, 158–68; Perrin, *Rediscovering*, 110–14; Jeremias, *Parables*, 176–80; Dodd, *Parables*, 93–95.

25. For the point here, the authenticity of v. 31 is crucial. Jeremias, *Parables*, 80, 125, and Perrin, *Rediscovering*, 119, treat it as authentic and in its proper context.

26. See also pp. 131–32 above. The authenticity of v. 28 in Matthew and v. 24 in Luke, upon which this point depends, seems secure: both occur in the reckoning scene with the third servant, upon which the focus of the parable lies and where the agreement between the two versions is greatest. Indeed, the two verses are verbally exact except for Luke's use of "pounds" and Matthew's use of "talents" and a slight change in word order.

27. There is a growing acceptance of the authenticity of this parable, even though some details are post-Easter community additions of an allegorical nature. See Dodd, *Parables*, 96–98; Jeremias, *Parables*, 70–77; Robinson, *Jesus and His Coming*, 59–60, who even suggests that it has been preserved in its original setting; Nineham, *Mark*, 308–11, who, after recognizing the usual objections to the authenticity, grants an authentic core; Derrett, *Law in the New Testament*, 286–312.

28. So, e.g., Gaston, *No Stone*, 476; Jeremias, *Parables*, 76.

strictly germane: "You will have no standing on that day." Moreover, the excluding/including process does not occur only at the last judgment, but had begun even then. This is pointed to especially by those parables linked to the table fellowship initiated by Jesus. Finally, the dual motif emphasized that it was those who thought of themselves as Israel who faced an absolutely decisive hour.

Destruction at the Hands of Rome

Eleven threats fall into this category.[29] They have already been examined in the previous chapter. In this category of threats, the judgment was to be accomplished through a historical agent (Rome). No verdict has yet been given as to whether that judgment, though accomplished historically, also was to begin the end of history. Little is said about that in the tradition, and it is self-evident that this was above all a threat to Israel in particular. Significantly, slightly over one-third of the synoptic threats of identifiable content fall into this category.

The Final Judgment

Two-thirds of the synoptic threats of identifiable content are contained within the previous two categories. The remaining third (twelve) demonstrate that Jesus did speak of history as having a general resurrection and final judgment as its boundary.[30] Here is the source of the fundamental problem: warnings concerned with the historical consequences for Israel of continuing to pursue the quest for holiness (categories one and two) are juxtaposed with predictions (apparently) of the imminent eschaton through a supernatural act of God.

Yet the problem is not posed by all of the sayings in this category. Indeed, the first six of the twelve sayings do not speak of imminence at all, and in fact are completely consistent with the claim that what Jesus threatened was a crisis facing Israel in particular.

With one exception, these first six are comparison sayings. The exception is Mark 9:43–48: if your hand, foot, eye causes you to sin, cut it off/pluck it out, for it is better to enter life maimed/lame/blind than to be thrown into *gehenna*. All that this passage need imply is that Jesus thought that the stakes were high, and perhaps that he accepted a division among humans of eternal duration. It implies nothing about a final judgment which was to come imminently upon his generation.

---

29. See appendix, table 4, p. 279 below.
30. See appendix, table 5, p. 280 below.

Nor do the five comparison sayings imply an imminent end to history. The first four compare this generation unfavorably with certain Gentiles. "It shall be more tolerable *on that day* for Sodom" than for that "town" which did not accept the messengers of Jesus (Luke 10:12=Matt. 10:15). "It shall be more tolerable *in the judgment* for Tyre and Sidon" than for Chorazin and Bethsaida, and Capernaum will be brought down to Hades (Luke 10:13–15=Matt. 11:21–23). "The Queen of the South *will arise at the judgment* with this generation and condemn it" (Luke 11:32=Matt. 12:41). Each of these implied a future judgment which would follow upon the resurrection of those long dead. Jesus, along with the majority of his compatriots, expected such an event. But the primary purpose of these passages was not to affirm a general resurrection and judgment. Instead, it is as if Jesus said to his hearers, "When the resurrection and judgment come (which you all — or at least most of you — accept), the men of Nineveh (Sodom, Tyre, Sidon, and the Queen of the South) will fare better than this generation." The commonly accepted belief was the background for what was truly startling, almost unbearably so: Gentiles (even Sodom!) would fare better at the last judgment than those who heard Jesus unresponsively.

Very importantly, there is no hint of imminence in these passages. It is not said or implied that this generation would live until the last judgment. Indeed, it is possible to read these passages as implying that this generation would *also* have to be raised before experiencing the last judgment: "with this generation" is most naturally taken with "will arise." The passage does not say, "The men of Nineveh will arise at the judgment and condemn this generation (which will live until then)," but, "The men of Nineveh will arise *with this generation* at the judgment...." Thus these four passages provide evidence that Jesus accepted the expectation of a final judgment, but no evidence that it was the final judgment which *soon* would face his hearers. Instead, whenever that judgment did come, that generation would discover to its shock that Gentiles of the past were less culpable than it was.

The fifth saying in this category, "Depart from me into the eternal fire," occurs in the parable of the sheep and goats (Matt. 25:31–46). The parable describes an elaborate last judgment scene: all the nations are assembled together before the king, who makes an eternal separation. If "all the nations" means "the Gentiles" (as distinct from Israel), as it often does, then the passage was not a threat to Israel in any direct sense since it concerned the basis on which the Gentiles would be judged. At the most its central claim might have been surprising to the adherents of the quest for holiness. Gentiles, even though not part of the people of God nor conscious of their good deeds, would be judged favorably for deeds of compassion to "one of the least of these."[31] If, on the other hand, "all the nations" includes Israel, then the saying indicated that one criterion would be applied to Gentiles and Israel alike. That criterion, significantly, was compassion;[32] and it implied that some (at least) of the Gentiles might fare better than some (at least) of Israel. In either case, there is no indication that the judgment was imminent, and it is clear that the major point of the parable was not that there would be a judgment (which was assumed), but that the criterion at the judgment would be deeds of compassion.

To reiterate, there is no inconsistency between the previous six threats and the first two categories of threats. All that is stated is that Jesus expected a final judgment in which decisions taken by that generation in response to a particular crisis would be seen to have not only historical but eternal consequences. Moreover, the first four comparison sayings, like categories one and two, singled out Israel in particular, and with their emphasis on "this generation," the threat was not directed primarily to individuals who faced judgment as individuals, but to "this generation" (contemporary Israel) as a collectivity.

There remain six son of man sayings that are threats. Two spoke of the son of man denying (Luke 12:8–9 par.) or being ashamed of (Mark 8:38) whoever denied or was ashamed of Jesus. The latter saying, though not the former, placed this in the context of the coming of the son of man. In neither case was the judgment or coming said to be imminent. What is said is that decisions taken for Jesus would be ratified by the son of man.[33] Two (Luke 17:26–27 par., 17:28–30) hark back to the days of Noah and Lot. Neither saying is yet a *coming* son of man saying; that was a step taken by Matthew (24:37–39). Noteworthy here is the use of the plural "*days* of the son of man" in Luke 17:26–27, which are compared to the *days* of business as usual before the flood, followed by *the day* when the flood came. Luke 17:28–30 uses the singular "*day* when the son of man is revealed," and compares it to the day when Sodom was destroyed, not to the days *preceding* destruc-

---

31. "One of the least of these *my brethren*" is ambiguous. See the discussion in Kümmel, *Promise*, 92–95. "My brethren" could mean simply a human being (so Jeremias, *Parables*, 207), or a follower of Jesus (so Manson, *Mission and Message*, 541–43).

32. Even though the word does not actually occur. See Tödt's discussion of the passage, *Son of Man*, 75–76 for the claim, "This rule made by Jesus (i.e., mercy) will be adopted by the Son of Man/Judge/King for the supreme judgment of the world."

33. And perhaps in the heavenly courtroom rather than in an earthly courtroom set up at the parousia? At least this is how Luke in Acts 7:55–56 interprets the martyrdom of Stephen. As Stephen faced his death, he saw Jesus *as son of man* standing at God's right hand, presumably ratifying *even then* the witness which Stephen had given.

tion (as the Noah saying does).[34] So either the sayings are to be taken together as pointing to *days* of the son of man, when humans are heedless, followed by *the day* when the son of man is revealed, a day which is compared to the flood and the destruction of Sodom.[35] Or, if the sayings are interpreted separately, they witness to a time when language about the son of man was inchoate. In either case, the emphasis of both sayings was on the obliviousness of that generation. If they, like people in the time of Noah and Lot, continued with business as usual, disaster would strike.

The remaining two son of man threat sayings spoke of the sudden unexpectedness of the son of man's day (Luke 17:23–24) or coming (Luke 12:39–40 par.). Though imminence is not explicitly stated, it is fair to assume it, for one does not give urgent warnings about an unexpected event that may be an indefinitely long time in the future. The note of imminence sounds most clearly in Matt. 10:23, which was not a threat but may have been either comfort to persecuted Christians or an admonition to hasty mission: "You will not have gone through all the towns of Israel before the son of man comes."

Finally, among the son of man sayings, the language of cosmic catastrophe is clear only in Mark 13:24–27: the sun and moon will no longer shine, the stars will fall, the son of man will come with clouds, and the elect will be gathered by his angels. This passage is not explicitly a threat, but it must be included if the basis upon which Jesus is claimed to have expected an imminent eschaton is to be examined.

This association of the coming of the son of man with cosmic catastrophe, presumably in that generation, is the basis for affirming that Jesus expected the imminent end of history as we know it, all accomplished by an unmediated act of God.[36] Though the basis is very narrow, it becomes very broad by a series of extensions. First, the theme of cosmic catastrophe is extended to other passages which speak of the coming of the son of man. Second, the theme of imminence is extended

---

34. Though, since Luke 17:28 does begin with "likewise," there may be an unstated but understood "so will it be in the *days* of the son of man." If so, then the saying speaks of days of business as usual in *the days* of the son of man followed by *the* (disastrous) *day* when the son of man is revealed.

35. To us the comparisons to the flood and destruction of Sodom point to supernatural intervention, but it is unlikely that this distinction would have been meaningful in the first century. Indeed, both of these events would have been understood as historical in one important sense — life did go on afterward, history continued.

36. It is, of course, an unresolved question whether Jesus spoke of the coming of the son of man in either of the two senses which these passages require if they are to refer to the imminent end of history: to refer to his own return as judge (or advocate) at the last judgment; or to refer to the arrival of a figure other than himself as judge (or advocate) at the last assize. This question is treated in a postscript to this chapter.

to those passages which do speak of a last judgment, so that it becomes imminent. And finally, the combined elements of imminence and universal world collapse and renovation are extended to that large category of threats of unidentifiable content. The crisis of which Jesus spoke is thus affirmed to be the final crisis of history.

Here then is the fundamental problem: how are categories 1 and 2, which speak of a contingent threat to Israel and which imply a continuing historical order, to be related to category 3: imminent inevitable universal catastrophe, resurrection, and judgment? A very common approach, as indicated earlier, is to dissolve or subordinate categories 1 and 2 in favor of 3. But this is highly questionable. Categories 1 and 2 embrace twice as many warnings as *all* of category 3. Moreover, within category 3 itself, the majority do not speak of an *imminent* world judgment and are completely consistent with an imminent threat to Israel in particular, followed at some indefinite time by the judgment which stands at the border of history.

Thus the exegetical base for affirming that Jesus proclaimed the eschaton to be near is very narrow. Nor can it be said that this narrow base must nevertheless be the point of departure on the grounds that these sayings have an indisputable claim to authenticity. In fact, the two which speak most clearly of an imminent end (Matt. 10:23, Mark 13:26) are regarded by a large number of scholars as unauthentic, notably including many who affirm an expectation of imminent world judgment.[37] Instead, the threat tradition of the synoptics justifies a different point of departure: Jesus did threaten, unambiguously, a crisis coming upon Israel, especially Jerusalem and the Temple. With this as a fixed point, two options, the second of which seems more likely, remain for reconciling category 3 with categories 1 and 2.

Option One. It is often rightly pointed out that an attack upon the holy city and the end of the age are associated in the pre-Christian tradition. This observation has served as one means of minimizing the significance of category 2. Category 3 is dominant, it is held, and the presence of the threats to Jerusalem (category 2) is explained on the

---

37. Among those judging Matt. 10:23 to be unauthentic: Bultmann, *Theology*, 1:42, 45; Manson, *Mission and Message*, 474, and *The Teaching of Jesus*, 221–22; G. D. Kilpatrick, *The Origins of the Gospel according to St. Matthew* (Oxford, 1946), 122; Perrin, *Rediscovering*, 201–2; E. Bammel, "Matthäus 10, 23," *StTh* 15 (1961): 79–92; Tödt, *Son of Man*, 60–62; A. J. B. Higgins, *Jesus and the Son of Man* (Philadelphia, 1964), 100–104; Hahn, *Mission*, 29, 41, 55 n. 5; R. H. Fuller, *The Foundations of New Testament Christology* (New York, 1965), 147. Mark 13:26 as unauthentic: Hahn, *The Titles of Jesus in Christology* (London, 1969), 33; Kümmel, *Promise*, 102–3; Perrin, *Rediscovering*, 173–85; Higgins, *Son of Man*, 33–36; Fuller, *Foundations*, 145; Taylor, *Mark*, 517–19; Nineham, *Mark*, 343, 356.

grounds that, consistent with the pre-Christian association of the two events, Jesus (or the early Christian movement) spoke *also* of the threat to the holy city, even though the real concern was the final end. What our fixed point of departure does is to turn this explanation on its head. The traditional association of an attack upon Jerusalem with the end of history explains why Jesus (or the early community) spoke *also* of the ultimate end, even though his primary concern was a historical threat.

What is the warrant for this claim? That which distinguished the future expectation of Jesus from his known contemporaries is that the coming assault by the Gentiles on the holy city would *be successful*. This does not suggest that the threats to Jerusalem were nearly adventitious, present only because of their traditional pre-Christian association with the ultimate end. Rather, this reversal of expectation suggests that the emphasis was on the threat to Israel, including the destruction of Temple and city, with *the end* present primarily because of its traditional association with an assault upon Jerusalem.

This is a possible way of accepting all three categories of threats, with the important proviso that the threat of historical destruction was dominant. That threat, if actuated, would usher in the time of the end. Yet this position has implications which may be regarded as difficult. From the fact that the destruction of Jerusalem was seen as contingent, it would follow that the imminence of the eschaton was also contingent, not inevitable within that generation. Moreover, category 1 implies a continuing historical order with sufficient time for the purposes and promises of Yahweh to be "given to others" if the leaders of Israel rejected the call issued by Jesus and his movement. This is difficult to reconcile with an imminent final end immediately consequent upon the destruction of the city.[38] But if these difficulties minimize this possibility as the expectation of Jesus, this option may nevertheless be important for accounting for the imminent expectation of the early church.[39]

Option Two. Returning to the fixed point that Jesus threatened the

---

38. Nor can this be resolved by supposing with Jeremias, *Promise*, 55–73, that the "giving to others" is accomplished by transcendent means. Jesus, he argues, expected that the Gentiles would be gathered (literally) by the angels of God. For a criticism of his position, see Hahn, *Mission*, 28–29. Among his telling points is the question: if Jesus affirmed that God himself would bring in the Gentiles by supernatural means, why did the disciples ever embark on such a mission?

39. There is reason to think that the destruction of Jerusalem and the Temple in the year 70 c.e. may have intensified apocalyptic expectation among early Christians. Mark's Gospel is written very near that time, and Mark 9:1 and chapter 13 as a whole (and perhaps Mark 1:15) may reflect a strong sense that "the end" was at hand. In this connection Gaston's remark, *No Stone*, 457, is illuminating: the early church did not, as it were, set and reset dates for the parousia; instead, "only one actual date was set for the parousia: the fall of Jerusalem."

imminent destruction of Jerusalem and the Temple, we now ask what imagery would be sufficient for a first-century Jew to describe a catastrophe of this magnitude. For this was not just any nation. According to the Hebrew Bible, Israel was Yahweh's chosen, the first born, the only begotten, the beloved, the people of God's desire, God's special possession and son.[40] The world was created for Israel,[41] and the threat of disaster for God's chosen people naturally called forth the imagery of world loss. Nor was Jerusalem just any city, but the mother of Israel,[42] where Yahweh had promised to dwell forever.

The religious loyalties of first-century Jewish people thus suggest that only the imagery of cosmic disorder and world judgment would have been adequate to speak of the destruction of Jerusalem and the Temple. To say that this language is symbolic is necessary in order to distinguish it from literal language, yet this should not lead to the presumption that it can adequately be translated into straightforward prose without loss, as if form and meaning were totally separable. For only language such as this can express the grief, love, urgency, and the sense of a decisive act of God which such a prospect engendered. Only such language can express the "radical cultural disorder," "the loss of meaning of inherited symbols and rites," the conviction that "the old order of life" was coming to an end and a new age being born,[43] which attended such an expectation.

The position maintained here, then, is that the transcendent imagery of category 3, which speaks of imminent universal disorder, is consistent with the threat of the destruction of Jerusalem and the Temple. Only such language was sufficient to express the significance of the destruction of Yahweh's beloved and Israel's mother.

Moreover, there are precedents in the Jewish tradition for the specific imagery contained in Mark 13:24–27, the darkening of sun and moon and the falling of the stars. The Hebrew Bible associates such astronomical phenomena with the day of Yahweh as judgment upon

---

40. These expressions occur in first-century Jewish writings as well, thus roughly contemporary with Jesus and the early Christian movement. See, for example, 2 Bar. 48:20; 4 Ez. 5:27–28, 6:58.

41. For example, 4 Ez. 6:55, 59; 7:11.

42. For Jerusalem as mother, see, for example, Is. 66:7–11; 2 Bar. 10:16; 4 Ez. 10:7; cf. Gal. 4:20.

43. The quoted phrases are from A. Wilder, "Eschatological Imagery and Earthly Circumstance," NTS 5 (1959): 239–40. Wilder's writings are consistently characterized by the attempt to relate apocalyptic imagery to the earthly events from which it arose, and he criticizes most students of eschatology (he cites Volz, Charles, Bousset, Althaus) for creating too great a disjunction between transcendental imagery and the historical process (230). See also his Eschatology and Ethics and "Social Factors in Early Christian Eschatology," in A. Wikgren, ed., Early Christian Origins (Chicago, 1961), 67–76.

a nation, whether that be Israel (Amos 8:9; Joel 2:10, 30–31), Egypt (Ezek. 32:7), Edom (Is. 34:4), Babylon (Is. 13:10), or the Gentile nations in general (Joel 3:15; 4 Ez. 5:4, 6). As language used to describe Yahweh's judgment on a nation, it does not intrinsically mean that history thereby would end.

Moreover, in a late first-century Jewish text written after the destruction of Jerusalem by Rome, the writer implored the sun and moon to darken themselves: "And do thou, O sun, withhold the light of thy rays. And do thou, O moon, extinguish the multitude of thy light." Why? Because "the light of Zion is darkened" (2 Bar. 10:11–12). Here a slightly different note is sounded, though it is still within the framework of "cosmic empathy" with decisive historical events: the loss of Zion ought to have astronomical consequences, here understood as mourning. Only such language can adequately express the magnitude of loss and anguish. More graphic demonstration of the relation between earthly event and cosmic imagery could not be wanted.[44]

In a quite different though still related context, Luke uses cosmic imagery to describe the birth of a new community rather than the end of an old. In Acts 2:19–20 Luke cites Joel 2:30–31 (signs in heaven and earth, blood, fire, smoke; sun shall be turned into darkness, moon into blood) *as having been fulfilled* at Pentecost. He does not say that part of the prophecy from Joel had been fulfilled and that part of it was yet to be fulfilled but, in v. 16, which introduces the extended quote from Joel, states, "This [i.e., the coming of the Spirit, the communication in diverse languages] is that of which Joel spoke." Though this conclusion can be avoided, Luke apparently thought these terms to be quite appropriate for speaking of God's decisive activity in history.[45] In short, the language of "cosmic empathy" can be adequately accounted

---

44. Much fruitful work remains to be done in this area. Besides the work of Wilder (see n. 43 above), see also two books by George Caird, *Commentary on Revelation*, and *The Language and Imagery of the Bible* (London, 1980), and his "Les eschatologies du Nouveau Testament," 217–27; Frost, *Old Testament Apocalyptic*; A. Sand, "Zur Frage nach dem 'Sitz im Leben' der Apokalyptischen Texte des Neuen Testaments," *NTS* 18 (1972): 167–77.

45. One could say that Luke should have ceased his citation of Joel with Joel 2:29 (Acts 2:18), but apparently continued through oversight, or perhaps the need to fill up his scroll. Or one could insist that his citation is divided into a present/future schema, despite the fact that there is no justification for this in the text; it is only by assuming that the language of cosmic disorder could not possibly refer to Pentecost that the notion of a present/future sequence is introduced. Finally, see Acts 4:31, where the coming of the Holy Spirit "rocks the house" (the "eschatological" earthquake); did Luke really think there was an earthquake? Or is this not instead another indicator that this language was a mode of thought and speech for characterizing decisive acts of God? For these two texts, see also Caird, "Les eschatologies," 225.

for by recognizing the contexts in which such language occurs: to speak of decisive changes in history brought about by God.[46]

Thus the language of cosmic dissolution need not imply the breakup of the created order and the imminent end of all things. But might it nevertheless do so in the case of Jesus? Against this, of course, is the previous survey which requires a historical judgment and a continuing historical order thereafter. But there is also one final point. In Mark, Q, Luke, and Matthew, the instructions for hasty evacuation are found in the midst of sections usually understood to pertain to the imminent eschaton. As noted in the previous chapter, hasty evacuation implies a historical localized judgment. Now either Mark, Q, Luke, and Matthew *all* failed to perceive the contradiction between this advice and the eschaton, which seems unlikely. Or they preserved the connection despite the fact that they perceived the inconsistency, presumably out of respect for the tradition, which is possible. Or, finally, there may be no contradiction because the sections as a whole originally referred to the impending destruction of Jerusalem and the Temple through a historical judgment. Indeed, this advice couched in nonmetaphorical terms should be the clue for determining the meaning of the metaphors and imagery of the contexts in which it appears. The texts themselves provide the warrant for offering a "demythologized" interpretation of the imagery of *Endzeit*.

Results

The threat tradition of the synoptics thus contains two elements. On the one hand, decisions taken for or against the mission of Jesus would have eternal consequences, to be actuated at the last judgment (e.g., Mark 9:43–48; Luke 10:12–15 par., 11:31–32 par., 12:8–9 par.; Matt. 25:31–46). Perhaps some of the threats of unidentifiable content belong here too. But this was not imminent, nor was this the primary source of urgency. What was imminent was the historical consequence of continuing to pursue the quest for holiness as separation (with its obverse of refusing to respond to Jesus): the threatened destruction of Jerusalem and the Temple (and, by implication, of the present leadership of Israel). *That* was the crisis which Jesus announced to his contemporaries. Here most of the threats of unidentifiable content can also be added:

---

46. It may be thought that the language of cosmic disorder is not the central problem, but rather the fact that the coming of the son of man is spoken of in such contexts. This will be treated in a postscript to this chapter.

the axe is at the root of the trees; the ruin of the house will be great; the blood of all the prophets will be required of this generation; he who thinks now is a time for building barns will discover that his life is required of him; make peace with your adversary before judgment occurs, or you will never get out; the fig tree which has not borne fruit will be given only a short respite before it is chopped down; worthless salt will be thrown out; like the contemporaries of Noah, this generation will be overtaken by catastrophe; the unmerciful servant will be delivered to the jailers; who warned you to flee from the wrath to come? The urgent imagery presses home to those responsible for Israel's direction that it is for them the last hour.

It is this that makes sense of Jesus' restriction of his mission to Israel, despite the fact that the Gentiles are also viewed as having a part in the promises of God. Jesus went to Israel alone because it was Israel alone who faced the crisis. Moreover, neither he nor the early Christian movement needed to go to the Gentiles, for if Israel responded, the Gentiles would be included. The kinds of structures which Jesus urged upon Israel — abandonment of holiness as separation, table fellowship which reflected the inclusive compassion rather than the holiness of God, the Temple as a house of prayer for all the nations — meant that Gentiles would share in the benefits. So too the "Jewishness" of the early Christian movement was not due to an in-principled particularism or conviction that the promises of God were only for Israel, but is explicable because it, like Jesus, saw the crisis as Israel's crisis. The early movement's insistence on circumcision, adherence to Mosaic food laws, payment of Temple tax, and "reluctance" to go to the Gentiles were not due to a failure to perceive the radicalism of Jesus, but were based on the hope that Israel might yet respond. Whether or not these allegiances were understood at first to have permanent validity, they were in any case necessary for a continuing mission to Israel.[47]

Finally, the perception that the future threat was seen as the consequence of the quest for holiness explains the source of Jesus' convictions regarding the future in a way in which the alternative cannot do. On the view argued here, the proclamation of threat arose out of a discernment of the present course of Israel. The logical pattern is "Because . . . therefore . . . unless"; e.g., "Because you have been unfaithful servants, therefore the destruction is at hand, unless you repent." On the alternative view, that Jesus proclaimed the imminent inevitable eschaton, the proclamation of judgment had no particular relationship to Israel's present course — it was simply coming.

---

47. So also Schmithals, *Paul and James*, 37, 47, 103.

The pattern has changed subtly: "Because the judgment is coming, be faithful stewards." This is a crucial difference. The judgment is no longer contingent, but inevitable — it is coming! There is no longer any organic connection between Israel's present course and judgment — the judgment is coming regardless. On this view, the conviction that judgment was imminent did not arise from a perception of Israel's present course, but came from elsewhere. But from where? The only alternative seems to be from apocalyptic calculation, not necessarily of dates, but at least of the conviction that the eschaton was near.[48] But this notion has rightly been rejected by most scholars as playing no part in the teaching of Jesus. And if not that, then it seems likely that Jesus' conviction came from a consideration of Israel's present historical situation, in light, of course, of the understanding of the purposes and promises of God in the Hebrew Bible. Thus again, the threat of destruction in the teaching of Jesus was organically related to those elements in Israel's life which Jesus found reason to criticize, viz. the quest for holiness.

Postscript: Jesus and the Coming "Son of Man"

Earlier we hinted that perhaps the chief reason for affirming that Jesus spoke of the imminent end of history is because he is reported to have spoken of the imminent coming of the "son of man." But did he speak of the coming of the "son of man" in either of the two senses which would entail imminent world catastrophe and judgment, namely, to refer to *his own* return as judge or advocate, or to a transcendent agent other than himself who would soon usher in the eschaton? There are weighty reasons for rejecting both possibilities.[49]

Did he speak of himself as the returning "son of man" who would come in the future on the clouds of heaven, gather the elect, preside at the last judgment, and so forth? Two negative arguments are highly persuasive. The first is the psychological difficulty, most emphatically put by John Knox: what kind of consciousness is attributed to Jesus if he is thought to speak of several stages of his own activity *after death*?[50] There is no difficulty in affirming that Jesus as a figure of history could anticipate events in his own historical future, including confidence that he

---

48. And even this may be a spurious alternative, for there is good reason to doubt whether any "apocalyptic calculation" is divorced from history.

49. Note that we are not here considering whether Jesus spoke of the "son of man" as present or suffering, but only whether he spoke of the future coming "son of man" as a transcendent figure, either himself or another.

50. J. Knox, *The Death of Christ* (London, 1959), esp. 54–60.

would be vindicated by God, but to attribute to him a consciousness of his *transhistorical* future in which he performs "the highest imaginable role in the eschatological drama"[51] is quite a different matter. Bultmann's point is well taken: Jesus would "have had to count upon being removed from the earth and raised to heaven before the final End . . . in order to come from there on the clouds of heaven to perform his real office."[52]

To some extent, this is a question of the "mental health" of Jesus.[53] Even more, it is a question of where he could have acquired such an idea about his own person. Knox's point has been recognized in the subsequent discussion,[54] but it has not been taken with sufficient seriousness.[55] Moreover, many scholars continue to affirm that Jesus did speak of himself as the supernatural coming "son of man," in part, perhaps, because of a wholesome reluctance to limit the ideas it was possible or impossible for Jesus (or any other person in a culture so different from ours) to entertain.[56]

Whatever may be thought psychologically possible for Jesus, there is a second reason for denying that he spoke of himself as the future vindicating "son of man," which may be designated "pedagogical." The Gospels indicate that his most intimate followers were not prepared for either his death or resurrection. Yet a second coming presupposes both death and an interval before the return. To think that Jesus spoke *of himself* as that future coming "son of man" both to the disciples (as promise) and to the crowds (as threat) is to admit that they could not

---

51. O. Cullmann, *The Christology of the New Testament,* 2d ed. (London, 1963), 156.

52. Bultmann, *Theology,* 1:29.

53. As Knox, *Death of Christ,* 58, puts it.

54. E.g., Hooker, *Son of Man,* 183–86, rightly contends that Knox's argument has force only when the "son of man" is thought of as a supernatural heavenly figure who will come with the clouds. Since she denies that this is the meaning of the term, Knox's argument is rejected. However, we would insist (as she also implies) that his argument has validity whenever Jesus is thought of as speaking of his own second coming.

55. E.g., Higgins, *Son of Man,* 19–20, notes Knox's argument and indicates that his own position will overcome it. Yet on pp. 202–3, he affirms that Jesus did speak "of performing Son of man functions in the future"; though Jesus *seems* to speak of the "son of man" as another, he really speaks of himself "*reinstalled* in his heavenly seat." Perhaps it is only an unfortunate choice of words, but with his use of the prefix "re," Higgins attributes to Jesus not only a consciousness of his transhistorical future, but also of his prehistorical past. Again one must ask: is this consistent with the affirmation of a human consciousness?

56. Knox, *Death of Christ,* 68–70, counters the suggestion that he is imposing modern categories on Jesus: (1) The implausibility is so great that even the widest differences in culture are irrelevant; (2) there is no analogous case in Jewish literature; though historical actors are found there with prophetic and even messianic consciousnesses, there is no precedent for a person (correctly or incorrectly!) identifying himself with a divine being seated (or to be seated) at the right hand of God, coming on the clouds of heaven.

have understood what he was talking about. He would have addressed "a future situation which had not even begun."[57] Whatever element of profound mystery is assigned to the teaching of Jesus, it is difficult to believe that he spent much time teaching about transhistorical events involving his person to people who had not yet understood the historical events which were prerequisite for being able to grasp at all the meaning of such speech. To put it tersely, both psychological and pedagogical reasons inhibit the affirmation that Jesus spoke of *two* comings *of himself.*

Did he then speak of the coming "son of man" as a figure other than himself who would soon introduce the final drama of history and vindicate his mission? For a large number of scholars, this has become a virtually assumed position.[58] For it to be maintained, it is absolutely essential that the pre-Christian Jewish tradition included the idea of a transcendent "son of man" destined to come at the end of time. Only if this is the case can Jesus have referred to this figure as the eschatological vindicator of his mission.

Such is recognized by Tödt, who has produced the most impressive exposition of the view that Jesus spoke of the coming "son of man" as a figure other than himself. His first chapter, entitled "The Transcendent Sovereignty of the Son of Man in Jewish Apocalyptic Literature,"[59] expresses his conviction that *bar nasha* ("son of man") in the first century designated the heavenly eschatological judge who would come at the end of time. A paragraph at the end of his chapter summarizes his conviction and position:

> The figure of a transcendent Perfecter, however, is exalted above all earthly sufferings. His power and sovereignty, untroubled by any earthly condition, accordingly lie in the future as part of the coming, the second aeon.... How could this transcendent figure be related to Jesus, who lived on earth and history?[60]

When once his question is posed against this background, the answer is inevitable: only as eschatological guarantor of that which was initiated

---

57. Robinson, *Jesus and His Coming,* 66; cf. Gaston, *No Stone,* 43: "The disciples did not even understand the necessity of his death; can they then have been given instructions about a second coming after Christ's death and resurrection?"

58. Probably a majority of German scholarship throughout the century. E. Schweizer, "The Son of Man," *JBL* 79 (1960): 120, speaks of it as "taken for granted in the whole German literature," though he does not accept it. Most important of recent works affirming this position are Tödt, *Son of Man;* Hahn, *Titles of Jesus,* 23–31; and in Anglo-Saxon scholarship, Fuller, *Foundations,* 119–25; Higgins, *Son of Man,* though he virtually controverts this on pp. 202–3.

59. Tödt, *Son of Man,* 22–31.

60. Ibid. 31.

by Jesus. And thus the meaning of "son of man" for Jesus is determined (in advance) by the background understanding of "son of man."[61]

But was "son of man" a title or designation of a supernatural perfecter or judge in first-century Judaism? The *only* evidence for this lies in the Similitudes of Enoch[62] (Enoch 37–71), the existence of which at the time of Jesus is doubtful. The evidence may be summarized as follows. First, the Similitudes are missing from all Greek manuscripts of the book of Enoch; they are found only in Ethiopic manuscripts, the earliest of which is either fifteenth or sixteenth century.[63] Second, the manuscripts found at Qumran include portions of every part of Enoch except the Similitudes.[64] Third, not only are the Similitudes absent from Qumran, but "son of man" as an apocalyptic designation is not found in any of the Qumran literature — a striking absence in the literature of an apocalyptically oriented group.[65] Fourth, though the Enoch literature as a whole was apparently much respected in both Jewish and Christian circles and is cited by or alluded to in Testaments of the Twelve Patriarchs, Jubilees, Jude, Justin Martyr, Barnabas, Irenaeus, Clement of Alexandria, Origen and Tertullian, reference is not once made to the Similitudes.[66] Fifth, several scholars have argued that the Similitudes are not pre-Christian, but come from a later time.[67]

---

61. Interestingly, Tödt, *Son of Man*, 32, recognizes the predetermination of the interpretation by the choice of background when commenting about those who see Daniel 7 as the primary background: "But a primary dependence on Dan. 7:13f. would determine the interpretation in advance. Thus, for example, this text yields decisive support for the 'communal interpretation' of the Son of Man." In the same way, his choice of background determines the answer he must reach.

62. Neither Daniel 7 nor 4 Ezra 13 provide evidence for the use of son of man to designate the transcendent vindicating figure of the future. In Daniel 7, *kebar enash* is not a term for a *vindicating* figure of the future, but is simply equivalent to the saints of the Most High who *are vindicated* by the Ancient of Days. In 4 Ezra 23, imagery from Daniel 7 is used, but the figure is simply "The Man"; that he is not called "son of man" suggests that son of man was not an apocalyptic title.

63. Charles, *Ap. and Ps.*, 2:165–66.

64. Summarized by J. T. Milik, "Problèmes de la littérature hénochique à la lumière das fragments araméens de Qumrân," *HTR* 64 (1971): 333–78, and his *The Books of Enoch: Aramaic Fragments of Qumran Cave 4* (Oxford, 1976). The Similitudes are missing from all eleven Enoch MSS found in Cave 4 (Enoch 1–36 are found in five; 72–82 in four; 83–90 in four; and 91–108 in two). Similarly, no part of the Similitudes is included "dans la masse innombrable des fragments" found in Cave 4, or in the other ten caves.

65. R. Leivestad in his provocatively titled study, "Der apokalyptische Menschensohn: ein theologisches Phantom," *ASTI* 6 (1967): 49, indicates that this was a major factor in his decision to question the firm conclusion of modern theology that "son of man" designated a heavenly figure of the *Endzeit*.

66. Leivestad, 52–53; see also the tables in Charles, *Ap. and Ps.*, 2:177–84.

67. J. C. Hindley, "Towards a Date for the Similitudes of Enoch: An Historical Approach," *NTS* 14 (1968): 551–65, suggests 115–17 c.e. Milik in both his article and his book (n. 64 above) argues for ca. 270 c.e. Milik's late date was unanimously rejected by

Thus there is no evidence that the Similitudes existed at the time of Jesus. If it is assumed that "son of man" was a designation for a transcendent perfecter and that the burden of proof lies with those who deny it, then this argument from silence may seem inconclusive. But this is the wrong way of putting the question. In the absence of *any* evidence that the Similitudes existed, the burden of proof must lie with those who say that "son of man" was such a designation. For this, there is not a whisper of evidence.[68]

In addition to the lack of evidence that the Similitudes existed, there is other evidence that "son of man" was unknown as a title for a supernatural judge of the last days. In an examination of the synoptic and Johannine "son of man" sayings, R. Leivestad has shown not only that none of them presupposes an apocalyptic titular background, but also that many become senseless if such a background is presupposed.[69] Moreover when the Jewish tradition does make use of Dan. 7:13–14, in which *bar enash* occurs, it does not refer to that figure as "son of man" but as "the man," or "cloud man."[70] This is extraordinary if in fact "son of man" (*bar nasha*) was a designation for the one coming with clouds; the clear inference is that it was not. One may speak of an "eschatological" use of Daniel 7, but not of a use of "son of man" as a designation of a transcendent perfecter. Finally, G. Vermes has shown that *bar nasha* was such a common expression (meaning "man," "someone," or used as a circumlocution in certain well-defined circumstances) that it would have been virtually impossible for somebody to invest it with titular significance.[71]

All of this indicates that there was no apocalyptic "son of man" in pre-Christian Judaism to whom Jesus could have referred as a coming

---

a group of New Testament scholars, as reported by J. H. Charlesworth, "The Society for New Testament Studies Pseudepigrapha Seminars at Tübingen and Paris on the Books of Enoch," *NTS* 25 (1979): 315–23; see esp. 322. Emerging instead was a date late in the first century. See also M. A. Knibb, "The Date of the Parables of Enoch: A Critical Review," *NTS* 25 (1979): 360–69, who favors the 40s of the first century c.e. D. W. Suter, *Tradition and Composition in the Parables of Enoch* (Missoula, Mont., 1979), suggests that the most likely date is the middle of the first century c.e., though granting that the range is from 25 B.C.E. to 70 C.E.; see pp. 23–32.

68. C. Colpe, *TWNT,* 8:403–81, grants that 1 Enoch, 4 Ezra, and Daniel cannot account for the apocalyptic son of man presupposed in much research, and so posits another source no longer extant. Perrin, *Rediscovering,* 260, aptly comments: "We remain unconvinced by this argument."

69. Leivestad, "Der apokalyptische Menschensohn," 59–98. He concludes (101), "Der apokalyptische Menschensohn ist eine theologische Erfindung der letzten hundert Jahre."

70. 4 Ezra 13; for rabbinic use, see G. Vermes, "The Use of Bar Nash/Bar Nasha in Jewish Aramaic," in M. Black, *Aramaic Approach,* 327–28.

71. Vermes, "The Use of Bar Nash/Bar Nasha," 310–28, and *Jesus the Jew,* 160–91.

figure who would vindicate his contemporaries' confession of him.[72] The coming "son of man" sayings *as references to a transcendent figure of the end time,* either to refer to Jesus himself in a transformed state or to another figure, disappear from the teaching of Jesus. And thus the claim that sayings about the coming "son of man" point to an imminent end, judgment, and new world evaporates.[73]

How then does one account for the sayings in the tradition (of which, it must be remembered, there are very few) which do speak of such a coming? This is a separate problem to which only the tentative outline of a solution can be given. To begin, *bar nasha* (whether as a circumlocution or in some other sense) must have been a memorable form of speech used by Jesus. Only if this is so can the distribution of its occurrences in the New Testament be explained. The resurrection, understood from the start as God's "Yes" to Jesus, was understood as the elevation of Jesus, *bar nasha,* to God's right hand, a belief which comes to expression in both Mark 14:62 and Acts 7:56.[74] With Jesus, *bar nasha,* now installed *ad dexteram dei,* it would be natural to assign

---

72. There are additional problems connected with the position represented by Tödt et al. even if *bar nasha* as a designation for a future figure be accepted. First, the assignment of sovereign priority to Luke 12:8–9 as the criterion for interpreting other "son of man" sayings is based on a circular argument; see P. C. Hodgson, "The Son of Man and the Problem of Historical Knowledge," *JR* 41 (1961): 96. Second, do the implicit claims of Jesus really permit the thought that he expected soon *another* coming one? Third, if Jesus did speak of the coming son of man as a figure other than himself, why did the resurrection convince the church that Jesus was *himself* the coming one? It should have convinced the disciples that he was *correct* in his imminent expectation of another, not that he was that other one. For this point, see E. Schweizer, "The Son of Man Again," *NTS* 9 (1963): 258, and *Jesus* (London, 1971), 19.

73. B. Lindars, "Re-Enter the Apocalyptic Son of Man," *NTS* 22 (1976): 52–72, argues that Jesus *did* speak of himself as the returning "son of man" and makes interesting use of the Similitudes of Enoch as he does so. Agreeing that the Similitudes provide no evidence for "son of man" as a *title* in pre-Christian Judaism and that Jesus therefore could not have spoken of "son of man" as a figure other than himself (see esp. 66, n. 1), he notes that the phrase in Enoch means simply "the man of the Danielic vision" (58), and that the Similitudes identify this "son of man" with Enoch. The Similitudes thus provide evidence that it was possible within Judaism to identify "an historical person with the agent of God's final intervention, conceived in Messianic terms, around the beginning of the Christian era" (59). In short, if Enoch could be thought of as the transcendent "man of the Danielic vision," then why not Jesus? The point is skillfully made. Lindars argues that Jesus himself made that identification on the grounds that *some* of the coming "son of man" sayings must be authentic in order to explain the existence of the rest (68). In our judgment, as argued below, the early Christian community is the more likely source of the identification of Jesus with the "man of the Danielic vision."

74. See the widespread use of Ps. 110:1 as a *testimonium:* Mark 12:36, 14:62; Acts 2:34, 5:31, 7:55–56; Rom. 9:34; Eph. 1:20; Col. 3:1; Heb. 1:3, 13, 8:1, 10:12, 12:2; 1 Pet. 3:11. See Dodd, *According to the Scriptures,* 34–35; Lindars, *New Testament Apologetic,* 45–51.

to him functions assigned to Yahweh in pre-Christian literature:[75] both as one who vindicates in history and as one who vindicates at the end of time.[76]

However tentative the above paragraph is, the essential claim of this postscript is firm. If Jesus spoke at all of the coming "son of man," he did not do so in either of the two senses which would entail an imminent eschaton. He neither referred to his own second coming, nor to the coming of *bar nasha* as another who would bring history to its conclusion. The traditions about the future coming of a figure known as "the son of man" cannot be used as evidence for Jesus' expectation of the future, even though they may disclose much about the developing images and beliefs of early Christians.

The case presented in this chapter is not intended to be completely conclusive. The traditions about the future in the synoptic Gospels are complex and not easily conformed to a single coherent schema. Undoubtedly modified by the early Christian movement, certainly with christological considerations in mind and perhaps also because of times of eschatological expectation and disappointment, these traditions are not easily disentangled into categories of authentic and unauthentic, especially since a single saying may have gone through several stages of development. Yet traditions which are clearly pre-70 and Palestinian, and others which may be regarded as such with a high degree of probability, indicate that Jesus warned in the most solemn terms, using language which echoed the prophetic strand of the Hebrew Bible, of the destruction of Jerusalem and the Temple by an invading military force, a destruction which was still seen as contingent, not inevitable. Thus the end to which he *clearly* referred, the last hour which he *certainly* announced, concerned the threat of historical catastrophe for his people.

Though it remains possible that Jesus did expect end-time events in some quite literal sense in the near future, our examination of the synoptic threat tradition displays the narrow base on which rests the dominant context for interpreting the teaching of Jesus in twentieth-century scholarship. The taken-for-granted status of the apocalyptic

---

75. And not only natural, but perhaps abetted by the possibility of variant interpretations of Dan. 7:22: "judgment was given *for* [i.e., in favor of] the saints of the Most High" (who are identified with *bar enash* in that chapter), or "judgment was given *to*. . . ." Thus Jesus, *bar enash*, one *for* whom judgment was given (in the resurrection), becomes the one *to* whom judgment is given. Though "for" is most likely correct, the alternative "to" was certainly known by the time 1 Cor. 6:2 was written.

76. For a different (though compatible) and more detailed account of how the early Christian movement came to speak of the risen Jesus as the vindicating son of man, see Perrin, *Rediscovering*, 173–99.

eschatological context clearly needs reexamination. Moreover, even if Jesus did expect the eschaton, the firm connections between his ministry — his teaching, actions, and prophetic warnings — and the historical course of Israel indicate, at the very least, that the expectation of the end, if genuinely there, is closely related to Israel's life as a community within history, and not to be sequestered from it. In short, the eschatological context, if correct, cannot exclude the historical but must somehow incorporate it.

CHAPTER NINE

Conclusion: Prophetic Conflict and Mystical Eschatology

At the beginning of this study the delineation of an overall understanding of the teaching of Jesus was compared to the construction of a building from the many stones of the synoptic traditions. The dominant understandings of Jesus on both the popular and scholarly levels, either as a primarily religious figure concerned with offering religio-moral teaching or making atonement for the world, or as a figure dominated by the conviction that the eschaton would come soon, have left many stones lying about as unusable.

Subsequent chapters made use of these discarded stones and built the foundation of an understanding of Jesus' ministry quite different from those which use other cornerstones. Moreover, the salvaged stones are not easily attributable to the stonecutters of the early Christian community. These aspects of Jesus' activity, all of which point to his involvement with the politico-religious course of Israel, on intrinsic grounds appear important — even central — and are yet incompatible with the other dominant contexts for understanding his mission.

In particular, Jesus' conflict with the Pharisees centered upon the adequacy of the quest for holiness as a program for Israel's national life. His choice of terrain upon which to do battle concerned those subjects (table fellowship, sabbath, Temple) important to Israel's survival and integral to its quest for holiness. Much of his teaching propagated an alternative paradigm with identifiable political consequences as a course for Israel. No less prominent were his action in the Temple as an indictment of Israel's course of separatist resistance, his undercutting of the Temple ideology as a pillar of resistance, and his portrayal of the future as one filled with the Roman threat. All of this provides evidence that Jesus' ministry concerned what it meant to be Israel in the setting of Israel's conflict with Rome.

In this concluding chapter I wish to outline a more comprehensive historical reconstruction of Jesus' ministry, one which makes central use

of these neglected stones. An interest in this greater whole was the original motivation for this quite specialized study, and the material treated
thus far provides one radius among several along which one may approach the center of the teaching and activity of Jesus. Moreover, since
the final test of any historical reconstruction is its comprehensiveness,
its ability adequately to accommodate the data which have good claim
to authenticity, it is appropriate to conclude this study with a fairly
comprehensive sketch.

To accomplish this goal, I will speak about the different roles in
which Jesus appears on the pages of the Gospel. Thus far we have employed the two categories of Spirit person and prophet. In addition, he
also appeared on the historical stage as a sage (a teacher of wisdom)
and proclaimer of the Kingdom of God. By summarizing what has been
said under the categories of Spirit person and prophet and then relating
that material to the two further categories of sage and proclaimer of the
Kingdom of God, I seek to draw the more comprehensive portrait.

Jesus as Spirit Person and Prophet

The central characteristics of a Spirit person have already been briefly
described: a person known for his or her intimacy with the sacred and
for the ability to perform miracles.[1] Here I wish to comment further
about the first dimension of a Spirit person's experience. Namely, a
Spirit person is not only a channel for primordial power, but *knows*
that power. Essential to a Spirit person's experience is the "breaking of
plane," frequently expressed as movement in a vertical direction. This
involves both alteration of consciousness and movement in a new dimension, often symbolized by a "celestial pole" which permits mystical
ascent to the heavens.[2] As such, a Spirit person's experience is one
form of mystical experience, a union or communion with God, or even
with "god beyond god," i.e., with Reality-Itself, that which lies behind
all conceptualizations, including all conceptions of God. Those who
have such experiences speak of them as ineffable, incapable of being
described precisely, for the experience is beyond thought, and beyond
the subject/object distinction and classification which both thought and
language presuppose.

Yet those who have such experiences also insist that it is a *knowing*,
and not just a feeling; it is a noetic and not simply a subjective emo-

---

1. See above pp. 88–89.
2. S. Larsen, *The Shaman's Doorway* (New York, 1976), 66.

tional state. The knowing is direct, immediate, intuitive, quite unlike the modern Western understanding of knowledge as necessarily involving observer and observed and thus subject/object separation.[3] Some mystics describe the experience as one of union in which self and God merge indistinguishably, others as a communion in which self and God interpenetrate but "particularity" somehow remains, a difference generally (though not universally) characteristic of Eastern and Western mysticism respectively.[4]

This way of knowing God was present in Jesus' milieu. As already noted, there were other Jewish Spirit persons contemporary with Jesus (those whom Vermes calls "Galilean charismatics"). Moreover, Jewish mysticism is known to antedate the time of Jesus. Though all of its extant literary products come from a later period beginning with the oldest Hekhaloth books from no later than the third century c.e. in Palestine,[5] Jewish mysticism clearly had its roots much earlier, at least as early as the first century b.c.e.[6] Furthermore, quite apart from tracing a literary tradition, it is clear that this way of knowing God is very ancient

---

3. One of the most comprehensive and yet compact descriptions of mystical experience is William James, The Varieties of Religious Experience (New York, 1961; originally published in 1902), 299–336, esp. 299–301. James stresses the noetic quality, as does the title of A. Greeley's Ecstasy: A Way of Knowing (Englewood Cliffs, 1974).

4. The difference between union and communion mysticism is difficult to explain. In mystical experience, the subject/object distinction of ordinary awareness disappears. For union mystics, everything becomes subject or, perhaps more accurately, everything becomes one (or "not two") beyond the subject/object distinction. For communion mystics, the subject/object distinction disappears, but it is not replaced by undifferentiated oneness. Instead, what might be called a subject/subject relationship emerges: knowing and being known by. For subject/subject as Buber's I-Thou, see M. Buber, I and Thou (New York, 1970). See also Ewert Cousins in Peter Berger, ed., The Other Side of God: A Polarity in World Religions (Garden City, N.Y., 1981), 79, who speaks of a "unity-in-difference" mysticism as "indigenous" to the Christian tradition. In the same volume, Michael Fishbane (p. 42) speaks of early Jewish mysticism as never, not "even at the ultimate point of beatific vision and spiritual adhesion," involving God and the mystic becoming "of the same ontological 'substance.'" Thus he sees early Jewish mysticism as communion mysticism.

5. G. Scholem, Jewish Gnosticism, Merkabah Mysticism, and Talmudic Tradition, 2d ed. (New York, 1965), 23–27.

6. G. Scholem, Major Trends in Jewish Mysticism (New York, 1961), 40–79. In addition to dating Jewish mysticism prior to the current era, Scholem notes its connection to apocalyptic thought (40–43, 73) and Pharisaic circles (41–42), its use of fasting and special postures of prayer (49–50), and its association with miraculous powers (50–51). Suter, Tradition and Composition in the Parables of Enoch, 14–23, connects the parables of Enoch, which he dates in the middle first century c.e., to the Hekhaloth tradition. Hengel, Jews, Greeks and Barbarians, 124, traces the special revelations of hasidic apocalyptic to mystical experiences. See also his Judaism and Hellenism, 1:207. Neusner, Early Rabbinic Judaism, 142, approvingly reports M. Smith's claim that mystical elements developed within Judaism in the pre-Christian Hellenistic period, and on p. 148 notes that we must suppose that Jewish gnosticism existed prior to 70 c.e.

in the Jewish tradition. Moses and Elijah were the two Spirit persons par excellence in the Hebrew Bible, and the prophets of ancient Israel knew God in this intimate way.[7]

That Jesus knew God in this manner is apparent not only from his sharing the general characteristics of a Spirit person, but from specific indications in the synoptic texts. The intimacy of his knowing is reflected in his addressing God in prayer as *Abba,* an informal Aramaic word used by very young children for their father, which may perhaps be translated "papa" and points to the intimate experience of the divine. The usage is very uncommon in Judaism, where the few parallels are found in rabbinic texts about other Jewish Spirit persons.[8] Closely related to this point, a Q text reports that Jesus spoke of the intimate knowing that occurs between father and son and uses this analogy to speak of Jesus' own experience of God: "No one knows the son except the Father, and no one knows the Father except the son."[9] The two halves of the statement are a Semitic idiom which means simply, "Only father and son really know each other," the Semitic way of speaking of a reciprocal relationship of knowing and being known by.[10]

Thus as a Jewish Spirit person, Jesus knew God. Out of this intimate knowing flowed his understanding of God's nature or quality, and his perception of what Israel was to be. Among the passages which give expression to Jesus' understanding of God's nature is the classic Q text:

> Look at the birds of the air. They neither sow nor reap nor gather in the barns, and yet God feeds them. Are you not of more value than they? And which of you by being anxious can add one cubit to your span

---

7. See A. Heschel's exposition of *daath elohim,* "knowing God," in *The Prophets* (New York, 1969), 1:57–60. Though Heschel avoids using the term "mysticism" in this context, *daath elohim* is a *direct* knowing *of* God, not a knowing *about* God.

8. For Jesus' use, see Mark 14:36. The term may also lie behind the unadorned "father" in Luke's version of the Lord's Prayer (Luke 11:2). That it was an important part of the prayer life of first-century Christians is indicated by its appearance in Rom. 8:15 and Gal. 4:6, documents composed in Greek for Greek-speaking audiences. It is reasonable to conclude that early Christian usage derived from Jesus' own use of the term. The classic study is J. Jeremias, *The Prayers of Jesus* (London, 1967), though he overstates the case for uniqueness. For parallels in texts about Jewish Spirit persons, see Vermes, *Jesus the Jew,* 210–13.

9. Matt. 11:25–27=Luke 10:21–22. Though its credentials as Q material are excellent, scholars tend to attribute it to the early Christian community instead of to Jesus, reading it as asserting the unique sonship of Jesus, a conviction clearly held by the post-Easter community. For a rehearsal of the arguments for and against authenticity, see J. G. Dunn, *Jesus and the Spirit* (Philadelphia, 1975), 27–34. Yet its language and content are at home in a pre-Easter Palestinian milieu (see esp. Jeremias, *New Testament Theology,* 56–61); and other Jewish charismatic men spoke of themselves as "son" in a sense that distinguished them from other Jews who were also called "sons" (see Vermes, *Jesus and the Jew,* 209).

10. Jeremias, *New Testament Theology,* 58.

of life? And why are you anxious about clothing? Consider the lilies of the field, how they grow. They neither toil nor spin. Yet I tell you, even Solomon in all his glory was not arrayed like one of these. But if God so clothes the grass of the field, which today is alive and tomorrow is thrown into the oven, will he not much more clothe you? (Matt. 6:26–30=Luke 12:24–28)

According to another Q text, Jesus said: "Are not five sparrows sold for two pennies? And not one of them is forgotten before God. Why, even the hairs of your head are all numbered" (Luke 12:6–7=Matt. 5:29–30). In these texts, marked by an imaginative and poetic appeal to nature, Jesus invited his hearers to see reality as characterized by a cosmic generosity. God feeds the birds, clothes the grass with lily blossoms, knows every sparrow, numbers every hair. Even that which has little value to human beings has value to God: the grass thrown into the oven, the sparrows sold in the marketplace five for two pennies. Reality is permeated, indeed flooded, with divine creativity, nourishment, and care.

To see God as gracious, nourishing, and encompassing is consistent with the Hebrew Bible and the tradition in which Jesus stood.[11] But the freshness of imagery and intensity of expression in these texts require more of an explanation than tradition. The most satisfactory explanation is that he knew God in his own experience.

The depiction of ultimate reality as lavishly nourishing care upon creation without regard to human valuation is intrinsically connected to the understanding of God as compassionate. The same cosmic munificence which clothes the grass also "makes the sun rise on the evil and the good, and sends rain on the just and unjust" (Matt. 5:45b), and is identical to the understanding of compassion described earlier. This perception flowed from Jesus' own subjective experience of the *mysterium tremendum* as gracious and compassionate, encompassing and present. As a Spirit person who knew the nature of the sacred, the "numinous," from his own experience, Jesus proclaimed the acceptance of the outcasts both in his teaching and actions. Moreover, his articulation of inclusive compassion as the paradigm for Israel to follow was similarly grounded in his own experience. Thus Jesus' basic "program" for the internal reform of Israel — "Be compassionate as God is compassionate" — flowed out of knowledge of God which he, as a Spirit person, was given in his own internal experience.

The sense of mission which he received as a Spirit person led him to undertake the role of prophet. As a prophet, he aggressively and

---

11. See, e.g., Ps. 139:1–18.

provocatively challenged the corporate direction of his people. Violating the taboos of table fellowship, subverting the sabbath, criticizing
traditions regarding the Temple, he reversed the expectations of the future held by his contemporaries. Motivated by a profound love for his
own people in a time when their future was at stake, he repudiated the
burgeoning momentum leading toward armed resistance to Rome and
called his hearers to the path of peace. His table fellowship, because it
included quislings and publicly enacted the breakdown of holiness as
separation, pointed to an understanding of Israel different from that advocated by those seeking a holy, separated nation. He also repudiated
the Temple ideology which augmented the dynamic of resistance with
the expectation of success. Contingent upon Israel's response, he promised peace instead of war, most evidently in Luke 19:42–44, in which
Jesus spoke not only of peace but, by contrasting the way of peace to
the impending destruction of Jerusalem, made it clear that peace was
not merely a depoliticized spiritual experience but embraced political
peace.[12] Peace as a consequence of response to Jesus was also implied
in Jesus' acted fulfillment of Zech. 9:9 in the entry into Jerusalem
narrative.[13]

The admonition "love your enemy" would have been understood, as
argued earlier,[14] as an explicit reference to the Roman enemy and an
unmistakable command to eschew the path of armed resistance. The
saying, a source of perennial debate in Christian ethics, was in fact intended not simply for personal relationships, but as "public policy" at
a particular time in history toward a particular state.[15] In an episode

---

12. See above pp. 199–201.

13. See above pp. 188–89. Further evidence for the Jesus movement's attitudes may
be found in the Lucan infancy hymns, which are likely to have had their *Sitz im Leben der
alten Kirche* in the Palestinian church, and which understand peace for Israel to be among
the potential consequences of Jesus' advent (Luke 1:79, 2:14). See H. L. MacNeill, "The
Sitz im Leben of Lk. 1:5–2:20," *JBL* 65 (1946): 123–30; Gaston, *No Stone*, 256–76. That
they have their origin in a Palestinian community does not depend on a linguistic argument for a Semitic origin; i.e., if one affirms with H. F. D. Sparks, "The Semitisms of
St. Luke's Gospel," *JTS* 44 (1943): 129–38, that the Semitisms are explicable as Lucan
"Septuagintalisms," this does not entail the view that the hymns are Lucan creations. In-
deed, Sparks himself (135–36), affirms that they are probably based on earlier tradition.
Also affirming a Christian community origin for the hymns (as opposed to a Baptist or
Lucan origin) are, among others, W. Wink, *John the Baptist in the Gospel Tradition* (Cam-
bridge, 1968), 60–72; D. Jones, "The Background and Character of the Lukan Psalms,"
JTS 19 (1968): 19–50.

14. See above 141–44.

15. It seems that often what Jesus meant by it is determined on the basis of whether
or not it can make sense as public policy in all periods of history. Since this would, it
is argued, often involve the suffering of innocents against whom unjust aggression had
occurred, it cannot be intended as public policy, but only for the Christian's personal
behavior, when s/he *alone* takes the consequences. For a statement of the dilemma, see

reported only by John but with allusive support in Mark, Jesus spurned the attempt of a desert gathering to make him king, that is, the leader of a national liberation movement, vetoing resistance as the way for Israel, though the incident also hints that Jesus was more concerned with national issues than is often affirmed.[16] Finally, the most famous pronouncement in this connection, "Render unto Caesar that which is Caesar's," must be regarded as answering the question about the tribute tax, even though it was probably not as important as it is usually claimed to be.[17] The tax was to be paid, and as such it was a pronouncement which radicalized anti-Roman elements could not have endorsed.[18]

To this disavowal of national resistance, two qualifications must be added at once. First, it did not imply a positive evaluation of Roman imperial order. For the Roman emperor was undoubtedly to be numbered among those who lorded it over their subjects, which was an object lesson of how not to behave.[19] It was Rome who committed atrocities, who would destroy Jerusalem, who would commit the abomination of desolation, who thereby, indeed, was Nebuchadnezzar *redivivus*, Antiochus *redivivus*. Rome was no more viewed as good than Assyria and Babylon were viewed as good by the preexilic prophets. And Herod Antipas, the local incarnation of Gentile power, was described contemptuously as "that fox."[20]

Secondly, because of this reversal of Israel's political aspirations,

---

J. Wood, *The Sermon on the Mount and Its Application* (London, 1963), 96–108. Whatever one says about its permanent application, one can say that, historically considered, it was intended as a collective posture at a particular time in history toward a particular state.

16. John 6:14–15; Mark 6:30–44. See Manson, *Servant Messiah*, 70–71; Blinzler, "Die Niedermetzelung von Galiläern durch Pilatus," 43–47; H. Montefiore, "Revolt in the Desert? Mark 6:30ff.," *NTS* 8 (1961–62): 135–41; Dodd, *Historical Tradition*, 212–17, and *Founder of Christianity*, 131–34.

17. Mark 12:13–17. It does not answer the broader question of what is Caesar's and what is God's. Moreover, it is inadequate as a basis for describing the politics of Jesus, as if this were the central political pronouncement of the ministry. The thrust of this study is that there is so much more which must be included under "the politics of Jesus."

18. Contra Kennard, *Render to God*, passim, and Brandon, *Jesus and the Zealots*, 345–49, both of whom argue that "Render to God the things that are God's" would have been understood to prohibit payment of tax to Caesar, since the wealth of the Holy Land was God's, not Caesar's. Yet in the context of handling a coin of Caesar's, "Render unto Caesar" must surely mean, "Go ahead and pay it." So also, among others, Stauffer, *Christ and the Caesars*, 112–37; W. L. Knox, "Church and State in the New Testament," *JRS* 39 (1949): 23; M. Rist, "Caesar or God (Mark 12:13–17)? A Study in *Formgeschichte*," *JR* 16 (1936): 317–31; Derrett, *Law in the New Testament*, 34–37. For research and bibliography, see C. H. Giblin, " 'The Things of God' in the Question Concerning Tribute to Caesar," *CBQ* 33 (1971): 510–14.

19. Mark 10:42–43 par.; cf. Luke 22:25–26.

20. Luke 13:32; on "fox," see Hoehner, *Herod Antipas*, 220–21, 343–47.

the injunction to nonresistance, and the advice to pay tribute, Jesus is widely held to be nonpolitical. But such a conclusion is incorrect. Jesus' attitude toward Rome was not based on an apolitical stance, but on the conviction that in the political affairs of the world the judging activity of God was at work.[21] Regarding his own society, he was intensely political in the sense which we have given to that term: he was concerned about the institutions and historical dynamic of Israel. The means which he used, including public revolutionary gestures, challenged current practice. The end which he sought was the transformation of the cultural dynamic of the quest for holiness into a cultural dynamic which would conform Israel to God as compassionate.

As a prophet, Jesus called Israel to a national reorientation in which both attitudes and institutions would be conformed to the inclusive compassion of God. Such a reorientation included a repudiation both of the path of resistance and of the quest for holiness which sustained it. This national reorientation is included in the word "repent," which, though it does not appear frequently in the teaching of Jesus, is joined to the programmatic summation of Jesus' preaching in Mark 1:15: "The Kingdom of God is at hand: repent." For repentance, though done by individuals, was not a turning from individual sins so much as a turning from commitments to a certain understanding of God and Israel to a transformed understanding.[22] It called for a departure from the established structures which had shaped and nurtured the existence of those who heard Jesus to a new understanding of Israel as a community of inclusive compassion, and to face a future that was largely unknown, with only the promise that ultimately God would vindicate them.

Repentance so understood entailed risks. There was not only a risk to the individual who responded, but also a risk to the existence of Israel. For the function of Torah and Temple *as institutions preservative of Israel's cohesiveness* would largely disappear if they were subordinated to the paradigm of compassion. Indeed, as we suggested earlier, the per-

---

21. See chapter 7 above, passim.

22. See the examination of the threat-warrant tradition in chapter 8, esp. pp. 215–17. The recognition that Jesus' message of repentance involved neither a turning from individual sins nor a turning to individual virtues, but rather included national shortcomings, helps to explain the frequently cited problem of why Paul and other epistolatory writers do not more often invoke the moral authority of Jesus when offering ethical instruction. The problem, identified by D. L. Dungan, *The Sayings of Jesus in the Churches of Paul* (Philadelphia, 1971), xvii–xxix, with citation of literature, is largely resolved by the recognition that the specific ethical teaching of Jesus did not consist of generalized morality or universally applicable laws for living, but concerned the specific politico-religious crisis of Israel. What he did say was often so related to the particularities of the Palestinian crisis that it could be used in another milieu only by modification and transformation, a process which by no means needs to be viewed as illegitimate.

ception of the importance of these institutions for Israel's survival was a fundamental reason for the opposition offered to Jesus by his contemporaries. What seemed threatened by the transformation of these institutions was national identity and national survival itself. Yet what was called for was a course of reckless abandon in a time when the destiny of Israel was at stake.

Thus, like the classical prophets of the Hebrew Bible, Jesus sought to divert his people from a course which was leading to catastrophe. Apparently knowing that the likely outcome would be his death, he went to Jerusalem during the season of Passover, there to make one final dramatic appeal to his people at the center of their corporate life.

Jesus as Sage: The Importance of the Heart

Jesus also appears in the role of sage, a teacher of wisdom. Sages are important figures in traditional cultures. Classic examples are Lao Tzu in sixth-century B.C.E. China, the Buddha, and the authors of the wisdom tradition in the Hebrew Bible: Proverbs, Job, Ecclesiastes. Vast in its scope, ranging from matters that are virtually questions of etiquette to ultimate matters such as human nature and the nature of ultimate reality, the source of sagely teaching is reflection upon existence from a particular perspective. To put that negatively, its source is not revealed esoteric truths from another world or deductions logically derived from an authoritative tradition (even though the tradition may affect the sage's reflection). The authority of the teaching depends upon its own perspicacity rather than upon some external authority. Frequently sages use analogies drawn from nature or common human experience to illustrate what they are seeking to communicate, thus inviting their hearers to see things a certain way rather than insisting that tradition or revelation dictates a particular way of seeing things. The parables and aphoristic sayings of Jesus (and other figures in his tradition) are good examples of this.

The perspective from which the astute observations flow is commonly age, that is, from reflection upon experience over many years. Frequently an older person, the sage has observed much and pondered long, and many cultures associate wisdom with "the elders." Occasionally and remarkably, sagacity is found in younger persons, as in Jesus and the Buddha. In such instances, the vantage point is obviously not the product of age. Rather, the transformation of perception is the product of their spiritual experience. The mystical perception of both self and world is *sub specie aeternitatis,* a vantage point beyond time from which ordinary consciousness and experience seem like a state of estrangement. Indeed, the stronger the mystical perspective, the more sharply ordinary existence appears to be a life of blindness, bondage, and misery, a plight which triggers compassion, sadness, and sometimes even anger. When this experience is combined with a sagacious intellect, the result is insight.

As a sage whose perception flowed out of his experience of the sacred, Jesus developed a set of teachings about God, the human predicament, and the way of transformation. In the previous sections, we have already briefly treated his understanding of God and of the *imitatio dei* which was to inform Israel's corporate life. In this section, we shall focus on his perception of the way of transformation.

Like the teaching of the other renewal movements, Jesus' teaching also involved an intensification of the Torah.[23] The other renewal movements intensified the Torah in the direction of holiness, emphasizing various forms of separation — from society as a whole, from the Gentiles, from impurity within society. Jesus, however, intensified the Torah primarily by applying it to internal dimensions of the human psyche: to dispositions, emotions, thoughts, and desires. Moreover, as we shall see near the end of this section, this internalization had immediate socio-religious and politico-religious consequences.

Jesus' application of Torah to internal dispositions can be seen most clearly in the antitheses of the Sermon on the Mount. Some of these most likely go back to Jesus himself, and all of them provide evidence for the stance of the Jesus movement. Not just killing but also anger is prohibited; not just adultery but also lust is enjoined (Matt. 5:21–22, 27–28). Such is also the thrust of the saying in the seventh chapter of Mark, which was analyzed earlier in the context of ritual washing of hands:

> Hear me, all of you, and understand. There is nothing outside a person that by going in can defile, but the things that come out are what defile.[24]

That is, what matters is what is within: true purity is a matter of inward purity. In Mark, the passage continues:

> Do you not see that whatever goes into a person from outside cannot defile, since it enters, not the heart but the stomach and goes out into the sewer? . . . It is what comes out of a person that defiles. For it is from within, from the human heart, that evil intentions come: fornication, theft, murder, adultery, avarice, wickedness, deceit, licentiousness, envy,

---

23. See above pp. 71–77 and Theissen, *Sociology of Early Palestinian Christianity*, 77–87.

24. Mark 7:15. See above pp. 110–13.

slander, pride, folly. All these evil things come from within, and they defile a person.[25]

Though almost certainly Marcan and not to be attributed to Jesus, the words are an appropriate commentary, extending the meaning of the previous saying and explicitly introducing the notion of the heart. Impurity is a matter of the heart, not of external behavior. Indeed, the latter has its source in the former. Conversely, true purity is purity of heart, as Jesus is reported to have said on another occasion: "Blessed are the pure in heart, for they shall see God" (Matt. 5:8).

The intensification of Torah by applying it to what is internal is thus seen most centrally in Jesus' teaching concerning the heart. In Jewish psychology, as disclosed in both the Hebrew Bible and the rabbinic tradition, the heart is "the psyche at its deepest level," "the innermost spring of individual life, the ultimate source of all its physical, intellectual, emotional, and volitional energies."[26] As such, the heart is the seat or source of thinking, feeling, and behavior, of intellect, emotion, and will. They do not shape or control the heart, but it shapes them. The rabbinic tradition affirmed that the heart in turn was ruled either by the "evil inclination" (ha-yetzer ha-ra) or "good inclination" (ha-yetzer ha-tob).[27] The power of the evil impulse was great: like a king, it ruled the 248 parts of the body. According to other images, the evil inclination ensnared the self with threads which, though thin as a spider's web at the beginning, soon became as thick as a ship's rope. Beginning as a visitor in the heart, it became a regular guest, and finally the host.[28] Thus one could have either a good or evil heart: the self at its deepest level could be inclined (or driven) either of two ways.

Jesus accepted this understanding of the heart and made it central to his perception of the human condition. In a passage attested by both Matthew and Luke, he said:

For no good tree bears bad fruit, nor again does a bad tree bear good fruit; for each tree is known by its own fruit. For figs are not gathered from thorns, nor are grapes picked from a bramble bush. The good person out of the good treasure of the heart produces good, and the evil person out of evil treasure produces evil; for it is out of the abundance of the heart that the mouth speaks.[29]

25. Mark 7:18b–19a, 20–23. See also p. 111 above.
26. R. C. Dentan, IDB, 2:549.
27. W. D. Davies, Paul and Rabbinic Judaism, 3d ed. (London, 1970), 20–35; Urbach, The Sages, 471–83.
28. Urbach, The Sages, 473.
29. Luke 6:43–45=Matt. 12:33–35; cf. Matt. 7:16–20.

As a sage, Jesus made a commonsense observation about nature: one gathers figs and grapes from fig trees and vines, not from thorn or bramble bushes. The application of the observation is obvious and far-reaching: the tree and its fruits are an image for the self (the heart) and its behavior: a good self produces good behavior. The rest of the saying makes explicit the connection to the heart: a heart filled with good treasure produces good, and one filled with evil treasure produces evil. Thus what matters is the kind of tree one is, the kind of heart one has.

Just as the rabbis spoke of the heart being inclined one of two different ways, so did Jesus. Identifying two comprehensive centers of ultimate loyalty, Jesus spoke of "treasures in heaven" and "treasures on earth," symbolic of the infinite and finite respectively, and added, "Where your treasure is, there will your heart be also" (Matt. 6:19–21; cf. Luke 12:33–34). That is, if one's treasure is in the finite, "where moth and rust consume and where thieves break in and steal," then one's heart will be preoccupied with the finite.

The same two fundamental orientations appear in a passage in which Jesus spoke of the impossibility of serving two masters: "You cannot serve God and mammon" (Matt. 6:24=Luke 16:13). "Mammon" meant "riches" and by extension connoted all of the finite. The heart could be centered in God or the finite, the servant (slave) of one or the other. Thus what made a heart pure or impure was its center.

Apparently, Jesus perceived most of his contemporaries as centered in the finite. In his parables, whose power depends upon the realistic portrayal of typical human behavior, people are concerned to receive what is theirs, undisposed to be generous to others, anxious about losing what they have, and fearful of defilement. In his teaching, he regularly identified four centers as most typically dominant in people's lives: family, status, possessions, and piety. The last perception is particularly interesting. The heart can center in its own piety, its own holiness or purity, whether one ostentatiously displays it or not, for the fault lies not in displaying the piety but in holding to it as the basis of identity and distinction from others. Such a heart is not pure, as the conclusion of the parable of the Pharisee and the tax collector shows: the tax collector, who appealed to the mercy of God and prayed for a pure heart, was praised instead of the Pharisee, who centered on his own purity.

Thus the problem was the heart: what mattered was a pure heart. Centuries earlier, the author of Psalm 51 identified the problem in the same manner: "Create in me a clean heart, O God, and put a new and right spirit within me" (Ps. 51:10). The hope for a transformed heart was the basis of the new covenant of which Jeremiah spoke:

> But this is the covenant which I will make with the house of Israel after
> those days says the Lord: I will put my law within them, and I will write
> it *on their hearts*; and I will be their God, and they shall be my people.
> No longer shall they teach one another, or say to each other, "Know the
> Lord," for they shall all know me, from the least of them to the greatest.
> (Jer. 31:33–34a)

Significantly, the passage combines the internalization of the Torah
"upon their heart" with *knowing* God.

What was needed was a new heart. But how was the heart to be
transformed? Obedience to the Torah was one way; indeed, the purpose
of the Torah was to "incline one's heart toward God." Immersion in
and meticulous observance of Torah in virtually every aspect of daily
life reminded one constantly of God and, with the Torah more and
more internalized within the psyche, oriented the heart toward God.
Moreover, it worked. As noted earlier, Judaism produced a number of
notable saints through this method.

However, this way had become normative among the religious, in
part because of the particular circumstances facing Judaism in the
Roman period and because of the particular intensifications of Torah
which had occurred, which had established holiness as the exclusive
way of being rightly related to God, and as a blueprint for society. But
as the normative way, this way cut off large numbers — perhaps most —
of the Jewish people from a relationship to God and was responsible for
the division within the people of God between righteous and outcasts.
Moreover, in Jesus' perception, it was possible to posture this way, to
follow the requirements of holiness without being transformed:

> Well did Isaiah prophesy of you hypocrites, as it is written, "This people
> honors me with their lips, but their heart is far from me." (Mark 7:6)

Jesus spoke of another way of transformation. Most basically, it was
the path of death: "If any want to become my followers, let them deny
themselves and take up their cross and follow me."[30] In the first century,
crucifixion was widely known in Palestine as a form of execution practiced by the Romans — a slow, torturous, agonizing death inflicted upon
those suspected of treason against the power which ruled the world.
Customarily the condemned were required to carry the horizontal cross-
beam to the place of execution; hence, "bearing one's cross" was a stark
symbol for death. The language of "following," "coming after," points to
the image of a way or path. To follow after Jesus, to follow his way,

---

30. Mark 8:34. See also Luke 14:26–27=Matt. 10:37–38, and the closely related
images of "drinking the cup" and being baptized with Jesus' baptism in Mark 10:38.

meant walking the road to death — to deny one's self and take up the cross.

Even though some of the early followers of Jesus were literally crucified, the saying was metaphorical, as the earliest commentary on it suggests: "Let them deny themselves and take up their cross *daily*."[31] As a metaphor for an internal spiritual process, the "path of death" involved the death of the heart centered in the finite and the birth of a new heart centered in God. The way of death can be described either as a dying to the world or a dying to the self: the person dies to the world as the center of security and to the self as the center of concern. From this death emerges a new heart or pure heart, centered in God.

Many of the images and contrasts in the teaching of Jesus expressed this basic pattern. To become as a servant was to cease to have a will of one's own, for servants/slaves in the ancient world were understood to be agents of their master's will. Their will had died.[32] To become as a child was to become as an infant, a newborn.[33]

In words preserved four times in the Gospel tradition, Jesus contrasted humbling and exaltation: "All who exalt themselves will be humbled, but all who humble themselves will be exalted."[34] Self-exaltation or self-elevation is a natural response of the self to culturally validated accomplishment, for the culture's standards have been internalized within the self through the process of socialization, and the self which meets those standards thus judges itself "good." In the Gospel contexts of this saying, these standards are religious and social.[35] The self in its own eyes thus "stands out" and becomes the basis for self-affirmation; it and its status have become the center. "Self-humbling" is the opposite. In the Hebrew Bible, to be humble was often associated with the objective state of poverty and affliction,[36] but by the first century referred primarily to a subjective state, though still carrying connotations of poverty. To be humble was not to claim status, but

---

31. Luke 9:23. Presumably Luke added "daily" as he incorporated Mark's text into his Gospel.

32. Mark 9:33–35; Mark 10:42–44=Matt. 20:25–27; cf. Luke 22:25–26, Matt. 23:11.

33. Matt. 18:2–4; Mark 10:15=Luke 18:17. The image seems closely related to the Johannine emphasis on being born again; see John 3:1–8.

34. Luke 18:14b; see also Luke 14:11, Matt. 23:12 and 18:4.

35. On two occasions, the context is self-exaltation through religious status: Luke 18:14b, the parable of the Pharisee and the tax collector; Matt. 23:12, the honor enjoyed by religious teachers. On another occasion, the context is self-exaltation through social (or religious?) status as indicated by the seating arrangements at a banquet (Luke 14:7–11). The other context is teaching on greatness (Matt. 18:1–4).

36. See, e.g., G. E. Mendenhall, *IDB*, 2:659.

to be internally without possessions, to be empty.[37] Self-humbling was thus self-emptying, and the passage may be paraphrased, "Those who empty themselves will be exalted; those who exalt themselves will be emptied, will come to naught."

The closely parallel contrasts of *first/last, finding one's life/losing one's life* made basically the same point. Those who make themselves first will be last, and those who put themselves last shall be first;[38] those who seek their lives will lose them, but those who let go of their lives will find them.[39]

The way as the path of death and rebirth of a new heart was embodied in the life and teaching of the early Christian movement. The apostle Paul, the earliest of the New Testament authors, wrote, "I have been crucified with Christ; it is no longer I who live but Christ who lives in me" (Gal. 2:20), and he affirmed that this experience was common to all Christians.[40] Such was also the case in the Jesus movement in Palestine, which grew directly out of Jesus' teaching. The symbolism of baptism, its ritual of initiation, points intrinsically to death and resurrection, to new creation: one was plunged beneath the waters of death, returned to the night before creation where one was created anew, born anew.

The Jesus movement in Palestine not only preserved the teaching of Jesus concerning the path of death, but arranged it into comprehensive patterns which emphasized the teaching even more sharply. Mark's Gospel as a whole can be construed as the Gospel of "the way"[41] and the massive central section of Luke's Gospel as a journey toward death.[42]

---

37. Cf. Phil. 2:5–11, where *"emptied* himself, taking the form of a servant," is parallel to "he *humbled* himself and became obedient unto death." Many scholars have argued that these words are from a pre-Pauline hymn, suggesting very early Christian tradition. In addition to the parallel between self-emptying and humbling, note the connection of both to *servant* and *death.*

38. Mark 10:31; Luke 13:30; Matt. 20:16.

39. Matt. 10:39; cf. Mark 8:35 par., Luke 17:33; cf. John 12:25.

40. See, e.g., Rom. 6:1–11; see esp. v. 3: "all of us."

41. Following the opening verse of the Gospel, which is really the title, Mark began his Gospel with a Hebrew Bible quotation suggesting that his Gospel concerned "the way." Each of the three occasions on which Jesus speaks of his impending death in Mark 8–10 is followed immediately by teaching directed to his followers concerning the way of death (Mark 8:31–35, 9:30–35, 10:32–40). The Gospel climaxes in the death of Jesus, which is understood as opening up access to the presence of God (Mark 15:38); i.e., the way into the presence of God is through death. That Mark's Gospel may be used cautiously as evidence for the Jesus movement's understanding flows out of the growing tendency among scholars to locate the composition of Mark's Gospel in Syria, part of the area included within the Jesus movement's activity; see, e.g., H. C. Kee, *Community of the New Age: Studies in Mark's Gospel* (Philadelphia, 1977), 100–105, esp. 105, where Kee speaks of "rural and small-town southern Syria."

42. Luke 9:51–18:14. Whether this may be used as evidence for the Jesus move-

The way of transformation of which Jesus spoke was akin to his own experience. Intrinsic to the spirituality of a Spirit person is the internal experience of death of self, sometimes involving a ritual of self-wounding, an ordeal, or participation in a myth of dismemberment that corresponds to inner psychic experience.[43] Jesus' ministry began with a ritual of death and rebirth, baptism; strikingly, the Gospels agree that on this occasion Jesus' identity as "son" was first disclosed. Moreover, the baptism was followed immediately by the temptation in the wilderness, which can be understood as a Spirit person's initiatory ordeal and encounter with the spirit world. Jesus himself had "died to the world," living without possessions, family, or home. Yet he did not make the details of his way normative, but only the basic pattern itself.

Put positively, the path of death involved trusting radically in the compassion of God and letting go of the self and the world as the basis of security and focus of concern. This way was simultaneously hard and easy. It was hard especially for those who were quite secure and who measured up to the standards of culture internalized within their psyches, whether the decisive standards were wealth, status, or observance of the Torah. For them to let go of those standards and the self which met them was very difficult. Hence the way was the *narrow* way: "The gate is narrow and the way is hard that leads to life, and those who find it are few" (Matt. 7:14; cf. Luke 13:24). Hence also the metaphor of death: dying is very hard and it is difficult to let go of finite centers. Yet it was also the easy way because it was a "letting go," a cessation of striving. Moreover, it may have been easier for some, namely, the poor and the outcasts. Riches were not a temptation for the poor (except in societies which stress upward mobility); the poor knew that the world offered scant measure of security. Righteousness was not a temptation for the sinner, social approval not a snare for the outcast. To die to a world in which one was poor, which pronounced one an outcast, was not as difficult as dying to a world in which one was financially secure, socially and religiously esteemed. Hence Jesus could say,

> Come to me, all who labor and are heavy laden, and I will give you rest.
> Take my yoke upon you, and learn from me; for I am gentle and lowly in

---

ment's point of view depends upon how one views the tradition which Luke received. Is the "journey toward death" section due to Lucan composition, or was it already present in "proto-Luke"? For an extended argument that the pre-Lucan traditions reflect the missionary activity of the Palestinian church (the Jesus movement), see Gaston, *No Stone*, 244–369.

43. Lewis, *Ecstatic Religion*, 70: "The shaman's initial crisis represents the healer's passion, or, as the Akawaio Indians themselves put it, 'a man must die before he becomes a shaman.'"

heart, and you will find rest for your souls. For my yoke is easy and my
burden is light. (Matt. 11:28–30)

The way of transformation thus involved becoming pure in heart
through dying to the finite and living by radical trust in God. The world
as the center of existence comes to an end. Even the form as well as the
content of much of the sagely teaching of Jesus seemed designed to jolt
his hearers out of their present world, their present way of seeing reality.
The aphoristic sayings and parables are crystallized flashes of insight
that also compel insight and frequently reverse ordinary understanding
by bringing it into judgment. In short, even the form of Jesus' wisdom
teaching mediated and invited end-of-world.[44]

Thus Jesus proclaimed a way of transformation that did not depend
upon observing the requirements of the Torah as understood by the
other renewal movements. Speaking of a divine compassion grounded
in his own experience of God, he proclaimed a way of transformation
whereby people could increasingly experience and live that awareness.
By undergoing that path, they began the process of becoming good trees
producing good fruit, of having hearts whose treasure was in heaven.
Thus Jesus internalized holiness, just as he internalized the commandments against murder and adultery. Holiness was a matter of the heart,
for what mattered was a pure heart. The way to purity of heart was not
exclusively or even primarily through obedience to the Torah, but the
path of dying to the self and the world.

Those commentators throughout the centuries who have affirmed
that Jesus was centrally concerned with the orientation and transformation of the heart are thus correct. What has not often been noted,
however, is that Jesus' teaching about the heart had a number of immediate socio-religious and historical-political implications in the context
of the Jewish homeland in the first century. Affirming that purity was
a matter of the heart cut the connection between holiness and separation as understood by the other renewal movements. That is, holiness
was to be achieved neither by driving the Romans from the land nor
by withdrawal from society nor by separation within society. Intensifying the Torah by applying it to purity of heart also destroyed the basis
for dividing society into righteous and outcast, for "once the norms
had been intensified ... so that they were quite beyond the possibility
of fulfillment," applying to internal disposition as well as behavior, no
one could claim that it alone was the "true Israel," for "all alike were

---

44. On the connection between the forms of Jesus' teaching and the "end of world,"
see esp. the work of William Beardslee and John Crossan, compactly reported by Perrin,
Jesus and the Language of the Kingdom, 48–56.

sinners."[45] Jesus' teaching thereby provided a ground for overcoming the fragmentation of Jewish society.[46] Moreover, Jesus perceived that the orientation of the heart — its most deeply seated commitments — had historical-political consequences. He saw that the most fundamental commitments of his culture were leading to a collision course with Rome. Finally, the basic quality of a heart centered in God — compassion — had political implications. Compassion was to be the core value of the people of God as a historical community. Thus Jesus' teaching as sage was not divorced from the conflict situation for which we have argued in this study, but was integral to it.

The Kingdom of God

One major stone remains to be integrated into the edifice, and it is a very weighty stone indeed. Jesus also appears in history as proclaimer of the Kingdom of God, a phrase which, in the judgment of virtually all scholars, was the center of his message.[47] Given its centrality, one might think it should be the starting point for a study of the teaching and intention of the historical Jesus and that treating it only at the end is odd. Yet, despite its centrality, it does not provide a good starting point. A century of scholarly activity has produced no consensus regarding its interpretation, suggesting some fundamental difficulties.

Much of the discussion has focused on whether Jesus proclaimed the Kingdom as present or future. Ambiguity attends some of the crucial sayings. For example, how is one to interpret the crucial verb in Mark 1:15: "The Kingdom of God *engiken?* Literally, it is to be translated "has drawn near" (perfect tense). But does that mean "has already come," or "is near — so very near — at hand"? Philological considerations seem unable to settle the question.

A different kind of ambiguity is posed by Luke 17:20–21:

---

45. Theissen, *Sociology of Early Palestinian Christianity,* 104–5; see also 79–80, 103–7.

46. Theissen, *Sociology of Early Palestinian Christianity,* 107, recognizes the connection between the particularities of the historical situation and this aspect of Jesus' teaching: though it "certainly points far beyond the particular historical context in which it came into being," it was initially "a contribution towards overcoming a deep-rooted crisis in Judaism."

47. Cf. J. Reumann, *Jesus in the Church's Gospels* (Philadelphia, 1968), 142: "Ask any hundred New Testament scholars around the world, Protestant, Catholic, or non-Christian, what the central message of Jesus of Nazareth was, and the vast majority of them — perhaps every single expert — would agree that this message centered in the Kingdom of God."

> Being asked by the Pharisees when the Kingdom of God was coming, he answered them, "The Kingdom of God is not coming with signs to be observed; nor will they say, 'Lo, here it is!' or 'There!' for behold, the Kingdom of God is in the midst of you."

If interpreted as an isolated saying separate from its Lucan context, the passage asserts the presence of the Kingdom. But in its Lucan context, where it is parallel to the subsequent saying about the day of the "son of man" arriving as suddenly as a lightning flash, it seems to refer to a future event.[48] But is Luke's context correct, or should the verse as a statement by Jesus be interpreted apart from its Lucan context? A decision can be made only by appeal to a criterion beyond this particular text.

Moreover, even many scholars who claim to use Kingdom of God as the starting point do not actually do so. For example, a number of scholars suggest that to the numerous sayings which speak of entering, being in, or possessing the Kingdom[49] (which do seem to speak of the Kingdom as a present reality), one must add the gloss "when it comes," so that what is spoken of is not a present entry, but "right disposition for *future* entry."[50] Or it is said that one should add an interpolation to all of the Kingdom sayings in order to make them refer to imminent universal judgment and renewal.[51] Not only does the possibility of making such a claim point to the ambiguity of the Kingdom sayings, but it also points to the influence of the interpreter's overall context — for what is the warrant for such a gloss, which the texts themselves do not include? Clearly the warrant is the conviction that the Kingdom sayings are to be interpreted within the context of imminent eschatology,

---

48. So, rightly, R. H. Hiers, *The Kingdom of God in the Synoptic Tradition* (Gainesville, Fla., 1970), 22–29.

49. See n. 64 below.

50. R. H. Fuller, *The Mission and Achievement of Jesus* (London, 1954), 31, in his analysis of Jesus' reply to the scribe in Mark 12:34. So also, Fuller argues, Luke 6:20 par. does not mean that the poor now possess the Kingdom, but promises to the poor *"future entry* into the Kingdom *when it comes"* (31, italics added); "receiving" the Kingdom in similar sayings means receiving "not the Kingdom of God as a present reality, but the present *proclamation* of the *future* event" (p. 30, second italics added). Hiers, *Kingdom of God*, 73, similarly argues that Mark 10:25 means that those "who *now* renounce all *will then* enter the Kingdom" (italics added), and 60, that Matt. 11:11 means that "the least in the Kingdom of heaven will be greater (then) than John is (now)." So also, earlier, Weiss, *Jesus' Proclamation*, 69, claims that Matt. 21:31 does not mean that tax collectors and harlots are already entering the Kingdom, but only that they have a head start on the way that leads to the Kingdom of God (when it comes). Cf. G. Lundström, *The Kingdom of God in the Teaching of Jesus* (London, 1963), 236, who refers all the entry sayings to the coming Kingdom.

51. Jeremias, *New Testament Theology*, 100: "when Jesus speaks of the *basileia*, he almost always includes the notion of the last judgment that is to precede it." Cf. Weiss, *Jesus' Proclamation*, 96–98.

which means that the Kingdom sayings themselves are not the starting point, even for many who give them prominence.

Thus, though the Kingdom of God was central to Jesus' proclamation, it is neither clear that one should begin with it, nor that many interpreters actually do. Instead, when a body of sayings remains subject to diverse interpretations, beginning at another point has merits, for it is a sound principle of interpretation to begin with what is clearest and then move to that which is more opaque, a procedure which this study has sought to follow. Jesus as a Spirit person initiated a renewal movement in the midst of a profound socio-religious crisis within Judaism, calling his people to the imitation of God's compassion as a program both for life within the community and for their relationship to those outside of the community. As a prophet, he warned them of the consequences of following their present course. As a sage, he taught that the way to a transformed heart, to purity of heart, was the path of death and rebirth. Is there an understanding of the Kingdom of God that is compatible with this overall picture? We shall argue not only that there is, but also that this overall picture in fact illuminates Jesus' proclamation of the Kingdom of God.

Scholarly discussion has emphasized that the phrase "Kingdom of God" is a *symbol* in the teaching of Jesus, not a concept.[52] That is, the phrase points to something beyond itself and is not an idea or "shorthand" for an idea, even though much scholarship has treated it as if it meant, in the noninclusive language of earlier in this century, "the brotherhood of man," or the imminent end of the world. In the former case, it would be shorthand for an ethical and social ideal, in the latter case for a conceptualized expectation. Rather, the function of a symbol is to evoke a *myth*.

That is, to the extent that a symbol is shorthand at all, it is shorthand for a myth, not an idea. Myth, here used in the sense articulated by Mircea Eliade,[53] is a story about the relationship between the two realms, the sacred and the profane, the noumenal and the phenomenal, the Real and the visibly real, the "holy" and the quotidian. Myth is the language for speaking about "the other realm" and its relation to this

---

52. See esp. Perrin, *Jesus and the Language of the Kingdom,* and the research which he reports. B. B. Scott, *Jesus, Symbol-Maker for the Kingdom* (Philadelphia, 1981), builds on Perrin's work, applying it particularly to the parables. Perrin stresses the difference between a *tensive* symbol and a *steno*-symbol (29–33). The latter represents something else in a one-to-one way and may thus be translated into its referent without loss, whereas the meaning of a tensive symbol is not exhausted by any one referent. Perrin concludes that Kingdom of God was for Jesus a *tensive* symbol. In the exposition which follows, Kingdom of God is treated as a tensive symbol.

53. See especially M. Eliade, *Myth and Reality* (New York, 1963).

realm.[54] Since a symbol functions linguistically to evoke a myth, it cannot be reduced satisfactorily to a single conceptual meaning any more than the myth itself can be, in part because a myth's meaning is not univocal and in part because myth as a "sacred narrative," especially when ritualized, mediates the reality of which it speaks. A symbol thus points to the particular way of seeing and relating to reality mediated by the myth.

To this function of symbol must be added a second. Namely, symbols do not simply point to narratival myths about reality, thereby only indirectly pointing to the real, but sometimes point directly to that which is symbolized. The most obvious example is the word "God" (and its equivalent in other languages and traditions), which seeks to point beyond itself to that which is known in ecstatic religious experience but which is ineffable.

Given that the phrase "Kingdom of God" is a symbol and not an idea, the proper question to ask is not, "What does the phrase *mean?*" but, "To what does the phrase point, or what does it evoke?" To answer this question, we must pay careful attention to the linguistic home of the symbol "Kingdom of God" in the proclamation of Jesus. Its linguistic home is twofold: the cultural-religious tradition in which Jesus stood, and the specific contexts in which, according to the Gospels, he used the phrase.

To begin with the former, though the phrase "Kingdom of God" is relatively uncommon in the Hebrew Bible, the correlative notions of God's kingship and Kingdom are widespread. Both are associated with the myth of salvation history, Israel's blend of the ancient Near Eastern myth of divine kingship and of its own historical experience. The myth of divine kingship, alluded to most clearly in a number of psalms[55] which may have been used in an annual divine enthronement ritual which Israel probably (though not certainly) observed, associates God's kingship especially with creation and restoration of creation. Basically, the myth affirms that visible reality has its origin, sustenance, and destiny in the other realm, in God. God as king created all that is, restores it yearly in the annual cycle of nature, and will one day effect a final restoration.

To put that slightly differently, all life began in the manifest presence of God (paradise) and will one day return to the manifest presence of God (paradise restored). This is Israel's version of the classic

---

54. Language becomes particularly difficult here. "Other realm" may suggest a spatial metaphor, as if one were speaking quite literally about two different worlds, but I am not inclined to think of it spatially but as another plane or dimension of reality. Ultimately, this becomes a metaphysical question which I am not disposed to treat.

55. E.g., Psalms 47, 93, 96–99.

cosmogonic-eschatological myth: the end shall be as the beginning, the Omega as the Alpha, the destiny of the world as the restoration of paradise. Moreover, the power which is the source and destiny of all that is, was known not only in nature but also in history: in the liberation of Israel from bondage in Egypt, in the giving of the land of Canaan to the freed slaves, in the destruction that began the exile in Babylon, and in the return from exile, a history that was destined to eventuate in the everlasting Kingdom of God, marked by righteousness, justice, and peace. Thus the myth of salvation history, which spoke of God as king, related the two realms at the beginning of history, at extraordinary moments within history, and at the end of history.

The birth of apocalyptic thought in the late postexilic period introduced a modification into the mainstream formulation of the myth. Historically conditioned by the apparent triumph of evil in the world (persistent occupation by foreign powers, persecution and even martyrdom of the righteous), apocalyptic writings generally heightened the distinction between the two realms into an antithesis. The present age was seen as the realm of evil, devoid of the divine, and the activity of God as king was seen as wholly past and future, but not in the present. The dawning of the new world — the Kingdom of God — necessitated the end of the old, the purgation of all evil through judgment and destruction, and re-creation. Thus, for much of apocalyptic thought, the other realm and this realm were linked at the beginning and end of history, but not within history. Yet apocalyptic expression continued to share a major conviction of mainstream salvation history: both affirmed that the two realms were not *ultimately* separated, and that the destiny of creation was the Kingdom of God. Thus the phrase "Kingdom of God" was a symbol not only for the other realm, but also for the destiny of this realm.

The second dimension of the linguistic home of the phrase "Kingdom of God" in the ministry of Jesus consists of the specific contexts in which he used the phrase. He spoke of the Kingdom of God in three such contexts: in connection with exorcisms, as something which could be entered or possessed, and in passages which refer to the future.

A saying universally accepted as authentic and commonly regarded as a central key for understanding Jesus' use of the symbol connects the Kingdom of God to exorcism:

> But if it is by the finger [or "Spirit"] of God that I cast out demons, then the Kingdom of God has come upon you.[56]

---

56. Luke 11:20=Matt. 12:28. Luke has "finger of God" and Matthew has "Spirit of God." N. Perrin and Dennis Duling, *The New Testament: An Introduction*, 2d ed. (New

Most discussions of this verse note that it is authentic, that it speaks of the Kingdom as present, and that it links the coming of the Kingdom to the casting out of demons and therefore to the defeat of Satan, the ruler of the present age, all of which is correct. Often overlooked, however, is a connection of signal importance. The passage joins Jesus' use of Kingdom of God to the religious experience of a Spirit person, for exorcism is a classic activity of a Spirit person. Essential to a Spirit person's experience, as known through cross-cultural studies, are two tiers of consciousness, ordinary and extraordinary.[57] Because these two tiers of subjective experience are both experienced as real, a two-tiered notion of reality flows directly out of the experience,[58] this realm and the other realm, the same two realms of which the myth of salvation history speaks. As a "delegate of the tribe to the other realm,"[59] the Spirit person connects the two realities, channeling power from the other realm to this one.

The explicit connection made by this verse between Jesus' exorcistic activity as a Spirit person and his use of the phrase "Kingdom of God" has an immediate implication. "Kingdom of God" here is Jesus' designation or "name" for the primordial beneficent power of the other realm, an energy which can become active in ordinary reality and which flows through him in his exorcisms. Expressed in language drawn from the religious history of Judaism, Jesus' exorcisms were the Kingdom (or kingship) of God manifested within the world of history. Expressed in language drawn from the intellectual tradition of the history of religions, his exorcisms were the "power of the holy" entering the profane world. The same reality is designated by both expressions.[60]

York, 1982), include it in the list of "at least three sayings about the Kingdom of God" whose authenticity is not challenged in contemporary scholarship. Exorcism is also connected to the Kingdom of God in the mission charge to the disciples (implicitly in Mark 6:7, explicitly in Luke 10:1–2 and Matt. 10:1–8) and in Mark 3:22–27.

57. See, e.g., Michael Harner, *The Way of the Shaman* (San Francisco, 1980), chapter 3, esp. 46–50.

58. Indeed, to speak of only two tiers may be an oversimplification. The celestial pole which the kind of Spirit person known as a shaman ascends may traverse several levels or dimensions of nonordinary reality. See H. Smith, *Forgotten Truth: The Primordial Tradition* (New York, 1976), esp. 34–59. Smith's intention is to describe the understanding of reality common to human experience in virtually every culture prior to the modern period. That understanding, shaped by the experience of holy men and mystics, and occasionally "confirmed" in the experience of ordinary people, reduced to its simplest form, included four levels or planes of reality: the ordinary or terrestrial plane, plus three extraordinary planes: the intermediate, the celestial, and the infinite. Nevertheless, to speak of two tiers makes the essential point: a Spirit person ascends or enters the nonordinary realm.

59. See above p. 88.

60. Utilizing the experience of Spirit persons as a means of illuminating Jesus' use of the phrase "Kingdom of God" has not often been done, perhaps because of the ethos

In short, the phrase "Kingdom of God" in this passage does not refer to a concept or ideal or belief, but to an actual though not physical reality: the beneficent power of the other realm. In the exorcisms, that power "comes": "But if it is by the finger of God that I cast out demons, then the Kingdom of God has come upon you."

The association of Jesus' use of the phrase with the nonordinary experience of a Spirit person is supported by the centrality of Kingdom imagery in Jewish mysticism of his time. Intimately connected with the throne vision in the first chapter of Ezekiel,[61] it was known as *merkabah* mysticism, "throne mysticism," an image obviously related to the symbol of God as King. To "ascend to the throne of God" in the "palace of the seventh heaven" is to enter "the place" where God is present, where God is enthroned as king. Essential to mystical experience of this type is the "perception of [God's] appearance on the throne,"[62] i.e., participating in that level of reality in which God's kingship is manifest rather than latent. Thus to enter the Kingdom of God was to enter the place of God's presence, the realm outside of time and history, the "time" before or beyond time. As such, it is a return to paradise, for paradise is the "time" beyond time in which God is manifestly present.

The phrase "Kingdom of God" is thus a symbol for the presence and power of God as known in mystical experience. It is Jesus' name for what is experienced in the primordial religious experience and his name for the power from that realm which flowed through him as a Spirit person. Thus one may say that Jesus as a Spirit person experienced the Kingdom of God, a reality which, because it is ineffable, can be spoken of only in the language of symbols.

The connections between this understanding of the symbol Kingdom of God and the rest of the material treated in this study are striking.

---

within which the scholarly study of the New Testament has developed. That ethos — Christian, Western, post-Enlightenment — has not been inclined until recently to take the religious experience of other cultures seriously and has tended to dismiss or explain away extraordinary phenomena, whether found in its own cultural history or in the experience of "primitive" cultures. Can the powers of another realm operate in this one? Jesus and his contemporaries, as well as people in most traditional cultures, believed so. Western intellectual history since the Enlightenment has most often assumed not, and thus scholars have generally not looked for illumination in traditions which make this affirmation.

61. See Fishbane in Berger, ed., *The Other Side of God*, 42: "One of the most arresting images of pure, concrete Yahwism is the throne vision in Ezek. 1" and "the earliest expressions of Jewish mysticism build on this symbolic structure."

62. Scholem, *Major Trends in Jewish Mysticism*, 44; see also his statement on p. 60: "The consciousness of these mystics" was irresistibly influenced by "the conception of God's Kingdom."

The experience of the Kingdom of God was the source of both Jesus' power and his transformed perception of existence, his insight. One may also surmise that it was the source of his sense of mission. As sage, he taught that the path of transformation was the death of self, the same death reported in mystical experience, and which he himself presumably experienced. There is also a connection to apocalyptic language, both historically[63] and psychologically. However, Jesus' use of the phrase did not point to the temporal end of the visible world, but to the end of the world of ordinary experience, as well as the end of the world as one's center and security. To enter that other reality, the new world, entails becoming completely empty of self. For that to happen, the self must come to an end, die to its world and die to itself.

The realization that Kingdom of God is a symbol pointing to an experiential reality known in Jesus' subjectivity provides the key for understanding the large number of sayings which speak of entering, being in, or possessing the Kingdom of God:[64]

Matt. 5:20: I tell you, if your virtue goes no deeper than that of the scribes and Pharisees, you will never *enter* the Kingdom of heaven.[65]

Matt. 7:21: Not every one who says to me, "Lord, Lord," shall *enter* the Kingdom of heaven.[66]

Matt. 21:31: Truly, I say to you, the tax collectors and harlots *are going into* the Kingdom of God before you.

---

63. See n. 6 above.

64. Mark 9:43–48; 10:15, 23–25; Matt. 5:20, 7:21, 18:3, 21:31, 23:13; Luke 9:62. The Kingdom as a "house" or realm which has a door through which one enters: Matt. 16:19, 23:13 par.; cf. Luke 13:24–25 par., 11:9–10 par. The Kingdom as a banquet in which one may participate or from which one may be excluded: Luke 13:28–29 par., 14:15–24 par., 22:29–30 par.; Matt. 25:1–12; Mark 14:25. The Kingdom as something one can be "in" or "out" of: Luke 7:28 par., Matt. 5:19, 18:1–4, 20:21; Mark 12:34. The Kingdom as something which one possesses: Mark 10:14; Matt. 5:3 par., 5:10, 21:43; Luke 12:32. See esp. S. Aalen, "'Reign' and 'House' in the Kingdom of God," *NTS* 8 (1962): 226–32; Gaston, *No Stone*, 229–38; H. Windisch, "Die Sprüche vom Eingehen in das Reich Gottes," *ZNW* 27 (1928): 163–92; G. E. Ladd, *Jesus and the Kingdom* (London, 1966), 191–213.

65. Translation from the Jerusalem Bible rather than RSV, which has "unless *your righteousness exceeds* that of the scribes and Pharisees." The latter translation suggests "out-excelling" the observance of the Pharisees, whereas what seems to be in mind is the internalization of the Torah, a connotation better captured by "unless your virtue goes *deeper. . . .*"

66. The use of the future here and in some of the other entry sayings does not necessarily imply that the Kingdom itself is future, any more than regulations for entry into a university couched in the future tense ("no one shall enter this university unless she has satisfied these requirements") imply that the university itself is a future entity; rather, the time of entry for some is future.

Matt. 23:13=Luke 11:52: Woe to you, scribes and Pharisees. . . . You shut
the Kingdom of heaven against people; for you neither *enter* yourselves,
nor allow those who would *enter* to *go in*.[67]

Luke 7:28=Matt. 7:11: Those who are least *in* the Kingdom of God are
greater than John the Baptist.

Luke 6:20=Matt. 5:3: Blessed are you poor, for yours *is* the Kingdom
of God.

Matt. 5:10: Blessed are those who are persecuted for righteousness' sake,
for theirs *is* the Kingdom of heaven.[68]

Behind the phrase "entering the Kingdom of God" or being in it is
the image of the Kingdom as a realm or house, or perhaps even palace,
which can be entered.[69] One may be in it or outside of it. Moreover,
Jesus spoke of it as a reality that could be entered or possessed in the
present.[70] These sayings are best understood in one or both of two ways.
On the one hand, the Kingdom as realm may point to the other realm,
the place of God's manifest presence. To enter the Kingdom thus refers
to the mystical experience of God, the return to the paradisal experience of life in the presence of God, the experience of communion with
God as *Abba*. On the other hand, the image "Kingdom" is intrinsically
corporate or communal, implying a community of people living as subjects of a king. As a symbol, Kingdom of God could thus also refer to
the community, and "entering the Kingdom" would refer to entering
that community. As such, it would refer not to an institutional community[71] but to a spiritual community, i.e., a community of those who
know "spirit," who know the embracing compassion of God in their own

67. See also p. 131 above.

68. In the exegesis of the last two sayings, commentators sometimes urge that, since
Aramaic has no copula, these sayings can legitimately be interpreted as if they were in
the future tense. Though such is possible, it must be said that the Greek translators (the
evangelists themselves?) of traditions preserved in both Q and M saw fit to use the present
tense here.

69. Jeremias, *TDNT*, 3:747: "entry into the royal dominion of God" is a specifically
Palestinian image. See Aalen, " 'Reign' and 'House' in the Kingdom of God," 233–40, for
the Jewish background; and 220–23, 228–29, for its use in the Gospels. See also Gaston,
No Stone, 229–40.

70. See note 66 above. Though the use of the future tense in some of these sayings
is compatible with the presence of the Kingdom, the use of the present in several is not
compatible with the notion that the Kingdom is wholly future.

71. Scholars have often been reluctant to speak of the Kingdom as a community,
in part to prevent an illicit identification of the Kingdom with a particular institutional
organization, the church. Yet some do speak of those who responded to the message of
Jesus as the Kingdom. See, e.g., G. E. Ladd, *Jesus and the Kingdom* (London, 1966), 239–
73, passim, who speaks of "community of the Kingdom" and "people of the Kingdom";
A. M. Hunter, *Interpreting the Parables* (Philadelphia, 1961), 64–74, who speaks of "men
of the Kingdom"; Manson, *Mission and Message*, 370; and J. Bright, *The Kingdom of God*

experience. Such a community is, in a sense, a community of the end-time — not in the sense of living in the time of the end, but of living already the life of the end, that other consciousness and style of existence that flow from knowing the sacred. They are the community of the new age, that is, a community living the life of the spirit.

A number of passages which speak of the difficulty or cost of entering the Kingdom of God connect Jesus' use of the phrase to his teaching as sage. After a rich man sorrowfully declined the invitation to sell all that he had, Jesus said to his disciples, "How hard it is to enter the Kingdom of God! It is easier for a camel to go through the eye of a needle than for a rich man to enter the Kingdom of God."[72] The way is difficult because it costs a person everything, as the twin parables of the hidden treasure and the pearl of great value[73] and the sayings on radical discipleship make clear.[74] The poor to whom the Kingdom belongs even now are the humble, that is, those who have undergone the path of self-emptying.[75] The way which Jesus taught as sage was the way into the Kingdom of God; as a realm or house, the Kingdom had a gate,[76] and the way into the Kingdom of God, to communion with God, was the path of death and rebirth, of self-emptying, which is the classical language of the mystical way. Thus, in the context of entering or possessing the Kingdom of God, the phrase symbolized either the experience of the other realm, or the community of those who knew the experience or possibly, sometimes, both.

There is yet a third category of Kingdom sayings. A number of them apparently speak of the Kingdom as a future reality. Most are illuminated by and consistent with the connotations of the symbol Kingdom of God already suggested; a few may strike new notes. As we begin to examine these sayings about the future, we need to note that as an element in Israel's myth of salvation history and divine kingship, the Kingdom of God can be imagined nontemporally as the other realm "above" or "below" time, outside of time. Or it can be imagined temporally as the destiny of history, even though that destiny is not imminent but brought about by divine intervention at some "time" in the future. The assumption that language employing future imagery necessarily im-

---

(New York, 1958), 220: "And those who heed it (Jesus' call) have entered the Kingdom, nay, *are* the Kingdom."

72. Mark 10:24–25. For the story of the rich man, see Mark 10:17–23.

73. Matt. 13:44–46. Though much contemporary scholarship stresses that these two parables emphasize the joy of discovery, both also stress the cost.

74. See, for example, Luke 9:57–62.

75. Luke 6:20=Matt. 5:3; for the connections between the poor, humbling and self-emptying, see above pp. 252–53.

76. Matt. 7:13–14; cf. Luke 13:23–24 and above, p. 254.

plies temporal futurity is unwarranted. Indeed, even the highly temporal
language of Jewish apocalyptic circles did not necessarily imply a temporal future; the everlasting Kingdom was not necessarily to "begin"
only at the temporal end of time.[77] Thus whether Jesus used Kingdom
of God as a symbol for the temporal future destiny of the world can
only be determined by looking at specific texts.

Mark's programmatic advance summary of the ministry of Jesus is a
good example of a future Kingdom saying whose relationship to tem-
porality can be interpreted in two quite different ways: "The time is
fulfilled, the Kingdom of God is at hand; repent." If the Kingdom is
thought of here as temporally future, coming at the eschaton and involving the "events" of resurrection and last judgment at that "time"
in the future, then it must be wholly future, no matter how near. But if
the symbol points here to the experience of God, then the saying means
in effect, "God is near, at hand, accessible to human experience." "Repent," the response called for, fits this understanding nicely, for repent
means to *return*, to return from the place of exile and estrangement
to the presence of God through a radical reorientation of one's most
fundamental posture. In short, the saying need not be interpreted to
refer to temporal futurity, and there are cogent reasons for preferring a
nontemporal interpretation.

In the second petition of the Lord's Prayer, Jesus taught his disciples to pray for a coming of the Kingdom which treats it as future:
"Thy Kingdom come."[78] The petition *may* refer to a temporally future
consummation visible in the external world, or it may be a petition
for the internal experience of entering God's presence, of having God's
presence come upon one. In fact, it could refer to both, namely, as a petition that the communion now known in the spiritual world may one
day characterize all of reality. But it need not be understood as a prayer
for the parousia understood as a temporally future event, even though
some early Christians *may* have understood it that way.[79] Similarly, the

---

77. Cf. Hengel, *Judaism and Hellenism*, 1:253: Within Palestinian Judaism, "the apocalyptic expectation of the end...is not so much to be understood schematically as a
unitary entity but as a view which contained many nuances. Thus in it salvation in the
present and the expectation of salvation in the future do not form exclusive opposites,
nor do a temporal conception of the future and spatial conceptions of heaven."

78. Luke 11:2=Matt. 6:10. The expansion of the second petition included by Matthew, "Thy will be done on earth as it is in heaven," can be interpreted either
eschatologically or ethically: thy Kingdom come on earth as it already is in the other
realm (May the life of this realm become as the life of the other realm); or, may the doing
of your will be accomplished on earth.

79. Here Perrin's comparison to the Kaddish prayer is illuminating. The prayer, in
regular use in Jewish synagogues at the time of Jesus, included the petition, "May God
establish his Kingdom in your lifetime and in your days and in the lifetime of all the house

difficult saying in Mark 9:1, "Truly I say to you, there are some standing
here who will not taste death before they see the Kingdom of God come
with power," need not be interpreted as referring to an expected but un-
arriving parousia. Mark apparently did not understand it that way, and
the saying of Jesus behind the Marcan redaction may not have either.[80]

In a Q saying whose core is almost certainly authentic, Jesus spoke
of the Kingdom using images generally associated with the eschaton:

> I tell you, many will come from east and west and sit at table with
> Abraham, Isaac, and Jacob in the Kingdom of God.[81]

The image of the "many" journeying from east and west alludes to the
biblical theme of the pilgrimage of the Gentiles to the God of Israel, to
the experience of Yahweh's glory or presence, a journey often associated
with the last days, as is the image of a banquet,[82] at which, according to
Jesus' words, figures of the distant past will be present. Yet the relationship between the Kingdom and temporal futurity is not clear. Nothing
suggests that it is to be soon. Moreover, though the coming of the many
from the east and west is future, the Kingdom itself is not necessarily
so, but may already "exist" as a realm beyond time, transcending time.

---

of Israel, even speedily and at a near time." As a prayer *used by a community*, the form
of the expectation would have varied from individual to individual, and some probably
would have understood it to refer to the imminent end of the created order. But as a
religious symbol, it was "plurisignificant" and its meaning could not be exhausted by any
one referent. Similarly, some early Christians may have understood the future Kingdom
sayings to refer to an imminent parousia. See Perrin, *Jesus and the Language of the Kingdom*,
28–29, 43, 47.

80. Chilton, *God in Strength*, 264–66, argues convincingly that in Mark's redaction,
the verse refers forward to the transfiguration. "Those standing here" are the three disciples who then witness the transfiguration in the next pericope. For Mark, the coming of
the Kingdom here is epiphanic, not eschatological. Behind the Marcan redaction, Chilton
argues somewhat more speculatively, lies a saying of Jesus which says, "There are those
who do not taste death before they see the Kingdom of God in power." "In power" belongs to pre-Pauline revelation language (p. 267), and the saying declares, in effect, that
there are those who do not die before they see the self-revelation of God.

81. Matt. 8:11–12=Luke 13:28–29. In both Matthew and Luke, the saying also addresses a threat to the hearers: in Luke, you will see "yourselves thrust out" of the
Kingdom; in Matthew, "the heirs of the Kingdom will be thrown into the outer darkness." Since the Q tradition strongly emphasizes judgment against Israel, the threat may
be part of the Q redaction; on the other hand, the "many from east and west" as referring to the Gentiles virtually implies a contrast to Israel or some within Israel so that
the warning may have been part of the saying from the beginning. Because the passage
uses banquet imagery, there may be a connection to the table fellowship controversies of
the ministry, either as a defense of Jesus' eating with the outcasts or as a threat to those
whose response is negative. One might paraphrase the passage as saying, "If, as the Scriptures say, even the Gentiles are promised communion with God in the table-fellowship
of the Kingdom of God, how much more so the outcasts within Israel," or, alternatively,
"Even if you do not respond, others will."

82. See esp. Isa. 25:6–9.

Here, as elsewhere, the reported words of Jesus do not point clearly to a future-temporal picture of the Kingdom, but leave ambiguous the relationship between Kingdom of God language and the temporal destiny of creation. Indeed, if one thinks that Kingdom here symbolizes a temporally future reality ushered in by the eschatological events of resurrection and last judgment, then one would have to think of Abraham, Isaac, and Jacob as presently dead, awaiting the resurrection. Yet elsewhere Jesus spoke of them as in some sense among the living (Mark 12:26–27). If instead we understand Kingdom as a symbol for the experience of God in the other realm which is outside of time, then this passage affirms that that experience is accessible to all, and that the realm entered in that experience transcends the polarity of the living and the dead as well as the polarity of Jew and Gentile.[83]

Finally, a few sayings do speak of Jesus as lord of the Kingdom and of a future day when the Kingdom would be established:

> In the *new world*, when the son of man *shall sit* on his glorious *throne*, you who have followed me will also sit on twelve *thrones judging* the twelve tribes of Israel. (Matt. 19:28)[84]

> *When* the son of man *comes* in his glory, and all the angels with him, *then* he *will sit* on his glorious throne.... Then [he as] the King will say to those at his right hand, "Come, O blessed of my Father, inherit the *Kingdom* prepared for you from the foundation of the world. (Matt. 25:31, 34)

The sayings provide evidence that some in the early Christian movement believed that the other realm would one day be externalized in the visible created world, and that Jesus would be the lord of that Kingdom. Some, perhaps many, believed that day would be soon. But there is no convincing evidence that Jesus believed that he himself would return as King of that Kingdom.[85] Even if he did believe that, the focus of his teachings was elsewhere. He emphasized a path of transformation for the individual by means of which entry into the Kingdom of God could be experienced in the present, and a path of transformation for the people of God, whose collective historical life was to embody compassion.

The picture of Jesus as the returning lord of a future Kingdom may belong to that stage of early Christian devotion and thought in which

---

83. See also Chilton, *God in Strength*, 199–200.

84. See the related passage in Luke 22:29–30, which also speaks of sitting at table with Jesus in the Kingdom of God.

85. See above pp. 231–33.

the Kingdom of God was transformed from a tensive symbol to a steno-symbol.[86] We may imagine that the intensity of the spiritual presence which flowed through Jesus and which continued to be encountered by his followers even after his death led some of them to think that the last days were at hand, and that he who was known and encountered in that other realm would soon return as King of the Kingdom of which he had spoken. But the evidence seems balanced against the notion that he himself thought in these terms.

Thus, in the clearly authentic sayings of Jesus, the phrase "Kingdom of God" never pointed unmistakably to a temporally conceived future, though it may allude to that in a few. Rather, when spoken of as coming, it was a symbol for the power or presence of the numinous breaking into ordinary reality,[87] either subjectively or objectively, as in the case of the exorcisms. As something that could be entered or possessed, it symbolized the experience of God or vision of God which transformed existence. Jesus proclaimed that the Kingdom was present, a reality active in the present and capable of being known in the present. As the transformative vision of God, it was the chief good for human beings ("Seek first the Kingdom of God," Matt. 6:33=Luke 12:31), the pearl of great value for which one would give everything (Matt. 13:45–46). It would not come with accompanying signs but was among or within people: "The Kingdom of God is not coming with signs to be observed . . . for behold, the Kingdom of God is in the midst [or within] you" (Luke 17:20–21).

In short, Jesus used the phrase "Kingdom of God" within the framework of what we might call an eschatological mysticism — a mysticism which used language associated with the end of the world. Or we might call it a mystical eschatology — an eschatology in which the new age was the other realm of mystical communion. Within that framework, Kingdom of God symbolized the experience of God, an experience known by Jesus himself. The Kingdom of God as the experience of God accounts for Jesus' teaching concerning the way of transformation and the course for Israel. Out of that experience flowed an awareness of a way other than the normative ways of the other renewal movements, one open to the outcasts and not dependent on holiness, but on self-

---

86. So Perrin, *Jesus and the Language of the Kingdom*, 60: the early church reinterpreted the coming of the Kingdom of God as the return of Jesus as "the son of man." The latter, Perrin notes, is most often a steno-symbol in the Gospels; and the former tends to become a steno-symbol when connected to "son of man." For the distinction between tensive-symbol and steno-symbol, see n. 52 above.

87. Cf. Chilton, *God in Strength*, 89: " 'The Kingdom of God' refers to God's *dynamic presence*." Italics added.

emptying and dying to self and world. Indeed, to enter the Kingdom of God requires the end-of-world of which Jesus spoke as sage.

Jesus' experience of God as King, in which God was known as the encompassing compassionate one, accounts for his substitution of compassion for holiness as the paradigm for Israel's collective life and was the ground of his conviction that his society was headed on the wrong course. Thus Jesus' experience and proclamation of the Kingdom of God were not disconnected from the cultural and political issues of his day, but intimately related. The connection was not simply negative, as challenge and criticism, but also positive. He sought the transformation of the historical life of the people of God so that their collective life would manifest compassion, the central quality of God. The eschatological mysticism of Jesus did not turn him away from the world, but instead was the basis for his passionate involvement in the corporate life and direction of his people. Thus the Kingdom of God is connected to history, not as a future historical event, but as the source of Jesus' paradigm for historical life: compassion.

Though a comprehensive treatment of the Kingdom of God sayings in the conclusion of this study is impossible, the more limited purpose of this treatment has been accomplished. I have sought to show that there is an understanding of the Kingdom of God consistent with what can be surmised about Jesus' spirituality, supported by linguistic usage in the Jewish milieu in which he stood, coherent with the Gospel texts in which the symbol appears, and integrated with — as opposed to antithetical to — the concern for history unearthed throughout this study.

The avenues of approach to the teaching of Jesus followed in this chapter converge in a remarkable way. Beginning with Jesus as sage leads to a picture of him as the teacher of death of self and end-of-world, whose language often functioned as mediator of that end, and whose teaching almost certainly derived from his own experience of the path. Beginning with Jesus as a Spirit person leads to a picture of him as an exorcist who experienced God in his own entry into the other world, and who used the phrase "Kingdom of God" as a symbol for the experience of God which was the source of his mission and the content of his teaching. Beginning with him as a person involved in conflict with the other movements of his day leads to a picture of him as deeply concerned to transform the historical existence of his people so that it embodied the compassion of God, a passionate concern grounded in his own experience of God as the embracing compassionate one. Each of these approaches is like a radius whereby one may approach the center. And, to change the metaphor, the new cornerstone for understanding the ministry of Jesus is what lies at the center. What is added by beginning with conflict is not simply a corrective to the overly eschatological emphasis of much New Testament scholarship in this century, but also a clear basis for affirming, consistent with the Jewish tradition, that the divine will is to be embodied within history: "Be compassionate as God is compassionate."

The Threat/Warrant Tradition of the Synoptic Gospels

TABLE ONE
The Threats Peculiar to Matthew

Reference	Threat	Warrant
5:19	Will be called least in the Kingdom of heaven	Whoever relaxes one of the least of these commandments
5:20	You will never enter the Kingdom of heaven	Unless your righteousness exceeds that of the scribes and the Pharisees
5:21–22	Shall be:... liable to judgment... liable to the council... liable to hell	Whoever: ...is angry with brother or sister ...insults brother or sister ...says "You fool!"
6:1–4	No reward from your father in heaven	Practicing your piety in order to be seen by others
6:15	God will not forgive you	If you do not forgive others
7:13*	Destruction	Entering the broad gate
7:19	Is thrown into the fire	A tree that fails to bear good fruit
12:36–37	On the day of judgment, you will be condemned	For careless words
13:24–30	Will be burned at the harvest	Weeds
13:40–42	Thrown into the furnace of fire, where people weep and gnash their teeth	All causes of sin and evil-doers
13:47–48	Will be thrown away	Bad fish
13:49–50	Thrown into the furnace of fire where people weep and gnash their teeth	Evil people
18:17	To be treated as a Gentile and a tax collector	If an offender refuses to listen to the church
18:23–35 (parable)	Delivered to the jailers	Mercy shown has not had its consequences
21:28–32 (parable)	Tax collectors and harlots enter the Kingdom before you	You have not worked in the vineyard
22:11–14	Bound and cast into the outer darkness where people weep and gnash their teeth	No wedding garment
23:33	Sentenced to hell	(warrant is Q: building the tombs of the prophets your fathers killed)
25:1–13 (parable)	Shut out of the wedding feast	The foolish maidens who were absent when the bridegroom arrived
25:31–46 (parable)	Depart into the eternal fire	I was hungry, etc., and you gave me no food, etc.
26:52	They will perish by the sword	Who take the sword

*This may be Q, though Luke 13:23–24 lacks an explicit reference to the broad gate that leads to destruction, suggesting that this may be Matthaean redaction.

Thus there are twenty threats peculiar to Matthew. Both the threats and the warrants attached to them present a pattern strikingly divergent from the threat sayings found in Mark, Q, and L. In Matthew the warrants point to generalized sins or sinners (entering the broad gate, bearing bad fruit, "all causes of sin and evildoers," "evil people") or specific sins (relaxing a commandment, anger, insults, saying "You fool," ostentatious piety, careless words, refusing church discipline). The exceptions to this pattern all occur in the parables peculiar to Matthew, plus Matt. 26:52. The warrants found in Mark, Q, and L, as we shall see, have very little to do with what are commonly considered sins in the sense of transgressions. The Matthaean threat tradition is also distinctive with a much greater emphasis on eternal judgment than in Mark, Q, and L. Indeed, there are more threats of eternal punishment in special Matthew alone than in the rest of the synoptic tradition combined. It seems appropriate to regard this distinctive Matthaean emphasis as due to his redaction, and to characterize it as individualizing and moralizing in nature.

TABLE TWO
Threats of Unidentifiable Content
(Mark, Q, L, Mp)

Reference	Threat	Warrant
1. Lk. 3:7 par. (Q)	Wrath to come*	—
2. Lk. 3:9 par. (Q)	Axe is at the root of the trees	Trees not bearing good fruit
3. Lk. 3:17 par. (Q)	Burn the chaff	—
4. Lk. 6:39 par. (Q)	Both will fall into a pit	If the blind lead the blind
5. Lk. 6:47–49 par. (Q)	Ruin of the house will be great	If it is built on sand
6. Lk. 11:49–51 par. (Q)	Blood of all the prophets will be required of this generation	Killing/persecuting prophets and apostles sent to them
7. Lk. 12:10 par. (Q)	Will not be forgiven	Blaspheming against the Holy Spirit
8. Lk. 12:41–46 par. (Q)	Put the servant with the unfaithful	If the servant acts irresponsibly
9. Lk. 12:47–48 par. (Q)	A severe beating	The servant who did not do the master's will
10. Lk. 12:57–59 par. (Q)	Imprisoned until you have paid the last copper	Not making peace before reaching the court
11. Lk. 13:6–9 (cf. Mk. 11:12–13, 20–21) (L, Mark)	Fig tree will be cut down (fig tree is cursed and withers — Mk.)	Not bearing fruit
12. Lk. 13:25–27 par. (Q)	Depart from my doorstep	Waiting until it is too late to enter
13. Lk. 14:8–11 (L)	Public shame at a banquet by being asked to take a lower place	If you seek a place of honor near the host
14. Lk. 14:34–35 par. (Q)	Salt will be thrown out	If it has lost its taste
15. Lk. 19:12, 14–15a, 27 (L)**	Slay these enemies before me!	Citizens not wanting a nobleman to become king

*The first three threats are actually from the preaching of John, but they are included both because Jesus' baptism indicates an initial identification with John's message of crisis, and because the church saw John's preaching as relevant to an understanding of Jesus.

**This accepts the suggestion of Robinson, *Jesus and His Coming*, 67–68, that there is a fragment here of a parable which the tradition has conflated with the parable of the money in trust; Robinson suggests that it be called "The Parable of the Prince Royal." So also Jeremias, *Parables*, 58–59; Gaston, *No Stone*, 354–55.

Reference	Threat	Warrant
16. Mk. 9:42 par. (Mk)	A great millstone hung round the neck and thrown into the sea	Causing a little one to stumble
17. Mk. 13:33–37 (Mk)	(Implicit)	If the master finds his doorkeeper asleep
18. Mt. 13:24–30 (Mp)	Bind them in bundles and burn them	Weeds
19. Mt. 13:47–48 (Mp)	Will be thrown away	Bad fish
20. Mt. 18:23–35 (Mp)	Will be delivered to the jailers	Not showing mercy to fellow servants
21. Mt. 25:1–13 (Mp)	Excluded from the wedding feast	Foolish maidens who were absent when the bridegroom arrived

TABLE THREE
Threats of Identifiable Content
The "Taken Away/Given to Others" Pattern

Reference	Threat	Warrant
1. Lk. 3:8 par. (Q)	God will raise up children to Abraham from these stones	Trusting in "We have Abraham as our father"
2. Lk. 4:24–27 (cf. Mk. 6:4) (L)	The prophet of God, activity of God, goes to others	No prophet is accepted in his own country
3. Lk. 13:28–29 par. (Q)	Many from east, west, north, south, will eat with the patriarchs in the Kingdom of God, but you will be shut out	(Implicit: nonresponse to Jesus)
4. Lk. 14:15–24 par. (Q)	Those invited will not taste the banquet	They refused to come when it was ready
5. Mt. 25:14–30 par. (Q)	Money entrusted to cautious servant will be given to others	Servant provided master with no return on it
6,7. Mk. 6:11, Lk. 10:11 (Mark, L)	Shake off dust on your feet as a testimony (i.e., they shall be as Gentiles)	If a town refuses the messengers of Jesus
8. Mk. 12:1–11 (Mark)	Tenants will be destroyed and vineyard given to others	Tenants refuse to give fruit to owner, killing his servants and son in the process
9. Mt. 21:28–32 (Mp)	Tax collectors and harlots enter the Kingdom of God before you	Not working in the vineyard

TABLE FOUR
Threats of Identifiable Content:
Destruction of Temple/City/Land

Reference	Threat	Warrant
1. Lk. 13:1–5 (L)	Fate of the Galileans whom Pilate slew, and of those killed by the falling tower in Siloam, shall be your fate	They were no more guilty (or no more innocent) than you: unless you repent, you shall likewise perish
2. Lk. 13:34–35 par. (Q)	Temple/city abandoned by the divine presence	Jerusalem kills the prophets
3. Lk. 17:31–36 par. (Q, L)	Invasion (you will have to flee suddenly, "Remember Lot's wife")	(Implicit: judgment on an apostate city; see p. 208 above)
4. Lk. 19:42–44	Enemies will surround and conquer you, and "not leave one stone upon another"	Jerusalem did not know the things that make for peace
5. Lk. 21:20, 21b–22, 23b–24 (L)	Jerusalem surrounded by armies and captured by Gentiles	(Implicit: these are "days of retribution")
6. Lk. 23:28–31	Days are coming when they will say, "Blessed are the barren"	(Implicit: Israel's present course will lead to a disastrous insurrection)
7. Mk. 11:15–17 (Mark)	Implicit: destruction of the Temple (see exegesis above, pp. 181–89)	You have made of it a stronghold of resistance
8. Mk. 13:2 par. (Mark)	There will not be left here one stone upon another	(Implicit: rejection of Jesus; see p. 193.)
9. Mk. 13:14–18 (Mark)	Desecration of Temple; cessation of sacrifice; sudden flight	—
10. Mk. 14:58, 15:29 (Mark; attributed to false witnesses, mockers; cf. John 2:19, Acts 6:14*)	"I will destroy this Temple and build another"	—
11. Mt. 26:52 (Mark)	Will perish by the sword	All who take the sword

*The four threats of Mark 14:58 et al. are here tabulated as one: see our exegesis on pp. 190–91. If they are counted as four, then the number of threats in this category increases accordingly and further increases the weight of categories 1 (table 3: the "taken away/given to others" pattern) and 2 (table 4: destruction of Temple/city/land) over category 3 (table 5: final judgment).

TABLE FIVE
Threats of Identifiable Content:
Final Judgment

Reference	Threat	Warrant
1. Mk. 9:43–48 (Mk)	Thrown into hell	Not cutting off or plucking out the offending hand, foot, eye
2. Mt. 25:31–46 (Mp)	Depart into the eternal fire	I was hungry, etc., and you gave me no food, etc.
3. Lk. 10:12 par. (Q)	More tolerable on that day for Sodom than for that town	If a town does not receive the messengers of Jesus
4. Lk. 10:13–15 par. (Q)	Tyre and Sidon will do better in the judgment than Chorazin and Bethsaida	Not repenting, despite the mighty works done in them
5. Lk. 11:31 par. (Q)	Queen of the South will witness against this generation in the judgment	Not repenting, though something greater than Solomon is here
6. Lk. 11:32 par. (Q)	People of Nineveh will witness against this generation in the judgment	Not repenting, though something greater than Jonah is here
7. Lk. 12:8–9 par. (Q)	Denied before the angels of God (by the son of man)	Whoever denies Jesus
8. Mk. 8:38 (Mk)	Son of man will be ashamed of them when he comes in the glory of his Father with the angels	Those who are ashamed of Jesus
9. Lk. 12:39–40 par. (Q)	Son of man, like a nocturnal burglar, will come upon you unexpectedly	Unless you are ready
10. Lk. 17:23–24, 37 (Q)	Son of man comes like a lightning flash; where the body is, there the eagles (vultures?) will gather	—
11. Lk. 17:26–27	Something analogous to the flood	Business as usual, as in the days of Noah
12. Lk. 17:28–30 (L)	The day when the son of man is revealed will be like the day when fire and brimstone rained on Sodom	Business as usual, as in the days of Lot

Bibliography

Aalen, S. "'Reign' and 'House' in the Kingdom of God in the Gospels," *NTS* 8 (1962): 215–40.

Abrahams, I. *Studies in Pharisaism and the Gospels*. Cambridge, 1917–24.

Albertz, M. *Die synoptischen Streitgespräche*. Berlin, 1921.

Allon, G. "The Attitudes of the Pharisees to the Roman Government and the House of Herod," *Scripta Hierosolymitana* vii (1961).

Anderson, H. "Broadening Horizons: The Rejection at Nazareth Pericope of Luke 4:16–30 in Light of Recent Critical Trends," *Int.* 18 (1964): 259–75.

Applebaum, S. "The Zealots: The Case for Revaluation," *JRS* 61 (1971).

Bacon, B. W. *The Beginnings of Gospel Story*. New Haven, 1909.

———. *Studies in Matthew*. New York, 1930.

Baeck, L. *The Pharisees and Other Essays*. New York, 1947.

Baird, J. A. *The Justice of God in the Teaching of Jesus*. London, 1963.

Baltzer, K. "The Meaning of the Temple in the Lukan Writings," *HTR* (1965).

Bammel, E. "Matthäus 10, 23," *StTh* 15 (1961): 79–92.

———, ed. *The Trial of Jesus*. London, 1970.

Banks, R. *Jesus and the Law in the Synoptic Tradition*. Cambridge, 1975.

Barbour, R. S. "Loyalty and Law in New Testament Times," *SJT* 11 (1958): 344.

Baron, S. W. *A Social and Religious History of the Jews*. 2d ed. New York, 1952.

Bate, H. N. *The Sibylline Oracles*. London, 1918.

Baumbach, G. "Die Zeloten — ihre geschichtliche und religionspolitische Bedeutung," *Bibel und Liturgie* 41 (1968): esp. 19–25.

Beardslee, W. A. "New Testament Perspectives on Revolution as a Theological Problem," *JR* 51 (1971): 15–33.

Beare, F. W. "The Sabbath Was Made for Man?" *JBL* 79 (1960).

Beasley-Murray, G. R. *Jesus and the Future*. London, 1954.

———. *A Commentary on Mark Thirteen*. London, 1957.

Becker, J. *Das Heil Gottes*. Göttingen, 1964.

Beker, J. C. "Biblical Theology Today." In M. Marty and D. G. Peerman, eds., *New Theology Number Six*. London, 1969.

Berger, P . *The Sacred Canopy*. Garden City, N.Y., 1969.

———, ed. *The Other Side of God: A Polarity in World Religions*. Garden City, N.Y., 1981.

Betz, O. "Jesu Heiliger Krieg," *NovTest* 2 (1958): 116–37.

Black, M. "The Patristic Accounts of Jewish Sectarianism," *BJRL* 41 (1958–59): 285–303.

———. *The Scrolls and Christian Origins*. London, 1961.

———. *An Aramaic Approach to the Gospels and Acts*. 3d ed. Oxford, 1967.

Blair, E. P. *Jesus in the Gospel of Matthew*. New York, 1960.

Blenkinsopp, J. "The Oracle of Judah and the Messianic Entry," *JBL* 80 (1961): 55–64.

Blinzler, J. "Die Niedermetzelung von Galiläern durch Pilatus," *NovTest* 2 (1958): 24–49.

Borg, M. *Conflict and Social Change.* Minneapolis, 1971.

———. "The Currency of the Term 'Zealot,'" *JTS* 22 (1971): 504–12.

———. "A New Context for Romans xiii," *NTS* 19 (1973): 205–19.

Börnhauser, K. *Studien zum Sondergut des Lukas.* Gütersloh, 1934.

Bornkamm, G. *Jesus of Nazareth.* New York, 1960.

Bowker, J. *Jesus and the Pharisees.* Cambridge, 1973.

Bowman, J. W. *Which Jesus?* Philadelphia, 1970.

Bowman, J. *The Gospel of Mark.* Leiden, 1965.

Braaten, C. *History and Hermeneutics.* Philadelphia, 1966.

Braaten, C., and R. Harrisville, eds. *Kerygma and History.* New York, 1962.

Brandon, S. G. F. *The Fall of Jerusalem and the Christian Church.* London, 1951.

———. *Jesus and the Zealots.* Manchester, 1967.

———. "Jesus and the Zealots," *StEv* 4=*TU* 102 (1968): 8–20.

———. *The Trial of Jesus.* London, 1968.

Branscomb, B. H. *Jesus and the Law of Moses.* London, 1930.

Bright, J. *The Kingdom of God.* New York, 1958.

Bruce, F. F. "The Book of Zechariah and the Passion Narrative," *BJRL* 43 (1960–61): 336–53.

———. *This Is That.* Exeter, 1968.

———. *New Testament History.* London, 1969.

Buber, M. *I and Thou.* New York, 1970.

Buchanan, G. W. "Mark 11:15–19: Brigands in the Temple," *HUCA* 30 (1959): 169–77.

———. *The Consequences of the Covenant.* Leiden, 1970.

Büchler, A. *Types of Jewish Palestinian Piety.* New York, 1968.

Bultmann, R. *Jesus and the Word.* New York, 1958.

———. *The History of the Synoptic Tradition.* New York, 1963.

Bundy, W. E. *Jesus and the First Three Gospels.* Cambridge, Mass., 1955.

Burkitt, F. C. "Jesus and the Pharisees," *JTS* 28 (1927): 392–97.

Burney, C. F. *The Poetry of Our Lord.* Oxford, 1925.

Burrows, M. *The Dead Sea Scrolls.* New York, 1955.

Cadbury, H. J. *The Peril of Modernizing Jesus.* New York, 1937.

———. *Jesus: What Manner of Man.* New York, 1948.

Cadoux, C. J. *The Historic Mission of Jesus.* London, 1941.

Caird, G. B. "The Mind of Christ: Christ's Attitude to Institutions," *ET* 62 (1950–51): 259–60.

———. *St. Luke.* Harmondsworth, 1963.

———. "The Defendant (Matthew 5:25f.; Luke 12:58f.)," *ET* (1965–66).

———. *Jesus and the Jewish Nation.* London, 1965.

———. "Les eschatologies du Nouveau Testament," *RHPR* 49 (1969): 217–27.

———. *Commentary on Revelation.* London, 1980.

———. *The Language and Imagery of the Bible*. London, 1980.

Calvert, D. G. A. "An Examination of the Criteria for Distinguishing the Authentic Words of Jesus," *NTS* 18 (1971–72): 209–19.

Carlston, C. E. "The Things That Defile (Mark 7:14) and the Law in Matthew and Mark," *NTS* 15 (1968–69).

Carmichael, J. *The Death of Jesus*. London, 1963.

Carmignac, J. "Les dangers de l'eschatologie," *NTS* 17 (1970–71): 365–90.

Carr, E. H. *What Is History?* Penguin Books, 1964.

Cassidy, R. *Jesus, Politics and Society*. Maryknoll, N.Y., 1978.

Catchpole, D. R. In E. Bammel, ed., *The Trial of Jesus*. London, 1970.

Charlesworth, J. H. "The Society for New Testament Studies Pseudepigrapha Seminars at Tübingen and Paris on the Books of Enoch," *NTS* 25 (1979): 315–23.

Charlesworth, M. P. *The Roman Empire*. New York, 1968.

Chesnut, J. S. *The Old Testament Understanding of God*. Philadelphia, 1968.

Clements, R. E. *God and Temple*. Oxford, 1965.

Coates, J. R. *The Christ of Revolution*. London, 1920.

Cohn, H. *The Trial and Death of Jesus*. New York, 1971.

Colpe, C. "East and West." In H. J. Schultz, ed., *Jesus in His Time*. Philadelphia, 1971.

Conzelmann, H. *The Theology of St. Luke*. New York, 1961.

Coser, L. *The Function of Social Conflict*. New York, 1956.

Cramer, A. W. "In All the Prophets I Awaited Thee," *NovTest* 8 (1966): 102–5.

Cranfield, C. E. B. *The Gospel according to St. Mark*. 2d ed. Cambridge, 1966.

Creed, J. M. *The Gospel according to St. Luke*. London, 1930.

Cullmann, O. *The State in the New Testament*. New York, 1956.

———. *The Christology of the New Testament*. 2d ed. London, 1963.

———. *Salvation in History*. London, 1967.

———. *Jesus and the Revolutionaries*. New York, 1970.

Dahl, N. A. "The Parables of Growth," *StTh* 5 (1952): 132–66.

———. "The Problem of the Historical Jesus." In C. Braaten and R. Harrisville, eds., *Kerygma and History*. New York, 1962.

Danby, H. *The Mishnah*. London, 1933.

Dancy, J. C. *A Commentary on 1 Maccabees*. Oxford, 1954.

Daube, D. *The New Testament and Rabbinic Judaism*. London, 1956.

———. *Collaboration with Tyranny in Rabbinic Law*. London, 1965.

———. *Civil Disobedience in Antiquity*. Edinburgh, 1972.

———. "Responsibilities of Master and Disciples in the Gospels," *NTS* 19 (1972): 1–15.

Davies, W. D. *Paul and Rabbinic Judaism*. London, 1948, 1970.

———. *Christian Origins and Judaism*. London, 1962.

———. *The Setting of the Sermon on the Mount*. Cambridge, 1964.

———. *The Gospel and the Land*. Berkeley, 1974.

Davis, M., ed. *Israel: Its Role in Civilization*. New York, 1956.

Derrett, J. D. M. "Korban Ho Estin Doron," *NTS* 16 [1969–70]: 364–68.

————. *Law in the New Testament*. London, 1970.

Dodd, C. H. *History and the Gospel*. New York, 1938.

————. "The Fall of Jerusalem and the 'Abomination of Desolation,'" *JRS* 37 (1947): 47–54.

————. *The Parables of the Kingdom*. London, 1961.

————. *Historical Tradition in the Fourth Gospel*. Cambridge, 1963.

————. *More New Testament Studies*. Manchester, 1968.

————. *The Founder of Christianity*. London, 1971.

Dougall, L. "The Salvation of the Nations," *Hibbert Journal* 20 (1921).

Downing, F. G. *The Church and Jesus*. London, 1968.

Dungan, D. L. *The Sayings of Jesus in the Churches of Paul*. Philadelphia, 1971.

Dunn, J. G. *Jesus and the Spirit*. Philadelphia, 1975.

Dupont, J. "La parabole des talents ou des mines," *RTPhil* 19 (1969): 376–91.

————. "Il n'en sera pas laissé pierre sur pierre (Marc 13:2; Luc 19:44)," *Biblica* 52 (1971).

Easton, B. S. *The Gospel according to St. Luke*. Edinburgh, 1926.

Eisler, R. *The Messiah Jesus and John the Baptist*. London, 1931.

Eliade, M. *Myth and Reality*. New York, 1963.

————. *Shamanism: Archaic Techniques of Ecstasy*. Princeton, 1970.

Ellis, E. E. "Luke xi. 49–51: An Oracle of a Christian Prophet?" *ET* 74 (1962–63).

————. *The Gospel of St. Luke*. London, 1966.

Eppstein, V. "The Historicity of the Gospel Account of the Cleansing of the Temple," *ZNW* 55 (1964).

Farmer, W. R. *Maccabees, Zealots, and Josephus*. New York, 1956.

————. "Judas, Simon and Athronges," *NTS* 4 (1958): 147–55.

————. "An Historical Essay on the Humanity of Jesus Christ." In W. R. Farmer et al., *Christian History and Interpretation*. Cambridge, 1967.

————. "The Revolutionary Character of Jesus and the Christian Revolutionary Role in American Society," *Perkins School of Theology Journal* 22 (1969): 37–59.

Fiebig, P. *Die Gleichnisreden Jesu*. Tübingen, 1912.

Filson, F. *A New Testament History*. Philadelphia, 1964.

Finkel, A. *The Pharisees and the Teacher of Nazareth*. Leiden, 1964.

Finkelstein, L. "Some Examples of the Maccabean Halaka," *JBL* 49 (1930): 21–25.

————. *The Pharisees*. 3 vols. Philadelphia, 1962.

————. *Akiba: Scholar, Saint and Martyr*. New York, 1975; originally published in 1936.

Fletcher, D. R. "The Riddle of the Unjust Steward: Is Irony the Key?" *JBL* 82 (1963).

Flusser, D. *Jesus*. New York, 1969.

Foakes, J., and F. J. and K. Lake. *The Beginnings of Christianity*. London, 1920.

Ford, J. M. "'Hast Thou Tithed Thy Meal?' and 'Is Thy Child Kosher?'" *JTS* 16 (1966): 71–79.

Förster, W. *Palestinian Judaism in New Testament Times*. Edinburgh and London, 1964.

France, R. T. *Jesus and the Old Testament*. London, 1971.

Frank, T., ed. *An Economic Survey of Ancient Rome*. Baltimore, 1938.

Fredriksson, H. *Jahwe als Krieger*. Lund, 1945.

Frend, W. H. C. *Martyrdom and Persecution in the Early Church*. Oxford, 1965.

Frost, S. B. *Old Testament Apocalyptic*. London, 1952.

Fuller, R. H. *The Mission and Achievement of Jesus*. London, 1954.

———. *The New Testament in Current Study*. London, 1963.

———. *The Foundations of New Testament Christology*. New York, 1965.

———. *A Critical Introduction to the New Testament*. London, 1966.

Gager, J. *Kingdom and Community: The Social World of Early Christianity*. Englewood Cliffs, 1975.

Gaston, L. "Sondergut und Markusstoff in Luk. 21," *ThZ* 16 (1960).

———. *No Stone on Another*. Leiden, 1970.

Giblin, C. H. " 'The Things of God' in the Question Concerning Tribute to Caesar," *CBQ* 33 (1971).

Ginzberg, L. "The Religion of the Jews at the time of Jesus," *HUCA* 1 (1924): 309.

———. *On Jewish Law and Lore*. Philadelphia, 1945.

———. "David in Rabbinical Literature," *JE* 4:453–57.

Glasson, T. F. *The Second Advent*. 3d ed. London, 1963.

Gnilka, J. "War Jesus Revolutionär?" *Bibel und Leben* 12 (1971): 67–78.

Goguel, M. *The Life of Jesus*. London, 1933.

———. "Luke and Mark: With a Discussion of Streeter's Theory," *NTR* 26 (1933).

Goodenough, E. R. *The Politics of Philo Judaeus*. New Haven, 1938.

Grant, F. C. *The Economic Background of the Gospels*. London, 1926.

———. *Ancient Judaism and the New Testament*. London, 1960.

———. *Roman Hellenism and the New Testament*. London, 1962.

Grant, R. M. "The Coming of the Kingdom," *JBL* 67 (1948): 297–303.

Greeley, A. *Ecstasy: A Way of Knowing*. Englewood Cliffs, 1974.

Grespy, G. "Recherche sur la signification politique de la mort du Christ," *Lumière et Vie* 20 (1971): 89–109.

Griffiths, D. R. *The New Testament and the Roman State*. Swansea, 1970.

Guignebert, C. *Jesus*. London, 1935.

———. *The Jewish World in the Time of Jesus*. London, 1939.

Guttmann, A. "The End of the Jewish Sacrificial Cult," *HUCA* 38 (1967): 147–48.

Haenchen, E. "Matthäus 23," *ZTK* 48 (1951): 38–63.

———. *Der Weg Jesu*. 2d ed. Berlin, 1968.

Hahn, F. *Mission in the New Testament*. Naperville, Ill., 1965.

———. *The Titles of Jesus in Christology*. London, 1969.

————. "Das Gleichnis von der Einladung zum Festmahl." In O. Böcher and K. Haacker, eds., *Verborum Veritas: Festschrift für G. Stählin*. Wuppertal, 1970, 51–82.

Hálevy, J. *Revue des Études juives* 4 (1882): 249–55.

Harner, M. *The Way of the Shaman*. San Francisco, 1980.

Hartman, L. *Prophecy Interpreted*. Lund, 1966.

Harvey, V. A. *The Historian and the Believer*. London, 1967.

Hengel, M. "War Jesus Revolutionär? Sechs Thesen eines Neutestamentlers," *EvKomm* 2 (1969): 694–96.

————. *Was Jesus a Revolutionist?* Philadelphia, 1971.

————. *Victory over Violence: Jesus and the Revolutionists*. Philadelphia, 1973.

————. *Judaism and Hellenism*. 2 vols. Philadelphia, 1974.

————. *Die Zeloten*. 2d ed. Leiden, 1976.

————. *Jews, Greeks and Barbarians*. Trans. John Bowden. Philadelphia, 1980.

Henry, P. *New Directions in New Testament Study*. Philadelphia, 1979.

Herford, R. Travers. *The Pharisees*. London, 1924.

————. *Judaism in the New Testament Period*. London, 1928.

Heschel, A. *The Prophets*. New York, 1969.

Hiers, R. H. *Jesus and Ethics*. Philadelphia, 1968.

————. *The Kingdom of God in the Synoptic Tradition*. Gainesville, Fla., 1970.

————. "Purification of the Temple: Preparation for the Kingdom of God," *JBL* 90 (1971).

Higgins, A. J. B. *Jesus and the Son of Man*. Philadelphia, 1964.

Hill, David. "On the Use and Meaning of Hosea vi. 6 in Matthew's Gospel," *NTS* 24 (1977): 107–19.

Hindley, J. C. "Towards a Date for the Similitudes of Enoch: An Historical Approach," *NTS* 14 (1968): 551–65.

Hirsch, E. G. "Sabbath," *JE* 10:558.

Hodgson, P. C. "The Son of Man and the Problem of Historical Knowledge," *JR* 41 (1961).

Hoehner, H. W. *Herod Antipas*. Cambridge, 1972.

Hoffman, P. "Die Versuchungsgeschichte in der Logienquelle," *BZ* 13 (1969).

Holland, D. L. *Jesus' Proclamation of the Kingdom of God*. Philadelphia, 1971.

Hollis, F. J. *The Archaeology of Herod's Temple*. London, 1934.

Hooker, M. D. *The Son of Man in Mark*. London, 1967.

————. "Christology and Methodology," *NTS* 17 (1970–71): 480–87.

————. "Interchange in Christ," *JTS* 22 (1971).

Hultgren, A. *Jesus and His Adversaries: The Form and Function of the Conflict Stories in the Synoptic Tradition*. Minneapolis, 1979.

Hunter, A. M. *Interpreting the Parables*. Philadelphia, 1961.

Isaksson, A. *Marriage and Ministry in the New Testament*. Lund, 1965.

James, W. *The Varieties of Religious Experience*. New York, 1902, 1961.

Jeremias, J. "The Present Position in the Controversy Concerning the Problem of the Historical Jesus," *ET* 69 (1957–58): 333–39.

————. *Jesus' Promise to the Nations*. London, 1958.

————. *The Parables of Jesus.* New York, 1963.

————. *The Eucharistic Words of Jesus.* London, 1966.

————. *The Prayers of Jesus.* London, 1967.

————. *Jerusalem at the Time of Jesus.* London, 1969.

————. *New Testament Theology.* London, 1971.

Johnson, S. *Jesus in His Own Times.* London, 1958.

Jones, A. H. M. *The Herods of Judaea.* Oxford, 1938.

Jones, D. "The Background and Character of the Lukan Psalms," *JTS* 19 (1968): 19–50.

Jones, G. V. *The Art and Truth of the Parables.* London, 1964.

Jónsson, J. *Humor and Irony in the New Testament.* Reykjavik, 1965.

Kallas, J. *Jesus and the Power of Satan.* New York, 1968.

Käsemann, E. *Essays on New Testament Themes.* London, 1964.

————. *Jesus Means Freedom.* London, 1969.

Käser, W. "Exegetische und theologische Erwägungen zur Seligpreisung der Kinderlosen Lk. 23:29b," *ZNW* 54 (1963): 240–54.

Keck, L. E. "Bornkamm's *Jesus of Nazareth* Revisited," *JR* 49 (1969): 1–17.

Kee, H. C. *Jesus in History.* New York, 1970.

————. *Community of the New Age: Studies in Mark's Gospel.* Philadelphia, 1977.

————. *Christian Origins in Sociological Perspective.* Philadelphia, 1980.

Kennard, J. S. *Jesus in the Temple.* Tokyo, 1935.

————. "'Hosanna' and the Purpose of Jesus," *JBL* 67 (1948): 171–76.

————. *Render to God.* New York, 1950.

Kenyon, K. M. *Jerusalem.* London, 1967.

Kilpatrick, G. D. *The Origins of the Gospel according to St. Matthew.* Oxford, 1946.

Kimbrough, Jr., S. T. "The Concept of Sabbath at Qumran," *RQ* 5 (1966): 487–98.

Klassen, W. "Jesus and the Zealot Option," *CJT* 16 (1970): 12–21.

————. "'A Child of Peace' (Luke 10:6) in First Century Context," *NTS* 27 (1981): 488–506.

Klausner, J. *Jesus of Nazareth.* Boston, 1964.

Klostermann, E. *Das Lukasevangelium.* Tübingen, 1919.

————. *Das Markusevangelium.* 3d ed. Tübingen, 1936.

Knibb, M. A. "The Date of the Parables of Enoch: A Critical Review," *NTS* 25 (1979): 360–69.

Knox, J. *The Death of Christ.* London, 1959.

Knox, W. *St. Paul and the Church of Jerusalem.* Cambridge, 1925.

Knox, W. L. "Church and State in the New Testament," *JRS* 39 (1949).

Koch, K. *The Rediscovery of Apocalyptic.* London, 1972.

Kohler, K. "Pharisees," *JE* 9:661.

Kraeling, C. H. "The Episodes of the Roman Standards at Jerusalem," *HTR* 35 (1942): 163–89.

Kümmel, W. G. *Promise and Fulfilment.* London, 1961.

———. "Norman Perrin's 'Rediscovering the Teaching of Jesus,' " *JR* 49 (1969): 49–66.

Kurfess, A. *Sibyllinische Weissagungen.* Munich, 1951.

Ladd, G. E. *Jesus and the Kingdom.* London, 1966.

Larsen, S. *The Shaman's Doorway.* New York, 1976.

Lauterbach, J. Z. "The Pharisees and Their Teachings," *HUCA* 6 (1929).

Leivestad, R. *Christ the Conqueror.* London, 1954.

———. "Der apokalyptische Menschensohn: ein theologisches Phantom," *ASTI* 6 (1967).

Leszynsky, R. *Die Sadduzäer.* Berlin, 1912.

Lewis, I. M. *Ecstatic Religion: An Anthropological Study of Spirit Possession.* Penguin, 1971.

Liberty, S. *The Political Relations of Christ's Ministry.* London, 1916.

Lightfoot, R. H. *The Gospel Message of St. Mark.* Oxford, 1950.

Lillie, W. *Studies in New Testament Ethics.* London, 1961.

Lindars, B. *New Testament Apologetic.* London, 1961.

———. "Re-Enter the Apocalyptic Son of Man," *NTS* 22 (1976): 52–72.

Linnemann, E. *Parables of Jesus.* London, 1966.

Linton, O. "St. Matthew 5:43," *StTh* (1964).

———. "The Parable of the Children's Game," *NTS* 22 (1976): 159–77.

Loewe, H. "Pharisaism." In W. O. E. Oesterley, ed., *Judaism and Christianity: The Age of Transition.* London, 1937, 1:179–88.

———. *Render unto Caesar.* Cambridge, 1940.

Lofthouse, W. "*Chen* and *Chesed* in the Old Testament," *ZAW* 20 (1933): 29–35.

Lohmeyer, E. *Das Evangelium des Markus* 15. Göttingen, 1959.

———. *Lord of the Temple.* Edinburgh and London, 1961.

Lohse, E. "Jesu Worte über den Sabbat." In *Judentum, Urchristentum, Kirche: Festschrift für Joachim Jeremias.* Berlin, 1964.

Loisy, A. *L'Evangile selon Marc.* Paris, 1912.

Lundström, G. *The Kingdom of God in the Teaching of Jesus.* London, 1963.

McArthur, H. K. *In Search of the Historical Jesus.* New York, 1969.

———. "The Burden of Proof in Historical Jesus Research," *ET* 82 (1970–71): 116–19.

McConnell, R. S. *Law and Prophecy in Matthew's Gospel.* Basel, 1969.

Macgregor, G. H. C. *The New Testament Basis of Pacifism.* London, 1953.

McKelvey, R. J. *The New Temple.* London, 1969.

Mackinnon, J. *The Historic Jesus.* London, 1936.

MacNeill, H. L. "The *Sitz im Leben* of Lk. 1:5–2:20," *JBL* 65 (1946): 123–30.

Maier, P. "Sejanus, Pilate, and the Date of the Crucifixion," *Church History* 37 (1968): 3–13.

———. "The Episode of the Golden Roman Shields at Jerusalem," *HTR* 62 (1969): 112.

Major, H. D. A., T. W. Manson, and C. J. Wright. *The Mission and Message of Jesus.* London, 1929.

Malherbe, A. *Social Aspects of Early Christianity*. Baton Rouge, 1977.

Manson, T. W. "Mark ii. 27f," *Coniectanea Neotestamentica* 11 (1947).

————. "The Cleansing of the Temple," *BJRL* 33 (1950–51).

————. *The Servant Messiah*. Cambridge, 1953.

————. *Jesus and the Non-Jews*. London, 1955.

Marriott, H. *The Sermon on the Mount*. London, 1925.

Marshall, L. H. *The Challenge of New Testament Ethics*. London, 1946.

Marty, M., and D. G. Peerman, eds. *New Theology Number Six*. London, 1969.

Martyn, J. L. Review of N. Perrin, *Rediscovering the Teaching of Jesus*. *USQR* 23 (1968): 133.

Menzies, A. *The Earliest Gospel*. London, 1901.

Merkel, H. "Jesus und die Pharisäer," *NTS* 14 (1967–68): 205–6.

————."War Jesus ein Revolutionär?" *Bibel und Kirche* 26 (1971): 44–47.

Michaels, J. R. "The Parable of the Regretful Son," *HTR* 61 (1968): 15–26.

Milik, J. T. "Problèmes de la littérature hénochique à la lumière des fragments araméens de Qumrân," *HTR* 64 (1971): 333–78.

————. *The Books of Enoch: Aramaic Fragments of Qumran Cave 4*. Oxford, 1976.

M'Neile, A. H. *The Gospel according to St. Matthew*. London, 1957.

Moltmann, J. *The Theology of Hope*. New York, 1967.

————. "Toward a Political Hermeneutics of the Gospel," *USQR* 23 (1968): 308–11.

Montefiore, C. G. *The Synoptic Gospels*. 2d. ed. London, 1927.

Montefiore, C. G., and H. Loewe, eds. *A Rabbinic Anthology*. London, 1938.

Montefiore, H. "Revolt in the Desert? Mark 6:30ff.," *NTS* 8 (1961–62): 135–41.

Moore, A. L. *The Parousia in the New Testament*. Leiden, 1966.

Moore, G. F. *Judaism in the First Centuries of the Christian Era*. Cambridge, Mass., 1927–30.

————. *Judaism in the First Centuries of the Christian Era: The Age of the Tannaim*. Cambridge, 1937.

Moule, C. F. D. "Sanctuary and Sacrifice in the Church of the New Testament," *JTS* 1 (1950): 29–41.

————. *The Phenomenon of the New Testament*. London, 1967.

Mussner, F. *The Miracles of Jesus*. Shannon, 1970.

Neusner, J. "Qumran and Jerusalem: Two Jewish Roads to Utopia," *JBR* 27 (1959): 284–90.

————. *A Life of Yohanan ben Zakkai*. 2d ed. Leiden, 1970.

————. *The Rabbinic Traditions about the Pharisees before 70*. 3 vols. Leiden, 1970.

————. "Pharisaic Law in New Testament Times," *USQR* 26 (1971): 337.

————. *From Politics to Piety: The Emergence of Pharisaic Judaism*. Englewood Cliffs, N.J., 1973.

————. *The Idea of Purity in Ancient Judaism*. Leiden, 1973.

————. *Early Rabbinic Judaism*. Leiden, 1975.

————. "First Cleanse the Inside," *NTS* 22 (1975–76): 486–95.

————, ed. *Christianity, Judaism and Other Greco-Roman Cults.* Leiden, 1975.

Nineham, D. E. *Saint Mark.* Penguin Books, 1969.

Nock, A. D. "The Roman Army and the Roman Religious Year," *HTR* 45 (1952): 239.

Olmstead, A. T. *Jesus in the Light of History.* New York, 1942.

Otto, R. *The Kingdom of God and the Son of Man.* London, 1938.

————. *The Idea of the Holy.* New York, 1958.

Parker, T. M. *Christianity and the State in the Light of History.* London, 1955.

Parkes, J. *The Foundations of Judaism and Christianity.* London, 1960.

Pawlikowski, J. T. "On Renewing the Revolution of the Pharisees: A New Approach to Theology and Politics," *Cross Currents* 20 (1970).

Perowne, S. *The Life and Times of Herod the Great.* London, 1956.

————. *The Later Herods.* London, 1958.

Perrin, N. *The Kingdom of God in the Teaching of Jesus.* London, 1963.

————. *Rediscovering the Teaching of Jesus.* New York, 1967.

————. *What Is Redaction Criticism?* London, 1970.

————. *Jesus and the Language of the Kingdom.* Philadelphia, 1976.

Perrin, N., and D. Duling. *The New Testament: An Introduction.* 2d ed. New York, 1982.

Pesch, R. *Naherwartungen: Tradition und Redaktion in Mk 13.* Düsseldorf, 1968.

————. "Der Anspruch Jesus," *Orientierung* 35 (1971): 53–56, 67–70, 77–81.

Piper, J. *"Love Your Enemies."* Cambridge, 1979.

Pittenger, N., ed., *Christ for Us Today.* London, 1965.

Plummer, A. *The Gospel according to St. Luke.* Edinburgh, 1896.

Poliakov, L. *History of Anti-Semitism.* New York, 1965.

Rawlinson, A. E. J. *The Gospel according to St. Mark.* London, 1925.

Reicke, B. *The New Testament Era.* London, 1969.

————. "Der barmherzige Samariter." In O. Böcher and K. Haacker, eds., *Verborum Veritas: Festschrift für G. Stählin.* Wuppertal, 1970.

Reimarus, H. S. *The Goal of Jesus and His Disciples.* Trans. G. W. Buchanan. Leiden, 1970.

————. *Reimarus: Fragments.* Ed. C. H. Talbert and trans. R. S. Fraser. Philadelphia, 1970.

Reumann, J. *Jesus in the Church's Gospels.* Philadelphia, 1968.

Rhoads, D. *Israel in Revolution: 6–74 C.E.* Philadelphia, 1976.

Richardson, A. *The Miracle Stories of the Gospels.* London, 1941.

————. *The Political Christ.* Philadelphia, 1973.

Richardson, P. *Israel in the Apostolic Church.* Cambridge, 1969.

Rist, M. "Caesar or God (Mark 12:13–17)? A Study in *Formgeschichte*," *JR* 16 (1936): 317–31.

————. "Jesus and Eschatology." In J. C. Rylaarsdam, ed., *Transitions in Biblical Scholarship.* Chicago, 1968. Pp. 193–215.

Rivkin, E. "Pharisees," *IDB* (1976): 657–63.

————. *A Hidden Revolution.* Nashville, 1978.

Robinson, J. M. *The Problem of History in Mark*. London, 1957.

———. *A New Quest for the Historical Jesus*. London, 1959.

———. *Twelve New Testament Studies*. London, 1962.

Ross, J. F. *IDB*, 2:306, 3:315.

Roth, C. *The Historical Background of the Dead Sea Scrolls*. Oxford, 1958.

———. "The Zealots in the War of 66–73," *JJS* 4 (1959).

———. "The Cleansing of the Temple and Zechariah," *NovTest* 4 (1960).

———. "The Pharisees in the Jewish Revolution of 66–73," *JSS* 7 (1962): 63.

Rowley, H. H. *Israel's Mission to the World*. London, 1939.

———. "The Herodians in the Gospels," *JTS* 41 (1940): 14–27.

———. "The Qumran Sect and Christian Origins," *BJRL* 44 (1961): 116–37.

Rubenstein, R. *My Brother Paul*. New York, 1972.

Russell, D. S. *Between the Testaments*. London, 1960.

———. *The Jews from Alexander to Herod*. London, 1967.

Rylaarsdam, J. C., ed. *Transitions in Biblical Scholarship*. Chicago, 1968.

Safrai S., and M. Stern, eds. *The Jewish People in the First Century: Compendia Rerum Iudaicarum ad Novum Testamentum*. 2 vols. Assen and Philadelphia, 1974.

Sand, A. "Zur Frage nach dem 'Sitz im Leben' der Apokalyptischen Texte des Neuen Testaments," *NTS* 18 (1972): 167–77.

Schalit, A. *König Herodes*. Berlin, 1969.

———. "Herod and His Successors." In H. J. Schultz, ed., *Jesus in His Time*. Philadelphia, 1971.

Schechter, S. *Some Aspects of Rabbinic Theology*. London, 1909.

Schmid, J. *The Gospel according to Mark*. Staten Island, 1968.

Schnackenburg, R. *The Moral Teaching of the New Testament*. London, 1965.

Schoeps, H. J. *Aus frühchristlicher Zeit*. Tübingen, 1950.

Scholem, G. *Major Trends in Jewish Mysticism*. New York, 1961.

———. *Jewish Gnosticism, Merkabah Mysticism, and Talmudic Tradition*. 2d ed. New York, 1965.

Schottroff, L. "Das Gleichnis vom verlorenen Sohn," *ZTK* 68 (1971): 27–52.

Schramm, T. *Markuss-stoff bei Lukas*. Cambridge, 1971.

Schultz H. J., ed. *Jesus in His Time*. Philadelphia, 1971.

Schulz, A. *Nachfolgen und Nachahmen*. Munich, 1962.

Schulz, S. "Markus und das Alte Testament," *ZTK* 58 (1961): 190.

Schürer, E. *The History of the Jewish People in the Age of Jesus Christ*. Ed. Geza Vermes et al. Edinburgh: vol. 1, 1973; vol. 2, 1979.

Schürmann, H. *Das Lukasevangelium* 1. Freiburg, 1969.

Schwarz, G. "Unkenntiche Gräber?" *NTS* 23 (1976–77).

Schweitzer, A. *The Quest of the Historical Jesus*. London, 1910.

———*The Mystery of the Kingdom of God*. London, 1914.

Schweizer, E. "The Son of Man," *JBL* 79 (1960).

———. "The Son of Man Again," *NTS* 9 (1963).

———. *Jesus*. London, 1971.

Scott, B. B. *Jesus, Symbol-Maker for the Kingdom*. Philadelphia, 1981.

Scott, E. F. *The Ethical Teaching of Jesus*. London, 1924.

―――. *The Crisis in the Life of Jesus*. New York, 1952.

Scroggs, Robin. "The Earliest Christian Communities as Sectarian Movement." In J. Neusner, ed., *Christianity, Judaism and Other Greco-Roman Cults*. Leiden, 1975. 2:1–12.

―――. *Paul for a New Day*. Philadelphia, 1977.

―――. "The Sociological Interpretation of the New Testament: The Present State of Research," *NTS* 27 (1980): 164–79.

Seitz, O. J. F. "What Do These Stones Mean?" *JBL* 79 (1960): 247–54.

―――. "Love Your Enemies," *NTS* 16 (1969–70).

Sherwin-White, A. N. *Racial Prejudice in Imperial Rome*. Cambridge, 1967.

Simkhovitch, V. G. *Toward the Understanding of Jesus*. New York, 1925.

Sleeper, C. F. "Political Responsibility according to I Peter," *NovTest* 10 (1968): 284.

Smallwood, E. M. "High Priests and Politics in Roman Palestine," *JTS* 13 (1962): 3.

―――. "Jews and Romans in the Early Empire," *History Today* 15 (1965): 316.

―――. *The Jews under Roman Rule*. Leiden, 1976.

Smart, J. D. *The Quiet Revolution*. Philadelphia, 1969.

Smith, B. T. D. *The Parables of the Synoptic Gospels*. Cambridge, 1937.

Smith, C. W. F. *The Jesus of the Parables*. Philadelphia, 1948.

Smith, H. *Forgotten Truth: The Primordial Tradition*. New York, 1976.

Smith, M. "Mt. 5:43: 'Hate Thine Enemy,'" *HTR* 45 (1952).

―――. "Palestinian Judaism in the First Century." In M. Davis, ed. *Israel: Its Role in Civilization*. New York, 1956.

―――. "The Dead Sea Sect in Relation to Ancient Judaism," *NTS* 7 (1960–61).

―――. *Palestinian Parties and Politics That Shaped the Old Testament*. New York, 1971.

―――. "Zealots and Sicarii, Their Origins and Relation," *HTR* 64 (1971): 1 and notes 1–8.

Snaith, N. *The Distinctive Ideas of the Old Testament*. London, 1944.

Sparks, H. F. D. "The Semitisms of St. Luke's Gospel," *JTS* 44 (1943): 129–38.

Stauffer, E. *Christ and the Caesars*. London, 1955.

―――. *Jerusalem und Rom im Zeitalter Jesu Christi*. Bern, 1957.

Stendahl, K. *The School of St. Matthew*. 2d ed. Philadelphia, 1968.

Suter, D. W. *Tradition and Composition in the Parables of Enoch*. Missoula, Mont., 1979.

Taylor, V. *The Gospel according to St. Mark*. 2d ed. London, 1966.

Theissen, G. *Sociology of Early Palestinian Christianity*. Philadelphia, 1978.

Tödt, H. E. *The Son of Man in the Synoptic Tradition*. London, 1965.

Tooley, W. "The Shepherd and Sheep Image in the Teaching of Jesus," *NovTest* 7 (1964–65): 22–23.

Townsend, J. T. "Matthew 23:9," *JTS* 12 (1961): 56–59.

Trible, P. *God and the Rhetoric of Sexuality*. Philadelphia, 1978.

Trocmé, E. "L'expulsion des marchands du Temple," *NTS* 15 (1968–69).

Turner, C. H. "Marcan Usage: Notes, Critical and Exegetical, on the Second Gospel," *JTS* 26 (1925).

Turner, H. E. W. *Historicity and the Gospels.* London, 1963.

Urbach, E. E. *The Sages.* Jerusalem, 1975.

van der Kwaak, H. "Die Klage über Jerusalem," *NovTest* 8 (1966).

van der Loos, H. *The Miracles of Jesus.* Leiden, 1968.

Vardaman, J. "A New Inscription Which Mentions Pilate as 'Prefect,'" *JBL* 81 (1962).

Vermes, G. *Jesus the Jew.* New York, 1973.

———. *The Dead Sea Scrolls.* London, 1977.

von Rad, G. *The Problem of the Hexateuch.* Edinburgh, 1966.

Weiss, J. *Jesus' Proclamation of the Kingdom of God.* Trans. and ed. R. H. Hiers and D. L. Holland. Philadelphia, 1971.

Westerholm, S. *Jesus and Scribal Authority.* Lund, 1978.

Wilder, A. *Eschatology and Ethics in the Teaching of Jesus.* New York, 1950.

———. *Otherworldliness and the New Testament.* London, 1955.

———. "Eschatological Imagery and Earthly Circumstance," *NTS* 5 (1959).

———. "Social Factors in Early Christian Eschatology." In A. Wikgren, ed., *Early Christian Origins.* Chicago, 1961. Pp. 67–76.

Wilson, S. G. "Lukan Eschatology," *NTS* 16 (1970).

Wilson, W. R. *The Execution of Jesus.* New York, 1970.

Windisch, H. "Die Sprüche vom Eingehen in das Reich Gottes," *ZNW* 27 (1928): 163–92.

Wink, W. *John the Baptist in the Gospel Tradition.* Cambridge, 1968.

Winter, P. "The Treatment of His Sources by the Third Evangelist in Luke xxi–xxiv," *StTh* 8 (1954).

———. *On The Trial of Jesus.* Berlin, 1961.

Wolfson, H. A. *Philo.* Cambridge, Mass., 1948.

Wood, H. G. "Interpreting This Time," *NTS* 2 (1955–56).

Wood, J. *The Sermon on the Mount and Its Application.* London, 1963.

Wright, G. E. *The Old Testament and Theology.* New York, 1969.

Yadin, Y. *Masada: Herod's Fortress and the Zealots' Last Stand.* New York, 1966.

Yoder, J. *The Politics of Jesus.* Grand Rapids, 1972.

Zahrnt, H. *The Historical Jesus.* London, 1963.

Index of Biblical References

Note: This index does not include texts cited in the footnotes.

Index of Subjects

Index of Modern Authors